THE BRITISH ARMY, MANPOWER AND SOCIETY INTO THE TWENTY-FIRST CENTURY

THE BRITISH ARMY, MANPOWER AND SOCIETY
INTO THE
TWENTY-FIRST CENTURY

Edited by

HEW STRACHAN
University of Glasgow

FRANK CASS
LONDON · PORTLAND, OR

First published in 2000 in Great Britain by
FRANK CASS PUBLISHERS.
2 Park Square, Milton Park, Abingdon,
Oxon, OX14 4RN

and in the United States of America by
FRANK CASS PUBLISHERS
270 Madison Ave, New York
NY 10016

Transferred to Digital Printing 2005

Website: www.frankcass.com

British Library Cataloguing in Publication Data

The British Army, manpower and society into the
twenty-first century
1. Great Britain. Army 2. Women and the military – Great
Britain 3. Sociology, Military – Great Britain
I. Strachan, Hew
355'. 00941

ISBN 0-7146-5005-6 (cloth)
ISBN 0-7146-8069-9 (paper)

Library of Congress Cataloging-in-Publication Data

The British Army, manpower and society into the twenty-first
century / edited by Hew Strachan
   Includes bibliographical references and index.
   ISBN 0-7146-5005-6 (cloth) – ISBN 0-7146-8069-9 (paper)
   1. Great Britain. Army – Recruiting, enlistment, etc.
   2. Sociology, Military – Great Britain.   I. Strachan, Hew.
UB335. G7 .B75 1999
306.2'7'0941 – dc21   99-045938

Typeset by Regent Typesetting, London

Contents

Foreword

The debate about how far an army should reflect the values and standards of society remains wide open. On one side, there are those who believe that the physical and psychological demands on a soldier in battle are enduring and unchanging – and that these dictate how a soldier should be trained and behave in peacetime. On the other side, there are those who believe that an army should closely reflect the culture of the society from which it draws its membership – and that to remain an isolated, backward-looking organisation will ultimately render an army irrelevant to the needs of the nation.

As Sebastian Roberts points out in his thoughtful article, fighting power comes from three components: conceptual, physical and moral. During the past 50 years of Cold War soldiering, the British Army, along with other NATO armies, has almost exclusively pursued the physical and conceptual components of fighting power. The physical component clearly needed to be emphasised during the period of East/West confrontation, as this was the best means of demonstrating the technical superiority of NATO over the Warsaw Pact. The second component, namely the conceptual, allowed the physical means at the disposal of NATO to be put to its best deterrent effect. All this successfully resulted in a NATO victory against the Warsaw Pact. However, it was a victory accomplished during a war of deterrence in which no shots were fired, and no one was actually exposed to the extreme violence and chaos of war. But in war it is often the moral component that predominates, and history is littered with examples of armies which were both physically and conceptually superior to their opponents, but who were nevertheless decisively defeated by armies which attached a greater importance to the moral component of fighting power than they did.

NATO's failure to pay sufficient attention to the moral component of fighting power during the Cold War has had a disastrous effect on its employability in time of war. The reluctance of NATO to deploy combat troops in Kosovo in March 1999 stemmed not just from a political reluctance to accept casualties – but, more importantly, came also from a recognition that the alliance lacked sufficient troops capable of fighting in a way that would ensure victory against the Serbs. For a ground war in Kosovo would have involved the same sort of close combat that was fought by the men of the British 14th Army in Burma during the Second World War, where every bunker had to be destroyed, every hilltop taken, and every village cleared of the enemy. The Japanese could never have been defeated by bombing or from a remote distance by precision-guided munitions . Over half a century later, the Nato bombing campaign in Kosovo demonstrated the same clear lesson – for the Serb army emerged largely unscathed after one of the most intensive bombing campaigns in history. Such battles can only be won by hard, aggressive soldiers capable of prolonged fighting with the rifle, bayonet and machine gun.

Fighting is an attitude of mind, and the willingness to kill and be killed comes from a blend of faith, trust in the leadership, harsh discipline and compulsion. It is this, combined with pride in the unit and comradeship, that creates the military ethos that sustains soldiers in time of war. In the British Army, the moral component of fighting power is founded on a distinct military ethos, deriving from the fundamental belief that soldiers are not merely civilians in uniform but form a distinctive group within society: no other group is required to kill other human beings or deliberately sacrifice their lives for the nation.

Troops who have become accustomed to a peacetime regime based on civilian practices involving restricted working hours, health and safety regulations, or the right of appeal to industrial tribunals outside the chain of command, cannot be expected to make the necessary physical or mental transition in time of war. Nor do modern forms of conflict based on technology render the fighting qualities of the individual soldier or small unit on the battlefield irrelevant. Indeed, conflict in the twenty-first century is more likely to involve peacekeeping and peace-enforcement operations than general war, and to perform successfully in the brutal and chaotic circumstances that prevail in these forms of modern conflict, a soldier will require all the disciplines and psychological preparedness of general war. Soldiers will also need to accept a greater moral responsibility and understanding of human rights than in general war, and the traditional discipline and standards of the British Army prepare them particularly well for these new forms of humanitarian war.

Today, the military ethos of the British Army, on which the moral component of fighting power depends, is not merely suffering from past neglect, it is being threatened by a mixture of cultural change within society, and by new national and international legislation. The importance attached in modern society to the pursuit of individual and minority-group interests – even when the consequences of this logic are damaging to the interests of the whole – has resulted in radical changes to the military ethos and disciplinary relationships within the armed forces. If an army is to perform successfully in war, its underlying ethos must, I firmly believe, be different from that of civilian society, whose beliefs tend to be faddish and certainly are not derived from the necessities of war. This does not mean that it needs to isolate itself from society or adopt a 'holier-than-thou' attitude. Nor will an army with an ethos that is different from that of society necessarily find it difficult to recruit soldiers – many people in civilian life welcome and admire military standards, as surveys continually demonstrate.

Undoubtedly, as memory of military service fades, the British Army does need to explain its purpose more clearly to the civilian community, and it has to spend more time in preparing people physically and mentally for military life. Thus the difficulty that the British Army has today in manning to its full established strength is not caused by low recruitment, but by poor retention. Political correctness and overstretch make poor retention officers.

Of course, the British Army must always be a good employer in terms of justice and fairness, for unless there is complete confidence and trust in the leadership, soldiers will not respond to the extreme demands made upon them. But there must be some limit as to how far an individual soldier can attend to his or her own interests in relation to those of the Army. This does not mean to say that there cannot be individuality or diversity of culture within the Army. Indeed, these qualities are essential to the fighting quality of an army and to military life. But the current debates taking place within the armed forces, and dealt with comprehensively in this book, concerning the wider employment of women, the extension of equal opportunities legislation within the Army – including the right of appeal outside the chain of command to civilian tribunals and the acceptability of homosexuals within the ranks – can properly be held only within the context of battlefield effectiveness.

In conclusion, an army at war cannot be just another civilian organisation, reflecting all the values and regulations of civil society. In times of conscription, when national survival is in peril, individual rights are inevitably suppressed to some degree, and justice and fairness are safeguarded by military law. I believe that it is the nature of conflict as much as the nature of society that should determine the characteristics of our armed forces.

This book provides a valuable opportunity to re-examine the relationship between the British Army and society. At the international level, NATO would also do well to look at the quality of its collective fighting power. Failure to act now will result in the British Army and NATO becoming incapable of confronting the challenges to world order that will occur in the twenty-first century.

General Sir Michael Rose
August 1999

Acknowledgements

In the first half of 1998 the Scottish Centre for War Studies in the University of Glasgow held four study days under the title, 'The British Army, Manpower and Society: Towards 2000'. The essays in this volume are the fruits of those study days.

The whole project has depended crucially on the support of the Army itself. The value of getting soldiers to discuss their profession in an academic environment, and of prevailing upon academics to expose their thinking to practitioners, ought to be self-evident. But until comparatively recently that idea was honoured more by lip-service than in practice. A principal reason for change has been the greater openness of the Army itself to intellectual debate. The establishment of the Higher Command and Staff Course at the erstwhile Army Staff College in 1988 enthroned the principle of higher education in a service environment. More negatively, the cuts consequent on the end of the Cold War and the strains of filling even a reduced establishment have forced the Army to look outwards as well as inwards for fresh thinking.

The first study day, held on 8 January 1998, considered the topic historically, and the papers then presented constitute the opening section of this book. The second day, 28 February 1998, addressed the current relationship between the Army and society in general terms. Major-General Jonathan Hall, CB, OBE, enthusiastically offered to incorporate those papers as the core of his annual GOC's Study Day for the Army in Scotland. By then Major-General Mark Strudwick, CBE, had succeeded him as GOC Scotland, and the Centre's debt to General Strudwick for his support and hospitality is enormous. That the day went so well was also due in no small measure to the administrative arrangements of Lieutenant-Colonel Val Hall and Major Stuart Hodges.

The third day, 21 April 1998, considered issues of integration – for women, ethnic minorities and homosexuals. The series concluded on 14 May with the implications of social change for the Army's fitness to fight. The papers from the final day make up the third part of the book, and the day itself was sponsored by the Strategic and Combat Studies Institute. The Centre has to thank Colonel Mungo Melvin, OBE, then the Institute's Director as well as Colonel, Defence Studies, and his superior, Major-General Tony Pigott, Director-General of

Development and Doctrine. Thanks to Colonel Melvin's good offices, the Strategic and Combat Studies Institute concluded the proceedings with the first of its dinners to be held outside the Thames Valley, at which the speaker was Dr John Reid, MP, then Minister of State for the Armed Forces, and the guests included the Principal of the University of Glasgow, Professor Sir Graeme Davies.

One of the reasons that the Centre focused on manpower issues was the migration of the Army Personnel Centre to Glasgow. Many of its staff attended the study days, and thanks are due to Major-General David Burden, CB, CBE, the Military Secretary, and to the Deputy Military Secretary, Brigadier Peter Grant Peterkin. Other soldiers who ensured the success of the whole venture include Brigadier Robert Gordon, CBE, Director of Public Relations (Army), and Brigadier Freddie Viggers, MBE, Director of Manning (Army). A sailor, Commander Simon Gillespie, had a role too; through his good offices we secured Dr Reid as a speaker.

Within the University of Glasgow, the secretaries of the former Department of Modern History, and now of History (Modern), Chris Fildes and Alison Peden, performed trojan work on the Centre's behalf.

Introduction

Hew Strachan

The British Army currently enjoys an international reputation for excellence. The end of the Cold War, which threatened its equilibrium by removing its principal strategic rationale, has ended up providing endorsement for its institutional strengths. A small but regular force was the odd one out in a Europe geared for conventional war between mass armies, but it is a role model in an age of peace enforcement and international interventionism. In 1997 France, so often Britain's enemy in the past, announced that it would emulate Britain in its conversion from conscription to professionalism. President Chirac described the British Army as 'among the best in the world'.[1]

The ironies in the situation are manifest. While Louis XIV and Napoleon used France's Army to establish it as Europe's major land power, Britain saw its Navy as its premier service. More recently, of course, the two nations have been allies, but the story of that relationship is not necessarily one of unalloyed triumph. Neither 1916 nor 1940 provided the French Army with unequivocal reason for taking the British Army as an example to be emulated.

France's enthusiasm for the British Army, however extraordinary in historical terms, seems perfectly logical in a contemporary context. Since the last conscript left the service in 1961, the British Army has been almost continuously engaged in operations of varying intensity, and it has brought two major wars – alone in the Falklands in 1982 and in alliance in the Gulf in 1991 – to victorious conclusions in short order. The admiration admitted by the French is a commonplace of British domestic perceptions. Opinion polls have continuously placed the Army at the head of the list of national institutions in terms of public confidence.[2]

The paradox that preoccupies the Army is that this popular respect does not readily transform itself into buoyant levels of recruiting. The establishment of today's Army is 120,000, and yet it cannot maintain its strength. This phenomenon is not as new as some of the debates surrounding it might suggest. The Army has a long history, but it has a short institutional memory. It can persuade itself that current practices have been hallowed by precedent when they have not been, and it can spend much time exploring paths and by-ways which it has mapped before. This may be the consequence of comparatively short postings: an ideal of 2.5 years or thereabouts in any job (which frequently becomes less) and a conviction that specialism is death to ambition both favour change over continuity. The situation is not helped by the fact the Army gives less attention to the promotion of serious military history than any major comparable force In these respects at any rate the popular image of the Army as bounded by tradition is unfounded.

A century ago, on the eve of the Boer War, the Army was held in as high regard as it is today. As the defender of the empire, it was the agent of civilisation and Christianity.[3] And yet then too it failed to recruit to establishment.[4] It certainly was not representative of society as a whole; those who were unemployed or paid only by the day were much more likely to enlist than those with skills or in white-collar jobs. The fact that most of its men came from the slums of industrial England meant that medical rejection rates were high.[5] After the Boer War, the decline of national fitness which military service revealed, and which urban-isation and its concomitants were deemed to have precipitated, prompted military pundits to pontificate about eugenics just as much as about tactics.

What erased this experience from the Army's institutional memory was conscription. In the two world wars Britain created a mass army. In both 1914–18 and 1939–45 the Army did reflect society. Indeed, the maintenance of conscription after 1945 until 1961 helped consolidate the view that this was the norm. But it was not. Conscription was an expedient, a response to a crisis. Its institutional impact on the Army was limited. Regular soldiers resented the amount of time spent training new recruits, and conscription's public justification was suspect when the direct threat to the British Isles seemed minimal. Between the wars, when the Army again reverted to professional enlist-ment, recruiting problems resurfaced. Leslie Hore-Belisha, the Secretary of State for War between 1937 and 1939, is remembered too often for his relationship with Basil Liddell Hart and too infrequently for his improvements in pay and conditions of service as he tackled the recruitment crisis.[6] When Duncan Sandys took the decision to abolish peacetime conscription in 1957, he predicted that the Army would not be able to draw in the 220,000 men which the Army Council felt was the appropriate size for the Army. He regarded 165,000 as realistic, and the Army struggled to reach the eventual target of 180,000.[7]

The truism that armies reflect the societies they serve is no more than that. In the British case it creates a false expectation. A small, voluntarily enlisted army can never fully reflect its parent society. The consequence of the abolition of conscription has been that this observation has become progressively more evident. Hopes to the contrary may have been buoyed by the fact that in with-drawing from empire the Army was coming home. But in reality Northern Ireland cut across any integrating effects such a redeployment might have had. First, it kept a large element of the Army there rather than on the British main-land. Second, until 1998 the terrorist threat forced the Army out of uniform in public places, and also restricted the public's access to military establishments. Even if soldiers were in the community, they were not visibly so.

Two factors helped postpone or alleviate the effects of this divergence. The first was that conscription had lasted long enough to ensure that most families embodied some military experience through their older generations, although obviously and significantly this was unlikely to apply to immigrants entering the country from the 1960s. In 1997 20 per cent of those aged 35–45 had direct links with individuals with military backgrounds; the same was true for only 7 per cent of those aged 16–24.[8] Second, although more arguably, the Territorial Army provided at least some evidence within the community of the Army's existence. From its low point in 1967, consequent on its restructuring as the Territorial Army and Volunteer Reserve, it gradually gained a higher profile in the 1970s and 1980s on the back of its reinforcement capability for operations in northern Europe. In the 1990s both the Gulf War and Bosnia made clear how dependent on the Territorial Army the Army had become for certain functions. The Territorial Army's difficulty was that home defence, its original rationale when it was formed 90 years earlier, was no longer its primary role. Significantly, the principal plank employed by its advocates against the cuts proposed in the 1998 Strategic Defence Review was less strategic than social – its function in bridging the gap between Army and society.

The return of full professionalism enabled the Army to revert to being what it had been in the nineteenth century, a more self-contained community. At the same time Britain emerged from the legacy of empire and two world wars, with the result that civilian society also changed. The military qualities of discipline, respect for authority, and self-denial lost the clear function they had possessed in the first half of the century. They were no longer necessary in the 1960s as they had been in the 1940s. The Army saw its increasing divergence from the values of civil society as evidence of its own virtue. Rising divorce rates, widespread drug abuse, and – probably most important of all – the elevation of individual satisfaction over community needs were interpreted as evidence of degeneration. Servicemen were not themselves immune from these trends but the Army collectively projected responsibility for them outwards, to the failures of civilian society. As worrying as the intangibles of cultural change were declining standards of physical fitness. In 1995 only 25 per cent of schools in Britain delivered a minimum of two hours' compulsory physical education.[9] Team games, which are closer to the values of co-operation and mutual dependence which the Army wishes to inculcate, have declined in schools both absolutely and in relation to individual sports. Alan Hawley reports in Chapter 15 of this book that in 1997–98 the Army accepted 21,864 recruits but rejected 8,795 on medical grounds. The current failure rate thus compares with that of the nineteenth century – even if it also reflects higher standards of diagnosis and higher expectations concerning public health.

One dilemma for the Army, as Iain Torrance argues in Chapter 14, is that it is now more moral than civilian society. There is continuity here too. Late-Victorian soldiers like Wolseley and Roberts, confronted by the Army's inability to attract a higher class of recruit, justified the Army's role in society in terms of its function as an improver. It provided schooling, health care, adequate housing and regular meals for the less privileged: in doing so it integrated them in the life of the nation. Today's Army has taken just this line in relation to racism. Having finally accepted that racism is endemic in the service, it has set out a comprehensive re-education programme. Its response to the problem, however belated, has been more thorough, more 'pro-active' and more determined than that of many institutions.[10] Significantly, however, it has not taken a similar approach to homosexuality. Confronted with evidence of massive intolerance within the services, the Ministry of Defence has used that as a justification for inaction, elevating the gut reactions of a macho culture into a principled policy.[11]

But high standards of public morality carry vulnerabilities. As the guardian of standards different from those now prevailing in civilian society the Army is much more exposed when its members fall from grace. Its susceptibility is compounded by its court-martial procedures. A legal system adapted for the trial of offences which are exclusively military but have no civilian counterpart, such as disobedience or desertion in the face of the enemy, is not necessarily appropriate for misdemeanours which also exist in civil law.[12] The court martial in April 1998 of Lieutenant-Colonel Keith Pople illustrates the point. Pople was charged with conduct prejudicial to good order and military discipline, and with conduct unbecoming of an officer. Essentially, however, the case was one of sexual harassment, an offence for which the civil courts provide a remedy. In securing his acquittal, Pople revealed his adultery with the complainant, a naval officer. The Army rejects the distinction between public conduct and private behaviour, between performance at work and demeanour off duty, prevalent in most workplaces. Adultery would not have brought him to a civil court, nor did it bring him to a military court, but it still effectively finished his career.

Courts martial make good copy, particularly when an officer charged with a sexual offence appears photogenically attired in uniform, medals and sword. The result is that press attention is focused, paradoxically, not on the Army's high moral standards but on those individuals who fail to maintain them. The Army therefore loses on both counts. It deters recruits because of its moral expectations and its traditional values, and at the same time it is seen as a haven for the stereotypes of loutish male behaviour, from sexual harassment to racism, from bullying to homophobia.

Civilian society has become more moral in this respect at least. It is less tolerant of various forms of discrimination, overt or indirect, than was the case when the Army was recruited by conscription. The subsequent divergence between the Army and civil society has therefore become particularly evident for three groups, each of them discussed in this book. First, women, who have been accorded equal opportunities in the civilian workplace, are eligible for only 70 per cent of jobs in the Army. Second, those from ethnic minorities, who in 1997 constituted up to 7 per cent of the United Kingdom population, make up only 1.4 per cent of the armed forces.[13] The Army discovered that, in following its declared policy of being 'colour-blind', it had been condoning racism. Third, homosexuals have found their ability to serve becoming more restricted rather than less so.

This last case illustrates in more graphic form trends which are less evident but nonetheless present elsewhere. Homosexual acts between male adults were not legalised until 1967. Thus, until that date, no formal division existed between civil and military law. Indeed in some respects the Army, particularly in the Second World War, was more relaxed in its attitude to homosexuality than was civil society. But the Wolfenden Report of 1957 inaugurated a progressive easing of public attitudes during the 1970s and 1980s. The Army, however, became less tolerant over the same period. By the early 1990s its policy was to remove from the service by administrative discharge not just those who were practising homosexuals but also those who confessed to being homosexual by orientation even if not practising. Here in microcosm was the Army reshaping its own community in its preferred image. In a classic illustration of the Army's capacity to invent tradition, it convinced itself that this had always been the case.

The Army has not been totally insensitive to these criticisms, at least in relation to women and to race. But in responding it has warned of the dangers to its own military effectiveness. The Army's values elevate the community over the individual because in war mutual dependence has to take priority over self-interest. Thus the Army deems adultery and homosexuality offences less for moral than for utilitarian reasons; they jeopardise the bonds of trust on which unit cohesion depends. Similarly, it rejects the implication that its social composition should be demographically determined. Conceivably, those from ethnic minorities may be reluctant to serve not because of racism within the Army but because of the expectations of their own cultures or because of the career ambitions dominant within their own groups. What this highlights is of general application. For many men and women the Army holds little attraction as a way of life; those of a less robust disposition are even less likely to appreciate a winter's night in a water-filled trench than the average soldier. The fact that the armed services make demands that are radically different from those of any other profession, including the requirement to face the possibility of death, has rationalised itself in the Army's assertion of its right to be different.

Currently, the Army tends to substitute the word 'right' with 'need'. Pragmatism is therefore emphasised over political theory. The Army is said to be out of step with civilian society for good functional reasons. The *Report of the Homosexuality Policy Assessment Team*, produced by the Ministry of Defence in February 1996, takes its stand against homosexuality entirely on the grounds of combat effectiveness. The core assumption concerning morale in the British Army is that soldiers fight less for their country and more for their comrades. Since 1945 the small unit has been seen, in both British and American literature, as the determinant in explaining why men keep going in battle.[14] The British Army's experience in the latter half of the twentieth century endorses this precept. But it also embodies an underlying contradiction.

The Army's combat experience since 1945 has been largely that of counter-insurgency, peace-keeping, and, latterly, peace-enforcement. By definition such tasks put a premium on the small group, and, if properly conducted, imply that casualties will be light. And yet, at least since the 1980s, the Army's doctrine has been developed on the basis of so-called high-intensity operations, with its acme the corps battle in manoeuvre warfare. This is a model derived from the fighting in north-west Europe in 1944–45, and sustained by the needs of the Cold War. Its combat application has been rare: arguably only a few hours in 1991. The case for making the exception the rule begins from the reasonable premise that at the sharp end the distinction between high intensity and low intensity is meaningless; both require a capacity for rapid and correct decision-making, and for a readiness to kill and be killed. The soldier trained for high-intensity warfare can rapidly adapt to other forms of conflict, but the converse does not apply: those prepared solely for gendarmerie or constabulary duties lack both the command structures and the equipment necessary for major war.

In reality, the adaptation from high-intensity war to low-intensity war may be more difficult than this argument implies. Regiments with particularly tough fighting reputations have found themselves more prone to be accused of using excessive force: the Argyll and Sutherland Highlanders in Aden in 1968 and the Parachute Regiment in Londonderry in 1972 are cases in point. Moreover, the other side of the coin is that small-unit morale and high-intensity operations may not be sustainable over the long term. Armies on the eastern front in the Second World War suffered casualties at such a rate that, if comradeship had been the principal key to fighting effectiveness, both the Soviet and German forces would have collapsed internally long before 1945.[15] Of particular relevance to the themes of this book is the observation that high-intensity warfare, as its name implies, develops its own inner drive in the minds of its participants. The fulfilment of its goals forges, for utilitarian reasons, a bond of mutual reliance, whatever the personal differences and sexual jealousies which may pertain between soldiers on the same side in more relaxed circumstances.[16]

The Army's case for its right to be different is therefore overdrawn. It has chosen to prepare itself for high-intensity warfare on the grounds that it can from there more readily adapt to circumstances at other points on the spectrum of conflict. But its rejection of conscription and of the principles of the mass army mean that it is structured as an army for low-intensity warfare and for the gamut of peacetime obligations. Having made these choices, ostensibly for operational and organisational reasons, it can rationalise its 'need to be different' in social terms. As the members of a small, long-service army, its soldiers prefer to serve with those of a like mind and like disposition. If they actually had to fight a hot war over a sustained period, they could not afford themselves that luxury – as their predecessors could not in either world war.

This argument may be too historically driven. The so-called 'revolution in military affairs', the introduction of smart technology and electronic warfare, may provide the material substitute for manpower. The United States Army seems to think so. But in that event the case for the small unit as the key to morale still remains vulnerable. The battle will be fought in depth and in three (or even four) dimensions: a model predicated on the infantry section or platoon no longer adequately reflects the nature of future war. In some sorts of fighting, physical fitness will take second place to technological dexterity.

Saying this is not the same as saying that manpower can now be traded off for machinery. Nor is it the same as saying that war has now become so physically undemanding that the Army can safely be shaped by the determinants of demography or political correctness. It is clearly in the interests of the society that the Army is called upon to defend that that Army should be constituted, even self-selected, in such a way that it fulfils its strategic objectives as effectively as it can. But one of the biggest constraints on the Army's efficiency remains manpower. And as the twentieth century closes the Army cannot get enough soldiers and cannot hold onto enough of those it does get. Its own preferred criteria for recruits will prevent it being able to fulfil the tasks it has been called upon to fulfil. The Army has to adapt to social change for reasons that have less to do with dogma and more to do with necessity.

In 1988, before the end of the Cold War, the Army was 1.5 per cent below full strength.[17] Furthermore, the age group from which the Army recruited was forecast to shrink by 20 per cent in the next five years. Under the acronym MARILYN (Manpower and Retention in the Lean Years of the Nineties), it set about addressing the problem – not least by becoming more flexible in its employment of women. The end of the Cold War and the consequent reduction in the size of the Army from 156,000, first to 116,000 and then to 120,000, therefore seemed to bring the Army's establishment and its recruiting base into line. In reality it did not. Throughout the 1990s the Army reported shortages of about 5,000 men, and it was suggested in 1997 that the underlying shortfall was 15,000 – in other words that the Army's strength was being kept up by improved retention of senior (and therefore) older soldiers rather than by fresh recruitment. On 1 April 1998 the actual figure lay between the two, with 109,800 in uniform.[18]

This consistent failure to meet even a lowered recruiting target is not satisfactorily answered in strategic terms. To blame the end of the Cold War for a public perception that the Army has no role is not consonant with the fact that the Army is now more actively engaged in operations which carry a high approval rating than it was before 1989. The Army maintains that 30 per cent of its strength is engaged on operations or about to be or has just returned from so being. Such an assertion begs the definition of operations, not least in relation to the discussion of high-intensity warfare above, but it also helps suggest that the reluctance to join the Army says less about its role, which is seen to be important and useful, and more about its nature as an institution.

The Army's readiness to respond to the call of equal opportunities is therefore pragmatic. It reflects its realisation that one substitute for a lack of white males is an appeal to blacks and females. Conveniently self-interest and good employment practice have combined. By realigning itself with civilian society it opens up its recruiting base. The cynic may conclude that its reluctance to confront the incorporation of homosexuals may reflect the Army's belief that comparatively few of the 6.1 per cent of males and 3.4 per cent of females who are homosexuals may want to enlist.[19]

In accommodating the demands of equal opportunities the Army is also embracing some of the language of political rights. This is less the community-based French concept which expresses iself in terms of the obligation of the citizen to defend his country and more the individualism espoused by British liberals which defines itself in terms of political equality. The individual's right to serve is an important counter to the Army's right to be different. In Chapter 8 Peter Bracken argues that a woman or a homosexual who has the same civil rights as the heterosexual can also claim, unless physically or mentally incapacitated, the comparable right to defend her or his country.

The idea of military service based on individual rights confronts a number of problems. One is indeed the notion that the Army is a moral community, not a collection of individuals. But another, and more profound one, is the absence of any historical relationship between citizenship and military service. This has been a major difference between Britain and France. In Chapter 13 Sebastian Roberts goes so far as to describe today's Army as a mercenary force; in one sense this is no more than an extension of its status as a professional body, but at another it is also a reflection of the fact that it incorporates soldiers who have no political rights as British citizens, including Irishmen and Gurkhas.

Rights are also germane to the position of junior soldiers. In the past the Army drew many of its long-serving other ranks from the Junior Leaders, units which bridged the gap between the school-leaving age and legal adulthood. Many attribute the current retention problems among non-commissioned officers to the lack of Junior Leaders. But their abolition conformed both to notions concerning citizenship and to United Nations directives. The former suggested that only those with the franchise, in other words aged 18 or over, should be required to serve their country. The latter, prompted by events in other continents, condemned the use of children in war. The trouble for the Army is that, by not being available as a job to those who leave school at 16, it forfeits the opportunity to recruit those who are at that stage seeking long-term careers. Junior service will now be revived through the establishment of an Army Foundation College. The fact that junior soldiers were not required to fight, and will not be so in the future, has not absolved this plan from criticism on the grounds of human rights.

The current Labour government has used the vocabulary of rights to explain and give coherence to its programme of political and constitutional change. Dr John Reid, when he was Minister of State for the Armed Forces, appreciated the force of rights-based arguments when he countered them by stressing that membership of society also carries obligations. His was a plea that Members of Parliament should recognise that 'the practice of war ... may imply the curtailment, in certain circumstances the negation of valued social rights'.[20] But a defence of the *status quo* based on the needs of war is hard to sustain when the practices are applied to issues derived essentially from the problems of peace-time. The Army's processes for administrative discharge, its rejection of those of homosexual orientation, and its procedures for managing the political behaviour of its members are all vulnerable to challenge in the European courts.

The rights at issue here are not those of civilians who wish to serve but of soldiers who have already opted to do so. Retention of those who have joined is as important an aspect of the Army's manpower problems and of its relationship to society as is recruiting. Its effects have caused Patrick Mileham (Chapter 17) to argue that Britain has not one army but two.[21] The first is that which is genuinely long service, whose members rise to senior commissioned or non-commissioned rank. The second is a short-service army, made up of people who serve much more limited engagements and which is by definition in need of constant renewal. Self-evidently the Army would need fewer recruits each year (and so put less strain on its fragile relationship with civilian society) if it could more fully satisfy the career aspirations of all those who had already joined it. One of the pressures on the Army as a community is the need to accommodate the social needs of existing members.

Some of the strain on the Army's own inner life is indeed external in origin. The expectation that fathers should be active in the home rather than absent on exercise; the need to accommodate the demands of two careers within the house-hold; the desire for domestic stability in the interests of the children's education; the cult of home ownership. In the nineteenth century the regiment saw itself as the soldier's family, and if he married its paternalism extended to his wife and children. But the shifting of that pattern is not exclusively the consequence of changes in society as a whole. The Army has played a part in its erosion, partly through a well-intentioned effort to apply what it has seen as best practice in other forms of employment.

The change in the background, education and expectations of officers has been particularly significant in this respect. The Army is much more meritocratic than Major Eric Joyce's paper for the Fabian Society, *Arms and the Man – Renewing the Armed Services*, allowed. Reggie von Zugbach and Mohammed Ishaq (Chapter 6) show that officers now come from a broader base of schools, even for those regiments which in the past have dominated the Army Board; the boarding public schools, whose dominance Joyce castigated, are less the models for secondary education and more the exceptions, as academic league tables give first place to day schools functioning as the old grammar schools once did. Most officers are now graduates, and their educational rite of passage is that of university rather than of Sandhurst. Those in technical arms are less restricted in career terms than was the case a decade or two ago. Officers' acceptance of a common culture is more conditional. Their attitude to mess life, if single, or to married quarters, if not, is much more critical. Common values are therefore not axiomatic.

The controversy surrounding Joyce's analysis of the social origins of the Army's officers obscured his much more important and substantive point, the conflict between management and command. Under the reforms introduced by Michael Heseltine in 1984, commanding officers are responsible for the management of their own budgets. The pressure from the Commission for Racial Equality and the needs of equal opportunities oblige them to monitor the careers of the men and women under their command as though they are personnel managers in large corporations. The Army has therefore embraced new management practices while failing to create the structures appropriate to them. Those promoted to command, presumably by virtue of their perceived potential to lead in war, are in practice required to deal with issues of severance, promotion and retirement. For this range of tasks they may not be the best people – or, if they are, they equally may not be the best commanders in combat.

The observation that good peacetime soldiers do not necessarily make good wartime warriors is hardly new. The purge of an officer corps at the beginning of a war, not just in the British Army, is a recurrent phenomenon. Command in war requires qualities of decisiveness, inner strength, and often sheer bloody-mindedness which are not so central in peace – and may even be at a discount when considering the personnel and welfare issues so central to the Army's public image, and to its recruiting and retention effort. The separation of the two functions goes against the instincts of an army shaped by the experience of colonial warfare and of regimental soldiering. But without such a separation the Army may continue to be reactive and defensive in the face of media scandal in peace, and may even fail in the exercise of its command function in war.

The Ministry of Defence has a poor record in the field of employee welfare. The ongoing saga of Gulf War syndrome is symptomatic of a whole range of related issues. Those who suffer injury and disability through their military service find themselves inadequately compensated and deprived of the forms of redress available to those in civil occupations. Post-traumatic stress disorder is recognised as a consequence of disaster in civil life, but has struggled to find incorporation within the pattern of military counselling.

The 1998 Strategic Defence Review was strong on the centrality of personnel issues but barely advanced policy in relation to them. Indeed some have argued that what it did was calculated to undermine the Army yet further. Recognising that the Army is in reality, at best, half a career, it promised to deliver a full educational programme, based on NVQs, for soldiers in service so as to prepare them for their lives after service. Enhancing subsequent civilian employability may boost recruiting but threatens to undermine retention.[22]

The proposal shows how much of a balancing act defence policy has to be. The fact that 25 per cent of those reported as homeless in April 1998 were ex-servicemen highlights the wisdom of the Strategic Defence Review. That so many soldiers should clearly have such difficulty in adapting from military to civilian life emphasises the difference between the two. But if the Army goes too far in its efforts to prepare soldiers to become civilians does it undermine its *raison d'être*?

Compromise may not make for intellectual coherence, but it is the solution to many things in life. The Army cannot be as different from society as it might like for reasons that are as much to do with pragmatism as with political correctness. But it is of course right to warn of the dangers inherent in adaptation of undermining the Army's own military effectiveness. An army that is manned by physically unfit, drug-dependent drag queens would be of no value. However, in conjuring up such caricatures as an argument against change, the Army itself misrepresents both the nature of civil society and those of its members who might actually be drawn to the military life. Moreover, it does itself a further disservice, because, in demanding that the entire Army conform to one interpretation of the nature of warfare, it may become the victim of its own propaganda, failing to prepare for the extraordinarily diverse nature of contemporary combat as much as for the variable and uncertain shape of future conflict.

NOTES

1. *The Times*, 8 November 1997.
2. *Daily Telegraph*, 23 September 1991; *The Times*, 26 June 1998; see also David Capitanchik and Richard Eichenberg, 'Defence and Public Opinion', *Chatham House Papers*, 20 (1983); J.C.M. Baynes, *The Soldier in Modern Society* (London: Eyre Methuen, 1972), pp. 56–65.
3. Olive Anderson, 'The Growth of Christian Militarism in Mid-Victorian Britain', *English Historical Review*, 84 (1971), pp. 46–72.
4. Alan Ramsay Skelley, *The Victorian Army at Home: the Recruitment and Terms and Conditions of the British Regular, 1859–1899* (London: Croom Helm, 1977), pp. 236–7; Edward M. Spiers, *The Army and Society 1815–1914* (London: Longman, 1980), pp. 38–9.
5. Spiers, *Army and Society*, p. 43.
6. Brian Bond, *British Military Policy between the Two World Wars* (Oxford: Clarendon Press, 1980), pp. 329–30; I am grateful to Mr Bill Buckingham for various other references on this point, as well as for drawing it to my attention.
7. Field Marshal Lord Carver, *Britain's Army in the 20th Century* (London: Macmillan, 1998), p. 408.
8. Figures given by Brigadier Freddie Viggers, Director of Manning (Army), in his presentation on 21 April 1998.
9. Arthur Bland, 'Are Our Children Going Soft?', *The Times*, 10 May 1996.
10. See, for example, *The Times*, 6 and 26 March 1998.
11. Ministry of Defence, *Report of the Homosexuality Policy Assessment Team*, February 1996, *passim*, but especially pp. 42–6, 149–51, 189, 195, 237.
12. Mark Barlow, 'Courts Martial: Time for an Independent Review', *Armed Services Forum*, 1 (February 1998), pp. 26–9.
13. Cm 3999, *The Strategic Defence Review* (London: Stationery Office, July 1998), supporting essays, 9–8, para 41.
14. For a consideration of this literature, see Hew Strachan, 'The Soldier's Experience in Two World Wars: Some Historiographical Comparisons', in Paul Addison and Angus Calder (eds), *Time to Kill: the Soldier's Experience of the War in the West 1939–1945* (London: Pimlico, 1997).
15. John Erickson, 'Red Army Battlefield Performance, 1941–45: the System and the Soldier',

and Jürgen Förster, 'Motivation and Indoctrination in the Wehrmacht, 1933–45', in Addison and Calder, *Time to Kill*; also Omer Bartov, *Hitler's Army: Soldiers, Nazis, and War in the Third Reich* (New York: Oxford University Press, 1991).

16. On this point J. Glenn Gray, *The Warriors: Reflections on Men in Battle* (New York: Harper & Row, 1970; reprinted University of Nebraska Press, 1998); T.E. Lawrence, *Seven Pillars of Wisdom,* is also relevant.

17. *The Times,* 3 November 1988.

18. House of Commons, 1997–98, 138–I, Defence Committee, *Eighth Report: the Strategic Defence Review,* I, para. 354.

19. Ministry of Defence, *Report of the Homosexuality Policy Assessment Team,* p.29.

20. John Reid, 'The Armed Forces and Society', *Journal of the Royal United Services Institute for Defence Studies* (April 1997), p. 33.

21. A point made by Patrick Mileham at the study day on 8 January 1998.

22. *Strategic Defence Review,* pp. 31–6; supporting essays, 9–1, 'A Policy for People', is fuller and more constructive.

PART I:
THE HISTORICAL CONTEXT

1

Liberalism and Conscription
1789–1919

Hew Strachan

Glasgow's Kelvingrove Park boasts the city's finest equestrian monument. It is a statue of Lord Roberts.[1] At first glance it confirms his reputation as an imperial soldier. The allegorical figures of war and victory which guard the base hail from south Asia as well as classical Greece. The battle honours are a roll-call of mid- and late-Victorian colonial wars – the Indian Mutiny, Umbeyla, Abyssinia, Lushai, Afghanistan, Burmah, South Africa. Marching along the friezes beneath the hooves of Roberts's charger are the soldiers he commanded. First the Indian Army, drawn not from the whole sub-continent but from what he himself called the 'martial races'. Second the regular soldiers of the British Army, voluntarily enlisted professionals recruited in the main from the lowest classes of home society and exiled overseas for the bulk of their careers. They are mute confirmation that the martial achievements of nineteenth-century Britain were not those of a nation in arms.

Closer consideration of the statue, however, reveals features which point not backwards in time but forwards, and not to the British empire but to the continent of Europe. Although the statue itself is a copy of one erected in Calcutta in 1898, the Glasgow version was unveiled on 21 August 1916. It is sur- prising enough that so much effort should have gone into so lavish a memorial in the middle of a world war. More relevant is the fact that 1916 was the year in which Britain formally adopted conscription and so definitively broke with the military institutions of its immediate past. Lord Roberts was being com- memorated not as a Victorian hero but as (in the words of the *Glasgow Herald's* leader writer on 22 August 1916) 'a prophet who, with more rapid strides than the majority of those who venture to instruct and inspire their contemporaries, has come into his own'. On one side of the base is the peroration of a speech given by Roberts in the city, in St Andrews Hall, on 6 May 1913: 'I seem to see the gleam in the near distance of the weapons and accoutrements of this Army of the future, this Citizen Army, warden of these isles, the pledge of peace and of the continued greatness of this Empire.'[2]

Roberts was greeted in Glasgow in 1913 with the honours accorded royalty but with an enthusiasm now reserved for pop stars or footballers. On 5 May he was given an honorary degree by Glasgow University. On 6 May a capacity audience of 5,000 filled St Andrews Hall to hear him speak: six times that number had applied for tickets and two overflow meetings had to be arranged. His speech was filmed and then played in the music halls and cinemas of the city and also of Edinburgh.

Roberts was speaking as President of the National Service League, an office he had assumed in 1905. The League itself had been set up in 1902 to call for conscription in peacetime for the purpose of home defence. It envisaged the creation of a second army, the first – the Regular Army – being committed to imperial defence and likely to be serving overseas in the event of a national emergency. This second army, Roberts told his Glasgow audience, should be 'drawn from all ranks and classes'. Its composition would therefore be very different from that which would three years later adorn the frieze on his memorial.

The popular and even sensationalist appeal of Roberts's call in 1913 rested on expedience: the remote possibility that the Royal Navy might fail to forestall an invasion. But the venerable field marshal also grounded his case in principle. 'In a democracy above all', he said, 'where the Government has become representative in the strictest sense of that word, and, in theory at least, is the mere agent of the national will, it is with the nation itself that the ultimate responsibility remains.'

The call for conscription was not unpopular. In 1910 the National Service League claimed the support of 105 MPs and by 1912 its membership was approaching 100,000.[3] The Liberal Secretary of State for War, R.B. Haldane, came under increasing Conservative attack. Haldane favoured the idea of a nation in arms, but wanted to achieve it through voluntary enlistment into the newly formed Territorial Army.[4] He therefore commissioned the Adjutant-General, Sir Ian Hamilton, to write a brief rebuttal of the case against conscription.

Hamilton's *Compulsory Service* (1910) infuriated Roberts, who replied in kind with *Fallacies and Facts: An Answer to 'Compulsory Service'* (1911). The book rejected the Liberals' equation of compulsory military training with despotism. Roberts associated conscription with the ideas of citizenship: the nation in arms would be the coping stone to democracy he averred.

> He alone possesses freedom, who can guard or maintain in arms his personal rights – and, by implication, can guard and maintain in arms the rights of the State. This principle, variously modified, governs the heroic period of English history. Obscured or obliterated, *pace* Mr Haldane, it governs English history now. It is inherent in the moral life itself; for it is but the political expression of the principle that man as man has duties as well as rights, and the higher he ascends in the scale of nature the more complex and varied those duties become.[5]

Most modern histories today cite the French revolutionary armies of 1793 as evidence to prove that conscription, constitutionalism and vigorous self-defence went hand in hand. But until the First World War itself gave practical effect to the Anglo-French entente, the long shadow of cross-channel enmity, the defeat of the French Army in 1870, and the volatility of the Third Republic's civil–military relations made France an intellectual prop of doubtful utility, at least in a constitutional context. Roberts preferred to hark back to the classical world. Athens, he told his readers, had declined when its citizens had ceased to be their own soldiers; Rome had flourished because its legions were made up of 'free-born citizens capable of bearing arms'.[6]

Between November 1912 and January 1913 Roberts was the centre of a small working party which met to discuss these matters. Their conclusion, 'that National Service was essential to security', rested on expedience, on the needs of home defence, rather than on principle. F.S. Oliver was given the task of drafting the group's findings for publication, but his work was overtaken by the outbreak of war and by the time that *Ordeal by Battle* was published in June 1915 the context had changed. Although the book's argument was in truth shaped more to the circumstances of peace than to those in which Britain now found itself, the delay in appearance enhanced its topicality and its sales.

Its fourth and final part, which contained the kernel of the National Service League's argument, was called 'Democracy and National Service'. But its strongest statement of political principle was to be found in Oliver's introduction:

> Democracy is not unlike other human institutions: it will not stand by its own virtue. If it lacks the loyalty, courage and strength to defend itself when attacked, it must perish as certainly as if it possessed no virtue whatsoever. Manhood suffrage implies manhood service. Without the acceptance of this principle Democracy is merely an imposture.[7]

But Oliver had put the cart before the horse. Britain did not have universal manhood suffrage in 1914; indeed it had the most restrictive franchise of any country in Europe, except Hungary. Only about 60 per cent of its adult male population enjoyed the vote, principally on the basis of residence and household occupation. Thus many, and possibly most, soldiers were not enfranchised. There was no equation between military service and citizenship. Although political reform was implicit in Roberts's and Oliver's calls for conscription, neither of them advocated it.

Roberts and Oliver were both Conservatives. But the party of progressivism and political change, the Liberals, was no more bent on franchise reform. Furthermore, it was deeply hostile to the concept of national service. For most potential political reformers conscription was not a corollary of liberalism but its antithesis. The fact that Britain's constitutional inheritance traced its roots to the 1689 settlement meant that its underlying premise was a check on the power of the state and the erection of a parliamentary bulwark against the dangers of militarism. Conservatives might favour conscription but would not urge suffrage reform; some Liberals might be persuaded to call for an extension of the franchise but they would also be the most likely to oppose conscription.

The situation was different in Europe. There manhood suffrage and manhood service were conceptually linked in a way that they were not in Britain. Indeed, Rousseau had forecast as much in the *Social Contract* in 1762. He was of the view that if the state treated its subjects as citizens, giving them the right to vote and to trial by jury, they in turn were under an obligation to shoulder a musket in its defence. The philosophers of the later French Enlightenment incorporated this thinking, evident most notably in its underpinning of the comte de Guibert's writings on tactics. Nonetheless circumstance rather than design was responsible for theory becoming practice in the wake of the French Revolution. Having failed to raise and retain a mass army by voluntary enlistment, the Committee of Public Safety fell back on conscription. Expedience was transmogrified into principle through the medium of revolutionary rhetoric. The phrases of Rousseau were drafted to support and justify a policy adopted for other reasons. To subsequent generations it mattered not that by 1798 the citizen soldiers were voting with their feet against continuous campaigning, nor that by 1812 Napoleon's army for the invasion of Russia contained fewer Frenchmen than representatives of other nations. What was more important was what people believed, and that included the notion that the French Revolution had inaugurated the nation in arms and that France's subsequent victories were attributable to the patriotic fervour of its citizens in uniform.

For much of the nineteenth century most of the European left therefore saw no incompatiblity between conscription and political progressivism. Indeed, as the manifestos of many revolutionaries in 1848 showed, the two could be linked. It was the professional and regular army that was seen as the threat to continental liberalism. Enlisted for long service and so detached from civil society, it could become the pliable tool of an autocratic monarch, available equally for political repression at home and for wars of aggression and acquisition abroad.

Jean Jaurès's *L'Armée Nouvelle*, published in its first form in 1910 and more widely in 1913, was the best known and most developed statement of the left's legacy from the French Revolution. Jaurès advocated the application of a Swiss-style citizen army, and did so in the belief that this was what would have resulted in France if the revolution had not been diverted from its 'normal democratic course'.[8] Jaurès pleaded for the integration of the Army and the nation, but he did so as a socialist convinced that such an army could only be used defensively. *L'Armée Nouvelle* was not translated into English until 1916, after the conscription debate in Britain had peaked, and it was abridged in the process. But Jaurès's assertion, so bizarre to English ears, survived: 'It is the workmen, the Socialists', he wrote, 'who demand that military service shall be universal.'[9]

France was both a republic and a democracy in 1914: Jaurès and his party were members of a state which, however imperfectly, embodied principles they wished to defend. On the other hand, Germany's constitution was sufficiently abhorrent to its socialists to ensure that, in theory at any rate, they were committed to its revolutionary overthrow. But in 1904 the leader of the German Socialist Party, August Bebel, still endorsed the prerogative of this same state to conscript men for the purposes of national defence: indeed he described his party as 'the most decisive defenders of the application of universal military service'.[10]

In Europe in 1914, political radicalism's complaint concerning conscription lay not with the principle but with the belief that its application in practice did not go far enough. Both Jaurès and Bebel would have drafted yet more men into the armies of France and Germany, so as to integrate them even more fully with their respective nations. But in Britain such thinking was associated with the right rather than the left. Although the Conservative Party refused to adopt National Service as policy, all but three of the 105 MPs who supported the National Service League in 1910 were Tory. By contrast, the Labour MP, Keir Hardie, believed that 'Conscription is the badge of the slave'. He declared in 1913: 'Compulsory military service is the negation of democracy. It compels the youth of the country, under penalty of fine and imprisonment, to learn the art of war. This is despotism not democracy.'[11] War did not shake such convictions. In 1915 the Trades Union Congress, fearful that military conscription would also signify industrial compulsion, overwhelmingly passed a resolution opposing National Service. Two years later, Ramsay MacDonald, the leader of the Independent Labour Party and, like Keir Hardie, a supporter of international socialism, rejected the case put forward by his now dead friend, Jaurès. He believed that the possession of an army, however enlisted, and even a citizen army, predisposed a nation to fight.

In this respect at any rate MacDonald was anxious not to align Britain with Europe. Part of the case mounted by those Liberal and Labour supporters who opposed conscription rested on the argument that it was alien to the British tradition. The supporters of conscription in 1915 contested this assertion. In their more romantic moments they harked back to the Anglo-Saxon fyrd. More relevantly they cited the Militia Act, which, at least in name, had only been suspended rather than positively repealed. The militia was dubbed the 'constitutional force', in recognition that it was a balance to the professional Army, a body commanded by the local gentry and thus a check on the power of the Crown.

The militia could indeed be raised by ballot rather than by voluntary enlistment. But the ballot had only been enforced in cases of dire national emergency – in the Seven Years War, the American War of Independence, and the Napoleonic Wars. It was a default mechanism: compulsion was not applied in peacetime and was in any case never applicable to the Regular Army itself. What had dictated attitudes to the militia in the eighteenth century was less constitutional propriety and more the needs of the developing British economy.

Scotland, as opposed to England, had no militia, and the eighteenth-century debate on its possible utility north of the border is particularly instructive.[12] Before the Union, in 1698, Andrew Fletcher of Saltoun attributed Scotland's comparative economic backwardness to the fact that too many young Scots preferred to go soldiering than to engage in more productive pursuits. He therefore favoured a militia in preference to a standing army: such an arrangement would provide an outlet for martial ardour without jeopardising national productivity. After the Act of Union, Adam Smith put the opposite case, *The Wealth of Nations* preferring a standing army. Smith saw professional armies as more competent than militias, and argued that they made for a more effective division of labour. Fletcher and Smith came to different conclusions, but they did so for the same reason – both sought economic efficiency rather than political utility.

This is not to say that the Scottish Enlightenment's debate over the nature of military service entirely ignored the sorts of propositions advanced by Rousseau. Smith still valued a martial spirit in the population as a whole, and David Hume, Adam Fergusson and Alexander Carlyle all saw the militia as a means of instilling 'virtue', believing that the capacity for self-defence was vital to a sense of freedom. But the point remains that the civic benefits and constitutional functions of military service were secondary to the economic imperatives.

Adam Smith and the Scottish Enlightenment, rather than Rousseau and the legacy of the French Revolution, were the roots from which nineteenth-century Victorian liberalism drew its intellectual succour. In the central debate concerning the relationship between the individual and the state, British liberalism began from the perspective of the individual and the need to protect his rights. On the continent of Europe the argument started from its opposite end: the collective needs of the community became the means to secure individual freedom. Nowhere was this contrast likely to be greater than in the area of military service, the most extreme instance of the subordination of the individual to the needs of the state.

What is therefore striking in the writings of the so-called English Utilitarians is how little attention they gave to military matters in general, and how infrequently, if at all, they saw military service as a means to emancipation rather than repression. The most significant exception to this generalisation was John Stuart Mill. In *On Liberty* Mill said that a citizen might be compelled to take a share in his country's defence. In 1867 he favoured the adoption by Britain of a Swiss-style citizen army. He referred to the example of the Union armies in America to show 'how a people will fight – when it is for themselves, for their own cause, for their own liberty, or for moral purposes which they regard equally with liberty'.[13]

Mill therefore equated the creation of 'a really national defensive force' with the idea of political freedom. Nonetheless he never went as far as Rousseau and the thinkers of the French Enlightenment. The second Reform Act was passed in the same year, 1867, and Mill advocated much greater working-class representation. It was a radical position. But he never linked his support of a wider franchise with the principle of compulsory military service. In 1871 he opposed Cardwell's Army Bill on the grounds that it perpetuated the regular, professional

Army, and embraced instead the principle of the nation in arms. In doing so, however, he was more concerned to counter the arguments of Smith's economics than to advance the cause of collective democracy: 'A citizen army in time of peace', he assured the Working Men's Peace Association, 'would cost the Government nothing except for the short period of its embodiment, and the loss of productive power by withdrawing from industry for a short time young men of that age would be scarcely felt.'[14]

Mill's assimilation of continental European socialism's thought on conscription may have been limited, but no other Liberal even came close to it in the years between the end of the Franco-Prussian War and the outbreak of the First World War. The British Army continuously struggled to recruit to its establishment in those years. Mill's case therefore rested on expediency as well as principle. However, the former could never drive the latter because the Army was not the bulwark of British home defence. The Army was an expeditionary force for employment in the empire. The Royal Navy was what prevented a French or, in due course, a German invasion. Furthermore, the corollary of a large navy – especially after the move from wood and sail to iron and steam, and even more after the adoption of the all big-gun battleship in 1905 – was high levels of expenditure. Over the same period Britain sustained higher average per capita spending on defence than any other state in the world.[15] It could do so because it had a fully developed system of direct taxation. The state opted to requisition the wealth of its voters rather than their time or their lives. Britain was enabled to trade the integrating effects of a nation in arms for the integrating effects of progressive taxation. Thus economic utility remained a conditioning factor in the formation of political principle.

When the First World War broke out the terms of the debate did not change. The primary issues remained those of economics, not of politics. Although conscription was introduced by a coalition cabinet in which Liberals dominated, and which had in Asquith a Liberal prime minister, constitutionalism and individualism were not the principal considerations. Having entered the war, those Liberals in government followed an agenda that was set by the needs of the war and the pursuit of victory, and not by a Gladstonian inheritance.[16]

The central question was – what was the best strategy for Britain? In answer, the deployment of forces between different fronts was less central and less divisive than post-war memoirs suggested. Rather, the key issue was the most effective management of resources. Britain had entered the war able to command the seas on behalf of the Entente. Allied to its maritime power was its position at the centre of the world's money markets: it could finance the war efforts of its allies by funding their overseas purchasing, and it could also produce munitions and equipment for its continental partners. To fulfil its role as the Entente's financier and armourer it had to sustain its own industrial base. Without that, not only would the manufacture of war-related equipment fall but so too would Britain's exports. If the pound then tumbled on foreign markets, the cost of Entente overseas purchasing would rise: in the short term British (and therefore Entente) credit would collapse and in the long term Britain's global economic position would be forfeit to the United States.

In 1914 Kitchener had set about the creation of a mass army through voluntary enlistment. He therefore added a third element to British strategy. But in doing so he drew men away from industry, so curbing output. By 1915 Reginald McKenna, the Chancellor of the Exchequer, and Walter Runciman, the President of the Board of Trade, feared that the pursuit of a mass army would undermine the economic pillars of British strategy. Lloyd George and the Conservative members of the coalition disagreed: they argued that Britain could do everything.

The debate threatened to shatter the coalition. But it was not a division over the principle of conscription; it was not a matter of the Conservatives and their unlikely ally promoting the needs of the state, and of Liberals defending the rights of the individual. The question was the proper size for the British Army given Britain's other contributions to the allied war effort. McKenna favoured 50 divisions, Lloyd George 70, and a deal was struck on 62. Conscription was a consequence of the commitment to a mass army, not its precursor.

Fiscal rectitude and good housekeeping may have been the only legacies of nineteenth-century liberalism in the cabinet (and even then only in a minority of its members), but broader principles were more in evidence on the party's parliamentary backbenches. Some of the opponents of the military service bills of 1915 and 1916 used the vocabulary of political rights. For them the success of Kitchener's appeal for recruits showed that a mass army could be raised through voluntary enlistment; the new armies proved that the Liberal state had the ability to adapt even to the demands of world war. One Liberal MP who resisted conscription, Richard Lambert, summarised these views: 'The basis of our British Liberty lies in the free service of a free people ... Voluntary service lies at the root of Liberalism just as Conscription is the true weapon of Tyranny.'[17] For Lambert and other Liberals, the war was a war against Prussianism and militarism; if Britain adopted Prussian methods to wage it, then it had effectively lost.

Although vocal, the proponents of 'old' liberalism were few in number. On 4 May 1916 the second reading of the Military Service Bill was passed by 328 votes to 36. Most MPs therefore accepted the proposition that in the last resort the state had the power to demand the services of all its citizens for the purposes of defence. The bill's only recognition of the rights of the individual – and a significant one in that it was unique among the belligerents in 1916 – was the allowance for conscientious objection.

Not once throughout the whole debate was F.S. Oliver's point taken up: compulsory military service was never linked to the introduction of universal suffrage. Nobody opposed conscription because its consequence would be a widening of the franchise, and nobody used the same argument as a reason for favouring it.

The easy explanation is that the left, which could be expected to support a wider franchise, opposed compulsion, while the right, which supported compulsion, opposed an increase in the electorate. Such an analysis is insufficient, not least because there is little evidence to support even an implicit acknowledgement that suffrage and conscription should be linked. Indeed the reverse is true. The manner in which compulsory military service was applied made it more likely that it would embrace those without political rights than those with.

Its first stage, the Military Service Act of January 1916, affected only unmarried men and childless widowers. The call up of married men was postponed, and so the really heated parliamentary debate took place over the conscription of men who were single. But unmarried men were precisely those least likely to have the vote: the overwhelming majority of voters were enfranchised through household suffrage, and they therefore tended to be those who had families and settled jobs. Secondly, the Act made men liable for call-up at the age of 18 and for overseas service at the age of 19; but nobody was eligible for the vote until he was 21. Neither point was used by the Liberal opponents of the bill.

Of course there is a superficial connection between the adoption of conscription in 1916 and the adoption of universal male suffrage only two years later, in 1918. But significantly the conferment of political rights followed, rather than preceded, the imposition of military obligations. Men were conscripted and possibly killed before they got the vote. Most important of all, the origins of the Fourth Reform Act do not in any positive sense lie in the debate over conscription.

The extension of male suffrage excited little interest before 1914, despite the Liberals' return to power in 1906.[18] Giving more men the vote would, after all, have only inflamed yet further the female suffragists. However, the outbreak of the war had the effect of disfranchising those who chose to serve. By joining up or even by moving into munitions production, those who were qualified by residence lost their votes. As each year of the war passed, the register became increasingly out of date, while the imminence of an election (which technically fell due in 1915) became more pressing. Parliament was confronted by a practical need – to update the register and in the process to ensure that those who had been displaced through war work were kept on it.

Conservatives became particularly anxious on this score: persuaded that those who had served in the Army were likely to vote Tory, they became more open to parliamentary reform than hitherto. In June 1916 Lloyd George, although he distanced himself from the detail of the bill after he became prime minister, wanted to make it a condition of his move to the War Office that those who served should be rewarded with the vote. Practicality was thus being elevated into principle. An ex-soldier could not, after all, be sensibly enfranchised for one election only. Unable to find a mechanism to meet its immediate objectives, Parliament found itself edging towards a more far-reaching measure.

The Fourth Reform Act conferred the vote on those who had been in the armed forces in two specific ways. First, those aged 19 who had seen active service were enfranchised, although they were not yet 21. Second, conscientious objectors were temporarily taken off the register. This was a retrospective decision, not reflected in the Military Service Acts of 1916, but reached in November 1917. It clearly flouted Liberal principles, in effect disfranchising conscientious objectors for five years between 1921 and 1926.

Universal male suffrage in 1918 was an independent development, whose final shape was affected by the fact that conscription was already in place; it was not the necessary or automatic concomitant of compulsory military service. By the same token, conscription was not the necessary corollary of universal male suffrage. In 1921 Britain reverted to voluntary enlistment.

Therefore conscription in the First World War, like the militia ballot in the eighteenth century, was a temporary expedient, adopted *in extremis*. Indeed, the issue of principle was comparatively unimportant in the debates of 1915–16 for precisely this reason – because no long-term change in policy was intended. When the victorious allies imposed a small professional army on the protesting Germans at Versailles in 1919, they reassured them that Germany's disarmament was but the first stage in a more general and multilateral process. The Americans and British were indeed keen to include a clause favouring voluntary enlistment in preference to conscription in the covenant of the League of Nations. But the French and Italians objected, the former arguing that 'compulsory military service ... appeared ... to be a fundamental issue of democracy, and was a corollary of universal suffrage'.[19]

That the British embraced the abolition of conscription with equanimity was not due simply to the fact that they were untrammelled by the legacy of its association with political rights; it was also because they saw voluntary enlistment as militarily and economically more effective. The Italian delegation at Versailles made the point: conscription – a manpower-intensive solution to defence – suited the poorer and more rural societies in ways which a competitively remunerated and well-equipped army did not. Britain abandoned the mass army at the end of the First World War in order to reduce defence costs, but it did so in the belief that new machinery – the tank and the aircraft – would act as a substitute for manpower.

The most forceful exponent of this trade-off in the inter-war years was J.F.C. Fuller. In an article on conscription published in *Encyclopedia Britannica* in 1929, Fuller declared that:

> The theory of conscription has run its course and is to-day growing out of date. A few years hence no conscript army will be able to face an organised attack by armed motor cars, let alone by tanks and kindred weapons. It will have its use solely as an army of occupation, a force of men which will occupy a conquered area but not conquer it. The fighting armies of the future will be voluntary, highly professional and highly paid, consequently comparatively small; this is the whole tendency of present day military evolution.[20]

Liddell Hart, as so often, seconded Fuller, but equally as often did it in his own way. Fuller was a fascist, Liddell Hart a liberal (at least with a small 'l'); he was also Vice-President of the National Council of Civil Liberties. Although an advocate of mechanisation, his analysis of war put morale, motivation, intelligence and intellect at its heart. He therefore argued that a free soldier fought better than a conscript. As Britain proceeded to reintroduce compulsory military service in 1939, Liddell Hart (who also rejected the continental commitment that was its corollary) wrote:

> Such a system entails the suppression of individual judgment – the Englishman's most cherished right. It violates the cardinal principle of a free community: that there should be restriction of individual freedom save when it is used for active interference with others' freedom. Our tradition of individual freedom is the slow-ripening fruit of centuries of effort. To surrender it within during the process of preparing to defend it against dangers without would be the supreme irony of our history.[21]

In the First World War Britain's Army was integrated with the nation as never before. If there is any sense in contemporary British society that the Army is an offspring of the nation, and that there is a need for the two to align their norms and practices, then it derives from the experiences of that war and of the war which followed it. But in 1916 the notion of the nation in arms was a new one, and after 1918 there was no necessity to see its message and its effects as anything other than a transient phenomenon. Britain fought the First World War, and adopted conscription to do so, without ever assimilating a link between military obligations and civic rights. In the process an opportunity to forge an enduring bond between Army and society was lost.

Most studies of modern armies and society begin with the French Revolution and its concept of the nation in arms. In 1880 the Third Republic opted to make 14 July, the day on which the Bastille had fallen in 1789 and on which royal power was – at least symbolically – ruptured, a public holiday. At first, the right disapproved, but by 1914 the parade fused the nation and the Army: it had become a popular celebration of patriotism, with the Army at its core but with the crowd integral to the occasion. France's soldiers belonged to the people.[22]

In Britain, on the other hand, continuity is to be sought not from the French Revolution but from the Scottish Enlightenment, with its idea of a small, professional army, standing apart from society. The freedom to pursue economic growth became a primary influence in shaping the country's military structure, while at the same time the fruits of that wealth themselves became the central pillar of the nation's strategy. Parliament huffed and puffed about its wish to curb the Crown's control of the Army, but in reality delivered less than its rhetoric promised. In Britain by 1914 the most significant annual military parade was the Trooping of the Colour. The date chosen was the monarch's official birthday, and the troops involved were drawn exclusively from the Crown's bodyguard. In essence this was a private occasion marking the relationship between the king and his troops. Staged in the comparatively confined area of

Horse Guards Parade, rather than along the length of the Champs Elysée, it was attended by privileged spectators who were essentially outsiders looking in on a more personal occasion. In 1913 Lord Roberts may have glimpsed an army of the people approaching from the distance, but after 1916–18 it marched out of view once more.

NOTES

1. Elizabeth Williamson, Anne Riches and Malcolm Higgs, *The Buildings of Scotland: Glasgow* (London: Penguin, 1990), pp. 55, 281.
2. There is a full report of Roberts's speech and of his visit to Glasgow in *Glasgow Herald*, 7 May 1913, pp. 9, 11–12. The account of the statue's unveiling is in issue 22 August 1916.
3. Rhodri Williams, *Defending the Empire: the Conservative Party and British Defence Policy 1899–1915* (New Haven, CT: Yale University Press, 1991), pp. 184–5; see also R.J.Q. Adams and Philip P. Poirier, *The Conscription Controversy in Great Britain, 1900–18* (London: Macmillan, 1987), pp. 1–47.
4. Edward M. Spiers, *Haldane: An Army Reformer* (Edinburgh: Edinburgh University Press, 1980), pp. 95, 98.
5. Field Marshal Earl Roberts, *Fallacies and Facts: An Answer to 'Compulsory Service'* (London: John Murray, 1911), pp. 196–7; also p. 208.
6. Roberts, *Fallacies and Facts*, pp. 199–202.
7. F.S. Oliver, *Ordeal by Battle* (London: Macmillan, 1915), p. xii.
8. Jean Jaurès, *L'Armée Nouvelle* (Paris: L'Humanité, 1915), p. 214.
9. Quoted in Denis Hayes, *Conscription Conflict: The Conflict of Ideas in the Struggle for and against Military Conscription in Britain Between 1901 and 1939* (London: Sheppard Press, 1949), p. 174.
10. Quoted in Jakob Vogel, *Nationen im Gleichshritt: der Kult der 'Nation in Waffen' in Deutschland und Frankreich, 1871–1914* (Göttingen: Vandenhoeck und Ruprecht, 1997), p. 223.
11. Quoted in Hayes, *Conscription Conflict*, p. 234.
12. For what follows see especially John Robertson, *The Scottish Enlightenment and the Militia Issue* (Edinburgh: John Donald, 1985).
13. Speech on 'Political Progress', 4 February 1867, at the Manchester Reform Club, in *Public and Parliamentary Speeches* (Toronto: Toronto University Press, 1988), ed. John M. Robson and Bruce L. Kinzer, *The Collected Works of John Stuart Mill*, Vol. XXVIII, p. 129. A recent discussion of these points is by April Carter, 'Liberalism and the Obligation to Military Service', *Political Studies*, XLVI (1998), pp. 68–81.
14. *Collected Works of Mill*, Vol. XXIX, p. 413.
15. Lance E. Davis and Robert A. Huttenback, *Mammon and the Pursuit of Empire: the Political Economy of British Imperialism 1860–1912* (Cambridge: Cambridge University Press, 1986), p. 160. For a corrective, see J.M. Hobson 'The Military Extraction Gap and the Wary Titan: the Fiscal Sociology of British Defence Policy 1870–1913', *Journal of European Economic History*, XXII (1993), pp. 461–506, who points to the dangers of per capita calculations. See, generally, Bernard Semmel, *Liberalism and Naval Strategy: Ideology, Interest, and Sea Power During the Pax Britannica* (Boston: Allen & Unwin, 1986).
16. This is a major theme of David French's writings; see especially, *British Economic and Strategic Planning 1905–1915* (London: Allen & Unwin, 1982), and *British Strategy and War Aims 1914–1916* (London: Allen & Unwin, 1986).
17. Richard C. Lambert, *The Parliamentary History of Conscription in Great Britain being a*

Summary of the Parliamentary Debates, etc., with an index and text of the Military Service Acts (London: Allen & Unwin, 1917), p. iv.

18. What follows relies on Martin Pugh, *Electoral Reform in War and Peace 1906–18* (London: Routledge & Kegan Paul, 1978).
19. Hayes, *Conscription Conflict*, p. 349.
20. Quoted in Hayes, *Conscription Conflict*, p. 357.
21. Quoted in Hayes, *Conscription Conflict*, p. 358.
22. Vogel, *Nationen im Gleichschritt.*

2

The British Army as a Social Institution 1939–45

Jeremy A. Crang

On the eve of the Second World War the small, peacetime Regular Army of some 220,000 men, was still, in many ways, a very traditional, conservative social institution. Certainly, under Leslie Hore-Belisha (who became Secretary of State for War in May 1937) efforts were made to improve the daily lot of the soldier. Faced with a recruiting crisis which was conceived of as being in large part due to the archaic nature of military life, measures were taken, for instance, to provide better barrack accommodation, raise the standard of Army cooking and enhance pay and promotion prospects.[1] Yet despite these changes the Army was to remain an essentially inward-looking organisation which shared few of the values of the civilian society it served.[2] 'The present-day army', observed one new recruit in the early months of the war, 'lacks every single one of those characteristics that make a democratic army.'[3]

During the Second World War, and for the second time in the century, this institution was forced to absorb a generation of civilians into its ranks. With the threat of war looming, in May 1939 the Military Training Act was introduced which required all men of 20 years of age to undergo six months training in the armed forces. On the outbreak of war in September this was superseded by the National Service (Armed Forces) Act which imposed a liability to military service on all males between 18 and 41 for the duration of the emergency.[4] While voluntary recruitment continued to play an important subsidiary role in filling the ranks, during the course of the war the Army absorbed nearly three million men, three-quarters of whom were conscripts.[5] Drawn from all occupational groups and social backgrounds, this mass army of civilians had to be moulded by the military authorities into an effective fighting force.

The aim of this essay is to seek to assess the impact of this process of integration on the Army as a social institution. In order to do this several aspects of the Army's social organisation will be examined: other-rank selection, officer selection, officer–man relations, Army welfare and Army education. The essay will begin by looking at the problems the Army faced in these areas and the solutions that were adopted. It will then say something briefly about the extent of social change in the wartime Army. It should also be noted that this investigation refers largely to the Army at home since that was where the bulk of it was stationed for most of the war. Indeed, it was not until after D-Day that the majority of the Army was overseas and even at the end of the war about one-third of soldiers were still serving at home.[6]

One problem the Army faced as a result of its great wartime expansion related to the selection of soldiers for the wide variety of occupations within a modern technological army. These included, for example, such diverse roles as a rifleman in the infantry, a gunlayer in the Royal Artillery, a tank driver in the Royal Armoured Corps and a skilled tradesman in the Royal Engineers. It was a question of placing the right man, as far as possible, in the right job. At the beginning of the war the procedure for selecting new recruits for particular roles in the Army was largely *ad hoc*. Men liable to be called up for military service under the National Service Act were called upon to register at one of the local offices of the Ministry of Labour and National Service. There each man was required to provide certain personal information, such as date of birth, occupation and employer, in order to assist in placing him with one of the three services. He was also able to express a preference for the service he wished to join although no guarantees could be given that he would be posted to his chosen service.

After the initial sorting of registration, men were summoned to a local recruiting centre. Each was medically examined and then interviewed by the recruiting officer of the service he hoped, or was destined, to join. If a man was interviewed for the Army, the recruiting officer recommended him for a particular arm, taking into account his age, medical condition, civilian experience and preferences. The recruiting officer's recommendations were then forwarded to the regional offices of the Ministry of Labour and National Service who endeavoured to allocate men to corps (or regiments) in accordance with the War Office's manpower requirements and, whenever possible, with regard to a recruit's family or territorial claims on service in a particular corps. In the first instance new recruits were posted to corps training units before being sent on to a battalion or equivalent unit. Under this system, a man's future role in the Army was, to a large extent, decided by a recruiting officer after a short meeting with the new recruit.[7]

It was crucial, particularly in view of the competing claims on wartime manpower and the pressing time factor that came to dominate every military task, that the Army efficiently used the manpower resources it had at its disposal. During the early years of the war, however, the existing selection system came to be seen as increasingly inadequate. First, there was no detailed record of the range of employments within the Army and the aptitudes and the temperamental characteristics necessary to carry them out satisfactorily; a problem compounded by the fact that few military occupations had a direct civilian equivalent. Second, there was no comprehensive assessment of how a man could most efficiently be employed within the Army. The recruiting officer's interview could only partially reveal a man's abilities, personality traits and capacity to learn. Moreover, these officers were untrained in interview techniques and there were no guidelines to ensure uniformity across the system. Third, there were difficulties with the way in which new recruits were enlisted into the Army. Under the existing procedure, recruits were allocated directly to corps. There was, however, a wide range of jobs to be undertaken in each corps. The Royal Engineers, for instance, needed not only skilled mechanical tradesmen, but drivers, storekeepers, clerks and domestic staff. To allocate a man to a corps was thus to make no recommendation as to the type of work he should undertake. What was more, if a man was misplaced the machinery of transfer was complicated. The loyalty of both men and commanding officers was often, in the first instance, a loyalty to their particular corps or regiment, and with their strong local associations and sectional interests, this could make the process of transfer difficult.[8]

Concern among the military authorities grew. Evidence began to accumulate about how inefficiently the Army was using its manpower resources. On the basis of tests conducted in Northern Command during 1940, it was estimated that 4 per cent of all intakes were useless for training as soldiers; 20 per cent of every infantry intake and 50 per cent of every Royal Armoured Corps intake had not the intelligence for full efficiency in the corps to which they had been allocated; and 20 per cent of every infantry intake and 50 per cent of every Pioneer Corps intake were capable of efficient service in a more skilled arm.[9] Not only did this misplacement have obvious implications for operational efficiency but also for soldiers' morale since men often became maladjusted through being employed either above or below their capacity. This resulted, on occasions, in recruits suffering psychiatric breakdowns.[10] Furthermore, there was growing public disquiet about the arbitrary methods employed by the Army, and in the summer of 1941 the government appointed Sir William Beveridge to inquire into the use of skilled men in the services. His committee's report, which was completed in the autumn, revealed that after two years of war less than half of the engineers joining the Army had been mustered in any engineering trade. The committee could cite, among others, a sheet metal worker sweeping barracks in the infantry and an electrical and mechanical engineer working as a cook for the military police.[11] Clearly, action had to be taken.

As a result of these concerns, in the summer of 1941 a new Directorate for the Selection of Personnel (DSP) was established in the War Office. Following a number of trials, the general service selection scheme was introduced a year later. Under the scheme, new recruits to the Army were enlisted, in the first instance, not into individual corps but into a General Service Corps and posted to Primary Training Centres. There they underwent six weeks of basic training and completed a battery of intelligence and aptitude tests. Each recruit was interviewed by a specially trained personnel selection officer who made 'training recommendations' for broad types of work (such as 'driving', 'signalling', 'combatant' or 'clerical') taking into account a man's wishes, civilian experience, medical category, temperamental characteristics and test scores; the minimum test scores for each recommendation having been devised after job analyses of all Army employments. Recruits with very low test scores, or who for some other reason were regarded as unstable, were referred to Army psychiatrists who could recommend special employment or discharge. The 'training recommendations' were then forwarded to the War Office which allocated men to corps (or regiments) on the basis of their individual recommendations, and ensured that each arm received a distribution of men by general intelligence. Account was also taken, where possible, of a recruit's family or territorial links with a particular corps. Recruits were then sent to corps training units accompanied by an agreed 'training recommendation' and a suggestion as to a specific job within that recommendation.[12]

The introduction of the general service selection scheme represented a significant advance on any previous other-rank selection system and brought with it the institutional recognition that recruits had different individual capabilities, temperaments and job needs, and that quality was as important as quantity. There was considerable evidence to suggest that the new scheme helped to ensure a more efficient use of the Army's manpower. Although it was difficult to compare directly the new methods with the old – adequate records for the period before the summer of 1942 were not available, and training failure rates were not strictly comparable over time because they tended to vary in accordance with the demand for and supply of manpower for the various arms – several follow-up studies nevertheless revealed that from the beginning of their Army careers men were being more suitably employed than before. As examples, the training failure rate for tradesmen fell from 17–27 per cent to 9 per cent, and for drivers from 16–20 per cent to 3 per cent. Other studies revealed that under the new system the training failure rate for signallers was 7 per cent, storemen 3 per cent and clerks 2 per cent. In 1944 a study of over 8,000 Army recruits, in several representative arms, found that the training failure rates averaged less than 5 per cent.[13] 'There is ample evidence', commented the DSP, 'that the proportion of men succeeding in each army occupation has been markedly increased since the introduction of the new system.'[14] There was also evidence of an improvement in morale. One Army commander observed:

> Although their tests at first sight seem gibberish, one point stands out – the men themselves believe in it. Previously, if a man fancied himself as a clerk, nothing would persuade him that he really ought to be a mechanic, but if the DSP tells him so he seems willing to admit that he must have been wrong. This has, of course, an enormous psychological effect in making men contented and keen at their work.[15]

While the military authorities tackled the problem of other-rank selection, they were also confronted with the question of officer selection. At the beginning of the war candidates for commissions were selected for officer training, after a period in the ranks, by a senior regular officer on the basis of a short interview. Successful candidates were sent to Officer Cadet Training Units (OCTUs).[16] It was vital, in view of the demands on officers in modern technological warfare, that competent men be selected as officers in sufficient numbers. As the war progressed, however, the officer selection system came to be seen as increasingly inadequate. Unlike other-rank selection, which was largely concerned with measuring mental abilities, officer selection was more a matter of appraising personality. Yet no matter how shrewd the senior officer appointed to select potential officers, a proper judgement could not be made on the basis of a short interview; and, in contrast to the previous war, there was less opportunity for selection on the basis of performance in battle. Furthermore, since the senior officers were untrained and appointed on an *ad hoc* basis, there was no way of knowing where the line was normally drawn between acceptance and rejection.[17]

In the summer of 1940 the War Office tried to solve this problem by replacing the senior officer's interview with an interview before a command interview board. These boards were headed by a permanent president, a full colonel drawn from the reserve, who was assisted by commanding officers seconded from local units. The presidents were chosen for their good judgement and by being permanent it was hoped that greater expertise and uniformity would be injected into the system. The establishment of the boards did little, however, to improve matters. Not only was there scant attempt to bring the presidents together to ensure common standards, but the boards did not ameliorate the inherent weaknesses in the interview technique.[18] In short, a candidate still stood or fell by the first impression he created. 'An awesome business,' related one candidate, 'not improved by the thought that one's entire future may be dependent upon the state of another man's liver.'[19] It became evident, moreover, that as the demand for officers outstripped the traditional public school sources, so the boards were poorly placed to assess candidates from a wider cross-section of the nation since the interviewing officers were confronted with men from social backgrounds of which they knew little. Unsurprisingly, the boards came to assume something of a reputation for allowing social bias to colour their judgements.[20] 'I was made to feel that my residence at a couple of English universities', wrote one puzzled interviewee, 'doesn't quite make up for the fact that my old headmaster didn't attend the Headmasters' Conference.'[21]

The military authorities became increasingly concerned. By the middle of 1941 a quarter of cadets were failing their officer training. Not only did this high failure rate have operational implications since it created a shortfall of new officers, but it also undermined morale since candidates were oppressed by the knowledge that a significant number of them would fail their officer training.[22] Furthermore, the cumulative effects of poor selection were evident in the number of officers who proved unable to shoulder the burdens of leadership and suffered psychiatric breakdowns.[23] Concern among the military authorities was set against a backdrop of growing public unease over the question of officer selection.[24] Plainly, steps had to be taken to improve matters.

In response to these concerns, in the spring of 1942 the military authorities introduced new War Office Selection Boards (WOSBs) which operated under the control of the DSP. The staff of the boards included a president (a senior regular officer), military testing officers (who were line officers of some experience), a psychiatrist and psychologist (assisted by sergeant-testers trained in psychological techniques). Under the new system, officer candidates reported to the boards, which were usually situated in large country houses, for a three-day selection process. Those attending the boards were required to conceal their badges of rank and were known only as numbers. During their stay the candidates completed a series of psychological tests designed to assess their powers of leadership. These included 'leaderless group' tests during which leaderless groups of candidates were observed as they completed designated tasks. Candidates were also interviewed by the psychiatrist who attempted to detect any unrecognised potential or underlying instability. At the end of the selection process, the board convened in order to assess the candidates. Those who satisfied the boards were sent on to officer training.[25]

The introduction of the WOSBs represented a more meritocratic system of officer selection than hitherto and seemed to give practical expression to the notion that every soldier had a field marshal's baton in his knapsack, and that ability, rather than wealth and the correct educational background, was the sole prerequisite for commissioned rank. Certainly, there was a good deal of evidence to suggest that the new procedure improved the efficiency of officer selection. During the summer of 1942, while the old and the new boards were working simultaneously, the opportunity was taken to compare the two systems by following up potential officers at OCTUs. Of those selected by the old methods, 22 per cent were rated above average and 37 per cent below average (13 per cent of these being markedly below average). Despite passing as great a proportion of the total candidates as the old boards, the corresponding figures for those selected by the WOSBs were 35 per cent above average, 25 per cent below average (8 per cent of these being markedly below average).[26] There was also evidence that the new methods created greater confidence in the officer selection process. Anonymous questionnaires revealed that an overwhelming proportion of both successful and unsuccessful candidates were satisfied with the procedure; complaints from those rejected by the boards tended to come mainly from public school candidates.[27] Overall, between 1943 and 1945 (a time in which it was generally conceded that the quality of Army intakes declined) the failure rate during officer training fell to 8 per cent.[28] The quality of officers also seemed acceptable. Although it was not possible to make a strict comparison with those selected under the old procedure, in follow-up studies of officers selected by WOSBs who were serving in the Mediterranean campaign, and in infantry units in north-west Europe, 76 per cent proved to be giving completely satisfactory service in the opinion of their commanding officers.[29]

The War Office also had to give consideration to the question of officer–man relations. The establishment of a close and comradely relationship between officers and men was of vital importance to the morale and fighting efficiency of the Army. As the war developed, however, it became clear that relations left a lot to be desired. The wartime conscript soldiers were more class conscious and generally better educated than their predecessors and were to look much more sceptically on the privileges of rank and the autocratic style of leadership that characterised the Army. In this respect the military authorities faced two particular problems. First, while the privileges accorded to officers were generally accepted if they were borne of military necessity, those for which there seemed to be little justification, apart from the assumption that gentility was concomitant with an officer's status, were resented by many of the soldiers. In the summer of 1942 it was reported that:

> The morale and fighting spirit of the Army as a whole would be enhanced if the ordinary soldier could be reassured that differentiations due to social tradition and the subordination involved in military discipline do not imply a fundamental conflict of interests. Anything, on the other hand, that strengthens his belief in the existence of a fundamental gulf or barrier between himself and his leaders has an immediate and marked adverse effect on morale.[30]

The second, and more important, problem was the poor standard of man-management on the part of junior officers. While most soldiers were prepared to concede the necessity of officers leading a somewhat detached life from their own and of following even the worst leader, it was clear that they were going to require tactful and sympathetic handling if their willing co-operation was to be maintained. But while it might have been thought that the new wartime officers, nearly all of whom had spent a period in the ranks, would bring a new degree of sympathy and understanding to their relations with their men, it was ironic that many of them seemed to go to great lengths to distance themselves from their subordinates. One soldier wrote of 'beardless young OCTU products, who are much too delighted with their new uniforms seriously to bother about such trivial matters as morale'.[31] The result was a worrying gulf between officers and men that threatened to undermine the solidarity of the Army. 'The problem', noted one report at the end of 1942, 'is largely one of officering: the troops are ready enough to feel friendliness, respect, and admiration for the right type of officer ... The troops' letters show, however, that such a relationship is far from universal.'[32]

The military authorities took steps to try to improve matters. Mindful of the readiness of Parliament and the press to attack the Army for perpetuating an outdated class system, some of the privileges of rank were restricted. Officers, it was instructed, were no longer permitted to reserve hotel bars and lounges for their own exclusive use;[33] the use of military transport by officers for recreational purposes was limited;[34] access to private medicine for those who could afford it was no longer to be the sole preserve of officers;[35] and attempts were made to equalise the living conditions of troopships which were a particular source of grievance to the rank and file.[36] Measures were also taken to improve man-management. The WOSB procedure included tests designed to assess a candidate's capacity to manage his men;[37] the syllabuses of OCTUs were modified to incorporate more training in man-management;[38] and commanding officers were encouraged to improve man-management practices in their units.[39] Furthermore, efforts were made to promote a more enlightened style of leadership. These were embodied in two pamphlets issued to officers: *The Soldier's Welfare* (1941) and *Comrades in Arms* (1942). While in former times the soldier's place might have been 'not to reason why but to do or die', officers were now instructed that recruits would come into the Army suspicious and resentful of authority and it would be necessary to explain the reasons for orders to maintain their full co-operation. Officers were advised that they had a duty to seek out the men's views on most matters affecting their welfare and that such action strengthened discipline and was not a sign of weakness. Officers were even encouraged to have 'free for all' discussions with their men over particularly controversial matters as a means of defusing discontent and getting to know each other's mind and temperament.[40] Underpinning this, in 1943 a system of weekly 'request hours' was instituted when men could approach officers informally over any matter that was troubling them.[41]

Over the war years, then, the military authorities made efforts not only to reduce some of the more indefensible inequalities between officers and men, but also to inspire a more democratic style of leadership which, in the view of one soldier, 'set the seal of approval upon the fullest *human* associations in place of the formal'.[42] Together these initiatives seemed like a blueprint for the breaking down of the old feudal relationship between officers and men. As the war went on there was evidence of an improvement in the relationship between the ranks. By the beginning of 1945 it was said that commanders generally were 'well satisfied with the relations between officers and men'.[43] A measure of solidarity seemed to have returned to the Army.

Welfare provision was another aspect of Army life that came under scrutiny in the War Office. At the beginning of the war the welfare of the soldier was regarded as first and foremost a matter for units and regimental officers. No official welfare organisation existed within the Army and what central services were provided were limited to a few basic amenities such as the NAAFI. Little or nothing, for instance, was provided to help cope with a soldier's personal or domestic concerns.[44] It soon became clear, however, that this was insufficient. The wartime soldiers brought with them a number of pressing welfare problems. The lack of amenities and recreational facilities was one issue that played on the minds of the soldiers. 'Ask any bachelor soldier what he most dislikes about army life', commented one officer, 'and I think he will tell you that it is the lack of any home comfort, the dreariness and lack of colour.'[45] A further problem was the enforced separation from families which often brought with it a host of pressing home worries. 'It is surprising to hear the chaps when they talk about their homes', confided another soldier. 'Many are married and have young children and even the toughest is full of concern for his wife and family.'[46] Indeed, the 'anxious soldier' was to become a recognisable character of the war.[47] It was clear that these matters needed to be addressed if the morale and fighting efficiency of the Army were to be maintained.

It was soon apparent, however, that the efforts of regimental officers alone would not be sufficient to cater for these welfare needs. Not only were they considered to be fully occupied in training the new troops, and thus less able to devote time to welfare matters, but some of the welfare problems that they had to deal with were outside the experience of the average junior officer.[48] Various voluntary organisations provided welfare support where they could but the service was patchy and uncoordinated.[49] It was in these circumstances that at the end of 1939 a network of voluntary Army welfare officers was set up across the country, and in the summer of 1940 a new Directorate of Welfare was established in the War Office to oversee welfare matters; a process expedited by Parliament's desire to see proper provision made for the forces.[50] Under the auspices of the welfare organisation a wide spectrum of services was built up. For a start, a range of amenities and recreational facilities was laid on for the soldiers. A network of canteens was organised; a hobby gardening scheme was devised; film shows were arranged; a central pool of artistes (or 'stars in battledress' as it became known) was formed to provide live entertainment; a broadcasting section was established to develop wireless programmes for the troops; and a host of Army newspapers was published around the world – from *The Orkney Blast* to *Eighth Army News*.[51] Various gifts were also distributed. According to one officer, the public's eagerness to ensure the comfort of servicemen led to the donation of some unusual items:

> One amazing parcel from friends in America included thick flannel night gowns evidently cut for giants and buttoning down the back from neck to heel, but our sincerest thanks go to the well-wisher who presented a pair of [ra]coon-skin underpants with the fur inside. One day we may hear from the soldier who wears them – probably a Provost Sergeant in Libya.[52]

In addition, assistance was provided for soldiers with personal and domestic worries. For troops concerned about the fate of their loved ones under the bombing, an air raid enquiry scheme was set up to provide prompt information about families in affected areas. A reconciliation scheme was instituted to help patch up differences between husband and wife before a family was broken up without good cause. An Army legal aid scheme was also launched to tender advice to soldiers on a range of civil matters. By the end of the conflict 175,000 cases of all types had been dealt with under the scheme.[53]

During the course of the war the War Office established a new welfare organisation in the Army and instituted a wide gamut of welfare services for the troops. What the war seemed to demonstrate was that proper provision needed to be made both for the soldier's recreation and the relief of his anxieties about personal matters if he was to function with full efficiency. There was a good deal of evidence to suggest that Army welfare contributed to the well-being of the troops. Not only did reports draw attention to a widespread appreciation of the welfare efforts made on their behalf, but one senior officer described the welfare organisation as 'an indispensable factor in maintaining morale, and that without it the modern soldier cannot be enabled to reproduce in his Army life conditions which, in his estimation, are sufficiently civilised to be tolerable'.[54]

Alongside welfare provision, educational provision also came under consideration. In the early months of the war official Army education virtually ceased and the bulk of the Army Educational Corps (AEC) was assigned to cipher duties. Education, it was believed, had no place in a wartime Army under active service conditions.[55] During the course of 1940, however, the military authorities were forced to reconsider their position. Not only was there a demand for educational provision from among conscript soldiers deprived of their normal peacetime studies, but there was a good deal of agitation in the press for suitable facilities to be provided. It was believed, moreover, that education could be used to sustain the morale of the troops while many of them sat around in Britain taking little active part in the war effort – a problem compounded by the withdrawal from Dunkirk. [56] Thus, in the autumn of 1940 a new scheme of education was introduced. Under the scheme, which was to be voluntary and take place in off-duty hours, a range of subjects was to be made available, including the humanities, utilities and hobby interests. The providers of education were to be serving teachers and lecturers, local education authorities and various universities and voluntary bodies. The AEC was to return to educational work to match demand with supply and a new Directorate of Education was established in the War Office to oversee the scheme.[57]

Although these activities were to continue throughout the war years, it soon became apparent that the voluntary scheme was not as effective as had been envisaged. Not only did the majority of soldiers have little interest in participating in voluntary education classes in their spare time on what were perceived to be mainly scholarly subjects, but the irregular duty hours, the movement of units around the country and the call-up of civilian tutors made it difficult to organise systematic education even for those that wanted it. By the spring of 1941 it was estimated that 80 per cent of troops remained untouched by educational provision. In the meantime, news of defeats in the Middle East and the prospect of a continued sedentary existence for many soldiers in Britain raised fresh concerns over morale.[58] It was in these circumstances that in the summer the military authorities announced another scheme of education for the Army. Under the scheme, which was to be compulsory and take place in training time, junior officers were to conduct weekly discussions with their men on current events, the aim being to inspire the troops by persuading them of the objectives for which Britain was fighting. A new Army Bureau of Current Affairs (ABCA) was set up in the War Office to administer the scheme, and the ABCA was to supply officers with two pamphlets on which discussions could be based: *War* and *Current Affairs*. The AEC was to act as the ABCA's local agents and give officers any assistance required. During 1941–45 soldiers were encouraged to discuss a wide range of subjects under the ABCA scheme, including such issues as the nation's health, education and social security.[59]

While the ABCA scheme was to remain in operation throughout the war years, by the summer of 1942 it was evident that there was still room for expansion in the field of Army education. For a start, the military situation was still depressing, with news of further defeats in the Middle East and Far East, and it was considered that something more needed to be done to sustain morale. Moreover, the ABCA scheme revealed just how ignorant of the country's history and institutions the average soldier was, and it was evident that some instruction in these matters was needed if current affairs discussions were to work effectively.[60] With these considerations in mind a further education scheme was set out in the autumn of 1942. Three extra hours of compulsory education were to be carried out each week over the coming winter alongside ABCA. One hour was to be devoted to military-related subjects such as map-reading; a second to hobbies or study for professional qualifications; and a third to a discussion of the British empire and the British way of life. This third hour, it was hoped, would provide a systematic course of civic instruction against which current affairs could be placed and would further motivate the troops by focusing on aspects of a Britain worth fighting for.

The scheme was to be run by the Directorate of Education and the Directorate was to supply reading material for the third hour in the form of a booklet entitled *British Way and Purpose* (BWP). Every effort was to be made to find instructors for the scheme from units themselves, but arrangements were put in hand for civilian education organisations and the AEC to help out where required. The winter scheme, as it became known, was put into operation over the winter of 1942–43 and was repeated in 1943–44. The BWP hour, however, was to continue throughout the year and remained part of the training programme for the rest of the war. From 1942–45 troops were invited to debate a wide spectrum of matters related to British democratic, social and economic institutions during this discussion period.[61]

During the course of the war the War Office initiated an impressive array of educational schemes for the troops. These represented a marked advance on anything previously available to the Army and an attempt by the military authorities to educate a generation of soldiers in current affairs and citizenship. What the experience of the conflict seemed to illustrate was that the modern soldier would no longer be motivated simply by appeals to duty or patriotism, but that as an intelligent being he needed to be persuaded of the positive objectives for which he was fighting. There was evidence to suggest that the ABCA and BWP hours assisted in improving the morale of the Army. Reports indicated that these discussions helped to bolster the troops' faith in the war effort and one commander concluded that they were 'a necessary part, in the broadest sense, of the armoury of the efficient solder'.[62]

Having examined some of the major aspects of Army life, we can see that a good deal of social change took place in the Army during the Second World War.

It became an institution seemingly more careful of human values, more responsive to the needs and aspirations of the ordinary soldier, and more democratic in spirit. 'The changes that have been made in the British Army in the past four years are very great', observed the soldier who had decried the undemocratic nature of the Army in the early months of the war. 'It is difficult now to remember how backward our Army was in 1939.'[63] In accounting for these developments, several factors seem to have been influential. First and foremost was the influx of civilians into the Army and the need to create from them a fighting force of high morale and efficiency to take on the Axis powers. It was no surprise that the bulk of reforms took place between 1940 and 1942 when military prospects were bleakest and new methods more readily employed. Public pressure also seems to have played its part with all aspects of Army administration subject to close scrutiny in Parliament and the press. The role of personalities was important too, and none more so than the Adjutant-General, General Sir Ronald Forbes Adam, who oversaw many of the reforms that were implemented. He emerges as a man with a deep understanding of the wartime citizen Army and as one of the most notable Army reformers of his generation. Finally, it should be noted that change did not occur within a vacuum. Parallel developments took place outside the Army such as the adoption of scientific management techniques in industry; the establishment of joint production committees of managers and workers; and the extension of welfare provision in the workplace. In this sense, the Army mirrored civilian society.

Although social change undoubtedly took place in the Army, questions do, however, have to be raised about just how profound this change was. Taking, for example, the new other-rank selection methods, it was clear that some of the more traditionalist elements within the Army remained unconvinced by the general service selection scheme. No doubt partly due to the fact that selection was conducted in isolation from the bulk of the Army and thus assumed an air of mystery, the view was still held that dull men made the best soldiers and that psychological tests placed unintelligent men who would make good fighters in non-fighting jobs. The involvement of the psychiatrist was seen as a convenient escape route for malingerers determined to evade military service.[64] The new methods were, moreover, regarded by some as undermining the regimental system. Not only was it said that by posting a recruit in the first instance into the General Service Corps so harm was caused by not introducing a soldier from his first day in the Army to the *esprit de corps* of individual corps and regiments, but the extent to which recruits were posted in accordance with their territorial connections was not always deemed satisfactory – particularly to the infantry.[65] In 1948 the Army dispensed with the general service selection scheme. Instead, the bulk of the procedure was to be carried out after recruits had been allocated to corps which, one officer noted, was like 'putting the cart before the horse'.[66]

The new officer selection methods also evoked a good deal of suspicion. In particular, the role of the psychiatrist at the WOSBs was singled out for special criticism. Not only was it argued that the psychiatric interview upset officer candidates by encroaching on matters of a personal nature, but that psychiatrists were dominating the selection procedure by virtue of their technical knowledge and ability to present evidence. Some of them, it was considered, had little experience of Army life and traditions and candidates were being rejected who would otherwise make suitable officers.[67] Given the strength of feeling on the issue, instructions were issued in 1943 that psychiatrists should interview no more than half of the candidates and that no questions on sex or religion would be asked.[68] In 1946 the decision was taken to withdraw psychiatrists and psychologists from the WOSBs and limit their staffs to the purely military assessors: a step described by one officer as putting the clock back to 'the Lewis gun age'.[69]

With respect to officer–man relations, questions have to be broached about the extent to which the gulf between officers and men was truly bridged. Although some of the inequalities between the ranks might have been revised, officers continued to be granted the right to a separate mess, to be valeted by batmen, and to a better general standard of day-to-day living than the soldiers. Moreover, despite efforts to improve matters, the standard of man-management on the part of junior officers continued to give cause for concern.[70] Of particular importance in this respect was the example set by commanding officers of units. Not only was it said that some did not realise how much more attention the wartime soldier required compared to his peacetime counterpart, but that others were simply not interested in their men and therefore did not ensure that their junior officers took an interest in them either.[71] A few officers clearly resented the new style of leadership that the War Office was trying to promote. One wrote of 'gutter inspired ideologies' which decried those qualities in a man which raised him above his fellows.[72] Despite reassurances that the subject of man-management was fully covered in the post-war Army, one former subaltern wrote of officer training as continuing to create an elite class, naturally designed to impose its will on all inferior classes, and of a fellow officer who likened his men to 'pets' that needed to be humoured with sugar and whipped when disobedient.[73]

Some doubts also have to raised about the effectiveness of Army welfare. Not only were there inherent difficulties in organising comprehensive welfare provision for all units scattered across the country, but a number of commanding officers regarded the welfare organisation as a 'spoon-feeding' establishment that interfered with their more important tasks and undermined the traditional responsibility of regimental officers for the care of the men.[74] Without their positive encouragement, it was evident that a number of junior officers either chose not to utilise the welfare assistance available to them, or simply remained ignorant of it. 'I am convinced', reported one commander, 'that many officers know little of the value and purpose of Welfare Officers, and therefore it follows that few of the men even know of their existence.'[75] Even when units were better informed, this could sometimes lead to a decline in the standard of welfare since it was said that 'the existence of a Welfare Department in the Army has led some officers to suppose that their obligation to do "welfare work" for their men has ceased'.[76] In 1948 the welfare directorate was dissolved as a separate and distinctive entity within the War Office and the following year the voluntary Army welfare officers across the country were stood down. This ensured that responsibility for the day-to-day welfare of the soldier would continue to lie first and foremost with regimental officers. 'The wheel', observed one officer, 'had come full circle.'[77]

As for Army education, questions need to be asked about how conscientiously the ABCA and BWP discussions were carried out across the Army. In the case of the ABCA, not only did many junior officers regard the task of leading discussions on current affairs as an unwelcome chore – sometimes merely reciting the discussion pamphlets as if they were Army regulations and doing little to encourage debate – but a good number of commanding officers regarded them as either having little relevance to the war effort, or as positively seditious, and did little to ensure that they were properly carried out.[78] If one applies this picture of indifference to BWP discussions as well – bearing in mind that they were more difficult to organise because there was a shortage of competent unit instructors to conduct these sessions, and the manpower resources of the AEC and the civilian educational organisations were limited – then it does seem that the provision of education was patchy at best.[79]

Indeed, while the War Office estimated that 60 per cent of units were successfully carrying out the ABCA and BWP discussions by 1943, another unofficial assessment put the figure as low as 10 per cent.[80] In the late 1940s it was decided to tailor the education syllabus more to the practical aspects of soldiering, and the discussion of domestic political issues in current affairs periods was phased out, the emphasis being placed instead on matters relating to the Army.[81]

Thus in the same way that some historians have raised doubts about the radicalising effects of the war on civilian society, so one can conclude that what social change took place in the Army was perhaps not quite as profound as at first sight. In relation to this, two particular points are worth noting. First, the Army continued to be controlled by regular officers who filled the majority of the posts of lieutenant-colonel and above. Well schooled in the values of the pre-war Army, a number of them half-heartedly carried out reforms they did not like, or simply ignored them.[82] Second, the military authorities had no really effective means of ensuring that reforms had been carried out beyond the testimony of the officers themselves. One soldier summed up the dilemma:

> The situation is that of a well-meaning Army Council distributing sensible plans which are never sufficiently well disseminated to become operative; and of their having no means whatever, beyond the word of the CO passed up through the usual channels, of finding out whether or not their schemes are being put into operation.[83]

In these circumstances, and bearing in mind that in a number of respects the Army put the clock back in the post-war years, there are grounds for being cautious about the extent of change. The Army might have become, in terms of its personnel and institutional values, more a part of the nation; but in many ways it remained a nation apart.

NOTES

1. Public Record Office, War Office papers [hereafter PRO WO], WO 277/12, *Manpower Problems*, War Office monograph compiled by Maj.-Gen. A.J.K. Piggot, 1949, p. 79; R.J. Minney, *The Private Papers of Hore-Belisha* (London: Collins, 1960), pp. 39–40, 46–7, 95, 179–80.
2. B. Bond, *British Military Policy Between the Two World Wars* (Oxford: Clarendon Press, 1980), pp. 35, 71.
3. Captain X, *A Soldier Looks Ahead* (London: Labour Book Service, 1944) [hereafter Captain X, *A Soldier*], p. 8.
4. PRO WO 277/12, *Manpower Problems*, pp. 7, 12; H.M.D. Parker, *Manpower: a Study of War-time Policy and Administration* (London: HMSO, 1957) [hereafter Parker, *Manpower*], pp. 54–5; *Ministry of Labour and National Service: Report for the Years 1939–1946*, Cmd. 7225 (1947) [hereafter *Ministry of Labour*], pp. 8–9.
5. PRO WO 277/12, *Manpower Problems*, p. 80.
6. PRO WO 163/48, War Office progress report, AE 59, Sept. 1940; PRO WO 163/50, War Office progress report, AC/P(41)28, May 1941; PRO WO 163/51, War Office progress report, AC/G(42)12, March 1942; PRO WO 163/52, War Office progress report, AC/G(43)11, March 1943; PRO WO 163/53, War Office progress report, AC/G(44)16, March 1944; PRO WO 163/45, War Office progress report, AC/G(45)6, March 1945.
7. *Ministry of Labour*, pp. 12, 21, 26; Parker, *Manpower*, pp. 150–3; *Parliamentary Debates* (Commons), 5th series, vol. 355 (1939–40), col. 432.
8. PRO WO 277/19, *Personnel Selection*, War Office monograph compiled by Col. B. Ungerson, 1953, pp. 4–8, 10, 12, 28–9; War Office Directorate for Selection of Personnel, 'Personnel Selection in the British Army', *Proceedings of the Eighth International Management Congress*, 1 (Stockholm, 1947)[hereafter DSP, 'Personnel'], pp. 451–2, 455.
9. Liddell Hart Centre for Military Archives, King's College, London, Adam papers [hereafter LHC Adam], viii, 'Various Administrative Aspects of the Second World War', 1960, chap. 2, pp. 1–2.
10. Lt-Col. J.D. Sutherland and Maj. G.A. Fitzpatrick, 'Some Approaches to Group Problems in the British Army', in *Group Psychotherapy* (New York, 1945), p. 206.
11. *Committee on Skilled Men in the Services. Second Report and a Memorandum by the War Office*, Cmd. 6339 (1942), pp. 14, 56–7.
12. DSP, 'Personnel', pp. 453–7; PRO WO 277/19, *Personnel Selection*, pp. 13, 27–45; P.E. Vernon and J.B. Parry, *Personnel Selection in the British Forces* (London: University of London Press, 1949) [hereafter Vernon, *Personnel*], pp. 43–6; R.H. Ahrenfeldt, *Psychiatry in the British Army in the Second World War* (London: Routledge & Kegan Paul, 1958) [hereafter Ahrenfeldt, *Psychiatry*], pp. 41–2; Privy Council Office, *Report of an Expert Committee on the Work of Psychologists and Psychiatrists in the Services* (London: HMSO, 1947), p. 10; WO 216/87A, AG to CIGS, 25 Aug. 1942.
13. PRO WO 277/19, *Personnel Selection*, pp. 48–9; DSP, 'Personnel', pp. 457–8; Vernon, *Personnel*, pp. 119–20.
14. DSP, 'Personnel', p. 458.
15. PRO WO 163/161, morale report, Nov. 1942–Jan. 1943, MC/P(43)2, 12 March 1943, p. 7.
16. PRO WO 277/12, *Manpower Problems*, War Office monograph compiled by Maj.-Gen. A. J.K. Piggot, 1949, p. 30.

17. PRO WO 277/19, *Personnel Selection*, p. 55; Vernon, *Personnel*, p. 53; WO 199/1644, A.E. Percival (43rd Div.) to Brig. F.B. Hurndall (Southern Command), 21 March 1940.
18. PRO WO 277/12, *Manpower Problems*, pp. 30–1; WO 277/119, *Personnel Selection*, p. 55; Brig. F.H. Vinden, 'The Introduction of War Office Selection Boards in the British Army: a Personal Recollection', in B. Bond and I. Roy (eds), *War and Society: a Yearbook of Military History*, vol. 2 (London: Croom Helm, 1977) [hereafter Vinden, 'The Introduction'], pp. 120–1; DSP, 'Personnel', p. 458.
19. H. Longhurst, *I Wouldn't Have Missed It* (London: J.M. Dent, 1945), p. 34.
20. J.R. Rees, *The Shaping of Psychiatry by War* (London: Chapman & Hall, 1945) [hereafter Rees, *The Shaping*], p. 64.
21. Gunner, RA, letter to the editor, *The New Statesman and Nation*, 22 (1941), p. 377.
22. Vinden, 'The Introduction', p. 120; LHC Adam, viii, 'Administrative Aspects', 1960, chap. 2, p. 7.
23. Rees, *The Shaping*, p. 64.
24. *Parliamentary Debates* (Commons), 5th series, vol. 367 (1940–41), cols 433–4; vol. 69 (1940–41), col. 1056; vol. 70 (1940–41), cols 96–7; B.S. Morris, 'Officer Selection in the British Army 1942–1945', *Occupational Psychology*, 23 (1949) [hereafter Morris, 'Officer Selection'], p. 220.
25. LHC Adam, viii, 'Administrative Aspects', chap. 2, p. 8; DSP, 'Personnel', pp. 459–60; Ahrenfeldt, *Psychiatry*, pp. 58, 60–3; Vernon, *Personnel*, pp. 53–63; S.W. Gillman, 'Methods of Officer Selection in the Army', *Journal of Mental Science*, 93 (1947), pp. 103–8; PRO WO 277/19, *Personnel Selection*, pp. 58–61.
26. Public Record Office, Cabinet papers [hereafter PRO CAB], CAB 98/28, 'Follow-up of WOSB Cadets at OCTU: Progress Report June 1943', RTC technical memorandum no. 4, PP(SC)(43)36, 19 Aug. 1943; Morris, 'Officer Selection', pp. 226–8; Vernon, *Personnel*, pp. 123–4; DSP, 'Personnel', p. 461.
27. Morris, 'Officer Selection', p. 226; PRO CAB 98/26, minutes of a meeting of the Expert Committee on the Work of Psychologists and Psychiatrists in the Services, PP(43)14th meeting, 14 Aug. 1943.
28. Morris, 'Officer Selection', p. 225; PRO WO 277/12, *Manpower Problems*, p. 31. It should be noted that in the summer of 1942 pre-OCTUs were introduced to which cadets were sent before being passed on to OCTUs. It is not entirely clear whether the figure of 8 per cent refers to the failure rate at pre-OCTUs, OCTUs or covers both sets of institutions. It is assumed that this figure refers to the combined failure rate. It should also be recorded that in 1942 instructions were issued (in view of the introduction of the WOSBs and pre-OCTUs) that OCTUs should only fail cadets on grounds of 'misconduct' or 'indolence'. It is not known how fully these instructions were implemented, or for how long they were in force, but they might well have had a distorting effect on failure rates at the OCTU stage.
29. Morris, 'Officer Selection', pp. 224–5; B. Ungerson, 'Mr Morris on Officer Selection', *Occupational Psychology*, 24 (1950), p. 55; B.S. Morris, 'A Reply to Colonel Ungerson', *Occupational Psychology*, 24 (1950), p. 59; Vernon, *Personnel*, pp. 124–5.
30. PRO WO 163/161, morale report, May–July 1942, MC/P(42)1, 11 Sept. 1942, p. 2.
31. Socialist Subaltern, letter to the editor, *New Statesman and Nation*, 21 (1941), p. 240.
32. PRO WO 163/161, morale report, Aug.–Oct. 1942, MC/P(42)3, 15 Dec. 1942, p. 1. For a fuller discussion of officer–man relations, see J.A. Crang, 'The British Soldier on the Home Front: Army Morale Reports 1940–45', in P. Addison and A. Calder (eds), *Time to Kill: the Soldier's Experience of War in the West 1939–1945* (London: Pimlico, 1997).
33. PRO WO 163/89, 'Use of Hotels: Segregation of Officers and Other Ranks', memorandum by AG, ECAC/P(42)136, 13 Oct. 1942; PRO WO 163/51, 'Use of Hotels: Segregation of Officers and Other Ranks', note by the joint secretaries, AC/P(42)11, 23 Oct. 1942; PRO WO 163/51, minutes of the 16th meeting of the Army Council, AC/M(42)5, 28 Oct. 1942;

PRO WO 163/89, minutes of the 90th meeting of the Executive Committee of the Army Council, ECAC/M(42)51, 18 Dec. 1942.

34. *Parliamentary Debates* (Commons), 5th series, vol. 379 (1941–42), cols 1221–2; PRO WO 163/161, minutes of the 13th meeting of the Morale Committee, 26 March 1943.

35. PRO WO 163/89, 'Medical Arrangements: Officers and Other Ranks', memorandum by FCB, ECAC/P(42)137, 14 Oct. 1942; PRO WO 163/89, minutes of the 82nd meeting of the ECAC, ECAC/M(42)43, 23 Oct. 1942; PRO WO 163/89, 'Medical Arrangements: Officers and Other Ranks', memorandum by AG, ECAC/P(42)146, 16 Nov. 1942; PRO WO 163/89, minutes of the 86th meeting of the ECAC, ECAC/M(42)47, 20 Nov. 1942; PRO WO 163/90, minutes of the 95th meeting of the ECAC, ECAC/M(43)5, 29 Jan. 1943.

36. PRO WO 163/161, morale report, Nov. 1942–Jan. 1943, p. 7.

37. H. Harris, *The Group Approach to Leadership Testing* (London: Routledge & Kegan Paul, 1949), pp. 123–47.

38. PRO WO 163/51, morale report, Feb.–May 1942, AC/G(42)24, 10 July 1942, p. 3.

39. LHC Adam, v/iii, 'Administration of Discipline', letter from AG to Corps District, Divisional, AA Group, District and Area Commanders, March 1943, pp. 3–4; PRO WO 163/162, minutes of the 24th meeting of the MC, MC/M(44)2, 25 Feb. 1942.

40. T. Harrisson, 'The British Soldier: Changing Attitudes and Ideas', *British Journal of Psychology*, 35 (1945) [hereafter Harrisson, 'The British Soldier'], pp. 35–6; Maj. R.A.C. Radcliffe, 'Officer–Man Relationships', *Army Quarterly*, 46 (1943) [hereafter Radcliffe, 'Officer–Man'], pp. 117–18; War Office, *The Soldier's Welfare* (1941), p. 4.

41. PRO WO 32/9487, AG to S of S, 12 Nov. 1943; PRO WO 32/9487, 'Request Hours', ACI 47/43, nd [1943]; LHC Adam, v/iii, 'Administration of Discipline', pp. 5–7; PRO WO 277/16, *Morale*, War Office monograph compiled by Lt-Col. J.H.A. Sparrow, 1949, pp. 33–4.

42. T. Harrisson, 'The British Soldier', pp. 35–6.

43. PRO WO 163/54, morale report, Nov. 1944–Jan. 1945, AC/G(45)12, 4 July 1945, p. 6.

44. PRO WO 32/14569, Future of Army Welfare Services: Twenty-First Report of the Standing Committee on Army Post-War Problems, APWP/P(46)4, 16 Jan. 1946; PRO WO 277/4, *Army Welfare*, War Office monograph compiled by Brig. M.C. Morgan, 1953, pp. 1–5, 10.

45. Captain X, *A Soldier*, p. 156.

46. Tom Harrisson Mass Observation Archive, University of Sussex [hereafter MOA], TC 29/2/E, 1 Sept. 1940.

47. Radcliffe, 'Officer–Man', p. 121

48. PRO WO 277/4, *Army Welfare*, p. 178.

49. PRO WO 277/4, *Army Welfare*, p. 6.

50. PRO WO 277/4, *Army Welfare*, pp. 7–8, 21, 23, 176–80; A Local Army Welfare Officer, 'Six Years of Army Welfare', *Journal of the Royal United Service Institution*, 91 (1946) [hereafter LAWO, 'Six Years'], p. 52.

51. PRO WO 277/4, *Army Welfare*, pp.11–12, 25, 50–6, 110–12, 127–31; Maj.-Gen. H. Willans, 'Army Welfare and Education', *Journal of the Royal United Service Institution*, 86 (1941) [hereafter Willans, 'Army Welfare'], pp. 253–4; LAWO, 'Six Years', p. 54; War Office, *The Soldier's Welfare* (1941), p. 36; R. Fawkes, *Fighting for a Laugh: Entertaining the British and American Forces 1939–1946* (London: Macdonald & Janes, 1978), pp. 39–50.

52. Its Co, 'The Depot at War', *Army Quarterly*, 45 (1942), p. 95; WO 277/4, *Army Welfare*, pp. 13–15; LAWO, 'Six Years', p. 54.

53. PRO WO 277/4, *Army Welfare*, pp. 25, 34–8; Willans, 'Army Welfare', pp. 249–50; War Office, *The Soldier's Welfare* (1943), pp. 48–56, 73–6.

54. PRO WO 32/14569, 'The Army Welfare Services after the War', memorandum by DAG(A), 16 June 1945; PRO WO 163/54, morale report, Aug.–Oct. 1944, AC/G(45)2, 17

Feb. 1945, pp. 2–3; PRO WO 163/54, morale report, Nov. 1944–Jan. 1945, AC/G(45)12, 4 July 1945, p. 7; PRO WO 163/54, morale report, Feb.–April 1945, AC/G(45)15, 20 Aug. 1945, p. 2.

55. PRO WO 32/4725, 'Role of the AEC in War', paper by DRO, nd [Feb. 1940]; Prince Consort's Army Library, W.E. Williams, *The History of Army Education* (1939–1945) (1949) [hereafter Williams, *Army Education*], pp. 5–6; Maj. T.H. Hawkins and L.J.F. Brimble, *Adult Education: the Record of the British Army* (London: Macmillan and Co., 1947)[hereafter Hawkins, *Adult Education*], pp. 91–2.

56. Hawkins, *Adult Education*, pp. 97–100; Lord Gorell, letter to the editor, *The Times*, 18 Jan. 1940, p. 7; H.A.L. Fisher, letter to the editor, *The Times*, 18 Jan. 1940, p. 7; A.D. Lindsay, letter to the Editor, *The Times*, 9 Feb. 1940, p. 6; Maj.-Gen. C. Lloyd, *Services Education* (London: Longman's, Green and Co., 1957) [hereafter Lloyd, *Services*], pp. 15–16; P. Summerfield, 'Education and Politics in the British Armed Forces in the Second World War', *International Review of Social History*, 26 (1981) [hereafter Summerfield, 'Education and Politics'], pp. 135–7.

57. PRO WO 163/412, Report of the Committee on Educational, Welfare and Recreational Needs of the Army, 7 May 1940, pp. 4–19, 30–1; PRO WO 32/9429, Education in the Wartime Army, Sept. 1940, summarised in ACI 1415, Nov. 1940; Williams, *Army Education*, pp. 8–9; Hawkins, *Adult Education*, pp. 100–5.

58. Williams, *Army Education*, pp. 10–11; W.E. Williams, 'Education in the Army', *Political Quarterly*, 13 (1942), pp. 252–4; N. Scarlyn Wilson, *Education in the Forces 1939–46: the Civilian Contribution* (London: Evans Bros., 1948) [hereafter Wilson, *Education in the Forces*], pp. 28–9; Col. A.C.T. White, *The Story of Army Education 1643–1963* (London: George G. Harrap and Co., 1963) [hereafter White, *The Story*], pp. 88–9, 95–6; LHC Adam, viii, 'Administrative Aspects', ch. 6, p. 3; Summerfield, 'Education and Politics', p. 138.

59. LHC Adam, viii, 'Administrative Aspects', ch. 6, pp. 3–4; LHC Adam, xii/iii, notes on ABCA, nd; PRO WO 163/84, 'Education in the Wartime Army', memorandum by DGWE, ECAC/P(41)37, 5 June 1941; PRO WO 163/84, minutes of the 16th meeting of the ECAC, ECAC/M(41)16, 9 June 1941; PRO WO 163/50, 'Maintenance of Morale in the Wartime Army by Means of Instruction Given to Unit Officers', note by the secretariat, AC/P(41)38, 12 June 1941; PRO WO 163/50, minutes of the 8th meeting of the AC, AC/M(41)8, 17 June 1941; PRO WO 32/9735, Current Affairs in the Army: the Outline of a New Plan, Aug. 1941; Williams, *Army Education*, pp. 97–8; White, *The Story*, pp. 97–8.

60. Summerfield, 'Education and Politics', p. 145; Williams, *Army Education*, p. 16.

61. PRO WO 163/89, 'Education in the Army during Winter 1942/1943', memorandum by AG, ECAC/P(42)101, 21 July 1942; PRO WO 163/89, minutes of the 69th meeting of the ECAC, ECAC/M(42)30, 24 July 1942; PRO WO 163/89, 'Education in the Army during 1942/43', memorandum by DGWE, ECAC/P(42)113, 18 Aug. 1942; PRO WO 163/89, minutes of the 73rd meeting of the ECAC, ECAC/M(42)34, 21 Aug. 1942; PRO WO 163/89, minutes of the 74th meeting of the ECAC, ECAC/M(42)35, 28 Aug. 1942; PRO WO 32/10455, 'The Winter Scheme of Education', memorandum by DAE, 7 Sept. 1942; Williams, *Army Education*, p. 16; PRO WO 163/89, 'Education in the Army during the Winter 1942/3', memorandum by AG ECAC/P(42)161, 28 Dec. 1942; PRO WO 163/90, minutes of the 96th meeting of the ECAC, ECAC/M(43)6, 5 Feb. 1943; PRO WO 163/92, 'Education in the Army during the Winter 1943/4', memorandum by AG, ECAC/P(43)99, 6 Sept. 1943; PRO WO 163/92, minutes of the 127th meeting of the ECAC, ECAC/M(43)37, 10 Sept. 1943; Wilson, *Education in the Forces*, pp. 58–9; Directorate of Army Education, *The British Way and Purpose: Consolidated Edition of BWP Booklets 1–18* (1944).

62. PRO WO 163/161, morale report, May–July 1942, p. 8; PRO WO 163/161, morale report, Nov. 1942–Jan. 1943, pp. 5–6; PRO WO 163/162, morale report, Aug.–Oct. 1943,

MC/P(43)13, 22 Dec. 1943, p. 7. For a fuller discussion of the development of wartime Army education, see S.P. MacKenzie, *Politics and Military Morale: Current Affairs and Citizenship Education in the British Army 1914–1950* (Oxford: Clarendon Press, 1992) [hereafter MacKenzie, *Politics*]. For a discussion of the debate over the influence of Army education on the 1945 general election result, see J.A. Crang, 'Politics on Parade: Army Education and the 1945 General Election', *History*, 81 (1996).

63. Captain X, *A Soldier*, p. 7.
64. PRO CAB 98/25, papers of the Expert Committee on the Work of Psychologists and Psychiatrists in the Services, PP(42)2, 17 Sept. 1942.
65. PRO WO 277/19, *Personnel Selection*, p. 50; PRO WO 32/11519, 'Further Notes on GS Postings and Infantry Regimental Connections', 28 May 1945; Jack Davies, letter to the author, Aug. 1988.
66. PRO WO 32/11185, 'Retention of the General Service Corps', na [DMP], 23 April 1944; PRO WO 32/12454, 'New Procedure for the Allocation of National Servicemen to Corps', memorandum by DMP, 16 Dec. 1947.
67. PRO CAB 98/29, minutes of a meeting of the Ministerial Committee on the Work of Psychologists and Psychiatrists in the Services, PP(43)1st meeting, 15 July 1943; PRO CAB 98/26, minutes of a meeting of the Expert Committee on the Work of Psychologists and Psychiatrists in the Services, PP(43)16th meeting, 11 Sept. 1943; PRO CAB 98/26, 'Criticism of the Psychiatrists at War Office Selection Boards', memorandum by Brig. H.A. Sandiford in consultation with Brig. J.R. Rees and Brig. A.D. Buchanan Smith, PP(43)39, 7 Oct. 1943.
68. Ahrenfeldt, *Psychiatry*, p. 64.
69. PRO WO 32/12134, Report by the Committee of Enquiry on the System of Selection of Officers for Emergency Commissions, 23 Sept. 1946; PRO WO 32/12134, D of A Psych. to DSP, 10 Oct. 1946.
70. PRO WO 163/161, morale report, May–July 1943, MC/P(43)11, 18 Sept. 1943, p. 4; PRO WO 163/162, morale report, Aug.–Oct. 1943, p. 2; PRO WO 163/162, morale report, Nov. 1943–Jan. 1944, MC/P(44)1, 24 March 1944, p. 1.
71. PRO WO 163/162, morale report, Nov. 1943–Jan. 1944, p. 2; PRO WO 163/162, morale report, Aug.–Oct. 1943, p. 3.
72. Maj. M.J.P.M. Corbally, 'The Officer-Producing Class', *Journal of the Royal United Service Institution*, 91 (1946), p. 205.
73. PRO WO 163/515, Final Report. Army Manpower Committee, Jan. 1949; S. Raven, 'Perish by the Sword: a Memoir of the Military Establishment', *Encounter*, 12 (1959), pp. 46–7. It should also be noted that a survey of the Sandhurst syllabus in 1960 found that only 14 hours, spread over two years, were devoted to instruction in leadership, which half of the cadets found of 'little use' or 'useless'. See J.E. Adair, 'New Trends in Leadership and Management Training', *Journal of the Royal United Service Institution*, 112 (1967), p. 317.
74. PRO WO, 199/1658, 'The Responsibility of the Unit Commander', memorandum by Brig. S. Collingwood, Southern Command, 25 March 1942; PRO WO 277/4, *Army Welfare*, pp. 1, 27.
75. PRO WO 163/162, morale report, Aug.–Oct. 1943, appendix 'A'.
76. Democritus, *What's Wrong With the Army* (London: W.H. Allen & Co., 1942), p. 60.
77. PRO WO 277/4, *Army Welfare*, p. 175.
78. PRO WO 163/161, morale report, Nov. 1942–Jan. 1943, p. 6; MOA, FR 948, 'Report on ABCA', 3 Nov. 1941, pp. 17; Lt.-Col. W.R.H. Charley (retd), letter to the author, Sept. 1988; Maj. F.C. MacMahon (retd), letter to the author, Oct. 1988; Rev. D.D. Caldwell, letter to the author, Nov. 1988; MacKenzie, *Politics*, p. 179; PRO WO 32/9735, Grigg to Cripps, Sept. 1942; PRO WO 277/16, *Morale*, p. 18; LHC Adam, v/iv, Adam to commanders, Sept. 1943, p. 3; MOA, FR 1485, 'Basis of Political Trends in the Army', 12 Nov.

1942, pp. 27–8; 'Notes of the Week', *The Economist*, 141 (1941), p. 748; Maj. B. Dobree, 'ABCA Gets Going', *The Spectator*, 168 (1942), p. 55; 'A Frustrated Army', *The Tribune*, 271 (1942), p. 10; G. Raybould, 'The Commanding Officer and Army Education', *The Highway*, 35 (1942), p. 10; Infantry Subaltern, Home Forces, letter to the editor, *New Statesman and Nation*, 25 (1943), p. 256–7; C.E.M. Joad, 'The Tide of Opportunity', *New Statesman and Nation*, 30 (1945), p. 122; White, *The Story*, pp. 99–100; Lloyd, *Services*, p. 19; Hawkins, *Adult Education*, pp. 295–8; Summerfield, 'Education and Politics', pp. 151–2; MacKenzie, *Politics*, pp. 96–9, 180.

79. Williams, *Army Education*, p. 17; A Correspondent, 'Army Education', *Journal of Education*, 75 (1943), p. 549.

80. PRO WO 163/53, morale report, Aug.–Oct. 1943, AC/G(44)4, 11 Jan. 1944, appendix 'B'; Williams, *Army Education*, p. 18; H. Ross, 'Army Education', *Fabian Quarterly*, 38 (1943), pp. 24–5.

81. White, *The Story*, pp. 184–5; MacKenzie, *Politics*, pp. 219–20.

82. At the end of 1942 it was reported that three-quarters of officers holding the rank of lieutenant-colonel and above were regulars or regular reserve officers. At the end of the war it was calculated that nine out of ten officers who had held the rank of brigadier and above had been regulars or regular reservists (these latter figures referring to officers 'otherwise than in Anti-Aircraft Command').

83. MOA, FR 937, 'Memo from an Army Officer', 31 Oct. 1941, p. 5.

3

A Rejected Strategy: The Army and National Service 1946–60

S.J. Ball

National Service had a short life. The National Service Act was passed in 1947 and the abandonment of conscription was announced ten years later. Throughout those ten years nearly all of the supporters of conscription viewed it as a temporary expedient, a necessary evil. The most concise formulation of this position can be found in the minutes of the Chiefs of Staff (COS) committee for June 1949:

> Regular forces backed by the necessary auxiliary formations and reserves provide undoubtedly the most economical and efficient method of meeting our commitments in peace and the requirements of our strategy in the early stages of a war. To use National Servicemen as we must at present to supplement the regular forces in their peacetime tasks is both expensive and inefficient because it results in an undue proportion of manpower being absorbed by training establishments at the expense of the front-line.

At one level, therefore, the brief life of conscription is relatively unsurprising: its survival rested upon an assessment of the current situation rather than any deep-rooted support. Attempts to describe this assessment have tended to take one of two approaches: the strategic or the political.

According to the first school, the rise and fall of National Service merely reflected changing strategic priorities. It was retained in 1947 because of a clear imperial strategy. The loss of India not only shrunk the British empire, it deprived it of a large pool of manpower. Yet the British government had no intention of relinquishing the rest of the empire. Whether it intended to build a 'third force' or create a partnership of equals with the United States, the formal and informal empire, together with the means to police and defend it, were vital. War plans assumed that even after the use of nuclear weapons a long drawn-out struggle would occur. Although forces in-being were needed to occupy Germany, there was to be no 'continental commitment'. Ten years later the strategic landscape had been transformed. Britain had its own nuclear force, there was a large continental commitment and long-war doctrines had been discredited. There was still an imperial strategy in place but it rested upon bases rather than colonies. Quite different forces were required.

The political interpretation denies the British government much in the way of strategic appreciation. Even in 1947 it attempted to pursue mismatched foreign and defence policies. Conscription was a political football kicked between military leaders and Labour back-benchers. The result was an unwieldy system of short-term universal military service when a longer-term selective service system would have been more sensible. Ten years later National Service was abandoned against the advice of the military purely in pursuit of political advantage. Harold Macmillan's new government was attempting to rebuild Conservative electoral fortunes after the Suez debacle. The termination of conscription was a relatively painless method of buying political popularity.

Both these accounts contain a measure of truth. In both 1947 and 1957 the logic of politics and strategy dovetailed. The factor which tended to be ignored, however, was the short-term needs of servicemen and commanders carrying out their duties. The result was 'overstretch' as commitments continued to outpace capabilities. This occurred despite increases in the defence budget. Defence spending was, in real terms, 156 per cent of the 1948 figure in 1952, 136 per cent in 1955 and still 107 per cent when Sandys had done his worst in 1959.

Commitments, of course, were a matter for the government of the day. Yet the ten years between 1947 and 1957 also saw the collapse of the influence of the Chiefs of Staff. The nadir of military influence was reached with the drafting of the 1957 Defence White Paper. The eventual fate of conscription was largely determined by the unwise means by which the military leadership attempted 'to get their business through', holding the government to ransom in the 1940s and then sacrificing their powerful position by creating strategic gridlock in the mid-1950s. Of course, the three services had clashing interests, but their inability to reach compromises in order to further the interests of all left the military with very little influence in 1957. As a result, National Service was ended by political fiat. But it is not impossible to imagine circumstances in which it could have been phased-out or replaced by a system other than an all-volunteer Army. Although the 1957 White Paper pleased none of the services it did reflect the balance of argument in the strategic debates of the 1950s. In this it marked a defeat for the Army, which had failed to develop a coherent long-war strategy which could have been the bulwark against the demise of conscription.

THE INTRODUCTION OF NATIONAL SERVICE

The National Service Act of 1947 was framed by two debates about strategy at the beginning and end of the year. These debates not only had an impact on the decision to retain conscription but defined the strategic tension within British defence policy which rendered the retention of National Service unstable.

It was quite possible to argue that in an age of atomic weapons many of Britain's commitments and force deployments had become otiose. In particular it seemed wrong to keep a large military establishment in the Middle East. This was indeed the contention of the new prime minister, Clement Attlee. He was critical of the size of the defence forces from the outset of his premiership. In February 1946 he formally broached this issue to his cabinet colleagues. Attlee questioned both the necessity of keeping the Mediterranean sea route open and Britain's ability to do so. The prime minister argued that the concept of defended lines of communication through the Mediterranean in time of war was out-moded. Not only had wartime experience shown that the Navy could operate only with the support of shore-based aircraft but these aircraft needed to be based in expensive areas such as Cyrenaica. Attlee did not believe Britain could afford to finance a large military presence in the Middle East and doubted whether it needed to. He argued that with Indian independence it would not be necessary to keep open a route to the sub-continent. In addition there was little point in keeping forces to defend Persia and Iraq since they were indefensible. Although the Foreign Secretary, Ernest Bevin, profoundly disagreed with Attlee's pessimism he was keen to move the British Mediterranean main base from an increasingly hostile Egypt to Mombasa in Kenya. It was thus left to the COS to carry the fight for the retention of a large British military establishment in Egypt. They argued that the British presence in Egypt was necessary in order to prevent the creation of a power vacuum in the Middle East. The argument went on throughout 1946. It was only resolved in January 1947 when the COS, led by the CIGS (Chief of the Imperial General Staff), Lord Montgomery, threatened their collective resignation. Thus the Middle East, in general, and Egypt in particular, became the third 'pillar' of British strategy along with the defence of the UK and the Atlantic ocean route.

The Middle East debate was largely hidden from public view but it did establish the context for the National Service debate, not least because the COS had inflicted a humiliating defeat on the prime minister. Attlee had been in charge of conscription issues for the coalition government in 1945. Then he had secured the acceptance of conscription in the short term, deferring any long-term commitments. At that time the post-war planners had outlined an Army with a seven-fold role: occupation forces; reoccupation forces; a strategic reserve; a United Nations force; imperial garrisons; a training organisation; and a cadre for expansion. Estimates of how large this force would be ranged from 275,000 regulars and 150,000 conscripts to an Army of 847,000. Of course each of the services drew up plans for large post-war forces, some more realistic than others. All, however, made the point that Britain would require a large military establishment. These plans, whatever their implicit meaning, rested upon the assumption that Britain would need its military establishment to act as one of the 'four policemen' rather than as a means of waging a Cold War.

Thus, when the continuance of wartime conscription was made the subject of a White Paper in May 1946 there was little dissent from the assumption that it would continue. The Cabinet Manpower Committee was more concerned with details. The COS proposed that men should be called up for three years, falling to

18 months in 1950. This would yield an Army of 389,000, with 180,000 regulars and the balance made up of conscripts, by 1951. In the spring of 1946 Cold War concepts were more to the fore. The COS maintained that such a reduced establishment would mean a rigorous pruning of commitments: they were criticised by Bevin who pointed out that precipitate withdrawals would mean the spread of Soviet influence. Arguments about the need for industrial manpower were also fully rehearsed. As a result the cabinet approved a two-year term of service for those conscripted in 1947 and 1948 with the assumption that any extension of the scheme would be based upon 18 months of service. This would yield an Army of six full-time divisions backed by eight to ten divisions in the Territorial Army.

Lord Montgomery did not find this arrangement satisfactory. If he was to create his 'New Model Army' he needed to know about manpower issues in the long term. He therefore pressed the government to bring in a new system. Most members of the cabinet were willing to accept the logic of the White Paper scheme. There would be universal male conscription. Each man's commitment to the forces would last for seven years; 18 months with the Colours followed by five-and-a-half years with the reserve. The main opponent of this scheme in the cabinet was Sir Stafford Cripps, the President of the Board of Trade and Minister for Economic Affairs, who argued against conscription on industrial manpower grounds. He received, however, little support.

The main debate revolved around the permanence of the new system. Although he had assured Alanbrooke in February 1946 that that year's Defence White Paper would pave the way to permanent conscription, Attlee refused to cede a permanent dispensation. Instead, legislation would establish conscription until 1954, thereafter it would be extended by yearly Orders in Council. Although Attlee had been defeated over the Middle East he had not recanted his views. He called existing policy a 'strategy of despair'. Although he had been forced to give way in the short term, the prime minister was confident that his ideas would be validated as the atomic age developed. In addition he suspected, rightly, that a permanent system of National Service would arouse much more opposition in his own party than the continuance of the wartime system to meet short-term contingencies. This is not to say that there was any political threat to conscription. Labour had an overwhelming majority in the House of Commons. The Conservative opposition and its leaders Winston Churchill and Anthony Eden were vocal supporters of conscription. What Attlee wanted to avoid were ructions within his own party which was already showing signs of the instability which would tear it apart in the 1950s. In particular the prime minister wished to appease the emerging Keep Left group, whose most notable member was Richard Crossman. Although Churchill labelled them 'degenerate intellectuals', Keep Left did not oppose conscription on principle but merely wished to limit the length of service. On 1 April 1947 72 Labour MPs voted against the National Service Bill and over 70 abstained. The government decided to perform a volte-face and reduce the length of service to one year.

Yet the importance of the amendment to the 1947 Act can be overstated. Military leaders certainly felt that they had been let down by 'windy' politicians, but in June 1947 Montgomery claimed that 'I have gained my way in all vital issues and I reckon the post-war Army is now well-launched'. Indeed on 2 April, as the government was on the cusp of decision, the CIGS had informed the Cabinet Defence Committee that the Army could cope with a one-year National Service system. It was the Chief of Air Staff, Lord Tedder, who had most vigorously opposed the 12-month term because the RAF would have to release technicians soon after their training finished. The Army's own 'degenerate intellectuals' such as Liddell Hart and Giffard Martel were more critical of Montgomery than Attlee for creating what Sir Orme Sargent called 'a glorified militia for home defence'.

Indeed, a much more insidious threat to the Army's role occurred in the summer of 1947. In mid-1947 an American loan of $3.75 billion was running out, yet under its terms the pound became convertible in July. After a disastrous run on sterling, convertibility was suspended in August. Senior ministers even talked of ousting Attlee. Instead, another round of cuts in defence expenditure was initiated. The cabinet agreed to cut the target figure for the size of the armed forces in March 1948 from 1,087,000 to 937,000 men. This would mean an Army of 527,000 men in 1948 shrinking to 339,000 in 1949. The Minister of Defence, Albert Alexander, estimated that Britain's long-term military establishment would be 450,000 regulars and 150,000 National Servicemen.

It was clear to each of the services after the convertibility crisis of 1947 that the pressure on the defence budget was to be more intense than they had feared. In consequence any attempt at a united front disappeared. The RAF feared that if short-term problems were given priority, the Air Force would be reduced to an Army support arm. In January 1947 Attlee and Bevin had decided that Britain would build its own A-bomb and advanced jet bombers to carry it. But these forces would not be available for a decade. Much could happen in ten years. The RAF was determined, therefore, to enshrine the primacy of the bomber force and long-term planning in the defence programme. They took their case independently, and successfully, to ministers. The Cabinet Defence Committee agreed that the Soviet Union would possess large atomic forces of its own in 1957. During the decade 1947–57 defence expenditure 'must be very severely limited if we are to survive as a first class power'. Given the destructive power of nuclear weapons priority had to be given to war prevention rather than war-fighting. In effect, this meant reliance on the American nuclear deterrent until 1955 and the British bomber force thereafter. Conventional forces were of little importance in the primary strategic mission. The Army was isolated. Albert Alexander told the Cabinet Defence Committee, 'I believe ... that the Navy and Air Force are right in their views that the plans to be considered by the COS and subsequently by ministers, ought to be plans related to preparation for war and not simply an assessment of what is required to meet peace-time commitments. The Army plans for a major war ought to be tabled and discussed.' The other services ridiculed Montgomery's suggestion that the role of the Army was to prevent the invasion of the UK. This debate was not fully resolved because Attlee ruled that no defence priorities should be articulated in public to prevent 'misunderstandings'. Yet it obviously had major implications for universal conscription. National Service might be necessary to meet immediate needs but it had little role in plans for a major war. This placed the Army at a constant disadvantage in ensuing defence debates.

Yet there was little chance that National Service would be abandoned. It did have critics in government, most notably Manny Shinwell, the Secretary of State for War and subsequently Minister of Defence, and Herbert Morrison, the deputy prime minister. Yet Shinwell's attempts to get consideration of a Regular Army were swept away by crises: Berlin in 1948 and Korea in 1950. Indeed the growing sense of Cold War changed the context in which National Service was discussed. If a large conscript Army had little role in protecting the United Kingdom it would be vital if Britain intended to enter into a major continental commitment as well as making major military deployments outside Europe. Shinwell himself was the most enthusiastic advocate of the continental commitment.

INTRODUCTION OF 18-MONTH NATIONAL SERVICE

In December 1947 the COS were informed that Bevin had had preliminary talks with the US Secretary of State, General George Marshall, about a security system for western Europe. They were asked to consider the role of the continental commitment. Montgomery pushed strongly for such a commitment. On 2 February 1948 he presented a paper to the COS which argued that:

> The political difficulties of forming the Western Union and ensuring that the countries concerned present a united front from the outset, will be considerable ... Our aim must be to build up a Union which has the necessary economic and military strength in the initial stage ... There is only one hope of achieving this object. We must agree that, if attacked, the nations of the Western Union will hold this attack as far East as possible e.g. on the Rhine. We must make it very clear that Britain will play her full part in this strategy and will support the battle on the Rhine.

Montgomery believed that the Western Union countries – Britain, France, Belgium, Holland and Luxembourg – should raise 45 divisions to make this strategy a reality, although even he admitted that a major American contribution would also be necessary. Montgomery was adamantly opposed by the other Chiefs of Staff and the prime minister but supported by the Foreign Secretary and the Minister of Defence. The result was a decision to draw up war plans for British forces to fight in Europe but no real change in policy. Since the British Military Governor in Germany, General Sir Brian Robertson, had only an armoured division and a weakened infantry division in the British Zone and a brigade in Berlin, he could do little more than plan a sacrificial effort.

It was the Berlin crisis of June 1948 which gave Montgomery the opportunity to argue that demobilisation of troops should be retarded, introducing, *de facto*, two years of National Service for each man. His colleagues of the COS disagreed. They wanted a temporary suspension of demobilisation so that they could retain their key tradesmen. The cabinet accepted the RAF/Royal Navy proposal. The suspension of demobilisation was, however, by its very nature, only a stop gap measure. The Chiefs of Staff argued that a longer-term solution was the extension of National Service to 18 months. Yet in practice conscription was already providing too many men for the services. The RAF and the Navy really needed some kind of selective service system which would allow them to pick and choose those who were recruited. It was Montgomery, with his vision of a mass Army to defend Europe, who pushed for universal two-year National Service. Indeed on 19 October 1948 he threatened the resignation of the military members of the Army Council if such a measure was not conceded. This threat fell a few days later when Montgomery demitted office as CIGS to become the chairman of the military committee of the Western European Union. The threat does, however, seem to have been reinforced by his successor, Sir William Slim, in pushing for the extension of National Service to 18 months. This was conceded, along with plans for raised medical standards and *ad hoc* deferments, by the cabinet in November 1948. In the new atmosphere of Cold War crisis opposition in Parliament was muted: 41 MPs voted against the second reading of the National Service Amendment Act. The 1947 revolt had thus come to nothing since the one-year servicemen were to have been recruited from January 1949, and effectively, the services went from two-year conscripts to 18-month conscripts. This was expected to yield an Army of 390,000 with 210,000 conscripts in 1949. This figure would rise to 240,000 conscripts as regular recruiting fell.

Although Sir William Slim had argued hard for this expanded conscript Army he believed that it would be most useful if deployed in the Middle East rather than in Europe. In May 1949, in response to the signature of the North Atlantic Treaty, he did suggest that Britain should undertake to earmark two divisions for deployment in Europe in the event of a war. By September, however, he wanted to tell the French that there was no hope of any British commitment and that this policy would only be reviewed if the United States agreed to deploy large-scale land forces in Europe. Thus the rationale for a conscript Army, with soldiers serving for 18 months, was thrust back on the short-term contingencies of Britain's imperial role.

THE INTRODUCTION OF TWO-YEAR NATIONAL SERVICE

This phase was, however, short-lived. The explosion of the Soviet A-bomb in August 1949 came as a severe psychological shock to the military establishments on both sides of the Atlantic. In addition it soon became clear that the political logic of NATO militated against the avoidance of any further commitments on the continent. The promise of British forces in Europe could become the 'sprat to catch the mackerel' of American forces in Europe. This was the view taken by the new Chief of the Air Staff, Sir John Slessor, and the new Minister of Defence, Manny Shinwell. It was therefore integral to the Global Strategy Paper which was drafted in the first six months of 1950. Yet although these discussions prepared the ground for a shift in British policy, the COS proposals were really very limited. The Chiefs accepted that the defence of the Rhine was part of the first 'pillar' of defence, the defence of the UK, and that the importance of the third 'pillar', the Middle East, could not be allowed to compromise this. In practical terms, however, they merely revived Slim's May 1949 proposal that Britain would earmark two divisions to be deployed in Europe within three months of the outbreak of war.

It was, of course, the outbreak of the Korean War in June 1950 which transformed judgements. With the Americans pressing for massive increases in defence spending and German rearmament, a solid British commitment seemed unavoidable. On 15 September 1950 Shinwell announced that Britain would send an armoured division to France in 1951 and earmark two further divisions as reinforcements for NATO. In October 1950, as part of NATO force levels discussions, Britain agreed to dispatch a further armoured division to the continent, thus creating a four division BAOR. In September the cabinet agreed to man these forces by reintroducing two-year conscription. Thus with only a brief hiatus in 1949–50 Britain retained two-year National Service, by various measures, throughout the era of post-war peacetime conscription. It is worth stressing how unusual this was. France and Germany, with their much stronger traditions of conscription, retained the one-year period of service.

It is also worth noting that the Korean War did not provide any arguments against conscription on the grounds of combat performance. The Army had not intended to make much use of conscripts in such an emergency. The force earmarked for Korea was 29 Brigade, a reinforced formation including tanks and artillery, kept in the UK as the strategic reserve. This brigade was designed to be filled out by picked men. Officers and men recalled from the reserve had seven years' experience with the Colours: by definition they could not be young post-war National Servicemen. National Servicemen aged over 19 *could volunteer* if they agreed to extend their service by six months. The ranks were filled out by Type Ks: serving or former National Servicemen who volunteered for 18 months as a regular. In March 1951 50 per cent of the brigade, and over 50 per cent of the infantry were recalled reservists or regulars retained after expiry. But 29 Brigade was slow to assemble: it did not reach Korea until the end of October 1950. The Americans, however, took the view that the timely arrival of a British platoon was worth a division later on. Thus the first Army formation to reach Korea in August was the under-strength and lightly equipped 27 Brigade from Hong Kong. Over 75 per cent of its complement was made up of National

Service officers and men. Yet the combat performance of the two formations does not seem to have been shaped by their different personnel profiles. Any differences seemed to have stemmed mainly from the differing size and equipment of the two formations.

The Korean War transformed the strategic side of the debate about conscription. If Britain was to maintain a large continental Army without reducing its imperial commitments National Service was essential. This commitment took place in the context of plans to expand the Army to 10 regular and 12 TA divisions by 1954. As the COS understood, however, it was very hard to disentangle oneself from the commitment once the context changed.

NATIONAL SERVICE AND NATO STRATEGY

The context changed quickly. There was little enthusiasm for the European force. Britain agreed to the Lisbon force goals of February 1952, which called for a NATO army of 96 divisions, without any intention of adhering to them. The new Conservative government had decided to scale-down the Attlee administration's rearmament programme. Although Churchill did not accept the intelligence estimate which posited a Red Army of 175 divisions he did believe that western Europe was indefensible. By December 1953 SACEUR had 39 divisions and 25 brigade groups under his command but many were at a very low level of readiness. In January 1952 the Chiefs of Staff advised that 'we must give the closest attention and priority to the development of atomic warfare to offset these deficiencies [in conventional forces] by the tactical use of atomic weapons in the field and for the attack of enemy airfields and submarine bases'. Yet the services could not agree on any coherent strategy which would involve a reduction of force levels. Even the 1952 Global Strategy Paper did not over-emphasise nuclear weapons and was amenable to various readings about force priorities. General Matthew Ridgway, SACEUR, maintained that even with enhanced atomic forces he would continue to need large conventional armies. As a result, the British government decided to rewrite NATO strategy to make clear that, since Strategic Air Command was fully operational, NATO forces were adequate even if 'they might not actually be sufficient to conduct a successful holding action should hot war break out'.

By the end of 1954 the fate of conscription was tied even more closely to the continental commitment. The initial period covered by the 1947 Act ran out at the end of the year. Conscription would now be a matter for yearly review. Although the Labour Party was exercising the privilege of opposition to call for the reduction of National Service to one year, it would take a major and unlikely parliamentary reverse for National Service to fall. Yet just at the time National Service came up for review and NATO adopted a more nuclear oriented strategy, MC 48 of December 1954, the British government entered into a permanent continental commitment. Between 1950 and 1955, NATO was obsessed by the question of German rearmament. In August 1954 the French National Assembly rejected the creation of a supranational European Defence Community. Britain and the United States were determined that NATO should not fall apart over this issue. A new policy was quickly hammered out at meetings in London and Paris: a new body, the Western European Union (WEU), would provide a vehicle for the FRG's accession to NATO in 1955. As part of these negotiations the Foreign Secretary, Anthony Eden, promised that Britain would maintain four divisions and a tactical Air Force on the continent. These forces would be committed to forward defence under the terms of MC 48.

National Service was not a major issue in the 1955 election. Indeed the Conservatives did their best to avoid entering into a bidding war with Labour. With the election safely won, however, they did subject the system to scrutiny. The years 1953 to 1956 were marked by a series of inconclusive defence reviews: the Radical Review, the Long-Term Defence Review, the Policy Review Committee. Few decisions were made but there were plans to reduce the armed forces from 835,000 to 700,000 men. This would involve an Army of 355,000, obviously too large for an all-regular force. In August 1955 Eden ruled that the forces in Europe were at the core of British defence policy. He conceded, however, that they had no military purpose. A year later 'he did not believe that the nation would continue to accept, after 1958, National Service as it now [was] unless the international situation deteriorated'. Studies of an all-regular Army proved inconclusive, however. The Army itself proposed a force of 200,000 but a Central Statistical Office assessment of recruitment suggested that the biggest all-volunteer force which could be maintained was 165,000.

To square the circle Britain needed to slash its continental commitment. But the government did not wish to use the economic escape clauses in the WEU. It wished to justify the reduction on strategic grounds. As a result, it pushed extremely hard for a new NATO strategic directive. By the end of 1956 it had succeeded. In December 1956 the government informed SACEUR that it intended to reduce BAOR from 77,000 to 50,000 men. Thus the government had done the groundwork for the end of conscription even before Duncan Sandys became Minister of Defence in January 1957. As the Permanent Secretary at the Ministry of Defence advised the minister in his initial briefing, Britain, in theory, should not make any military commitment to NATO at all but continued to do so merely for political reasons. The Ministry of Defence believed that BAOR could be shrunk to a force of 43,000 men.

END OF NATIONAL SERVICE

It was Sandys, however, who cut the Gordian knot. In February 1957 he ruled that:

> In reviewing our defence plans, my starting point has been the Government's declared intention to end National Service as soon as practicable.

> For the purposes of this review, I have assumed that there would be no
> call-up later than 1960 and that consequently the last national servicemen
> would leave the forces in 1962.

In fact, of course, the government's intention to end National Service had
been very vague before Sandys made his snap decision. In the minister's view
armed forces of 380,000 men should suffice. He estimated that this would yield
an all-regular Army of 165,000 by 1962: 80,500 troops, including a strategic
reserve, would be stationed in the UK, 50,000 in Germany, 14,000 in the Far East,
12,000 in the Middle East and 8,500 in transit.

Of course the Chiefs of Staff were aghast, not least because they had not been
consulted. As the VCIGS, Sir William Oliver, pointed out, their last firm advice
to the government had been that Britain needed a military establishment of
450,000 men. Yet Sandys's assault on constitutional propriety can be overstated.
Macmillan was certainly cashing in the chips of the previous government. It had
not escaped his notice that he had to hold a general election by the spring of 1960,
just as National Service would end. But, in fact, the Chiefs of Staff were hopeless-
ly divided. Sir Dermot Boyle, the Chief of the Air Staff, was the most
fervent proponent of the 'trip-wire' strategy. Lord Mountbatten could tell a lost
cause when he saw one and was already compromised. In any case they had more
pressing concerns, the demise of manned aircraft and the Navy in the eastern
Atlantic.

The CIGS, Sir Gerald Templer, was thus isolated and frustrated. Yet even the
General Staff were more concerned with ensuring that the Army had the most
modern equipment rather than in preserving National Service *per se*. That was
why the continental commitment was so important: forces outside Europe might
be lightly equipped. Despite the public attempt of the former Secretary of State
for War, Antony Head, to reverse the complete abandonment of conscription,
the Army accepted that after April 1957 there was no hope of reviving it. Instead
the General Staff concentrated its energies on a guerrilla war against the demise
of a militarily significant continental commitment and on ensuring that forces
outside Europe would be well equipped. NATO provided many opportunities
for subverting the minister's intentions. Although bound by his new strategic
directive SACEUR, General Lauris Norstad, mounted an energetic campaign,
supported by the General Staff in Britain, to preserve a force of 30 well-equipped
divisions under his command. In January 1958 the reduction of BAOR to 55,000
troops was announced and in May a support costs agreement was signed with
the FRG which envisaged the presence of only 45,000 troops by 1961. But
Macmillan also acceded to Norstad's request that 5,000 men of the strategic
reserve would be stationed in Germany rather than the UK. Although Norstad
made many enemies in both the British and the American governments his views
won more acceptance when an acute crisis threatened Berlin in August 1961. As
a result, the draw-down of British forces was frozen at the 55,000 figure. It
should be noted, however, that although some British Army officers in Europe

did not believe in the early use of nuclear weapons and 'gave at least equal emphasis in training for conventional operations' neither the Army nor SHAPE was thinking in terms of war with conventional weapons. Both expected the forces in Europe to be heavily armed with tactical atomic weapons.

As the Chiefs of Staff had warned Sandys in February 1957 it was unlikely that Britain would be untroubled by crises which would make the 165,000 man Army look too weak. Berlin was one example which closed off the room for manoeuvre Sandys had assumed in 1957. At the end of the Conservative period of government in October 1964 there was also a war in Borneo. The defence budget in 1964 was 109 per cent in real terms of the budget in 1959 when Sandys left office. The all-regular Army at the end of the East of Suez period in 1968 had over 189,000 men. It was not until the end of the Callaghan government in 1979 that the Army's strength dipped below the 165,000 ceiling set by Sandys.

CONCLUSION

National Service was the product of a consensus that embraced both political and military leaders. Within both groups, however, the consensus was fragile. Once National Service became subject to yearly renewal in 1955 its long-term future was questionable. The 1957 decision to abolish conscription was, nevertheless, based upon contingency. The 1957 Defence White Paper itself made provision for the reintroduction of National Service. This never became an issue because regular recruiting proved more buoyant than the government had estimated in the mid-1950s. If problems with regular recruiting had arisen Sandys's critics on the Conservative backbenches would have had more ammunition to use against him. Yet it seems doubtful that the decision would have been reversed even then. The Conservative Defence Committee numbered little more than 30 MPs and was far from unanimous on the specifics of policy. It is worth noting, however, that Sandys's window of opportunity was small. In 1956 Eden had said that National Service would be reformed by 1958 if there was no change in the international situation. The second Berlin crisis blew up in November 1958. If conscription had not already been abandoned the Macmillan government might have felt reluctant to announce its cessation before 1962 when the crisis subsided. Since the services were not finally purged of National Servicemen until 1964, if Macmillan and Sandys had opted to end conscription slowly and by stealth it might have survived at least until the end of the 1960s. It is impossible to tell what ramifications this would have had.

National Service might have put down deeper roots in the military establishment if strategic debates had taken a different course. It was perhaps typical of Britain that both military and government should look to the long term and high technology to frame their policy. If actual commitments had driven defence policy, National Service would have been much more difficult to dislodge. The most likely basis for long-term conscription, however, would have been a genuine 'continental commitment'. If Britain had ever intended to pursue its Lisbon conference commitments whilst retaining a global role, conscription would have been indispensable. Although there was little support for such an option, the conventional defence of Europe seems, in retrospect, far from a specious strategy. In this case National Service could have had a more profound influence on British politics than it, in the end, did.

4

Recruiting the Professional Army, 1960–90

John Baynes

When the last National Servicemen were called up in the late summer of 1960 there were widespread concerns among those interested in defence matters as to whether the decision to end conscription and rely on voluntary enlistment could keep the armed forces, in particular the Army, at a proper strength. In 1961 Professor M.R.D. Foot wrote in his book *Men in Uniform* a warning about the future:

> For all the ancient traditions of the armed forces of the Crown, they are now embarked on a new voyage that is set about with perils. The dropping of compulsory national service is a gamble; the odds are no doubt in favour of success, but success is no certainty.[1]

As things have turned out, it has been possible to rely on voluntary recruiting to keep the armed forces up to strength, or nearly so, at least for the three decades under study here. But in spite of the steady reduction in the size of these forces throughout the period they have been constantly cursed by a problem also noted by Foot:

> The butter of forces in being is going to be spread exceedingly thin over some parts of the bread of British commitments in the coming few years. Too thin a spread produces severe overstrain for regular forces, lowers their morale and hence their fighting quality, and must be avoided.

Most officers and other ranks who have served since 1960, or are serving now, would add a loud 'Amen' to that.

Throughout the 30 years under review here recruiting has shared with the British economy a pattern of ups and downs, to some extent copying the vagaries of the latter as it has followed its 'stop-go' course. As the strength of the forces has risen to a satisfactory level the funds available for the recruiting organisations have been cut back. In due course a dearth of manpower has followed, and the efforts to find recruits have been started up again. This has been the case in respect of the Army more than the other services, although the Royal Navy has had its problems. What follows in this paper, however, will apply only to Army recruiting.

Although the emphasis will be on the search for volunteers to come in 'off the street', the importance of internal recruiting must not be forgotten. This had, and still has, two aspects. The positive one is the effort to persuade those already serving on specified terms to extend to longer engagements, the 'carrot' being either an increased rate of pay or a bonus paid after entering the new period of service. Action along these lines was being taken back in National Service days in the 1950s, and many conscripts were persuaded to sign on as three-year regulars to get extra pay; in fact this was a major source of so-called regular recruits. The negative aspect is the attempt to prevent men and women leaving before their proper demobilisation date. This was not a serious problem until, as part of the liberalisation of Army conditions in the 1970s, the right was given to other ranks to apply for PVR, or premature voluntary retirement, subject to a year's notice and the Army's right to withhold it for operational necessity on active service. PVR has tended to be a temptation to those most confident of civilian employment and so by definition the ones the Army is most anxious to retain: the bright 25 to 30-year-old NCOs (non-commissioned officers), and the skilled tradesmen trained at great cost. Officers have traditionally been able to apply for transfer to the reserve at any time, subject to certain obvious limitations, such as a national emergency or the recent completion of a long period of special training, but their retention was not a serious problem during the 30 years being considered, though it may have become one more recently.

We will shortly be looking at the disbandments and amalgamations in the Regular Army and the Territorial Army in the second half of the 1960s. Two points are worth making in connection with such cut-backs. First, the surplus personnel from broken-up units serve temporarily to bring up to strength the untouched ones into which they are posted. Second, governments like to claim credit for the cuts, either for saving the tax-payer's money or for making the forces 'leaner and meaner'. The result in each case is harmful to the essential search for new young recruits: money is withheld from the recruiting organisation because many units seem to be fully manned, and the outside world gets the impression that there is no future 'in going for a soldier'. In extreme cases publicised reports of reductions lead to a belief that a branch of the Army has disappeared altogether.

1960–70

In 1962 the last National Servicemen were demobilised, and the Army was left to face the future without any powers of conscription for the first time for 24 years. In the early part of the decade the fears of the pessimists proved unfounded, with recruiting figures at a peak in 1962, as shown in the statistics of enlistments over five years in Table 1, extracted from my book *The Soldier in Modern Society*.[2]

Table 1

TABLE OF ENLISTMENTS

Year	Men	Junior soldiers	Total
1962	29,813	6,794	36,607
1963	18,058	5,823	23,881
1964	23,853	6,535	30,388
1965	20,307	5,436	25,743
1966	19,950	5,838	25,788

The strength of the Army in 1962 was 183,000 adults and 9,700 juniors. It dropped slightly in 1963, and then was held to an average of 172,000 and 9,000 for the rest of the 1960s. Missing from these totals is the Brigade of Gurkhas, still composed in those days of the four infantry regiments, the 2nd, 6th, 7th and 10th, as well as Gurkha engineers, signallers, and transport drivers.

The Gurkhas played a major part in the now largely forgotten campaign in Indonesia, which lasted from 1962 to 1966. This was a classic operation of its kind, setting the seal on earlier successes in Malaya and Kenya. In the middle of 1965 Britain had 60,000 troops in Borneo, which was the same number as the USA had in Vietnam. As the Americans were preparing to escalate into the disaster that their war in Indo-China eventually became, the British were nearing the end of their little known confrontation with the Indonesians. Our lack of equipment and of public relations were blessings, in that the soldiers had to use their feet rather than aircraft, and nobody at home knew or cared much about what was going on.

With an effect not unlike the party's victory in 1997, though less extensive, Labour won the General Election of 1964, ending 13 years of Conservative dominance. With stirring talk of the 'white-hot, technological revolution' about to begin, Harold Wilson promised a new approach to many of Britain's problems. In the realm of defence, Labour's intentions were explained in the White Paper of February 1965:

> The present Government has set in train a series of studies on defence policy; these will cover the effects on force levels and capabilities of a number of different possible courses of action.[3]

Before considering the first important step taken by the government as a result of these studies mention should be made of what might be called 'the spirit of the 1960s': to some a wonderful throwing away of outmoded restrictions and traditions; to many others a downward lurch into scruffy idleness, typified by the drug-taking hippy. The proportion of those who rejected the old order grew from a tiny minority into a large one. Harold Macmillan is reputed to have compared this wave of iconoclasm to a situation in a school where 'the beaks have given up, and the lower boys have taken over'. Nobody could fail to be aware of these disruptive activities, except the very few people not owning a television set, as both the BBC and ITV brought to their screens not only news of strange events but satirical programmes, which many older people considered outrageous. It was in the 1960s that television firmly established the hold on the population that has been such a feature of the years that have followed.

Returning to the studies put in hand by the government, the first step was the announcement of a complete reorganisation of the Territorial Army. As the regular Brigade Major of a Territorial Army brigade in south-west England I was deeply involved in this process, which was carried out between the end of 1965 and 1 April 1967. Put briefly, it meant the reducing of most regiments and battalions from unit to sub-unit size throughout the country: regiments to squadrons or batteries, battalions to companies. Hundreds of small drill-halls were closed, and headquarters such as the one I worked in also disappeared. The outcry was vehement from serving and retired Territorials, often backed up by local councils and other groups. Much pleasure was found in rude comments about the two senior officers in the Ministry of Defence who were responsible for arranging the reorganisation. These were the aptly named Generals Hackett and Carver.

Under-funded, and under-recruited in most units, the Territorial Army with its 20-year-old, wartime weapons and equipment was due for this shake-up, and I for one, though I kept my opinions to myself, was glad to see it. The Volunteer Reserve, known at first as TAVR, and more recently back to Territorial Army again in general speech, was an infinitely better military force. New hardware of all kinds, a much stronger regular staff, and opportunities for annual camps overseas brought great improvements to the reformed body, which was given a clear role as immediate reinforcement to the Regular Army.

In spite of these improvements the TAVR never reached its full target-strength of 81,000, although certain units were well recruited. Two factors were at play. One, mentioned earlier, was the government's wish to draw credit from making cuts and reducing defence expenditure; the other was the publicity sought by, and given to, the vociferous objectors to change in the old Territorial Army. The result was that the population at large came to believe that everything had been disbanded and that a reserve Army no longer existed.

The second step taken by the new government following its studies of defence policy was to announce a reduction in overseas commitments. The withdrawal from east of Suez was to be speeded up, making the final year 1971 rather than 1975, with the first exodus being the departure from Aden in 1967. The retreat from this colony, after just under 100 years of British rule, was an affair of less dignity than many might have wished. The result of the cutting back of commitments was inevitable. After a period when the air had been thick with rumours, the first disbandments since the Southern Irish regiments in 1922 were announced. Starting the process on 14 May 1968, the 1st Battalion The Cameronians (Scottish Rifles) slipped out of the Army's muster-books, after

279 years' unbroken service, at an impressive ceremony at Castle Douglas, Lanarkshire on the exact spot where it had originally been raised. Three other battalions followed in the same year, and four more were warned that they would be reduced to company size in 1969. Among these was 1st Battalion The Argyll & Sutherland Highlanders, whose supporters ran a much publicised campaign to 'Save the Argylls'. In the end salvation came from an unexpected source to be discussed shortly, and the Argyll company was eventually restored to battalion strength.

The reductions in the Territorial Army and the Regular Army were not encouraging to potential recruits, and numbers coming forward to join started to drop sharply, reaching an absolute 'low' in 1968 (see Table 2).

Table 2

RECRUITMENT IN THE LATE 1960S

Year	Men	Junior soldiers	Total
1967	15,868	5,604	21,472
1968	11,474	5,392	16,866
1969	13,789	6,503	20,292

Apart from the ill effect of the publicity given to the reductions, two other factors had a bearing on the difficulty in finding suitable recruits: the high rejection rate at the Army Careers and Information Offices (ACIOs), and the rates of pay that were slipping behind the national average. Of those men who wanted to join in 1967 32 per cent were turned away, for the reasons shown in Table 3.

Table 3

CAUSES OF REJECTION IN 1967

	%
Failing relatively simple selection tests	8.6
Admitted record of crime or court appearance	9.6
No vacancy, usually for trades in technical arms	2.5
Medical reasons	11.7
Total	32.4

A further 21.7 per cent voluntarily withdrew their applications to join at the last minute, just before attestation was completed. So in all there was just under a fifty-fifty chance of seeing a potential recruit who came into an ACIO finally being sworn in.

The question of pay was one of the main preoccupations of the Ministry of Defence during Denis Healey's reign there in the last years of the 1960s. Close links were established with the National Board for Prices and Incomes (NBPI) set up by the government in 1967, with some of the staff of the Board's *Standing Reference on the Pay of the Armed Forces* being Ministry of Defence civil servants on secondment to it. This group gathered much useful information about military careers and professional attitudes as well as coming forward with some ideas on improving conditions. One was the introduction of the military salary, enabling basic rates of pay to be comparable to civilian wages while making the serviceman pay for food, accommodation, etc. which had previously been hidden benefits. Another introduction was the 'X' factor, a weighting in favour of service pay to make up for the inevitable disruption caused by the nature of the military way of life. As long as the government wished to give strong support to the services it could set the scales in both these areas in a generous manner, and did so when they were first introduced. The trouble was that both could be manipulated in another, meaner direction, and were to be from time to time in years that followed.

One reason why so much effort could be devoted by the Ministry of Defence to matters such as pay and conditions of service was the absence of more warlike problems to be solved. Making himself something of a hostage to fortune, Mr Gerry Reynolds, Minister for the Army, stood up in the House of Commons on 5 March 1969 and announced:

> In the last 12 months we have lost, thank goodness, the best recruiting sergeant one normally has. British forces have not been in action anywhere in the world. No one has been killed or wounded in action anywhere in the world in the last 12 months – the first time this has happened in this century. I hope that goes on for many more years ...[4]

Within months civil disorder broke out in Northern Ireland. It is worth remembering that it began as a result of a long period of apparently good relations between the Protestants and Catholics in the province, leading the prime minister, Captain O'Neill, to make a trip to Dublin to begin a hoped-for improvement in relations with the Republic of Eire. Inspired by this gesture, a strong body of Catholics began a civil rights march through the counties along the border. Entering a strongly Protestant region, they were met by opposition. Tempers flared and rioting started, quickly spreading to many other areas, and soon out of the control of the police and the few soldiers of the permanent garrison in the province. More troops were rushed in and gradually began the troubles that have carried on at varying levels of intensity for the past 30 years. The long-quiescent IRA soon came to life again, to be answered by the building-up of Protestant paramilitary groups.

1970–80

The early 1970s saw the worst of the violence in Northern Ireland. On 6 February 1971 the first British soldier was killed on duty: by the end of the year another 47 had died. The following year saw the regular troops in Ulster at a peak strength of 21,266 at the end of July, backed by the mobilisation of 9,000 members of the Ulster Defence Regiment (UDR), the part-time organisation which had been raised locally in 1970. Following this massive application of force the successful operation code-named 'Motorman' restored order in certain parts of Belfast and Londonderry which the IRA and various Protestant groups had made into 'no-go' areas. By the end of 1972 6,000 soldiers had left the province, but the bloodshed throughout the year had been horrendous; 129 soldiers, including 26 members of the UDR and 17 of the Royal Ulster Constabulary (RUC), had been killed, along with 321 civilians; 578 soldiers and 3,902 civilians were injured or wounded. In addition 1,853 bombs were found, of which 471 were made safe by the outstandingly brave members of the Army bomb disposal teams. Shooting incidents were recorded at 10,630 – six times as many as in 1971.

However sad it is that such a story of savagery and destruction has to be told about events in a part of the United Kingdom, the Army found salvation from prospective decline into virtual disappearance through the Ulster disorders. The Argylls and the other battalions reduced to company size were re-formed at full strength, and for the rest of the decade the demand for units to serve in the province was constant, though increasingly hard to meet as time went by, and the word 'overstretch' began to be part of the British military vocabulary.

In 1971 a change was made in the way in which new recruits were received into the ranks when two Recruit Selection Centres (RSCs) were set up to handle applicants for all branches of the Army. One was in Scotland, and another and bigger one at Sutton Coldfield, in the Midlands near Birmingham. The journalist Dennis Barker visited the latter in the later 1970s while writing his book *Soldiering On*, published in 1981. Noting that 'It did not make instant friends with everyone in the British Army, much of which is geared to the virtual autonomy of regiments. The regiments used to choosing their own men had some initial suspicions',[5] he went on to show that after a few years its advantages had become accepted. A major one was that no time and effort was wasted taking an unsuitable man through a part of his depot training before having to discharge him as unsuitable. During a period of three days at an RSC either party could change its mind, and Barker found that 'the Selection Officers of Sutton Coldfield say that many of the men who back out of their own accord have thereby saved the Army the trouble of giving them the shove'.[6]

Although recruits had been coming forward in good numbers in the early 1970s, partly as a result of the interest and excitement of events in Northern Ireland, by the time Barker was writing he described the selection machine at Sutton Coldfield as 'a machine which had a target of 7,000 candidates every six months when I visited it, but which at that time was dealing with only 5,600, largely owing to lack of applicants'.[7]

By 1977 the British economy was entering one of its 'stop' phases, and Denis Healey, now Chancellor of the Exchequer, had been forced to apply for help to the International Monetary Fund to bail the country out. This body demanded strict control of public spending, so national and local government employees at all levels felt the squeeze on their wages, leading to the 1978–79 'winter of discontent' that brought down the Labour government. The services, already behind most of the nation before the squeeze, found that their pay rates had dropped to a level that made joining them, especially the Army, an unattractive proposition. One of the early actions of Margaret Thatcher's new Conservative government, following its victory in the 1979 General Election, was to give significant pay rises to the armed forces and the police.

1980-90

There was a lull in 1980 in the disorder in Ulster, following two serious incidents on 27 August 1979; the murder of Earl Mountbatten and the double killing at Warrenpoint of 18 men of the Parachute Regiment and 12 of the Queen's Own Highlanders. The lull did not last long, and in 1981 hunger strikes by convicted terrorists in H-block at the Maze prison sparked off serious rioting in April, as a result of which 600 extra soldiers were sent to the province in May, bringing troop levels up to 11,500. Violence came to London later in 1981 with a nail-bomb attack on the Irish Guards band in a bus outside Chelsea barracks. On 20 July 1982 bomb attacks on the Household Cavalry and the Royal Green Jackets band killed eight soldiers and wounded 51.

While these losses were serious enough in so-called peacetime, there were greater casualties suffered during the war in the Falklands from 2 April to 14 June 1982. 'So extraordinary an event was it', wrote Max Hastings and Simon Jenkins in *The Battle for the Falklands*, 'that even after men began to die, many of those taking part felt as if they had been swept into fantasy'.[8] By the time the Argentinians surrendered on the afternoon of 14 June, 28,000 members of the three British services had been involved in the war, and of these 10,000 from the Army and Royal Marines had been landed on the islands. In all, 255 men were killed, of whom 123 were from the Army and 27 were marines. Of the 777 wounded, 464 were soldiers. The success of this amazing short campaign, conducted 8,000 miles from Britain with exemplary efficiency and courage by the armed forces, gave rise to a wave of euphoria throughout the nation, soon dubbed the 'Falklands factor'. It was used by Margaret Thatcher to win a resounding majority in the 1983 General Election, and it was one of the major reasons why Army recruiting was so buoyant up to the mid-1980s.

There were several factors, not all stemming from the Falklands victory, that inspired plenty of good-quality young men and women to join during these years. At the practical level there was the improved standard of Army pay, coupled with continuing large-scale unemployment throughout northern and western England and Scotland, traditionally the best recruiting areas in the country. At what might be termed the emotional level there was an upsurge of patriotic fervour and admiration for the armed forces. Partly this sprang from constant viewing of military activities on television, both from Ulster and the Falklands, and partly a general sense of national confidence following the gloom of the late 1970s. (It would be interesting to know whether unemployment caused by the long miners' strike of 1984–85 had any effect on recruiting in the mining areas.)

Halfway through the 1980s the picture began to change. The recession of 1981 had been followed by a boom, and unemployment was falling rapidly, making competition for suitable young trainees increasingly fierce among all potential employers. About this time those responsible for manning the Army began to be aware of an impending difficulty likely to make the situation worse still, the 'demographic trough'. Awareness of the effect that this would have on recruiting led to the Adjutant-General forming a special committee to study the problem. In 1988 it produced its report under the title MARILYN (Manning and Recruiting in the Lean Years of the Nineties). The opening paragraph sets the scene:

> In common with the other NATO nations, the United Kingdom faces a decline in the number of young people within the overall population. By the year 2003 there will have been a reduction of about 20 per cent of those aged between 15 and 29, compared to 1987. It is from this age-group that the army recruits its officers and soldiers. Allied to this the economic outlook has been brightened and unemployment is falling, so that the competition for resources will be even more fierce.[9]

While looking to the future, the people involved in recruiting were coming across a different problem of more immediate concern, summed up in two quotations from Antony Beevor's book *Inside the British Army*. In respect of young men he records that:

> Sergeants were also dismayed at the change in the recruits they had been getting since about 1987. (Right across the Army almost everyone puts their finger on that year, although nobody can give a satisfactory explanation.) Not only has there been a significant decline in the quality of recruits, but their attitudes are completely different. They are not necessarily insubordinate, one sergeant explained, they just don't understand what authority or rank mean. Like many instructors, he felt that they had little grasp of reality and that their expectations of the Army were based on film fantasies.[10]

Similar views were expressed to Beevor about young women at the WRAC Centre at Guildford:

> Over the last three years NCO instructors have noticed a change in the new recruits which parallels that remarked upon with such feeling in the rest of

the Army. Many of the girls have never learned to look after themselves: their mothers have done everything for them, and few know how to cook, wash their clothes or sew on a button. Quite a few cannot even wash themselves properly, so NCO instructors have to start with lessons in basic hygiene.

This general lack of awareness baffles women NCO instructors as much as permanent staff at male depots, and they too date the dramatic decline from around 1987. 'They'll ask you the first thing that comes into their heads', said one sergeant. 'It's not that they're stupid. But they've got no idea about anything. To get them to understand that in the Army they've got to do what they're told is really hard ... they just don't seem to understand about rank.'[11]

Along with this mental ignorance and aimlessness found in recruits of both sexes went physical unfitness, a particularly serious problem in the case of the majority of male entrants. Bedevilled by the fact that a recruit could pull out of training with relative ease, even though enlisted for a period of several years, the Army could not 'knock into shape' these pathetic youngsters in the traditional ways that most officers and NCOs would have wished. Ever conscious of the shortage of suitable applicants explained in the MARILYN report, the authorities had to treat them all with the greatest care.

In 1988 new initiatives were considered. After nearly 18 years in existence the RSC at Sutton Coldfield had been closed down, but St George's Barracks were retained and given a new charter as a residential centre. Ten-week preliminary education courses were begun in 1989 to help the promising young men who had failed the comprehension tests at their ACIOs, but in other ways seemed suitable. The two-week course devoted purely to physical development, which had already been running successfully for some time, was retained. Among the 600 recruits who had passed through this physical course by the autumn of 1989 a big drop in wastage during the further training was noticed. There are two objections to running these remedial units for recruits already enlisted, however valuable the work they do for the nation at large as well as the Army. First, they are expensive to run, both in skilled manpower to staff them and in straight cash terms to set them up and maintain them; second, those who fail to make the grade must be discharged, which means that all the time and money spent on them up to the moment of rejection is wasted – for the Army at least if not perhaps for the individual concerned.

New ideas were developed at other training centres and depots in 1989. Having gone through, and mostly enjoyed, a more rigorous spell of recruit training 43 years earlier in 1946, I found reports of these schemes at once something of a joke and something to be sad about. The *Daily Telegraph* on 12 January 1990 reported that:

A more gentle approach to Royal Marine training, with instructors discussing orders with recruits, has resulted in a 20 per cent increase in trainees passing the physically demanding course at Lympstone in Devon.

'There is no question of us reducing the standards of the regiment and the course training is just as hard with as much pressure put on, but like everybody else we're facing the demographic problem. We need to get through as many people as we can', said the spokesman.[12]

What Sergeant Ainslie, MM, Cameron Highlanders, my platoon sergeant in training with the 30th Training Battalion at Cameron Barracks, Inverness in 1946 would have thought of 'discussing orders with recruits' is beyond my imagining, but demographic problems were not his concern, even if he or any of us knew what they were in those days.

The depot of the Parachute Regiment also reported a big improvement in the retention of recruits under training in 1989, with 45–50 members of each intake successfully completing training compared with a figure of 25–30 previously. One cause of this success was devoting 90 per cent of instructors' efforts in the recruits' first week to a careful familiarisation programme, with little emphasis on military training until late in their course. Strange though such ideas may seem to those of us reared in a more robust age, they can only be commended if they produce the right results.

During the late 1980s the events with the greatest impact on the long-term structure of the Army, and so of its manpower needs, were the beginnings of the break-up of the USSR under the pressure of Gorbachev's *perestroika*, and following from it the demise of the Warsaw Pact. By the end of the decade the fear that 'Ivan might come over the fence' had virtually disappeared, so that touring the units of BAOR in the autumn of 1988 Antony Beevor found a distinct lack of enthusiasm for the British presence among the Germans. He wrote:

> NATO forces had already begun to find local communities reacting towards them as though they were an occupying army. Faced by relatively restrained German protests about British tanks continuing to churn up the Soltau area after 30 years, the commander of 7th Armoured Brigade said that he could hardly blame them: how would people in Britain react if German tanks were allowed to exercise round our villages and over our farmland?[13]

From the lifting of the threat of Russian invasion of western Europe came in due course the reductions in NATO force levels, and thence the cut-back in the British services that have been such a feature of military life in the 1990s, some of whose implications are explored in the chapters which follow.

NOTES

1. M.R.D. Foot, *Men in Uniform: Military Manpower in Modern Industrial Societies* (London: Weidenfeld, 1961), p. 148.
2. J.C.M. Baynes, *The Soldier in Modern Society* (London: Eyre Methuen, 1972).
3. *Statement on the Defence Estimates, 1965* (Cmnd 2592, 1965), p. 5.
4. *Report of Parliamentary Proceedings* (*The Times*, 6 March 1969).
5. Dennis Barker, *Soldiering On* (London: Sphere Books, 1983), p. 169.
6. Ibid., p. 164.
7. Ibid., p. 168.
8. Max Hastings and Simon Jenkins, *The Battle for the Falklands* (London: Michael Joseph, 1983), p. vi.
9. MARILYN, *Report*, abridged and unclassified version, p. 1.
10. Antony Beevor, *Inside the British Army* (London: Chatto & Windus, 1990), p. xxi.
11. Ibid., p. 330.
12. Toby Moore, *Daily Telegraph*, 12 January 1990.
13. Beevor, *Inside the British Army*, p.160.

PART II:
THE ARMY AND SOCIETY

5

The Army and Modern Society

Antony Beevor

For foreigners especially, 1997 appeared to be the moment when the British apparently discovered tears, and hugging, and popular democracy for the first time. Unfortunately, the vast journalistic outpourings on the subject of 'Year One of the People' has played up the notion of a sudden revolution, triggered by the death of Princess Diana. This gross simplification distorts the origins of recent changes in our society. It is vital, therefore, that we re-examine from recent beginnings the pattern of developments which have come to affect the armed forces the most.

During the 1960s – that period of student rebellion, protests against the Vietnam War and alternative lifestyles – the British Army remained singularly untouched by the outside world. When dancing in discos, young officers sang about wearing a flower in their hair if going to San Francisco, but the whole idea was a faraway joke. They continued to live in a self-contained society, virtually impervious to the fads and political fashions of the rest of the country outside.

The year 1970 saw the introduction of new salary structures and married quarters made available on a much wider basis for junior ranks. To maintain recruiting, the Army had to compete with civilian employers. Little thought was paid to the likely long-term effect. Any suggestion that social issues might one day affect recruiting, training, promotion and even deployment was considered ridiculous.

During the 1970s, the huge demands of Northern Ireland meant that training was restructured in packages, and training establishments geared up, with far higher turnovers. The Army suddenly became far more professional, taking on a much higher proportion of graduates. Yet the greatly increased recruitment of graduates had a much deeper effect than ever imagined at the time. Graduates were more career conscious and they tended to keep in closer touch with their civilian contemporaries. The Army started to lose much of the cultural isolation which had been its largely self-imposed lot until then.

Throughout the 1970s and right into the first half of the 1980s, one inconsistency seems to have received very little attention. The Army was modernising almost all of its professional practices, but little attempt was made to reassess the corresponding effect on cultural and moral values. Even as late as 1988 and 1989, many senior officers were still arguing that it was the duty of the armed forces to remain half a generation behind civilian society.

It must not be forgotten that the British Army, which evolved from a regimental base, with gentlemen buying officers' commissions, was essentially an amateur organisation with an increasingly professional system grafted on to it. So the sudden modernisation experienced in less than two decades, without a corresponding shift in social values, was bound to create internal strains, to say nothing of external contradictions with the society from which both officers and men were drawn.

The question of mutual trust and collective values lay at the heart of the culture shock which hit the Army in the second half of the 1980s. The institutions which had sailed untouched through the so-called revolutionary 1960s found themselves shaken by an utterly different ethos. A new generation was joining. Many young officers had little understanding or sympathy for tradition and convention.

Commanding officers noted with dismay that the one thing that subalterns wanted to do was to move out of the officers' mess as soon as possible and into a flat like their civilian contemporaries. An officers' mess was seen as an anachronism, an atrophied relic from Edwardian country-house mentality. This and the requirement to dress and behave like gentlemen was seen as another crumbling facade.

Many junior officers were also dismayed at the prospect of married life in the services. Graduate officers tend to marry graduates, and graduate wives did not take kindly to what many described as 'the Stepford Wives conformity' of coffee mornings and the garrison dinner party circuit.

As the Army rapidly discovered, it was not just graduate wives who wanted to maintain a career. The vast majority of officers' and NCOs' wives had careers which they were loath to give up. A second income was vital to pay the mortgage. It later came to be needed as a safety net in case of redundancy. During the 1980s, Army wives started to resist the disruptive pattern to their lives and changes of schools for their children. Weekend commuting became a way of life for a sizeable minority, at times perhaps even a majority. Military establishments became deserted at weekends save for those stuck behind on duty, or junior ranks without money or transport.

In the eyes of younger officers, the unit was no longer a surrogate family, and service life was no longer a vocation. It was just another career. And like any other career, it had to deliver. The romantic dreams of former generations of young officers of commanding their regiment in some hazy distant future had passed. It was now just a step, albeit a very important one, on the career ladder.

The clash between this new wave of personal ambition and the old ethos of collective loyalty was bound to be deeply unsettling. It would, of course, be utterly unjust to paint a picture of rampant careerism all round, but against the background of civilian society, where the notions of success and failure had sharpened dramatically, an officer, just like his civilian contemporary from university, had to become ambitious and career-conscious, if only as an act of self-preservation. Many officers remarked that loyalty to the Army could no longer be just a one-way process.

The acceptance of the unit as a surrogate family was also challenged, because married men wanted to spend far more time with their real family. This was especially true of officers and NCOs with young children, who did not want to feel obliged to spend the bulk of their free time on the rugby field or socialising in the mess. Wives also became far more outspoken on the subject. In the Army, the demands of the emergency tours arms plot meant that they were already liable to spend many months on their own, so when their husbands were in camp, the least the regiment could do was to let them spend their off-duty hours at home.

Yet while on one hand there were wives and husbands wanting a more stable life, on the other, there were still young unmarrieds wanting adventurous experience at a time when the services were withdrawing from bases abroad. An increasingly home-based service life appeared much more mundane, and even more akin to civilian life. Meanwhile, the growth of the mass travel industry, long-haul as well as European, also meant that the Army's traditional appeal of seeing exotic places was losing its edge.

It was not just young officers who appeared to be a slightly different breed. Around 1987, NCOs in training establishments noticed a significant change in their intakes. Certain characteristics of the new soldier recruits stood out. Most notable were an inexperience, even ignorance, of authority; a lack of touch with reality; and what can only be described as a rootless ambition. A majority of their recruits demonstrated a longing for instant professionalism and instant gratification, but they gave up easily. This video generation had a relatively short attention span and wanted to fast forward through anything which bored it.

The following gameboy generation, and – worst of all – the forthcoming 'virtual reality' generation, once the entertainment industry makes the next leap in technology, are likely to be even more out of touch. These developments may prove a far greater liability in operational terms than we can yet assess, with a strong possibility that the true experience of war after all the amusement-arcade simulation may be even more disorientating and shocking than at present. There is emotional, as well as operational, chaos when sophisticated systems fail. This is a very important area which cries out for more detailed study.

Part of the problem comes from the way the fantasy diet of the film industry has led the younger generation to believe that it can have incredible adventures without real physical danger. The popular press, meanwhile, has encouraged people to believe that we should be masters of our destiny, and that if anything goes wrong, somebody else must be responsible. We live in an age when people and governments believe that anything dangerous, from food poisoning to sport, should be controlled. Yet the Army has to recruit and train for the most unpredictable and dangerous of all occupations.

Even the chaos of battle is no longer regarded as an excuse. Tragic accidents, such as casualties from friendly fire, are no longer accepted as acts of God. And as the Ministry of Defence (along with the National Health Service) has discovered to its cost, we have not just entered a very secular age, we have also entered a very litigious one. If the police are to be followed as an example, we will see a mounting rate of cases dealing with thwarted promotions, hurt feelings or stress on operations. How long will it be before we have counselling detachments blistered on to every unit?

If 'no win, no fee' solicitors' deals become widespread, as appears to be the case, then the legal situation may well slip out of control. Not surprisingly, a new breed of solicitor has emerged ready to specialise in such fertile areas. There is a risk that court challenges could swamp the system if we follow this route. Recruits who cannot stand the course could, in increasing numbers, allege discrimination in some form, the physically challenged, the mentally challenged, even the cosmetically challenged, since an unflattering remark from their drill sergeant about their appearance may be enough to bring a claim for emotional injury. Individuals aggrieved by a decision not to promote them could bring a case. And we now cannot rule out the possibility of single soldiers – the maritally challenged – bringing actions if they are refused a married quarter to live in with their girlfriend. The problem is that not even a team of QCs revising every article in the Manual of Military Law and Queen's Regulations could be certain of making them watertight. Even the basic system of military justice is under threat.

The Army tends to be judged today not on its true professional performance, but on peripheral matters. The answer to that basic question, 'How is the Army seen?' comes on two levels – the general and the particular – a division which reflects the split personality, or split perception, of the public itself. On a general level, the British Army is without doubt one of the most highly respected institutions in the country. It is internationally admired for its professionalism and its standards, but on side-issues it is bound to be vulnerable. One might well argue that it is doubly vulnerable. Its high standards and its attempts to maintain traditional values of loyalty and duty in a society, whose own values have changed with bewildering rapidity, offers a very tempting target for the new journalism of calculated disrespect.

Today, only a tiny proportion of the population has any direct experience of the Army as it is today, so their images of it are even more liable to be influenced by press and television as well as thoroughly outmoded stereotypes. I do not intend to get bogged down here in that chicken and egg debate over the degree to which 'public opinion' is a reflection of 'published opinion', but two things are clear. First, the media, for commercial reasons, want dispute and 'issues' to make news. And second, newspapers especially feel a desperate need to spot trends and shifts in public mood. This helps them to capitalise on causes, and – at least in theory – harness a tide of public opinion. The notion of the crusading newspaper also serves another purpose: it salves the conscience over unscrupulous muck-raking and the distortion of facts to spice up stories.

The media has sensed the way the social mood is moving in the 1990s. It is, by and large, in a politically correct direction. In journalistic terms therefore, when an issue of egalitarianism or individual rights emerges, it is now a ball worth picking up and running with for all its copy value.

The British Army, both from its origins, and as a result of its necessarily hierarchical structure, has long believed in respect for rank as an essential part of discipline. But there is a widespread mood in this country, especially among the young, which has little patience for past practices. Values based on deference and hierarchy and collective loyalty are portrayed as ridiculously old-fashioned. Organisational structures in the civilian world are flattening, with a previously unimaginable informality in a rapidly changing workplace. But the Army's basic human needs – those of mutual trust, cohesion and respect for authority – have not changed, and cannot change if an effective war-fighting capability is to be maintained. The Army, unable to get the message across, is therefore bound to be seen as out of step with the times.

We have also entered, it would appear, an age of paradox in which the public rapidly rises to moral judgement on anyone in public life, yet increasingly believes that private conduct should be 'value-free'. Corporate bodies and their leaders are by definition responsible for anything which goes wrong, but individuals are seen essentially as victims of their own conditioning or genes. The basic Army ethos of personal responsibility and respect for the *status quo* extended to respect for the institution of marriage, but, as you all know, this has very recently been redefined. Adultery and divorce in themselves are no longer grounds for disciplinary proceedings, only adulterous behaviour which directly threatens group stability. Yet we are still likely to see more cases of appeals to the European Court by those disciplined on the more specific grounds of adultery within the military community. A former Director General of Personal Services once told me how shaken he was by the totally unrepentant tone of one officer, so charged. 'But if I was in Unilever', this officer retorted, 'nobody would give a bugger.' This is a clear example of the process of the Army's civilianisation, which has accelerated since those reforms in 1970 which first brought the Army into a direct comparison with civilian employment.

The Army is in a desperately difficult position. The unrelenting pressures of service life lead to more and more breakdowns of marriage. In many cases, adultery is not the cause, but the sadly inevitable symptom of family disruption, personal frustration and loneliness. Careers are destroyed as well as families. The other problematic development is the greatly increased deployment of women serving alongside men. (Before I am accused of sexism, let me quickly add that the problem is far more male-based than female-based.) In any case, the consequences are not surprising. A highly physical organisation like the Army is bound to be sex-obsessed. To make matters worse, the British are always said to be the people who tend to throw off constraints the most when away from home.

It is all very well introducing no-touching, or so-called 'six-inch', rules, but they can never be more than an ineffective dam.

The subject of women and combat service will continue to be vexed for some time. We have only to look westwards to the problems of the US Army. The idea that the future reaches Britain from across the Atlantic began during the Second World War. Since then, it has come to be seen as a second prevailing wind. Military culture shock, however, has come a long way since informal salutes and nylon stockings. The recent doctrine of equal opportunity is a much more important reason for keeping a sharp eye on developments across the ocean.

Only the Americans, we might have said even just a few years ago, could have set up an establishment called DEOMI – the Defense Equal Opportunity Management Institute. DEOMI is located at Patrick Air Force Base near Cocoa Beach, on the east coast of Florida. Its mission accomplishment slogan is 'Human Readiness Equals Combat Readiness'.[1] The whole issue is taken so seriously by the US Army that there is even a section in confidential reports, marking whether or not the officer in question is personally committed to equal opportunity. Those classified as reactionaries face blocks on further promotion. 'A tick in the no-box is a killer', was the way one officer who has done the course put it to me.

The establishment started life in 1971 as the Defense Race Relations Institute after a very bad period of racial tension in the US Army. It then became DEOMI eight years later, broadening its activities to cover the integration of women. A new impetus was provided by the 'Tailhook' sexual harassment scandal involving navy fliers. Altogether DEOMI has trained some 15,000 'equal opportunities advisers' as well as instructors at establishments such as West Point. The institute can also be called in to organise a 'Military Equal Opportunity Climate Survey', to assess attitudes whenever a 'human relations problem' is identified. Those sergeants and officers selected for training are not supposed to become commissars of the new doctrine, so much as counsellors to improve 'unit cohesion'. Most candidates are chosen for having the right out-look in the first place, but a suspicion lingers that DEOMI might also serve as a re-education camp for 'social dinosaurs'. A couple of generals from the US Marine Corps who had expressed illiberal thoughts were sent there for instruction in equal-opportunity new-speak.

The United States armed forces, despite major efforts to establish an equality of treatment, is still lurching from scandal to scandal. Fundamental adjustments of attitude in less than a generation are proving extremely hard both in the country which invented political correctness, and over here. But one thing is certain: the British Army cannot possibly turn back for a whole range of reasons. Apart from any legal issues, both here and in the European Community, the armed forces desperately need to recruit women, not just to make up manpower deficiencies, but also because in a world which will be increasingly technological and communications dominated, they need their skills.

A major change of policy, which the British Army still refuses to accept, is the recruitment of homosexuals. The Army's reaction, which appears purely visceral to outsiders, focuses mainly on the threat of sexual tension within the barrack block, and the consequent effects on group cohesion on operations. Servicewomen need privacy and protection from sexual harassment within their own quarters, it is argued, so same-sex service personnel, obliged to live together, with shared showers and rooms, must be allowed the same sense of security. It is an argument which may be rejected outside the Army, but there can be little doubt about the strength of feeling on the matter within.

The basic issue is not whether homosexuals make good or bad soldiers. Even Evelyn Waugh, who was both outspokenly homophobic and courageous to the point of fearlessness, once wrote to a friend: 'Buggers are jolly brave as I saw in the war.'[2] The debate is essentially over the degree of disruption to the military system.

Personally, I fear that the Army missed an important opportunity back at the beginning of 1993, when the suggestion of following the Australian Army's formula was rejected. The Australians managed to avoid specifics by never mentioning the words 'homosexual' or 'heterosexual' in their equivalent of the Discipline and Standards Paper. Instead they use the formula of 'unacceptable sexual behaviour' without defining it. The interpretation has been left to commanding officers. This seems to have succeeded in heading off a row over anti-homosexual discrimination. Whether conflict will be whipped up at some stage in the future due to a particular case, one cannot of course tell. But they were right in deciding that a low-key approach offered the only chance of a relatively smooth transition. This placed the matter firmly in the sphere of military necessity, while keeping it out of the political arena. The British Army, on the other hand, by nailing its colours to the mast in the Discipline and Standards Paper of October 1993, allowed the issue to become politicised in this country and thus greatly reduced its own room for manoeuvre in the future.[3]

The problem in this country now is that the more high-profile the argument becomes, the more difficult the situation will be to handle if and when – and I would certainly calculate that it is a question of when – the Army has to concede defeat, almost certainly as a result of a court case. There is no doubt about the intensity of loathing for homosexuals in the ranks, especially in infantry regiments. The arrival of open homosexuals might well dwarf the bullying scandals of the late 1980s. And if that happens, there is no point the Army saying to press or politicians, 'But we warned you.' Commanding officers will still be held responsible.

In the circumstances, the Army has two options. It can try to fight to the finish, but this risks a humiliating and very dangerous outcome, should it fail to convince. Or it can deploy all its arguments, as cogently as possible, yet meanwhile prepare for the fateful day by studying in advance ways to take the heat out of a very inflamed situation.

Psychiatrists tell us, and I am sure they are right, that a loathing of homosexuals comes primarily from a fear of one's own homosexual potential, however slight. One thing is undeniable: nothing breeds greater violence than suppressed fear. The other great fear in this case, will be stimulated by grossly exaggerated ideas about homosexuals as Aids carriers. It was with this in mind that I suggested five years ago at the Army and Society seminar at the Staff College, that, to prepare the ground in advance, compulsory blood testing should be introduced as soon as possible for all entrants, or on the orders of a commanding officer.

The Army's arguments will be dismissed by more and more people, especially the young, on the grounds that its values are out of date and that it is just trying to defend macho values. Whether the Army likes it or not, this is a generation issue, even more than one of personal politics, and every army, by definition, needs the younger generation.

It is understandable that the British Army feels aggrieved. The equal opportunity lobby has quite clearly targeted the armed forces because they represent the commanding heights of the employment sector. If the armed forces are compelled to comply with the needs of every minority group, then this can be imposed across the board to the rest of the country.

The Army is also exasperated by the idea it should have to reduce its own exacting standards of behaviour to the declining levels of morality in society as a whole. The services, more than any other organisation, need their own rules to allow them to cope with circumstances and pressures which have no parallel in civilian life. The problem is that very few politicians, on either side of the House of Commons, have had military experience and understand the issues involved. Politicians, for their own very different party reasons, cannot acknowledge that the job – literally a matter of life and death – really is radically different from any other.

Conservative speeches under the government of John Major resounded with staunch support. These went down well in the constituencies and at party conferences. What Tory MPs could not admit, however, was that the armed forces, the epitome of Conservative values, also represented very similar collective loyalties to those which they had destroyed in the trade union movement. It is no coincidence that the collapse of the traditional officer class went hand in hand with the accelerated disintegration of the organised working class. These were part of historical processes, linked to the cultural and technological revolutions which coincided with the collapse of the Warsaw Pact.

Labour front-benchers face different contradictions. They have made all the right sorts of defence noises, yet deep down they knew even before the 1997 election that the armed forces, especially the infantry, cannot be expected, by the very nature of the beast, to become politically correct overnight. There is no future, whatever wishful thinkers may say, in an international gendarmerie trying to counsel warring factions. Peace-enforcement requires war-fighting qualities, nothing less. The problem that we are concerned with here today is that the atavistic nature of the fighting group is likely to resist externally imposed change.

Perhaps the greatest shift in British society over the last ten years is the new definition of citizenship. In the past, citizenship was bound up with patriotic duty, loyalty and responsibility. Everything has now been turned upside down within little more than a decade. First came Thatcherite individualism. It was followed from 1991 by Major's rhetoric of citizenship, which, unintentionally, gave a populist twist in a different direction. This encouraged the notion of individual rights without any idea of individual responsibility.

All of this, followed by notions of a 'stakeholder' society, has led to a revised idea of democracy based on individual rights rather than collective duties. The Army is no longer allowed to be self-selecting. It has to acknowledge an ill-defined 'right to serve'. As the ultimate expression of the state, it is now expected to represent society in all its diversity: social, sexual, racial and, perhaps in the not so distant future, the 'differently abled'.

This notion of deliberately mirroring an increasingly varied society runs contrary to past practice, when the traditional regimental system looked for similarity and compatibility. The Army, unfortunately, had until very recently failed to see the writing on the wall. Insufficient attempts were made to tackle racism, and many recruits suffered badly as a result. The Household Division in particular did not take the problem seriously and utterly failed to foresee how the issue would boomerang. The British Army is now genuinely determined to improve its record, but finds itself trapped in a vicious circle, partly because of earlier procrastination, and partly because the whole issue of racism has been polarised and polemicised.

Racism is unfortunately, but inevitably, present in all parts of our society, and probably in every other society. Yet what people often seem to forget is that it covers a very wide spectrum, from an insensitive remark right through to deliberate racial violence. Perhaps inevitably, the approach of race relations organisations, like the Commission for Racial Equality, tends to ignore historical and cultural circumstances. Their approach is clear: racism is racism, whatever the situation. This approach, whether intentionally manipulative or not, may well make genuine long-term solutions to the problem more, rather than less, difficult. For example, the British Army has long had what might politely be described as a robust sense of humour. Drill sergeants can be merciless in their comments, usually about a recruit's appearance and origins, be he tall or short, fat or thin, dark or fair, Geordie or Jock. The jokes were often pretty cruel, but they were part of the toughening up process, and, above all, part of the bonding process.

Drill sergeants now have to be very much on their guard. To call an Afro-Caribbean recruit 'Chalky' is now considered a racial insult, whatever the tone in which it is said. Some, perhaps many, remarks really were deliberate racial insults, and should *never* have been allowed. But the main point is that it will be very hard to achieve a true bonding process of the fighting group if the majority has to be acutely sensitive to the reactions of the minority. Increased official protection of the minority is obviously necessary, but politically correct policing may well fail to persuade the majority to change its attitude and accept ethnic minorities as a true part of the group. It may even provoke a backlash. But that, quite obviously, is no excuse for doing nothing.

The vicious circle seems to affect every aspect. Publicity about a handful of bad cases of harassment has deterred members of ethnic minorities from applying. This means that there are even fewer good recruits coming in, just when the Commission for Racial Equality wants to put on the pressure with targets, both for recruitment and promotion of ethnic minorities. However well meant, positive discrimination, especially if it involves promotion targets, is likely to prove counter-productive. Any suggestion that a soldier from an ethnic minority might be promoted because of his colour will arouse strong feelings in the barrack block.

It is absolutely right to make every effort to increase the proportion of ethnic minorities within the Army. But one also has to acknowledge that the recruiting objectives must be practicable. Attracting ethnic minorities will always be difficult, however much race relations in the Army improve. Afro-Caribbean culture has long tended to be anti-authoritarian, while few members of the Asian community have been attracted to service in the British Army even if they come from a warrior caste. As a result, the mismatch between the 1 per cent ethnic representation within the Army, and the 6 per cent in British society at large, will almost certainly prove impossible to eliminate. It can only be reduced.

The Commission on Racial Equality report on the Household Cavalry also argued implicitly that the regimental system, with its traditional culture and sense of identity, is essentially exclusive and thus hostile to those of ethnic minorities. Regimental history and traditions are seen to encourage the spirit of colonial wars. Even the regional character of regiments is seen as wrong, because it is said to discriminate against racially different outsiders. And according to the Commission on Racial Equality, the encouragement of family links to a regiment apparently amounts to 'unlawful indirect racial discrimination against ethnic minority applicants'.[4]

The Commission on Racial Equality, with little experience or knowledge of the Army, cannot be expected to sympathise with or even to understand the tribalism of the fighting group. As a result, its agenda is to impose civilian multi-cultural solutions, which almost by definition, means no culture of any sort, on an organisation with a very strong culture of its own. The idea that race relations can be improved through social engineering laid down in a *ukase* imposed from Whitehall is optimistic to say the least. The Commission on Racial Equality strongly criticised the suggestion of two commanding officers that recruits from racial minorities should be introduced in groups to make them feel less isolated. They were deemed to have issued 'racially discriminatory instructions'.[5] Yet their recommendation is, in the circumstances, a matter of common sense. Commanding officers have to live in the real, and rather imperfect world. A single black recruit arriving in a regiment is more than likely to attract the attention of one or two racial bullies who alone can make his life hell. His conspicuous solitude and his palpable sense of vulnerability unfortunately encourage the bully even more, just like in a school playground.

The emergence of so many forces for change – social, technological, economic and geo-political – in such a short space of time caught the British Army as well as the monarchy and other institutions off-balance. The Cold War, acting as splints on the body politic for 40 years, allowed some underlying changes to be ignored. Britain was probably the country most exposed to the force of these changes. Over the last two centuries we have undergone a low-intensity class conflict. This enabled us to avoid the revolutions which plagued the continent, but it produced an ossifying stand-off, strikingly similar to that of the Cold War itself.

Old virtues and cultural assumptions, especially notions of discretion and hypocrisy, have been turned inside out. Long-established institutions like the services have suddenly found that the ground has shifted under their feet. The new rules of the game – or rather lack of them – have proved bewildering. The almost impossible task for the British Army is to judge on which issues it should stand firm, and which changes should be conceded in good time. Decisions made off the back foot are usually bad ones. The vital point is that the British Army must never attempt to set itself up as a moral beacon for the nation, and attempt to justify a code of conduct based on moral principles. That will be seen as Cromwellian, and it will set the Army up as an Aunt Sally for the media. The Army does not have to mirror society, as the equal opportunity lobby insists, but it must not run counter to it, and cannot make a point of being both different and morally superior, as some officers would like to proclaim in the belief that it would help recruiting. Every point on which the Army decides to stand firm must be selected purely on the grounds of operational necessity and argued solely in those terms.

Ideally, it must try to make sure that it obtains the understanding and support for its positions in advance of the moment of crisis, but this will be hard. Civil servants and government ministers, whatever their political party, do not take kindly to senior officers publicly expressing their opposition to a particular policy. If any claim a right to, then their strong disapproval of Major Eric Joyce speaking out of turn will be thrown back at them. Their resignation will be expected and the whole exercise may well prove to be little more than a kamikaze option. It may obtain support in a few newspapers, but the rest are bound to caricature the issue. No officer contemplating such action should understimate the distorting headlines which will follow, probably along the lines of 'Brasshats blow their Top'.

The British Army is not simply being forced to mirror contemporary society. It increasingly runs the danger of being bogged down by attitudes which are utterly inimical to conventional military values. One might well argue that the day the British soldier becomes a model of caring citizenship is the day that he can no longer be counted on to hold the pass against the thug and tyrant. It is a subject which deserves the widest possible debate so that civilian society is fully aware of the implications.

NOTES

1. Defense Equal Opportunity Management Institute pamphlet (undated) provided 1994 by Defense Attaché US Embassy, London, and interview with DEOMI graduate.
2. Evelyn Waugh, letter February 1966, *Mr Wu and Mrs Stitch*, A. Cooper, ed., (London: Hodder & Stoughton,1991), p. 324.
3. The Discipline and Standards Paper, D/AG/4/5/1 dated 21 October 1993.
4. Commission on Racial Equality, Race Relations Act 1976 – Formal Investigation (Household Cavalry) 5.1.1.(a), March 1996.
5. Commission on Racial Equality, Race Relations Act 1976 – Formal Investigation (Household Cavalry), 5.1.1.(e), March 1996.

6

Officer Recruitment: The Decline in Social Eliteness in the Senior Ranks of the British Army

Reggie von Zugbach de Sugg
and Mohammed Ishaq

In his major paper, 'The Educational Background of British Army Officers', Otley[1] showed how men from what he termed 'the hegemonic stratum' of British society came to dominate the officer corps of the Army. Otley examined the educational background of British Army officers over the period 1855 to 1971 and argued that reference to the educational background was an appropriate method by which to measure the social eliteness of a group in British society. His tool of analysis was attendance at one of the British 'public schools' in general and at one of the Great Public Schools, which he referred to in his category of 'major boarding schools' in particular.

From this analysis, Otley felt able to predict that a change was taking place in the composition of the British Army's officer corps. While, at the time of his writing the Army was governed by an elite drawn from a socially elite background, Otley detected a trend whereby, for the first time since the Cromwellian era, the command of the Army was likely to pass into the hands of men drawn from 'the subordinate stratum' of society.

This paper seeks to take over from where Otley left off and to examine the senior ranks of the British Army, from the time of Otley's writing up to 1996 – four years after the 'Options for Change' reorganisation of 1992 – in order to determine whether Otley's predictions have been fulfilled.

Was Otley right? From his detailed analysis of the background of British Army officers, he made two predictions. First, he argued that the higher ranks of the Army, at any given time, would be drawn from a more socially elite background than the junior ranks. To some extent, this tendency can be accounted for by the residue of any past bias towards social eliteness. However, as Otley shows in his examination of the complete range of the officer ranks of the Army, the tendency for the higher ranks to be drawn from more socially elite backgrounds holds good even at the most junior levels of the Army, where historical trends have not yet had time to bring their influence to bear.

Otley's major prediction, however, was that the British Army would come more to reflect society in the composition of its leadership. In short he foresaw a British Army where the patriciate would no longer provide the majority of its senior generals.

FRAMEWORK FOR ANALYSIS: OTLEY'S SURVEY

The picture of the British military elite with which Otley[2] leaves us is clear. His findings, acknowledged from the work of Wakefield, show an army whose generals are heavily drawn from an elite educational background, indicating a patrician origin. Otley's data, illustrated in Table 1, give the percentage of general officers in two groupings: major-generals and lieutenant-generals and above, who attended HMC (Headmasters' Conference), i.e. public, schools and those attending major boarding schools, serving in 1971.

Table 1

THE EDUCATIONAL BACKGROUND OF THE BRITISH MILITARY ELITE
IN 1971 (PER CENT)

Officer category	HMC schools	Major boarding	Sample size, N =
Lt-Generals and upward	90.6	75.0	32
Major-Generals	66.3	51.7	89

Source: Otley, 'The Educational Background of British Army Officers', *Sociology*, 7 (1973).

Before proceeding to the findings of this study it is necessary to point out that there were methodological flaws in Otley's analysis, which, if extrapolated, would bias the effect of future investigation. Otley was wrong in taking, at face value, Wakefield's classification of 'lieutenant-generals and upwards'.[3] While his source, Wakefield, had been careful to exclude the honorific field marshalship extended to members of the royal household, he failed to take account of the fact that former serving field marshals hold their rank for life. While these officers may appear in the *Army List* as serving officers, they exercise no formal function in the operational administration of the Army. Thus, their inclusion serves only to bias the samples in favour of the past.

Second, the inclusion of non-combatant officers of the medical, legal and dental arms offers a bias of another sort. In the samples involved in both this and Otley's studies, such officers have held purely technical posts, in the rank of lieutenant-general and major-general, but officers of these non-combatant arms have never played a major part in either the strategic or operational management of the Army.

THE OBJECTIVES AND METHODOLOGICAL APPROACH OF THIS STUDY

This study looks at the background of Britain's senior Army officers over the 21 year period immediately following Otley's predictions. It examines the educational background of 143 general officers in two samples, 1974 and 1996, that is immediately after the publication of Otley's study and at a point four years following the major reorganisations of the 'Options for Change' 22 years later.[4]

The categories of generalship that we have used in this paper differ from those of Otley's study in order to take into account the criticisms highlighted above. In order to avoid confusion between the rank of 'general' and the generic category of 'general officer' this paper uses the NATO terminology by which the general officer ranks are referred to by a 'star' rating:

Brigadier	– One Star
Major-General	– Two Star
Lieutenant-General	– Three Star
General	– Four Star
Field Marshal	– Five Star

The paper is concerned with serving officers of two-star rank and above. Unlike Otley and the other studies on which he drew in his paper, we have divided the samples into four categories. Otley's major-generals are analysed under the category 'two-star generals'. Otley's category of 'lieutenant-generals and upwards' is divided between separate analyses for three-star generals on the one hand and for four- and five-star appointments, taken together, on the other. At both the two- and three-star levels, officers of the non-combatant arms are excluded from the analysis. The category 'four- and five-star appointments' excludes not only five-star officers holding honorary rank, as in Otley's study, but also five-star officers who, at the time of the sample, had ceased to hold active appointments.

To the analysis by rank, this paper adds a further refinement. In the study *Power and Prestige in the British Army*,[5] an inner power elite of British general officers was identified, whose members are responsible for the determination of military policy. This group, which we have termed here the '*Promenente*', is particularly relevant for the purposes of this study, in that it represents the inner elite responsible for the selection of officers for promotion to the general ranks of the Army – members of the British Army's Number One Selection Board. In short, it is an elite group which selects its successors.

The samples are taken from the *Army List* of the years 1974 and 1996. It begins in the year after the publication of Otley's paper and ends four years after the implementation of the 'Options for Change' reorganisation, being the latest data available for analysis at the time of writing. The time gap is such that each sample may be seen as being independent of the others. Over the period of 22 years, officers from one sample will have retired and a completely new list of officers will form the basis of the subsequent analysis (see Table 2).

Table 2

NUMBER OF OFFICERS IN EACH SAMPLE

Sample category	1974	1996
Two star	69	35
Three star	11	10
Four and five star	12	6
Promenente	6	6
Total officers	92	51

Otley's study[6] follows a tradition that uses educational background as a means of determining the eliteness of social background when examining the membership of British institutions. The key category in this tradition is attendance at one of the non-public sector British 'public schools', which in modern terminology are designated 'HMC – Headmasters' Conference' schools.

This category is problematic for those who seek to analyse social background. While the category HMC schools includes the 'great public' boarding schools, such as Eton and Harrow, which are the preserve of the British patriciate, it also admits a variety of types of school, many of which are local day schools whose pupils come from a very mixed social background. Otley himself acknowledges this problem, albeit in passing, by reference to a category which he calls 'major boarding schools'.[7] He further refines this by reference to what he refers to as the 'elite schools' – Eton, Harrow, Marlborough, Rugby, Winchester, Cheltenham, Clifton, Haileybury and Wellington.[8]

In the analysis of the background of officers for this study, we have followed the traditional dichotomy by distinguishing between officers from an HMC educational background and others. We have further built upon Otley's 'elite school' category to include in it the elite Roman Catholic schools of Ampleforth, Downside and Stoneyhurst, together with the Scottish boarding school, Gordonstoun, which has recently been favoured by the attendance of members of the royal family.

It is argued, however, that even this refinement of the category of HMC schools is not sensitive enough to detect the changes that may take place in British institutions over a relatively short period. Thus, in this paper, we have followed the *Power and Prestige* approach in attempting to refine the analysis still further by isolating certain elite schools as categories of analysis in their own right,[9] and the samples are also categorised under the headings of a group of schools, 'Eton, Harrow and Winchester'.

The *Power and Prestige* study also included a further refinement for the examination of the school background of British institutional groups – the

'S Index'. This was derived by the examination of the background of 2,403 members of the titled aristocracy of the United Kingdom as ascertained from *Who's Who* entries in 1974. The justification for this approach is documented in the text of *Power and Prestige in the British Army*.[10] Suffice it here to say that the S Index allows inclusion of non-HMC schools which would otherwise be rejected from analyses and offers a pragmatically based weighting as to the importance of any individual school in the determination of eliteness of social background, for the purposes of comparison. The list of schools included in the S Index, together with the weightings associated with each school entry, is given in the Appendix to this paper.

Otley's study touched only lightly upon the role of university education as an insight into the determination of the social origins of the British generals. This study includes in its analysis a survey of the university educational background of general officers in the samples. Analogous with the HMC approach to school background, the analysis looks at the proportions of general officers of the sample who attended the universities of Oxford or Cambridge. Again, drawing upon the tools of analysis from the *Power and Prestige* study, a 'U Index' is used, derived from the same sources as the S Index and based upon the same criteria (see Tables 3 and 4). The institutions included in this analysis are listed in the Appendix to this paper. The categories for analysis of the samples of senior officers in this study are thus:

HMC — per cent attendance at an HMC school.

EPS — per cent attendance at an 'elite public school'.

EHW — per cent attendance at Eton, Harrow or Winchester.

UNI — per cent attendance at a university.

OX — per cent attendance at Oxford or Cambridge.

SI — index of eliteness of school education.

UI — index of eliteness of university education.

Table 3

THE EDUCATIONAL BACKGROUND OF SENIOR BRITISH ARMY OFFICERS IN 1974 (IN PER CENT EXCEPT FOR SI AND UI)

	HMC	EPS	EHW	UNI	OX	SI	UI
Promenente	100	83	50	50	50	17.6	6.67
Four and five star	92	58	25	42	33	5.83	3.34
Three star	82	55	36	18	18	14.1	2.07
Two star	77	32	10	32	26	3.24	1.94

Table 4

THE EDUCATIONAL BACKGROUND OF SENIOR BRITISH ARMY OFFICERS IN 1996 (IN
PER CENT EXCEPT FOR SI AND UI)

	HMC	*EPS*	*EHW*	*UNI*	*OX*	*SI*	*UI*
Promenente	83	33	17	67	33	2.00	1.30
Four and five star	88	33	17	33	33	1.53	0
Three star	70	20	20	30	20	1.74	0.78
Two star	54	6	3	43	17	0.40	0.26

ANALYSING THE DATA

Otley's study claimed to have identified a marked tendency for the higher
ranks of the British general officers to be drawn from a more socially elite group
than the more junior generals – the higher in the military rank structure, so the
fewer officers drawn from a 'subordinate stratum' background would hold
senior military posts. This hypothesis is examined by reference to Tables 5 and 6,
in which the junior general officer categories for each year are compared with
their next senior in terms of elite representation. An increase in proportion of
officers in the junior of two categories compared is marked by a plus sign, '+'. A
decrease in representation is marked by a minus sign, '−'.

Table 5

COMPARISON OF CATEGORIES FOR 1974

	HMC	*EPS*	*EHW*	*UNI*	*OX*	*SI*	*UI*
Four and five star to three star	−	−	+	−	−	+	−
Three star to two star	−	−	−	+	+	−	−

Table 6

COMPARISON OF CATEGORIES FOR 1996

	HMC	*EPS*	*EHW*	*UNI*	*OX*	*SI*	*UI*
Four and five star to three star	−	−	+	−	−	+	+
Three star to two star	−	−	−	+	−	−	−

From the above tables, it will be seen that Otley's thesis as to the greater eliteness of the higher general officer ranks of the British Army over the more junior general officer ranks is generally correct both for the time at which he was writing and for the situation 22 years later. The thesis holds, even when the bias towards eliteness in Otley's senior general categories is corrected. Thus, HMC representation in 1974 fell from 92 per cent at the four- and five-star level to 77 per cent at the two-star level (see Table 3). In the same year, the percentage of generals educated at elite public schools fell from 58 per cent to 32 per cent between the two categories and the S Indices were 5.83 and 3.24 respectively (see Table 3).

The thesis remains correct in the later 1996 sample too (see Table 4), even after the 'Options for Change' reorganisations had eliminated a number of two-star appointments that were reserved for officers drawn from the technical arms where, as we have shown elsewhere, HMC school representation is at its weakest.[11]

HMC representation in the 1996 sample fell from 88 per cent at the four- and five-star level to 54 per cent at the two star level (see Table 4). In that year, elite public school representation fell from 17 per cent to 3 per cent between the two categories and the S Indices were 1.53 and 0.40 (see Table 4).

While Otley's thesis as to the higher the rank, so the more elite the background of its members, is generally correct, it will be noted that the three-star categories in each sample year show a tendency to include a greater proportion of officers from the three front-rank elite schools – Eton, Harrow and Winchester – than is found in the four- and five-year categories. This is also reflected in the S Indices for each year (see Tables 3 and 4). In 1974, 36 per cent of three-star officers were drawn from these schools as opposed to 25 per cent of the four- and five-star category. In 1996 the relevant percentages were 20 per cent of the three-star category and 17 per cent for the four- and five-star generals. In both cases, this must be seen against a background of a decline in the elite public school representation against the next highest rank category. It would thus seem that the social process which lies behind Otley's thesis may be partially suspended at this level. A disproportionate number of general officers from an ultra elite background make the jump from the two- to the three-star level; however, they fail to make it into the most senior ranks. This phenomenon is consistent with the findings of the paper 'Who are the British Generals', which documents the domination of the senior ranks of the British Army by officers drawn from a small group of regiments which recruit heavily from the elite public schools – Eton, Harrow and Winchester.[12]

Before moving to the major of Otley's theses – that relating to the changes that occur in the social make-up of the general officer ranks over time – it is of value to draw attention to another feature of the educational background of the generals looked at in this study, namely university education. From the above tables, it will be seen that the proportion of university graduates follows a similar pattern. In each case, there is a higher proportion of graduates at the higher levels of generalship than the lower, until one comes to the two-star rank, where the possession of a university degree becomes more common. In the earlier, 1974 sample, the 'Oxbridge' component showed an increase at the two-star level. This would be explicable, given the pre-1963 make-up of British university provision. Recourse to the U Index, however, shows that this in no way invalidates Otley's thesis as to the social eliteness of higher ranks as the index is shown to decrease for each category.

A similar picture may be drawn for the 1996 sample. Here, the higher-rank categories demonstrate a greater proportion of graduates, except at the two-star level. The representation of the 'Oxbridge' category decreases at all levels. One 'glitch' may be noted. It will be seen that the U Index for three-star officers increases. This is consistent with the corresponding S Index findings noted above and can be attributed to the same interpretation.

Otley used categories of general officer that were contaminated by past bias. His educational background categories were crude and he excluded the evidence that could be drawn from university education. However, using methodologies that correct these omissions, in terms of his 'The higher the fewer' thesis, Otley's thesis appears to be correct for samples taken after the time of his writing.

The second and more interesting of Otley's theses about the composition of the British general officer corps relates to the likely direction of change in its social composition over time. In this study, we have sought also to examine how far Otley's predictions of a British Army led by men drawn from the 'subordinate stratum' have been realised.

Table 7

COMPARISON OF CATEGORIES OF GENERAL RANK (1996 AS PERCENTAGE OF 1974 REPRESENTATION)*

	HMC	*EPS*	*EHW*	*UNI*	*OX*	*SI*	*UI*
Promenente	83	40	34	134	66	11	26
Four and five star	90	57	68	79	0	26	0
Three star	85	36	56	167	111	12	38
Two star	70	19	3	134	65	12	13

Note: *Percentage figures have been derived by taking the 1996 figures and dividing them by their corresponding 1974 figures.

Analysing the data in Table 7 will reveal that there is a definite shift in the direction that Otley predicted in 1973. From the inter-sample analysis, it can be seen that, in terms of each method of analysis, the eliteness of each category has been eroded over the time elapsed. The most useful tools appear here to be the S and the U Indices. While the changes in HMC and elite public school representation may appear to be less than radical over the 22 years elapsed between the samples, these indices make it clear that a definite shift away from the 'hegemonic stratum' has taken place in the senior leadership of the British Army.

As would be consistent with Otley's thesis as to the eliteness of higher ranks, the major changes appear to be taking place at the junior levels. The grip of the public school system in general and of the elite public schools in particular is shown to be diminished most at the two-star general level. Here, at the level from which the future senior leadership of the British Army will emerge, is shown to exist a population that is much less drawn from a patrician background than would have been the case at the time when Otley was making his predictions as to the future generalship of the British Army.

If there is a prediction from these data, it would appear that the graduate from a non-elite, university background is beginning to displace the elite, HMC-educated officer at the senior levels of the British military system.

CURRENT REALITIES

The above data may be looked at in a different way. In 1974, Otley predicted a future British Army the senior officers of which would be drawn from a background that was not 'hegemonic'. Twenty-three years later, what do we find?

1. Of the generals who will select their successors 83 per cent come from a public-sector school background: 33 per cent of these generals attended one of 13 elite public schools and 17 per cent went to one of three ultra-elite schools; 33 per cent of these officers were educated at either Oxford or Cambridge.

2. Table 8 illustrates that the decline in social eliteness, as measured in terms of educational background, is evident when comparing cadets in 1974 with those in 1997. The percentage of cadets having attended elite schools declined in 1997 in comparison to 1974. This is better demonstrated through the Debrett scale and the S Index, which both record marked declines.

Table 8

EDUCATIONAL BACKGROUND OF SANDHURST CADETS, 1974 AND 1997

Educational institution	1974 (N = 446)	1997 (N = 234)
HMC (Headmasters' Conference)	44%	44%
EHW (Eton, Harrow, Winchester)	7%	6%
Wellington	3%	2%
EPS (elite public schools)	19%	13%
Debrett	38%	24%
S Index	1.76	1.48

CONCLUSIONS

This paper essentially reopened the debate on officer recruitment, more specifically the educational background of senior British Army officers, in order to determine the extent of social eliteness embedded within the senior ranks of the British Army. Although Otley examined in some detail the educational background of British Army officers in his 1974 paper, this study has attempted to fill the vacuum left over since he produced his paper. Otley offered a number of predictions which could not be ignored. This study has brought the issue up to date and while it has shown Otley's predictions to be correct it has made a number of refinements. First it has eliminated the flaws in Otley's methodology which provided a bias in favour of the past. In addition, by including the *promenente*, the study very relevantly takes into account these inner elite officers who will select their eventual successors. Furthermore, it has refined the analytical tools by adding the S and U Indices.

The major findings which emanate from this study show that over a period of time – in this case 1974 to 1997 – all ranks of the Army have become less elite. This also holds true for cadets. Very importantly, in line with Otley's predictions, the Army today has become more, and is becoming more, representative of society. The process of social change has contributed to this development. At the same time the study negates the thesis of Major Eric Joyce, who has argued that the old elite still runs the Army and that the trend is still the same.[13] It is fair to say therefore that today we have a new model of the Army leadership: one which is simultaneously socially *less elite* and more representative of the society which it serves. Perhaps an interesting analogy can be drawn with a recent report in the media[14] regarding the Conservative Party which revealed an exact opposite trend to the one which we have isolated in this chapter. The report of the Tory reform group said that a vast majority of Conservative MPs come from a narrower cross-section of society than was the case 20 years ago. Changes to selection procedures in 1980 led to fewer MPs educated at state schools. Of the Tories elected at the last election 64 per cent were educated at private schools. It appears that the process of social change has not left its mark on the Conservative Party

While the evidence in this paper is conclusive, sometimes it is not statistics but perceptions which dominate the mind. In other words the perception among some of the public is that the Army is an old-fashioned institution managed by old-fashioned, and socially elite personnel, a view which perhaps would be more appropriately applied to Conservative MPs. There is no doubt that some of these perceptions are fuelled by instances of racial discrimination in the British armed forces,[15] and by recent statistics which show that ethnic minority representation in the British Army is very low.[16] In fact the government has vowed to increase the recruitment of non-white people in the British Army. However, it is hoped that the evidence presented in this paper will go some way towards reversing such perceptions.

NOTES

1. C. Otley, 'The Educational Background of British Army Officers', *Sociology*, 7 (1973), pp. 191–209.
2. Ibid.
3. Wakefield's work is referred to in Otley 'The Educational Background of British Army Officers'.
4. See *A Report by the House of Commons Defence Committee*, 'Options for Change: Army', HMSO, March 1992.
5. Reggie von Zugbach, *Power and Prestige in the British Army* (Aldershot: Gower/Avebury, 1988).
6. Otley, 'The Educational Background of British Army Officers'.
7. Ibid.
8. Ibid.
9. See Zugbach, *Power and Prestige*.
10. Ibid., pp. 85–6.
11. Ibid.
12. Reggie von Zugbach, 'Who are the British Generals', *Defense Analysis*, 9(3) (1993), pp. 289–310.
13. Eric Joyce, 'Arms and the Man – Renewing the Armed Services', *Labour in Action*. Discussion paper 37, Fabian Society.
14. Reported in *BBC World Service News*, 24 January 1998.
15. There have been numerous reported cases of racism and racial discrimination in the armed forces. See the *Sunday Times*, 1 February 1998, pp. 7 and 12; Eric Joyce, 'Arms and the Man – Renewing the Armed Services', and the *Daily Telegraph*, 21 March 1997, p. 5.
16. Reported in *BBC World Service News*, 29 January 1998. See also the *Sunday Times*, 1 February 1998, p. 12.

APPENDIX

SCHOOLS FORMING THE 'DEBRETT'S INDEX LIST AND THE WEIGHTINGS
ASSOCIATED WITH THESE

Eton	46.82	Beaumont	0.61	Millfield*	0.23
Harrow	7.96	Canford*	0.61	Cheam*	0.15
Winchester	5.15	Dartmouth*	0.61	Tonbridge	0.15
Wellington	2.80	Sherborne	0.53	Campbell	0.15
Stowe	2.27	Malvern	0.53	Hurstpierpoint	0.15
Radley	2.05	Repton	0.45	Rossall	0.15
Downside	2.05	Haileybury	0.45	Eastbourne	0.15
Charterhouse	1.59	Lancing	0.45	Clifton	0.08
Rugby	1.59	Gordonstoun	0.38	Cranleigh	0.08
Ampleforth	1.52	St Paul's	0.38	City of London	0.08
Marlborough	1.36	Fettes	0.38	Felsted	0.08
Bradfield	1.29	Pangbourne*	0.30	Milton Abbey*	0.08
Osborne*	1.14	Blundells	0.30	Sandford*	0.08
Oundle	1.06	Loretto	0.30	Royal Masonic	0.08
Westminster	0.98	Brighton	0.30	Oratory	0.08
Shrewsbury	0.91	Leys	0.30	Kings, Canterbury	0.08
Cheltenham	0.68	Bedford	0.23	Bedales	0.08
Uppingham	0.68	Stoneyhurst	0.23	Dulwich	0.08
Greshams	0.68	St Lawrence's	0.23	Mill Hill	0.08

*= non-HMC schools

INSTITUTIONS INCLUDED IN THE U INDEX AND THE WEIGHTINGS ASSOCIATED
WITH THESE

Trinity, Cantab	24.96	Trinity Hall, Cantab	1.87
Christ Church, Oxon	14.94	Corpus Christi, Cantab	0.17
New College, Oxon	8.15	Pembroke, Cantab	0.17
Magdalene, Cantab	7.81	University College, Oxon	0.17
Balliol, Oxon	6.96	Kings, Cantab	0.15
Magdalene, Oxon	3.40	Brasenose, Oxon	0.14
Trinity, Oxon	2.55	Trinity, Dublin	0.14
Jesus, Cantab	2.04		

7

Transforming Wives into Spouses: Changing Army Attitudes

Christopher Jessup

In 1860, returning to the barracks from the cemetery where she had just buried her soldier husband – a victim of cholera – the new widow met the sergeant major, who immediately proposed marriage to her. She burst into tears, and her suitor apologised for raising the matter so soon. However, it was then explained to him that what caused the tears was that she had already accepted a proposal from a lance corporal on the way back from the funeral.

This apocryphal story is quoted by Mona Macmillan, a fourth-generation service wife, in her chapter on 'Wives of the Armed Forces' (p. 94) in *The Incorporated Wife*,[1] which reviews the changing circumstances and roles of wives in a variety of occupations – diplomatic, the police, academia and the armed forces. What the position of wife had in common in these different environments was the expectation that personal ambitions and opportunities would be subordinated to the greater benefit of her husband's career. In return for this sacrifice, various types of reward were provided – some financial, others primarily of status. What *The Incorporated Wife* also revealed is how wives have increasingly rejected this type of marital relationship in recent years.

The Army's attitude to marriage has changed dramatically over the last 150 years. Initially this could be characterised as outright hostility and denial that the Army had any responsibility for wives and children. Gradually this phase was replaced by a view which saw utility in incorporating and subordinating wives to Army values. More recently, marriage has been welcomed as a positive and normal life event in which soldiers are entitled to engage. Moreover, it has also been recognised that the satisfaction or otherwise of wives and family members has an important impact on retention rates. Ironically, such institutional concern with the well-being of families has occurred against a background of wives themselves identifying fewer benefits in retaining a close association with the Army, and wanting instead to disengage from its paternalistic clutches.

Reviewed in this chapter are some of the stages in the process of interaction between wives and the Army:

- rejection of marriage by the Army;
- toleration/incorporation of marriage;
- subordination/exploitation of wives and families;
- support and containment;
- voluntary disengagement from the Army by wives.

However, Army attitudes to wives have not been transformed solely by internal developments. External changes in UK civilian society in female employment rates, the increased proportion of women (and men) with better educational qualifications, alterations in marriage, cohabitation and divorce, and the continuing transformation of gender roles within households have also, and unavoidably, affected Army policies and practice.

These developments have combined to raise serious questions about the ongoing relationship between the armed forces and service spouses. Will the marital partners of soldiers in 2010 retain any links with the Army? Will Army geographical communities disappear, to be replaced by what Morris Janowitz[2] has called 'professionals in violence' living as owner-occupiers amongst civilians, and commuting daily to work? Does the Army need to worry any further about marital partners, or has the point of total disengagement between the Army and the private lives of its employees been reached? These are some of the issues addressed here.

MARRIAGE AND THE ARMY 1850–1970

Marriage and the Army became a subject of considerable public comment during and immediately after the Crimean War (1853–56). There were two principal concerns. First, that the wives and families of gallant soldiers suffered appalling neglect and poverty. Second, that by discouraging marriage the Army was actively promoting prostitution. Such a practice became increasingly unacceptable to the propagandists of Victorian family values.

Until 1867 only 6 per cent of soldiers could marry and bring their wives into barracks. Such wives were classed as 'married on the strength', and it was only these wives who received any official Army recognition or entitlements. In 1867 new Army regulations specified who could be married on the establishment. These were: all regimental sergeant majors, 60 per cent of other sergeants and 7 per cent of lower ranks. There were no direct bans on officer marriages, but the informal rules – quoted by Veronica Bamfield in *On the Strength: the Story of the British Army Wife*[3] were: 'Subalterns must not marry; Captains may marry; Majors should marry; and Colonels must marry.' Subalterns who nevertheless married without the Commanding Officer's permission could find their wives being ostracised by order of the Commanding Officer's wife to reinforce the authority of her husband.

Despite political and media pressure to encourage marriage, the Army remained reluctant to do so. It recognised that marriage and family ties were serious competitors with its own demands for total commitment. In the 1970s, this conflict was described by L. Coser as a struggle between greedy institutions.[4] As an employer, the Army demands unwavering availability from its staff – it is greedy for their time and energies. But families are equally demanding. Quite correctly, therefore, the Victorian Army identified marriage as a serious threat to the loyalty of soldiers. Given that there were strong social pressures preventing the maintenance of prostitution as the mechanism for satisfying soldiers' sexual needs, marriage could not be entirely avoided. However, the 1870 Army Reform Act – which abolished the purchase of commissions – also introduced the six-year contract of engagement. In part the hope behind this was that it would be attractive to young men who would be competent soldiers but prepared to remain single for such a period of time. This appears to have happened, since a War Office committee reporting on 'The Married Establishment' in 1881 found that in many regiments the proportion of soldiers married was below the permitted quota. It was also true, however, that investment by the Army in sporting and educational facilities from the 1870s onwards meant that there were competing attractions for soldiers other than alcohol and prostitution.

For those soldiers who were allowed to marry on the strength, initial facilities were poor. In the 1850s, men could house their wives and children in the corners of barrack blocks – the origins of married quarters. But such families had no privacy. They were screened from the dormitory accommodation of unmarried men only by canvas. The realisation that married women could be in such close proximity to unmarried soldiers aroused both prurience and moral clamour. It was obvious that wives could hardly avoid seeing, hearing and smelling soldiers in various states of dress. And when wives themselves were ill, or in childbirth, the accommodation was self-evidently totally unsuitable. What persuaded the Army, however, to provide separately located quarters was the ease with which infectious illness travelled from the married corners of barracks to the majority of single soldiers in adjacent dormitories.

Despite an increasing proportion of soldiers marrying with permission, their rates of pay were low and not adequate to support wives and families. That this was considered a desirable state of affairs was made abundantly clear during the Crimean War by Lord Panmure, then Secretary of State for War, who said in Parliament:

> Every endeavour is made by the government to discourage the marriage of soldiers, whose pay is calculated as only sufficient for maintaining them in health and military efficiency ... Every soldier's wife must therefore depend on her own industry for her maintenance, whether her husband is in this country, in a colony or at the seat of war. (*The Times*, 26 July 1855, quoted in Trustram, *Women of the Regiment*, p. 155)[5]

Until 1873 soldiers were exempt from an obligation to maintain their wives and children. Even after legal changes in 1873, soldiers could only be required to support families married on the strength. Other wives had no option but to seek support from the Poor Law. This was a constant source of dispute between the War Office and the Poor Law authorities during the last 40 years of the nineteenth century – especially when recruiters encouraged men to join up as a means of evading responsibilities to maintain wives which would fall on them if they remained civilians. As a recruiting tactic, its contemporary counterpart would be for the armed forces to indemnify all recruits against any maintenance liability being pursued by the Child Support Agency.

Even where soldiers were legally liable to maintain families after 1873, it was in practice very difficult for the Poor Law authorities to enforce any payment orders since they could not seek to imprison defaulters or discharge them from the Army, nor could they confiscate military equipment or uniforms. Effective enforcement of maintenance orders was impossible unless the War Office agreed to make stoppages from soldiers' pay.

Subordination of families to regimental interests

Although financial security was not the lot of most soldiers' families, there were nevertheless some advantages in being within the Army – provided they were on the strength. Once the early barrack accommodation had been superseded by purpose built or adapted accommodation, the quality of housing enjoyed by Army families was vastly superior to that experienced to labourers in expanding Victorian cities. Regimental schools were also provided. These were paid for by the officers, with their wives normally selecting and monitoring the instructors. Such schools were seen as a fruitful source of future recruits, and soldiers' children probably received more and better education than their civilian counterparts between 1850–90. In 1887, schools were reorganised on a garrison basis. From that date parents were made responsible for ensuring that children attended school – well before such obligations were laid on civilian parents – and if children arrived late or not at all, the fact was reported to the Commanding Officer.

In 1871 separation allowances were introduced, which soldiers were required to supplement out of their pay after 1882. Widows' allowances – a gratuity of one year's pay – began in 1881, although in India widows received a gratuity of six months' pay somewhat earlier.

Soldiers' wives also found employment with regiments in washing, sewing and nursing. Pay was poor, but benefited both the wives and regiments, who were provided with a cheap, reliable and available source of labour. In effect, by the mid-1880s the Army provided a range of services and support for families which few other employers offered. This was especially true overseas, above all in India where the Army had to design and provide health and welfare services for its own personnel. By delivering a quasi-welfare state to families, the Army found an effective way of ensuring that they subordinated their own desires and interests to those of the regiment. It behoved wives to encapsulate and propagate the values of the regiment, since their well-being depended crucially on their husbands remaining within it.

In addition to statutory provisions, much philanthropic activity was undertaken by officers and their wives to improve family welfare. Officers were expected to produce non-public funds to achieve charitable ends for soldiers and their families. Officers' wives – who were not expected themselves to be in paid employment – were vital in sustaining such benevolent regimental functions. They visited married quarters to offer congratulations on the birth of a child, or condolences when one died. The Commanding Officer's wife was at the apex of this regimental welfare system, exercising informal control over other wives and ensuring that the regiment's systems of family support operated efficiently.

India: the ex-patriate model of social interaction

Veronica Bamfield, describing life in India, claims:

> The extraordinary thing about Army life in India was that it remained entirely unchanged for three generations ... nice bungalows, servants, ponies, pets and picnics ... It was all so ordinary, so established: Camberley, Catterick and Colchester set amid cannas, hibiscus and queen of the night, with no servant problems and lovely leisurely life of morning bridge and tea parties and the Club. The Club, that pivot of cantonment life, with its tennis courts, the children's playground, the Bar, the ballroom, the billiards room and the library, and the regimental bands playing the evening. (*On the Strength: the Story of the British Army Wife*, p. 122)

This idealised life was, of course, how officers' wives perceived India. Kipling's soldiers and their wives had less idyllic experiences. Nevertheless, in India the Army established the ex-patriate model of community living which has served it so well. Isolated by language, culture and by its imperial role, it was entirely appropriate that the Army recreated miniature versions of England abroad. The regiment as family replaced absent kin and provided not only practical support but also group solidarity and a sense of belonging. The social class structure of Victorian England could be replicated without the complications caused by industrialisation back in Britain. The hierarchy of military rank could also be applied to wives as well, who acquired roles within the community by virtue of their husbands' appointments. Such roles were unpaid, but they offered status, respect and a clear place within the community. As Hew Strachan[6] has pointed out, the regiment was itself a microcosm of a landed society in which deference was rewarded by concern for the welfare of the soldiers. Living in India gave particular impetus to such a paternalistic relationship, since the isolation of the Army community from any meaningful interaction with local customs and cultures preserved a pattern of social life from external threat. That wives should subordinate their own interests to those of the regiment was therefore a natural consequence of ex-patriate living.

For some wives, incorporation into the regiment as a new family member actually involved initiation rites analogous to those demanded of husbands too. Describing the living conditions and variable quality of married quarters in Gibraltar in 1931 to which families of the Royal Welsh Fusiliers were allocated, Bamfield reports:

> The casual treatment of wives was a well known characteristic of the RWF – a regiment that considered its wives lucky to be married into it ... No other regimental wives ate a raw leek in public on the first St David's day of their married life. A civilian who knew the regiment well remarked he reckoned its wives qualified for danger money. (Bamfield, *On the Strength*, p. 139)

MARRIAGE AND THE ARMY SINCE 1970

In the last quarter of the twentieth century, the Army has become a society in which a majority of its members marry during their service. Its ability to distance itself from patterns of social change affecting civilians has also been much reduced. These developments have been recognised in several studies and in many practical responses from the Army to its new circumstances.

Army Welfare Inquiry Committee (Chairman John Spencer) Ministry of Defence 1975[7]

Commissioned in 1974 by the Army Board, this was a comprehensive review of the changing composition of the Army and the consequential need for welfare and support services. The Committee's report pointed to the growing number of married personnel in the Army; to the extreme youth of many wives; reviewed the adequacy of support systems for families; and recommended the establishment of an Army Social Work Service to provide professional supplementation to the in-house systems of regiments.

In fact the central recommendation of the Spencer Committee was not adopted. No social work service, analogous with that established in the Navy as the result of the *Report of the Naval Welfare Committee*[8] (1974) was set up. Instead the Army developed the Families Housing and Welfare Service, which became operational in 1977. This provided a comprehensive housing but initially limited welfare system to Army families. The major innovation introduced by the Families Housing and Welfare Service (FHWS) was the introduction of Army Welfare Assistants. These were serving NCOs – initially female only – drawn from a variety of Army backgrounds who received six months' training before operating in roles similar to those of assistant social workers in civilian life. Only eight Army Welfare Assistants were established in 1977, but by the time the welfare element of the FHWS was incorporated in the new Army Welfare Service in 1996, the number of such staff – now termed Army Welfare Workers – had grown to 44. Only with the establishment of the Army Welfare Service did professional social workers become fully integrated into the Army's welfare system – nearly 20 years after the Spencer Report.

Although the *Army Welfare Inquiry Committee* highlighted major social changes impacting on the Army and stimulated some appropriate responses, it had no remit to alter attitudes towards wives or other family members. Such issues were, however, addressed by the two-part *Army Wives Study* – the Gaffney Report.[9] Historically, this has been of great significance. For the first time the Army acknowledged the vital importance of wives in military communities, and began the process of examining its institutional expectations of wives and the extent with which these coincided with the ambitions of requirements of present-day Army wives themselves.

The Army Wives Study

Part One (*The Findings*) was published by the Ministry of Defence in June 1986; Part Two (*The Way Ahead*) followed in April 1987. The Gaffney Report was the outcome of a husband and wife team. The voluminous terms of reference given to Colonel and Mrs Gaffney covered two sides of A4. They were given six months to produce a report for the Adjutant-General, and the main aim of the study was identified as being: 'To determine those specific aspects of Army life which cause problems and aggravations for wives, and to recommend changes in the areas identified.'

The approach stipulated in the terms of reference was: 'To conduct a survey to ascertain: first what aspects of Army life cause the worst problems and difficulties so far as wives are concerned; second, what changes most wives wish to see.'

Among the many issues which the Gaffneys were required to consider were:

- the loss of employment opportunity for wives;
- the adequacy of garrison amenities;
- the role of wives and whether the Army places excessive demands on them;
- particular problems faced by very young wives away from home for the first time;
- an assessment of the contribution made by the Federation of Army Wives Clubs, the Families Housing and Welfare Service and the Soldiers', Sailors and Airmen's Families Association (SSAFA.).

The philosophy underlying the Report (commissioned by the Adjutant-General) was also spelled out in the terms of reference.

> Because of the nature of the profession, the Army's wives are very closely affected by their husband's choice of career. Frequent postings, much enforced separation, heavy dependence on military facilities ... all affect wives as much as they do the soldier – possibly even more so in some instances and often very much to their disadvantage.
>
> It therefore behoves the Army much more than an ordinary employer to make sure that wives (and families) are properly cared for both within and by the Army system ... particularly as we still look to our wives to play a major part in the many voluntary welfare activities that make such an important contribution towards high morale – and therefore also towards efficiency.

With such a limited time frame to complete the study, the Gaffneys judged it impossible to conduct a large postal survey. They therefore resolved to meet and discuss with as many wives in as many Army locations as possible. In the event, they met and received opinions from over 2,000 wives associated with 50 different units and distributed throughout all Districts in England, the British Army of the Rhine, Northern Ireland and Hong Kong.

These were all wives accompanying their husbands, and the Gaffneys acknowledged their inability to sample the views of wives currently separated. Because the sample was large, the Report authors felt the wives they met with to be reasonably representative, and they developed considerable skills in spotting those situations in which units fielded wives who were considered reliable and likely to produce safe opinion.

Overall the Gaffneys concluded:

> In spite of the generally critical tone of much of what was said by wives, there was no doubt of their good will towards the Army. Most had come to criticise constructively.

Having examined the extent and nature of welfare support systems for wives and families, the authors reiterated their belief that the regimental system would remain the basic structural feature of the British Army, and would continue to play through its Commanding Officer a key role in promoting family welfare.

However, not all was well with this traditional and vital support system. The Gaffneys decided: 'there are faults with the operation of the regimental system which often distort the relationships between wives and the Army' (6.1).

Many wives experienced regimental concern as paternalism: 'they could decide few things for themselves and were not consulted in major decisions which affected them. They felt they were humoured much of the time and allowed to do just enough to keep them happy' (6.2).

The expectation that the wives of certain key members in a regiment should provide welfare support and advisory services to young wives was resented, both by those expected to perform these unpaid tasks and by those who would be the recipients of such charity. The Gaffneys also uncovered considerable anxiety about the consequences of seeking official help for personal problems inside the regiment for fear that this would endanger husbands' careers.

Reviewing self-help activities amongst wives, the Gaffneys described the prototype Help Exchange agencies then being trialled in Munster and Hohne. These experiments proved successful and blossomed into HIVEs (Help, Information, Volunteer Exchange) currently offering information and support at almost all Army locations. They also reported favourably on the Federation of Army Wives Clubs, formed in 1983, which later became the Federation of Army Wives and in 1996 the Army Families Federation.

Under the heading *Wives' Concerns,* three main areas were distinguished:

Loss of identity

> It was said to us by many wives that they feel their treatment by the Army relegates them to second class status. (8.2)

In particular, the designation W/O (wife/of) was found offensive and demeaning, and the Gaffneys recommended that its use be officially discouraged.

Wives' rights

A number of practices were identified by wives as belittling and constantly reaffirming their lack of rights or legal status. These included their inability to receive letters in the British Army of the Rhine – mail normally followed the husband even when he was away; the requirement to have the husband's permission to obtain a ticket for the Army library service; and, above all, the lack of rights in respect of any married quarter a wife occupied with her husband. The Report recommended the issue of identity cards to wives in their own right to avoid some of these situations.

Postings

Wives accepted that postings were an unavoidable feature of Army life, and many welcomed changes of location on a regular basis. They were highly critical, however, of the timing of many such changes, which they felt were badly managed in respect of school terms. The Gaffneys reported:

> ... (wives) feel helpless when plans are constantly changed at short notice. Forecasting of leave and advance notice of postings are not well managed on the whole, especially in the case of trickle posted soldiers in support arms. (8.4)

There were two main conclusions reached by the *Wives Study.* First:

> Our deployment and movement policies are themselves the cause of turbulence and disruption of married life in the Army. We concluded that greater stability for families could only come through longer

average tour lengths and the ability to be able to identify with a particular geographical area in the UK. (9.1a)

Second:

The Army is slow to change its attitudes ... We believe that what we are observing now is the Army trying to come to terms with the new status of women ... [however] the most common reaction from Army officers to proposals for change is a fear of the loss of the control they enjoy at the moment. We concluded that this attitude is the most fundamental cause of the unhappiness of wives as a group. (9.1b)

Part Two of the *Wives Study*, published in April 1987, included detailed recommendations seeking to address many practical concerns of wives. These included, *inter alia*, wider consultation on the decoration and furnishing of married quarters; changes in rules controlling the movement of personal belongings between the UK and overseas stations; and changes to the methods of charging for damage in married quarters. The Gaffneys repeated their view that wives' concerns could only be adequately addressed if the Army:

- adopted postings intended to produce what was then being described as a more stable Army;
- took positive action to recognise wives as adults who happened to be married to soldiers, principally by abandoning the term W/O and by issuing identity cards.

What actions did the Army take in response to the Gaffneys' Report? A number of practical measures designed to improve the life quality of wives, and therefore families, were introduced. Identity cards for wives and more generous rules on the delivery of furniture and personal belongings of personnel moving between the United Kingdom and western Europe improved the quality of Army life. District Commands in the United Kingdom issued instructions that 'wife/of' should no longer be used. In reality, though such a description is no longer officially sanctioned, its use remains widespread within Army culture. That wives' opinions became viewed as sufficiently significant to merit analysis through the *Continuous Attitude Survey* process could also be seen as a tribute to the *Army Wives Study*. Perhaps above all what the Gaffneys achieved was to alert the Army to the existence of the post-deferential society in which traditional expectations about wives were no longer valid.

CHANGES IN EMPLOYMENT PATTERNS AND GENDER ROLES

A major concern in the *Wives Study* was that the Army should acknowledge the employment expectations of its wives. The Gaffneys demonstrated the changing picture of employment by women – especially married women – and warned the

Army that its ability to retain skilled, trained personnel would be adversely affected if wives were denied opportunities to engage in paid employment available to their civilian counterparts.

Female employment in Britain declined after the Second World War until the 1960s. Since then it has increased steadily, primarily – but not exclusively – through the provision of part-time work. Paid employment for wives after marriage is now a standard expectation of currently unmarried young people, and a reality in most married households (see Table 1).

Table 1

ECONOMIC ACTIVITY RATES OF MARRIED WOMEN IN GREAT BRITAIN

	In employment (%)	*Unemployed* (%)	*Not in work* (%)
1981	55	5	40
1986	59	7	34
1991	69	4	26
1996	67	4	29

Source: Employment Department statistics.

An important response to the *Army Wives Study* was the decision to extend the regular *Continuous Attitude Surveys* of soldiers and officers to wives as well. Begun in 1983, these surveys sampled substantial numbers of serving personnel primarily to provide data on morale and motivation. Extending the process to wives was an acknowledgement of the important contribution wives made to the morale of husbands, and to retention decisions. The first *Wives Continuous Attitude Survey*[10] (1994) included questions on employment status and intentions which revealed the following information: in employment 54 per cent; unemployed 18 per cent; not in work 28 per cent.

The most recent survey (1996) asking the identical question found: in employment 62 per cent; unemployed 13 per cent; not in work 25 per cent.

Although Army wives might appear to be at a slight disadvantage in the employment market, the *Continuous Attitude Survey* figures do not distinguish the ages of the wives responding, nor, crucially, of their children. Given the relative youth of Army communities – the mean age of wives responding to the 1996 survey was 32 – it is reasonable to compare Army wives' employment rates with civilian wives with pre-school or primary school children. For Great Britain in 1996 see Table 2:

Table 2

ECONOMIC ACTIVITY RATES OF WOMEN IN GREAT BRITAIN WITH CHILDREN AGED

	0–4 (%)	5–10 (%)
In employment	48	65
Unemployed	5	5
Not in work	47	30

Though a substantially larger proportion of Army wives are unemployed – and seeking work – compared with civilians, the overall difference in employment opportunities between them and civilians appears to be lessening. This probably reflects the higher proportion of Army families based in the UK since 1991. Such a geographical distribution certainly increases wives' employment chances since it locates them in the more favourable UK market. Any increase in paid work by wives owes nothing to Army policy since – unlike the American services – no spouse employment assistance programmes operate within the British armed forces. The only job search system for wives within the Army is delivered by the Army Families Federation (previously the Federation of Army Wives).

Neither the *Continuous Attitude Survey* nor Department of Employment data tell us anything about the *quality* of employment available. Service wives were highly vocal in the *Wives Study* not only about the limited work opportunities available but the poor quality of what could be found. The difficulties for wives in pursuing their own careers is voiced regularly in all the *Continuous Attitude Surveys*.

In 1997, for the first time, the Defence Evaluation Research Agency[11] was asked to carry out a *Spouse Attitude Survey*, and this was incorporated in a combined Report also featuring responses from soldiers and officers. Concern that Army policies continue to affect spouse employment opportunities continued to be strongly expressed. Invitation to comment on the statement 'Changes in postings have meant my own career opportunities have suffered' produced the following responses: strongly agree 64 per cent; neutral 11 per cent; strongly disagree 10 per cent; not applicable 16 per cent.

The *Offcers and Soldiers [Army] Continuous Attitude Survey* (1997)[12] also demonstrated that concern about spouse employment was shared by serving personnel. Asked to reflect on the impact of Army service on families and children, all rank groups saw the area giving most cause for dissatisfaction as the effect on their spouse's or partner's career.

In 1997 the Army Families Federation carried out an *Accompanied Service Survey*.[13] This was intended to review the difficulties attaching to accompanied service, with an invitation to produce solutions. Two hundred and forty Army Families Federation members replied – including one male spouse. The disruption of spouse career patterns was identified as the second greatest problem currently inherent in accompanied postings – the first was the disruption of children's education. Respondents commented critically on the difficulties of developing and maintaining a career, and as the Army Families Federation commentary pointed out:

> Very few careers are portable, and most Army spouses find themselves doing part-time jobs, frequently at a more menial level than their qualifications warrant. (Army Families Federation *Accompanied Service Survey*, p. 4)

Spouse comments also referred to the loss of lifetime earnings resulting from working only in low quality employment, and a concomitant reduction in pension entitlements. Some argued that such lifetime losses should be acknowledged and compensated for through their partners' pay and allowances.

Discontent amongst spouses is clearly reflecting very strong dissatisfaction about the quality of employment opportunities open to Army spouses and the mismatch between skills and work available. Spouses in the Army demonstrate a trend towards higher educational achievements which can be observed throughout British society. Precise comparisons between civilians and Army personnel are not possible because the major source of data about Army wives – the *Continuous Attitude Surveys* – do not measure exactly the same educational achievement categories used in civilian studies. Nevertheless, the 1996 *Continuous Attitude Survey* found that:

- 23 per cent of wives had A Levels (or equivalent);
- 19 per cent had a first or higher university degree;
- 28 per cent possessed secretarial/IT qualifications;
- 28 per cent possessed nursing or other professional qualifications;
- 11 per cent had no formal qualifications.

This compares with data on the United Kingdom population as a whole for 1995 which found that 75 per cent of women aged 16–59 had qualifications obtained at school, college, work or government training schemes. This suggests that the proportion of women married to Army husbands without any qualifications may be somewhat lower than civilian wives.

Finally, a new issue for spouse equality was addressed by at least one respondent to the May–August 1996 study who commented:

> Husbands should be able to take time off to take children to hospital, doctors etc. when the wife is in full-time employment. Why should we put our jobs on the line when kids are taken ill?

The relocation of more wives in the UK clearly increases their chances to develop existing careers and job skills – hitherto a particular problem for wives with professional qualifications. The price that the Army will pay for this integration into the employment market, however, is the distancing of the partners of service personnel from Army functions and voluntary activities.

CHANGING GENDER ROLES

Changes in employment patterns and educational attainments have also been accompanied by modifications in gender roles. To a considerable extent, these may still be changes in *expectations* rather than reflecting reality. 'British Social Attitudes' studies reveal marked discrepancies between what men and women wish to see and what actually happens. Nevertheless the expectations that men and women have about roles they will play – both domestically and profession-ally – affect the Army like any other section of British society. And if the demands of the Army frustrate the ambitions of couples to organise husband and wife, mother and father roles as they wish them to be, then this becomes a further possible area of conflict with an employer perceived as overbearing and intrusive.

In 1973 Phyllis and Michael Willmott published *The Symmetrical Family*.[14] They argued that segregated marital roles – in which men earned money and women managed homes and children – were being replaced by shared roles – in which both marriage partners had equal activity and responsibility for domestic and employment functions. The Willmotts predicted that Britain was rapidly moving towards symmetrical household and employment functions where gender was becoming of less significance.

The extent to which role symmetry has occurred is the subject of considerable dispute. The caring, sharing New Man has been more evident in discussions on family change than in the kitchen or undertaking the shopping according to feminist critics of the Willmotts. That changes in gender roles have happened is not disputed by feminists, but it has been primarily a change involving women playing a greater part in the employment scene rather than men increasing their housework activities. And a recent study by the Family Policy Study Centre on *Parenting in the 1990s*[15] concluded that in Britain New Men remained largely mythical because they were working long hours in order to retain jobs. The pattern of lengthening working hours for men, with one in four fathers claiming to work more than 50 hours per week, has undoubtedly slowed down any movement towards symmetry in household roles. But it also remains true that currently unmarried young people envisage future marital relationships for themselves in which equality and role sharing feature heavily on the agenda. Employment insecurity may militate against turning such ideals into reality for the time being, but it does not eliminate them. The political pressure to enable gender equality to co-exist with employment demands remains, and employers whose requirements frustrate such goals will face criticism from their staff. Thus although adverse developments in the British economy in the early 1990s may have diverted attention from gender role changes and so diminished potential conflict between the Army as an employer and the preferred lifestyle of Army households, it remains likely that most members of Army communities will continue to share gender aspirations common to the rest of British society. Employment demands which prevent those goals being achieved – and obviously separation is a major factor here – will provoke further tension between the Army and its families.

CONCLUSIONS

In their summary on the views expressed in the first *Wives Continuous Attitude Survey*, the Report's editors made the following points:

- Army wives were dissatisfied with most aspects of their lifestyle.
- Attitudes to wives and employment continued to be the areas where the greatest levels of dissatisfaction were shown.

As the Army has moved towards recognising the transformation of wives into spouses, and new patterns of family formation not exclusively based on hetero-sexual couples, have these concerns also been addressed? Dissatisfaction with spouse employment remains high on the agenda. Although objectively Army spouse employment rates appear similar to civilian married women with dependent children aged under 11, there remains a widespread perception that the quality of work available to Army spouses is inferior, that this has lifetime implications in terms of lost earnings and associated employment rights, and, above all, denies opportunities for spouses to pursue personal careers. Stability for extended periods of time – three to five years – within the United Kingdom is probably the only way in which the Army could assist such ambitions. In default of that occurring, Army families may increasingly create such stability for themselves by moving into owner occupation, so avoiding disruption to children's schooling as well as enabling spouses to achieve careers in their own right. (For a review of these issues, see Chapter 9 'The Challenge of New Social Structures' in the author's *Breaking Ranks*.)[16]

But there is clearly a risk of the Army paying a high price for such decisions – either in terms of marital breakdown or because families choose to end their separated existence by leaving the Army altogether. It is unlikely that most partners will face this situation with the equanimity reported by one wife responding to the 1997 *Army Continuous Attitude Survey*:

> I have had no difficulty in pursuing my own career whilst my spouse has been in the Army, but this has meant personal sacrifices such as only living together for three years out of our ten year marriage and my having to take the majority of responsibility for looking after his children.

Discontent about the short length of postings, and about inappropriate posting dates routinely occurring during school terms, continue to be prominent in spouse concerns as the *Army Families Federation Survey* shows. These were, of course some of the key issues identified in the *Army Wives Study* a decade earlier.

Both the 1994 and 1996 *Wives Continuous Attitude Surveys* invited respondents to reflect on the impact of Army life on their marriages. In both studies 38 per cent of wives agreed that: 'I have experienced problems with my marriage that are related to my husband being in the Army'; and 71 per cent (1994) and 78 per cent (1996) agreed that 'I feel the Army expects me to behave in a certain manner.' Only 17 per cent (1994) and 16 per cent (1996) supported the proposition: '"Army Wives" are treated well by the Army.'

Such responses do not suggest that fundamental discontents about paternalism and dependency status disclosed by the Gaffney Report have been overcome. On the other hand, only 19 per cent of wives in the 1996 *Continuous Attitude Survey* admitted that they did not enjoy Army life at all – the other 80 per cent found it either enjoyable or tolerable. Thus spouses are not all in revolt or unhappy with Army living. Maintaining contentment amongst the majority will be a major challenge in managing human resources for the Army in the next decade.

Supporting Army families will require that four different types of Army community be acknowledged:

• single;
• unmarried but cohabiting;
• young married living in service family accommodation (the term which has replaced 'married quarters');
• older married living in owner-occupied housing.

For the Army to engage fruitfully with its married communities, it will have to recognise that there are contradictory criticisms underlying the comments made about family support services. On the one hand there is resentment at paternalism, which is experienced as both archaic and belittling. For these spouses, what they want is to be recognised as adult civilians with no allegiance to their partner's employer.

Other – perhaps younger, less experienced – spouses are critical that the Army does not appear to be doing enough. Far from being left alone as coping adults, they welcome support in what they otherwise find an alien culture and a lonely world where partners are frequently absent.

What is also abundantly clear is that spouses often find themselves in direct conflict with the official policy of accompanied service. Accompanied service at first sight sounds eminently desirable, but what it in practice means is a high degree of turbulence. Moving every 18 months is a common experience for many Army families at present. The Army Families Federation *Accompanied*

Service Survey reveals very clearly the opportunity costs – in terms of employment earnings forgone, the struggle to obtain Job Seekers Allowance and the damage to careers. However, the major complaint from spouses about accompanied service is that it is in fact anything but accompanied. Army spouses find that relocating with their partner in no way guarantees being together. As one Army Families Federation respondent, explaining the sequence of events which left her in Germany and her husband in Northern Ireland and then Bosnia, commented:

> ... out of 104 weeks (I was in Germany), we spent 29 together. Who was posted to Germany? I challenge anyone to persuade me to leave my family, friends, dog and a country whose language is my mother tongue for another such 'accompanied' posting.

Spouse careers and accompanied postings are in principle contradictory objectives. Perhaps because this has tacitly been recognised, the Army has never itself assisted spouses to find employment. But it is the discontinuities within accompanied postings which will end the system by spouses themselves abandoning it. If such postings continue to include substantial periods when marital partners are in fact on their own and forced into single parent mode, many will choose to stay unaccompanied. In their own homes. As was tartly commented by one of the owner-occupier Army Families Federation respondents:

> Why should I pay more rent to live in a shed in a part of England where I don't want to be with a husband who is never there?

Recognising spouses may involve abandoning expectations of accompanied service as the norm. Gender role changes and the need for two-earner households mean that counting on spouses to forgo careers and follow their Army partners to new pastures every two years is increasingly unrealistic. Such a policy fits poorly with the contemporary demands that adults must be responsible for their own personal happiness and satisfaction, not vicariously dependent for these rewards merely as the partner of somebody else. These drives for independence and personal responsibility which characterise women's attitudes in particular are not easily compatible with Army policies which are reluctant to embrace spouses as independent civilian adults over whom the Army has no legitimate claim.

Campaigners on behalf of family welfare in the United Kingdom have endeavoured to persuade government departments of the crucial importance of analysing the impact on families of proposed policy changes. Requesting what are termed *Family Impact Statements,* this approach demands that policy proposals be considered in the light of what the consequences would be for families. The intention has been to elevate family welfare to the forefront of government decision-making, and to attempt to ensure that different government agencies and departments operate consistently towards particular sections of society – in this case, families. The Army's current Human Resource Strategy based on the triple objectives *Obtain, Retain and Sustain* could fruitfully incorporate *Family Impact Statements* within its overall concerns. This would, of course, give prominence to the supporting tail rather than the operational teeth. But it is abundantly clear that operational effectiveness cannot be delivered without attention to the well-being and morale of spouses and families. Army policies inevitably do impact on families. Can they in future do so in more user-friendly ways?

The Army of the future will be more heterogeneous than its predecessor, both in terms of gender and ethnicity. Its variety of communities will each need different methods of support to sustain them. Benevolent paternalism has offered positive advantages in the past. What methods of social integration can be created to replace it with acceptable alternatives? What outreach mechanisms need to be developed to provide solidarity and support and a sense of belonging for spouses living off base? Membership of an Army community in the past has often brought with it many advantages, particularly a strong sense of belonging. A major challenge for the Army is how to replicate such supportive practices for a new century.

NOTES

1. H. Callan and S. Ardener (eds), *The Incorporated Wife* (London: Croom Helm,1984).
2. M. Janowitz, *The Professional Soldier: a Social and Political Portrait* (Glencoe, IL: Free Press, 1980).
3. V. Bamfield, *On the Strength: the Story of the British Army Wife* (London: Charles Knight, 1974).
4. L. Coser, *Greedy Institutions: Patterns of Undivided Commitment* (New York: Free Press, 1974).
5. M. Trustram, *Women of the Regiment: Marriage and the Victorian Army* (Cambridge: Cambridge University Press, 1984).
6. H. Strachan, 'The Early Victorian Army', *English Historical Review*, XCV (1980), pp. 782–809
7. *The Army Welfare Inquiry* (Spencer Report) (London: Ministry of Defence, 1975).
8. *Report of the Naval Welfare Committee* (Seebohm) (London: Ministry of Defence, 1974).
9. *The Army Wives Study* (Gaffney Report) (London: Ministry of Defence, 1986/7).
10. *Wives Continuous Attitude Surveys* (Army Personnel Research Establishment, 1994).
11. *Spouse Attitude Survey* (Defence Evaluation Research Agency, 1996).
12. *The Army Continuous Attitude Survey* (Defence Evaluation Research Agency, 1997).
13. *The Accompanied Service Survey* (Army Families Federation, 1997)
14. P. and M. Willmott, *The Symmetrical Family* (London: Penguin 1973).
15. *Parenting in the 1990s* (Family Policy Studies Centre, 1996).
16. C. Jessup, *Breaking Ranks: Social Change in Military Communities* (London: Brassey's, 1996).

8

Women in the Army

Peter Bracken

The Army is not at ease with itself. Nowhere is this more evident than in its relationship with the women that serve in it. To be critical of the Army is to risk being dismissed as unpatriotic. The Army is established to defend society, and maintaining its fighting capability is considered more important than, say, any observance of the prevailing view of equality of opportunity. No doubt this observation explains the standing of soldiers in the mind of the British public. In any index of regard they lie in the top quartile, among doctors, nurses and firemen – and quite beyond the reach of politicians, journalists and solicitors, to name just three other professional groups. It is my view, however, that the sacrificial symbolism of military duty has neutered criticism of the Army for too long, and that this gloss can no longer be maintained. Moreover, it is in the interests of a modern Army that it should not be.

This chapter is broader than its title alone suggests. There are three sections to it. In the first, I shall consider the relationship between Army and society. There is a tension in this relationship, as indeed there is between most organisations and society. The tension is born of a juxtaposition of value orientations that by its very nature needs to be negotiated and managed. I will argue that the Army has, in the main, failed in this task of management. The result of this failure is a worrying dislocation from the values and tolerances of wider society such that the Army now finds itself unable to recruit, retain and resettle service personnel.

The second section considers the treatment of women in the Army. Whether one is for or against the employment of women in the Army, the fact is that ever greater areas of the military are being opened up to them. But we should not overlook that it is only a trend. We are approaching the millennium and yet until recently more than half the Army was closed to women. The policy change on 1 April 1998 still means that 30 per cent remains closed to them. Twenty-two years after the Sex Discrimination Act, the question of whether women should be allowed to serve in the Army should not be controversial. Besides, the headline changes – welcome though they most certainly are – should not disguise the day-to-day experience of women in the military and the limited career prospects for the 6 per cent who serve in it.

Finally, in the third section, I will address the overarching issue of the Army's culture. I will argue that the military is a strong culture organisation and that many of the social disputes it has faced over the years stem from the maladaptive qualities of this culture. I will outline briefly the mechanisms which sustain it; but my main concern will be to establish that it is fundamentally at odds with the spirit of equality of opportunity, which if nothing else celebrates diversity. I will argue that its culture is distinguished by its homogeneity and expresses this quality in its preference for heterosexual, male, white Christians. The problematic truth is that women – and blacks and gays for that matter – are seen as inimical to the *esprit de corps* that bonds white brothers in arms.

ARMY AND SOCIETY

The relationship between organisations and the society in which they operate is characterised to a greater or lesser extent by tension. Tension is inevitable because wider social values and norms are more inclusive than those which inform the much more focused purpose of organisations. For this to be otherwise, organisations would need to be microcosms of society, which they never are – even if some aspire to be.

The issue of equal opportunities exemplifies this tension. It does so for the simple reason that the principles it articulates are at the leading edge of social change and are people-centred, whilst the orientation of organisations subordinates people to function and utility. The Army is like any other organisation in this respect. But because the role of the Army is unique in that it is designed to function in times of crisis, the tension at the civil–military interface is particularly accented. Operational effectiveness is the rubric that governs the Army's purpose and it is currently used to justify, for example, the exclusion of women from certain teeth arms and of homosexuals from enlisting in the ranks in any capacity.

Managing this tension between the perceived military requirement for operational effectiveness and the pressure to conform to wider social trends is an ever-present Army dilemma. This difficult task has been managed badly. The evidence for this judgement is twofold. First, the Army has repeatedly found itself on the wrong side of the law. It is true that the Army meets the letter of the law as defined by the Sex Discrimination Act of 1975, but it has been disregarding the spirit of the law. The law does not deal in absolutes: it is a continuously evolving prescription and in many ways its pronouncements reflect and sometimes presage emerging trends or values; whatever the outcome of legal rulings, the cases themselves constitute to a greater or lesser extent barometers of change. As such, institutions should develop an ear for the law and encourage a proactive change culture. The Army could not be further from this ideal.

The force of law is neglected at one's peril, as the Army has found, literally, to its cost. The ongoing litigation concerning the dismissal of 5,000 pregnant women from the services between 1978–95 is likely to cost the Ministry of

Defence upwards of £55 million.[1] Likewise, the humiliating threat of a non-discrimination notice following a damning report by the Commission for Racial Equality into racial discrimination in the Household Cavalry[2] has only recently been lifted. And we may speculate, too, on the probable cost of a likely reversal, by the European Court of Human Rights, of the services' exclusionary policy towards homosexuals. Nearly 2,000 men and women have been discharged from the armed forces because of their sexuality in the past 20 years, and compensation may exceed £300 million, quite apart from the estimated £70 million wasted on training.[3] This consideration may be behind the latest press speculation that gays may soon be allowed to serve in the ranks – so long as they are not 'active' in what is seen as improper behaviour. The argument that the Army has been negligent in its management of the tension at the civil–military interface is supported by a second and self-evident observation: the recruitment, retention and resettlement difficulties that the Army faces are symptomatic of a troublesome dislocation from the values and norms of wider society. The Army is not alone in experiencing this dislocation; the monarchy is also having to modernise in the face of public disdain for its outmoded ways, and the established Church is seen as increasingly irrelevant to the needs and expressions of mainstream communities. But the consequences for it are much the greater.

The real texture of military service – one in which recruitment and promotion is conditional upon social class, gender, race and sexual orientation to an extent intolerable in any other profession – has long been evident to serving and retired officers. But it is now being appreciated by a wider constituency, not least the young people from whom the Army recruits. According to the Defence Analytical Services Agency,[4] in 1985 16–24 year olds constituted 46 per cent of soldiers and officers across the three services. By 1995 this proportion had fallen to 33 per cent. The cause is only partly demographic; indeed, the effect of the demographic trough is diminishing as the manning crisis in the Army deepens. The larger factor at play is the perception among young people that the Army, especially its older and more celebrated regiments, is both out of date and out of touch. The consequences for the Army are cumulatively catastrophic. The Army is nominally 5,000 under strength, but this is a conflated statistic that disguises the fact that there is a 15,000 shortfall in the youngest age bracket and an 8,000 surplus (and growing) in the remainder to 40. The infantry is most depleted, this at a time when the government's Strategic Defence Review has recommended an increase in manning levels. To put it mildly, this is an inauspicious conjunction of trends. To put it bluntly, the Army is withering at its roots. There are signs that this situation is set to improve: officer recruitment is at an all-time high, and female recruitment is running this year at a record 14 per cent of total intake. But officers and women represent a small proportion of overall Army strength and the trend will have to be maintained and replicated in the wider Army for years to come if it is to meet its projected manning levels.

Worrying, too, is the haemorrhage in retention levels. Most infantry battalions, for example, have experienced a serious exodus of soldiers despite, for the best part of this decade, a less than propitious civilian job market, and the extent of the problem threatens the operational capability, if not survival, of some English and Welsh regiments. Premature Voluntary Retirement (PVR) rates amongst regular officers are increasing by 10 per cent per year, fewer soldiers are extending beyond the three-year minimum, and the number of officers applying for regular commissions is diminishing. Moreover, retiring service personnel imbued with the culture of the military find their outlook incompatible with the values of civilian life. A 1995 study conducted by the Army code-named 'Operation Overview'[5] established that the unemployment level of ex-soldiers was almost 20 per cent 12 to 14 months after leaving, compared with a national unemployment rate at the time of less than 9 per cent. The armed forces may boast the 'best trained workforce in Britain' but few organisations seem to agree.

TREATMENT OF WOMEN

The Army's relationship with wider society provides the context for the following analysis of the treatment and experiences of servicewomen. On this subject there are some positive things to report, for the Army has made progress in support of its efforts to be an equal opportunities employer. The drive to integrate women into the Army, for example, has achieved much: male and female officer cadets and recruits now undertake the same training courses; the Women's Royal Army Corps – once a potent symbol of their detachment from the mainstream Army – has been disbanded and women are now 'cap-badged' according to their regiment or (more likely) corps; the distribution of women across a wide range of skilled appointments (engineering, electrical and so on) exceeds their proportion in equivalent occupations in wider society; and perhaps most indicative of all, the exclusion of women from the combat arms – the great remaining bastions of male preserve – has been breached: women are now admitted to the Royal Artillery and according to press reports their exclusion from the infantry and armoured corps may be lifted, at least in principle, sooner rather than later.

The reasons for the delay in granting full integration are unclear. Until recently I understood that Army top brass were 'holding back from instituting this final form of equal opportunity because they believe British society as a whole is not yet ready for it'.[6] The admission that the Army must move with the times is a progressive and revealing development. But, whilst it is encouraging that the Army is developing a listening social and cultural ear, the idea that the Army could present itself as the vanguard of emerging social trends is not only incredible, it is also sophistical. Indeed, its past record on this issue suggests quite the opposite: that chief among organisations it has sought to set itself *apart* from emerging lifestyles and moral values. In short, the Army's calibration of the social pulse has, on the contrary, been less than adequate, with consequences I have already outlined.

It is better to see this reason, therefore, as a masquerade for the deeper problem the Army has with full integration; *it doesn't believe it will work.* Indeed, it views the extension of female employment to the artillery as an experiment, the results of which will determine access to the infantry and armoured corps. According to the Director of Manning (Army) (private communication) there is even the possibility that the Army will reverse the decision to let women serve in the artillery if the effect of their service on operational effectiveness is judged ill. This is naive. But the point is that the Army's commitment to full integration is far from certain, even if political pressure will, ultimately, force it to bite the bullet.

Furthermore, the headline-catching changes – including, it should be acknowledged, the first female combat aircraft pilots and sea-faring commanders – should not disguise the humdrum but nonetheless real day-to-day experiences of most serving women. A commitment in principle to wider female integration does not necessarily mean wider opportunities in practice. The experience of ethnic minorities tells us this much. The reality for women is not dissimilar.

Women make up just over half of the population of the UK yet constitute just 6 per cent of the Army's total strength. The highest-ranking female officer was until very recently a colonel, and there is no female representation on the Army Board. Moreover, women are over-represented at major level and below.

Of course, these facts and figures do not in themselves constitute evidence of sex discrimination in the Army. The composition of the services will only reflect that of the population when the different groups within it 'have an equal interest in joining and an equal ability for meeting the military's eligibility requirements'.[7] This is currently not the case and is never likely to be for a host of cultural, legal and political reasons. Thus, the absence of proportionate distribution is not *ipso facto* evidence of discrimination. However, the *size* of the anomalies is cause for legitimate concern and needs explaining. What we need to do is contextualise our observations on the representation and career progression of women in the Army. But how should we do this?

Official statistics on the incidence of sex discrimination are extremely hard to come by. Indeed, any assessment of discrimination based on these alone would suggest that the military has a clean bill of health. The 5,000 plus cases of sex discrimination which have arisen since the Treaty of Rome's Equal Treatment Directive was applied to the Sex Discrimination Act in 1991 relate to ex-servicewomen, dismissed between 1978–95 for falling pregnant. My own questionnaire (see below) did not report a single case of sex discrimination which was not dealt with at unit level, where it was unlikely to be recorded, if at all, as anything other than offences 'prejudicial to good order and discipline'. Officially, sex discrimination does not exist, except in the legal discrimination that still excludes women from the infantry and Royal Armoured Corps.

Where else can we turn to ascertain the extent of sex discrimination? An obvious source is newspapers. Indeed, it would not be exaggerating the case to say that they have been crucial in maintaining an undercurrent of public scepticism in the face of Ministry of Defence assurances that discrimination is nothing other than isolated events perpetrated by deviant individuals. It is true to say, however, that aside from the furore caused by the retrospective illegality of the Ministry of Defence's policy of sacking pregnant servicewomen, the issue of sex discrimination has attracted much less press attention than racial discrimination. This is partly of course because the position of women as soldiers has improved over the years. Has sex discrimination become a non-issue in the Army?

It was to answer this question that a sex discrimination questionnaire was distributed. This was the first occasion a survey of this kind had been conducted in the Army and its findings should trouble senior management. What interests us most is the incidence of documented sex discrimination. Based on a large sample of UK-based females – 16 per cent – over half claimed that they had been victims of sex discrimination as defined by the Sex Discrimination Act.

By any standard this is a disturbing figure. Alone it would substantiate the long-felt suspicion, and the hitherto spattering of anecdotal evidence, that sex discrimination permeates the Army. A male control sample of equivalent size, however, was also taken to enhance the credibility of the survey. It found that 93 per cent of servicemen had never been victims of sex discrimination. This figure will surprise few. But it was important to establish if only to focus more sharply the experiences of servicewomen. For the record, then, it would appear that male sex discrimination is not an issue in the Army.

In the small instances that sex discrimination is cited by men, furthermore, it is invariably provoked by claims of 'reverse' discrimination: lower physical thresholds in annual fitness tests, for example, or of special treatment meted out to women – the leniency and first-name terms they purportedly enjoy from the higher ranks, and the pointed allocation of menial, load-bearing jobs to males. Since my survey, of course, the legitimate complaint that men had to meet higher physical standards has been removed. The favouritism females experience, however, almost certainly remains. But I would argue that it is better accounted for as a further manifestation of discrimination against servicewomen. The assumption behind favouritism is that women cannot cope with the Army's tougher regime; in other words, the action both confirms and reinforces the prejudice. Thus, reverse sex discrimination may, ironically, be a product of the attitude of male managers towards servicewomen. Likewise, the disputes over servicewomen's uniform and hair length, or their dispensation to wear make-up and jewellery – all cited by servicemen in the questionnaire as further instances of reverse discrimination – speak rather more volubly about the ambivalence of the military towards women-as-soldiers: the Army, it appears, still expects its servicewomen to be visibly feminine.

In contrast to these symbolically important but nonetheless peripheral observations by servicemen, female respondents cited the whole gamut of forms sex discrimination may take. Gestures, oral and written abuse, physical harassment and psychological abuse accounted for 80 per cent of the total incidences reported.

This amounts to almost half of the total female sample and suggests strongly that discrimination is not only manifest in the denial of career opportunities but also stains the warp and weft of Army life. The same forms of discrimination were cited by only 1.9 per cent of the male sample population. In addition, asked about the prevalence of sex discrimination in the Army regardless of whether they had been a victim of it or not, 85 per cent of female soldiers claimed that there was either a 'lot' or 'some'. Only 12.4 per cent thought that there was 'little' or 'no' sex discrimination, in contrast to male respondents, 40 per cent of whom felt that there was little or none.

A large number of the servicemen and servicewomen who took part in the survey annotated their responses. Their remarks ranged from the empathic to the sinister. Many of the comments made by servicemen related to the impossibility of equality in an Army predicated on strength and, ultimately, violence ('sticking someone in the guts with a bayonet', as one senior officer put it). But for some this simply meant that true equality of opportunity must await 'gender-free' physical standards. Well, their time has come. In setting gender-free tests, however, the Army needs to be sure they reflect what a soldier is likely to be called upon to do. Service chiefs increasingly predicate their commands on scenarios collectively entitled 'Operations Other Than War'. Peace-keeping and peace-enforcing operations invoke definitions of military effectiveness quite different from those associated with high-intensity conflict, and for which women are equally, arguably better, suited. Besides, the distinction between the combat arms and the support arms is fast losing its logic in an age when technology has transformed the spatial dimension of the battlefield: killing has become reassuringly remote. And as Enloe notes: 'If "the front" is not where combat exclusively occurs, there is no way to ensure the survival of the essential masculinity of the military as an institution and the gendered basis of militarist ideas which legitimise it.'[8] She wrote this in 1988, and her prognosis is finally coming home to roost. In addition, the physical issue does not explain the discrimination servicewomen face as members of non-teeth arm units, where strength matters less and in which the vast majority currently serves.

This did not, however, deter other servicemen from drawing less understanding conclusions on the matter of female physical capabilities: 'their position is in the home, rearing children and not donning uniforms and weapon', remarked one lieutenant-colonel (he made a point of giving his name and rank). Another soldier commented that 'they should not be allowed in [the Army], or if so they should go AGC' (Adjutant-General's Corps, which primarily oversees education, pay and personnel matters). In a similar spirit, one serviceman claimed discrimination given the allowances made for pre-menstrual tension! A minority of servicemen, on the other hand, reflected on the relationship between the Army and wider society. One concluded, for example, that 'the Army must be seen to accommodate the changing culture of its personnel pool'.

The comments from servicewomen were altogether more desperate and plaintive, largely on account of the impotence they felt in the face of the range of discrimination which confronted many of them. The overwhelming impression the reader is left with is that female soldiers have little faith in the importance senior ranks attach to the issue of sex discrimination specifically and equal opportunities in general. And whilst the vast majority are prepared to soldier on regardless, most are also less than sanguine about the current situation.

These findings are the context in which we should account for the pattern of representation and career progression I outlined earlier. At its most basic level, it suggests that few women wish to enlist in the Army, and even fewer progress within it, because it is discriminatory. At the time of writing this chapter, it was also announced in the press that the Army is to relaunch itself as the 'People's Service' after private research found that Army life was seen as time-warped and its culture old-fashioned, robotic and repressive. My research suggests that this perception is sound. The same press release also noted that the Army wants to avoid what officers see as 'synthetic' rebranding exercises: 'the only way to change a damaging perception is to change the damaging policy or practice', said the spokesman.

This is why our analysis now has to dig deeper. How can we explain the findings of my research at a time when the Army angles to present itself as an equal opportunities employer and has in place a directive which endorses the principle that everyone, regardless of their arbitrary attributes, should have the opportunity to progress in life as far as their preferences and abilities will take them? The explanation is to be found in the structural flaws of the equal opportunities directive, and in the limitations of Army culture. I will discuss the cultural issue in my final section.

By structural I mean that the principle on which the equal opportunities directive is based is inadequate and that the procedures to implement the principle are flawed, though vastly improved since the issue in July 1997 of the Adjutant-General's equal opportunities action plan.

The Army is behind the curve on the issue of principle because the principle it articulates is predicated on the cult of the individual. Equality of opportunity is seen as the right to make the most of the capacities with which the individual is blessed, and requires that the Army select on the basis of relevant merit only. So far so good. But this formulation ignores the differences in opportunities as exist between groups. In other words, there are structural sources of dis-advantage which manifest themselves in group inequalities, and these have to be tackled before true equality of opportunity can flourish. Women are one such group, ethnic minorities another.

For this reason, the drive towards equality of opportunity has, for several years, been advancing a more radical agenda, one that embraces the concept of positive action. Positive action is designed to address the well-established fact that individuals from certain groups find it harder to fulfil their career potential than people from other sections of society. It includes such measures as encouragement (through, say, sensitive advertising), remedial training (for example, special pre-training courses which seek to equip disadvantaged individuals with entry-level competencies), improved working arrangements (especially in relation to maternity matters) and monitoring (to ensure that the measures are working).

On the face of it, the Army has moved to meet the demands of this more radical agenda. Advertising campaigns are now specifically targeting women and individuals from minority groups; targets have been set for the recruitment of both women and ethnic minority soldiers; monitoring is now in place so that the success of equal opportunities policies can be measured and evaluated; and remedial training is in force at training establishments which will benefit women in particular.

But doubts remain about the Army's commitment to the principle of positive action. Whilst acknowledging the progress the Army has made, we should not be blind to the reasons that have brought the changes. Those reasons relate to compulsion, be it through law, the threat of law, or for more pragmatic reasons relating to staffing levels. The Army's outlook, in other words, is characterised more by reactive management than strategic vision. Moreover, we should not ignore the *resistance* that has preceded the capitulation. It wasn't just that the Army *neglected* the victims of discrimination. For years, for example, the Army denied that they had a race problem, and it engaged in protracted legal man- oeuvrings to thwart the essential justice that the spirit of the law demanded. Commitment is the handmaiden of success in any project, and commitment is rarely born of compulsion.

What is more, nearly all of the positive measures that the Army has introduced date from 1997. Many have yet to be properly implemented, or will take time to have effect. They remain, in other words, more intention than fact, a plan rather than reality. My survey takes account of the experiences of women during the course of their careers over several years past. This was during a period when complaints about sexual harassment or discrimination were dealt with within the chain of command, 'with the possibility that the perpetrator of the grievance and the person to whom the complaint was advised were one and the same'; or when the complaint was to be considered by someone 'responsible for the command management climate in which the discrimination existed'.[9]

And even now, the Army refuses to grasp the nettle. Thus, in defence of its decision to ring-fence the infantry and Royal Armoured Corps from its policy of integration the Army reasserts arguments breathtaking in their insensitivity to changes in outlook now widely embraced by society. Do we have to debate, again, the discrimination inherent in the suggestion that women are unsuitable for employment by dint of their capacity and proclivity to give birth? Debate the practicalities of this, of course. And if it means introducing a higher manning and training margin, as it will, then so be it. Likewise, if this has cost impli- cations, then they, too, should be met.

By the same token, is it fair to highlight the fact that women in the Army have over twice the rate of bedded sickness compared with their male counterparts without taking into account the regime of discrimination and harassment that many of them confront and suffer? And should we use the practical problem of providing equipment that meets the female form or shape as a justification for their exclusion from service? The Army marshals these arguments, and more, not, as it should, as the catalyst for action which helps bring women on board, but as part of a case against access. And even when it recognises that it may be forced to accept a policy of open employment, it finds comfort in the knowledge that the physical requirements for entry into the infantry and Royal Armoured Corps are likely to render the problem, in the Army's phrase, 'self-managing'. In other words, the Army needn't worry about conceding the principle of open employment because in practice nothing much will change. So much for the spirit of positive action.

My final observation in this section relates to the Army's condoning of chauvinism within its rank and file. If soldiers wish to identify with the cult of the machismo, that is for them. But for the Army to use the supposed adverse reactions of men to any perceived softening of combat arms to defend single-sex units is to elevate prejudice above justice. If some men cannot operate professionally with women in their midst, this is a problem for them, and they should not be indulged at women's expense. The affair between Colonel Pople and Commander Pearce has been used by commentators, including John Keegan, to argue that integration has gone too far. On 12 April 1998, in a piece impoverished in imagination, Keegan wrote in the *Sunday Telegraph* that: 'The Pople–Pearce case demonstrates that integration ... is inimical to respect for rank, to the operation of authority and eventually to military efficiency. It is ultimately inimical to the delicacies of morality by which professional armed forces work.' Given that Pople and Pearce were staff officers when they met, and as desk-bound as you are likely to get, one can only assume that Keegan feels that any female contamination of the services is unacceptable. What he seeks is to quarantine the Army against temptresses in uniform, to protect what he describes, in an uncomfortably intimate passage, as the raw sexuality of men from sirens in short skirts. Pearce, whatever the merits of her case, has been demonised as a sexual distraction whose bedroom appetite was the downfall of Pople; a case, perhaps, of Adam and Eve Part Two.

ARMY CULTURE

I now turn to my third and final section. May I remind the reader that I am trying to provide an explanation for the disparity between the stated commitment of the Army to end discrimination and the reality that confronts servicewomen? At the heart of the problem lies what I will describe as a malaise in Army culture.

The Army is a strong-culture organisation. In theory, strong-culture organisations are distinguished by their members' alignment with, and adherence to, a strict set of values and norms. As O'Reilly and Chatman[10] note, these values and norms are intensely held and often result in enhanced commitment. They are established by a variety of mechanisms. Not least, strong-culture organisations tend to recruit people who have personalities and interests which coincide with their outlook, that is to say, they recruit 'similar others' – the Army does this to some extent, for example, given its bias for selecting officers from public school. In addition, strong-culture organisations create 'strong situations' which are characterised by norms that are difficult to violate. Army training establishments are a case in point. New recruits soon learn that there are uniform expectancies, or appropriate response patterns – ways of doing things – deviancy from which is likely to result in excessive censure. And then there are subtle psychological mechanisms which clarify expectations and create consensus or similarity in outlook; these may exploit the insecurity born of being new, when the desire to fit in is usually most acutely felt, and may take the form of 'informational salience', which calls attention to or teaches important norms.

These mechanisms, then, lead members to behave in normatively consistent ways. And they encourage leaders not so much to manage the members but to manage and exploit the culture itself. Well, you might ask, so what? This may be vaguely interesting theory, but what has it got to do with women in the Army? The point is that strong-culture organisations tread a fine line. Commitment to an organisation's values and norms may seem, on the face of it, a good thing. Indeed, it may be the case. But only if these values and norms are strategically appropriate. Huge difficulties arise if they are not, and if members' investment in them prevents them from perceiving a need to realign their values and norms. The Army, in my opinion, finds itself on the wrong side of the fine line with the result that an inertia and obsessive conformity disfigures its culture. Army personnel, and critically its more senior members, are failing to perceive the need for change in response to wider social shifts.

But the problem goes deeper than this. The military hierarchy as it is presently constituted is largely incapable of effecting a change in a culture that they themselves embody. Officers are not trained how to manage change, still less cultivate it – the foci of managers in successful civilian organisations and professions. Instead, their training is predicated on a narrow definition of leadership that exemplifies all that management is not: heroic, intuitive, impulsive. Little wonder, therefore, that the Bett Review[11] tacitly recognised the need for a professional management ethos. It is implied in many of its findings and especially in the most far-reaching of his recommendations, the establishment of a Services Personnel Board. This new body has, in theory, the potential to develop a new approach to management, one in which leadership is subsumed within it: leadership is not a strategic concept; management is.

Industry has long recognised this and has practised leadership at the operational level, with management focusing on the overarching issues of resourcing, governance and policy. The relevance of this to the topic of equal opportunities should be clear: the new concept replaces an *ad hoc*, parochial and largely anecdotal concept of management, the perceived Cinderella of its brother, leadership, with one in which human resources issues can be professionally addressed.

Leadership has an important place under the rubric of management, but only if we invest it with the meaning it deserves – the galvanising and release of potential and ideas, not the ritualised and oppressive display of status, authority and power that currently informs the term. Moreover, the pied-piper leadership style that underscores the sacrificial potential of service during war is singularly unsuited to the job during peace. And peace has visited the British military for most of the years since the end of the Second World War. It is manifestly absurd to run organisations of service size on the basis of a contingency alone: its leading warriors need to be peacetime managers too, and sadly most are not up to it. Too many top brass confuse real leadership with the maintenance of anachronistic standards of behaviour, standards defined by the monarch in Queen's Regulations, including some which royalty itself is finding hard to uphold – fidelity, integrity, solvency and so on.

This focus on leading by upholding standards is a management dead-end. It is the military equivalent of the previous government's 'back to basics' campaign, a focus which not only places an unseemly premium on avoiding detection, but which does not acknowledge the inherent dynamism of values, or the relativism which complicates their legitimacy: values may change and can mean different things to different people. The Army brooks no such outlook. Rather it equates discipline with uniformity and thus seeks its military ideal: heterosexual, male, white Christians. Herein lies a fundamental problem with strong social control mechanisms: they find a level of least resistance. They encourage a reductionism that leads, almost inevitably, to homogeneity – for the simple reason that members from similar backgrounds and from similar groups are more readily processed into an homogenised military ideal. Women fall foul of this insidious equation, as do blacks and homosexuals; they impede, in other words, the over-bearing monoculture that unites white servicemen. For this reason, the culture of the Army is also fundamentally at odds with the justice of equal opportunities which celebrates merit through diversity.

In defence of its decision to resist convergence with the accepted standards of equality of opportunity the Army pleads that it is a special case; that it is unique in that it is designed to function in times of crisis, in conditions in which the rules and values of society have usually broken down, where survival and victory are the pre-eminent concerns. All of this is true. But equally, the Army is established precisely to defend society, and thus by extension its values and tolerances: in an important sense, the Army embodies – or should embody – society's outlook.

CONCLUSION

This chapter has attempted to place the issue of servicewomen within the broader context of the relationship between Army and society. The issue is among several others at the cutting-edge of this relationship and is therefore well placed to illuminate its nature. In broad terms, the Army is damagingly out of step and time with wider social trends, and this is reflected in its legal wranglings and inability to recruit, retain and resettle service personnel. The experiences of women in the Army reflect this condition, and also reveal deeper reasons for it: namely, the Army's impoverished definition of equality of opportunity and, more generally, the maladaptive qualities of its culture. Sooner or later, the Army will be obliged to move from its current policy of wider employment of women to open employment. Rather than resisting but ultimately retreating in the face of this inevitability, the Army should, as a minimum, accept it.

But the Army could and should do more. How it might do so relates to the issue of citizenship. Citizenship is founded upon the principle of equality, and anyone who meets its eligibility requirements is deemed to hold the same rights. These rights are unconditional; they are not linked to utility in terms of organisational effectiveness or marketplace economics. In other words, citizenship enjoys a moral imperative – justice demands that individuals have the right to exercise their citizenship. And as Mason observes, 'the centrality of equality to citizenship means that equal opportunities issues are, *in principle*, at the heart of a genuine extension of citizenship rights'.[12] The relevance to the Army of these observations should be clear: there are few more potent expressions of citizenship than the right to serve in a great institution of state, one established moreover to defend that state. Indeed: 'Given their key role as defenders of the nation's territory, constitution, values and, ultimately, citizenship, the armed forces are uniquely placed to set the standards for the nation as a whole in the realisation of the principles on which that citizenship is founded.'[13] The Army, in other words, has within its gift the capacity to lead others in a commitment to deliver genuine equal opportunities for all. The latter is no romantic objective. It represents a key aspiration for modern Britain. In helping to achieve it, the Army would be replacing its anachronistic (and debilitating) orientation to society with one fit for the millennium. And fit for its servicewomen.

NOTES

1. House of Commons, *Statement on the Defence Estimates* (Cm 3223) (London: HMSO, 1996).
2. Commission for Racial Equality (CRE), *Ministry of Defence (Household Cavalry): Report of a Formal Investigation* (London: CRE, 1996).
3. See Christopher Jessup, *Breaking Ranks: Social Change in Military Communities* (London: Brassey's, 1996).
4. Ministry of Defence, *UK Defence Statistics* (London: HMSO, 1996).
5. Project Overview – Unemployment amongst Army leavers, D/ETS2c/2755 (1995).
6. *Guardian*, 8 July 1996.
7. L. Gorman and G.W. Thomas, 'General Intellectual Achievement, Enlistment Intentions and Racial Representativeness in the US Army', *Armed Forces and Society*, 19 (4) (1993), pp. 611–24.
8. C. Enloe, *Does Khaki Become You?* (London: Pandora, 1988), p. 153.

9. S.W. Crawford, 'Race, Ethnicity and the Army: Racial and Ethnic Minority Representation and Integration in the British Army', unpublished Defence Fellowship thesis (University of Glasgow, 1996).
10. C.A. O'Reilly and J.A. Chatman, 'Culture as Social Control: Corporations, Cults and Commitment', *Research in Organisational Behaviour*, 18 (1996), pp. 157–200.
11. Michael Bett, *Independent Review of the Armed Forces' Manpower, Career and Remuneration Structures* (London: HMSO, 1995).
12. D. Mason, 'Diversifying the Uniform: Citizenship, Equality of Opportunity and the British Armed Forces', unpublished paper (University of Plymouth, 1996).
13. Ibid.

9

The British Army and Homosexuality

Stephen Deakin

Some of the most sensitive issues in public policy today are those concerned with sexual and gender politics.[1] It is not surprising therefore that the Army's policy towards homosexuality causes some controversy.[2] Whilst civilians are largely free to practise homosexuality as long as they are adults and do so in private, the Army's stance, like that of the other services, is one of total exclusion of known homosexuals. The Army argues that it is a special case since it derives much of its fighting power and effectiveness from high morale, team work and leadership that stems from and is based upon trust, mutual respect and social cohesion. It argues that the admission of homosexuals would undermine these qualities and hence lessen its ability to defend the nation-state. Its critics argue that the Army's policy is prejudiced and discriminatory, that homosexuals should have the right to serve their country as members of the armed forces, that the Army's community will not be harmed by the admission of homosexuals and that the Army should be bound by the same law as civilians in this area. Each side in this dispute has strong arguments and it is very unlikely that a solution can be found that will satisfy each of them.

HISTORICAL BACKGROUND

For a long period, almost certainly due to the predominance of Christianity, homosexual practice was illegal in Britain, since it was regarded as both immoral and harmful to society. However, there was growing pressure, after the Second World War to abolish this prohibition. In 1954 the Wolfenden Committee was appointed to consider the legal position of homosexual practice and prostitution and it reported in 1957.[3] With regard to homosexual practice the Committee concluded that, in some circumstances, it should no longer be a crime. One of the Committee's key arguments was to identify an area of private morality in which, it argued, the law should not intrude and in which, consequently, there should be individual freedom of choice. The government rejected this proposal because it argued that public opinion was not ready for this change. However, a decade later, the Sexual Offences Act 1967 changed the law and allowed that in most cases homosexual practice conducted between two consenting adults, over the age of 21, in private, was no longer a crime. The Criminal Justice and Public Order Act 1994 lowered this age to 18 years. Section 1 (2) of the 1967 Act delineated what is meant as private; a sexual act is not done in private if more than two people are present nor if it is done in a lavatory to which the public have access. The result of this 1967 Act is that, in many circumstances, adult civilians have legal freedom to practise homosexuality if they so wish.

A notable exception to this new liberty were members of the armed forces; they were explicitly excluded from the immunity provided by the Sexual Offences Act 1967. Section 1 (5) of the Act maintained that the newly decriminalised homosexual acts in civilian law would, nevertheless, remain criminal for military personnel subject to military law. Military law regards both known homosexual and lesbian orientation, or activities, as incompatible with military service. Admitting to being a homosexual or being found behaving in this way leads to dismissal from the Army. There is, however, no specific offence of homosexuality in military law, the charge is usually one of disgraceful conduct of an indecent kind, or conduct prejudicial to good order and discipline, or scandalous conduct by officers. Hence, under the provisions of the 1967 Act, if two adult consenting civilians engage in homosexual behaviour in private they are not guilty of a criminal act; but military personnel doing so break military law.

This distinction between civilians and military personnel is not simply a theoretical one, military authorities have taken the offence of homosexual or lesbian behaviour seriously and they have often acted to enforce military law. For example, statistics of courts martial and discharges for homosexual activity were provided for the 1990–91 Select Committee on the Armed Forces Bill. It found that in the previous four years 22 servicemen had been dismissed from the Army, nine from the Navy and eight from the Royal Air Force on conviction of homosexual activity. An additional 296 people, over half of them female, were discharged by administrative action, although no formal disciplinary charge was made against them of homosexual activity.[4]

The 1990–91 Select Committee on the Armed Forces Bill recommended a change of policy that was accepted by government.[5] The Committee acknowledged the strength of military objections to allowing homosexual activity in the services on the grounds that this would weaken units' fighting effectiveness.[6] It did, however, call for a change in military law in relation to homosexual practice. For, it suggested, 'we see no reason why Service personnel should be liable to prosecution under Service law for homosexual activity which would be legal in civilian law'.[7]

This proposal was accepted by the government in 1992 when the Minister of State for Defence Procurement outlined the change in policy which was to be made, and which was later implemented in the Criminal Justice and Public Order Act 1994.[8] Section 1 (5) of the Sexual Offences Act 1967 was to be repealed and homosexual acts that were not criminal under civil law were no longer to be criminal under military law. Hence military personnel no longer commit a criminal offence if they engage in homosexual activity which is not illegal in civilian law. (One exception to this, found in the Criminal Justice and Public Order Act 1994, is that a homosexual act which occurs in circumstances where, for example, heterosexual or homosexual behaviour is inappropriate is still liable to constitute an offence.) However, the Minister emphasised that although military personnel would no longer be prosecuted under military law for activity which was legal in civilian law they would still be discharged from the service. So even though a criminal offence no longer exists for military personnel found engaging in homosexual acts, evidence of such activity either in the workplace, or privately elsewhere, will result in discharge from the military by administrative process. This means that the person concerned must leave the service, but that their dismissal papers will make no mention of homosexuality, they will not have a criminal record and subsequent employers will be unaware of the reason for their leaving. The Minister stressed that this decriminalisation measure was aimed at making military and civil law more compatible and that there was no intention in so doing of altering policy towards homosexuals in the military.

A further development in policy, in 1994, was the publication by the Ministry of Defence of its 'Armed Forces Policy and Guidelines on Homosexuality' paper.[9] The policy emphasised that homosexuality is incompatible with military service but stressed that homosexuals should receive psychological support and sympathetic treatment since disclosure of their sexuality could lead to pain and possibly even self-harm. In 1993 the Army restated its policy in an important internal policy document, *The Discipline and Standards Paper* that covered a number of personnel and moral issues and with regard to the issue of homosexuality it stated that, 'Anyone who admits to, or displays the orientation of, or indulges in homosexuality will be required to resign or be discharged.'[10] The election of a Labour government in 1997 may lead to policy changes in this area as may the challenge to the policy, by former service people dismissed on grounds on homosexuality, that is currently, at the time of writing, being considered by the Court of Human Rights in Europe.

The existence of the Army is approved by Parliament every year, and in practice this leads to a five-yearly examination of military procedures and discipline through the Select Committee on the Armed Forces Bill and subsequent parliamentary debate. The reports of the five-yearly Select Committee on the Armed Forces Bill are an important source of information for the arguments used about the British military and homosexuality. It appears that the issue of homosexuality and the military was first discussed by the Committee in 1966.[11] Since then in each successive report the issue has assumed greater prominence and the submissions of the Ministry of Defence and those representing the homosexual case have become ever more sophisticated. In what follows use is made of the latest 1995–96 Select Committee Report, henceforth referred to as the 1996 Report, as a source from which to identify those arguments that currently seem to emerge strongly from discussion of the issue.[12] The Committee called as witnesses the Ministry of Defence, Rank Outsiders, a pressure group representing homosexuals in the military, and Stonewall, a national organisation committed to legal equality and social justice for homosexuals. Stonewall's evidence to the Committee is complex and sophisticated and it is used here to represent the current homosexual viewpoint in this debate.

THE CASE FOR HOMOSEXUALITY

Stonewall's case to the Committee involved a detailed rebuttal of the Ministry of Defence's testimony. However, there are two principal arguments that seem to be central to its submission: they are equal treatment and human rights, and secondly, the right to sexual privacy. There is also an important argument that is missing from Stonewall's presentation: group rights. Stonewall wished the Committee to begin its analysis with the principle of equal treatment and non-discrimination against homosexuals;

> ... our starting point, in looking at this issue, and we hope, indeed, the starting point of the whole Committee, is that discrimination on any grounds not related to individual merit and capacity is morally wrong and economically wasteful.[13]

And,

> Everyone is entitled to equal treatment and, at work, to be assessed on merit against objective criteria, not on the basis of prejudice and stereotyping. The question which the Select Committee must ask is whether there are any compelling arguments, based on evidence, as opposed to prejudice and stereotype, to justify Parliament allowing the armed forces to continue to depart from this principle?[14]

Stonewall supported its case by appeal to Article 14 of the European Convention on Human Rights, which forbids discrimination on many grounds, including sex.[15] Consequently, Stonewall argued, there is nothing about lesbian and gay homosexuals as a group that justifies the ban on their serving in the military.[16]

That people should be treated equally and have equal rights and that they should not be discriminated against in the workplace is so much part of contemporary thinking that it seems simply a self-evident, unassailable, argument. That anyone, women, heterosexuals, or homosexuals, should be treated other than on the grounds of merit and individual capacity is seen as wrong. Sexuality is viewed as an irrelevant ground for discrimination in contemporary British civilian society. The results of such arguments often give us what we want: none of us wishes to be treated unequally, or unfairly, or to be discriminated against on irrelevant sexual grounds. However, no public policy is cost free and in the context of this debate about homosexuals and the Army some of the standard criticisms of rights-based thinking generate interesting issues.

One of the most well-known critics of rights thinking is the conservative philosopher Edmund Burke in his *Reflections on the Revolution in France* (1790).[17] Burke did not deny natural rights, but he saw them as simply conventions arising out of custom and practice rather than from them being anything intrinsic to humans. Burke argued that society was a complex organic institution that benefited from the application of tradition, conventions, prejudices, sentiment, experience and wisdom on a case-by-case basis, rather than from the application of universal abstract principles such as the rights of man that allow individuals to govern themselves.[18] The outcome of this conservative tradition is liable to be quite different from that of the equal rights, equal treatment practice. In a conservative Burkean-style community there will likely be equality before the law rather than equal rights, because the community will wish to discriminate and to treat some people unequally to achieve community goals. Ideals such as promoting public morality, the individual moral character of citizens, making judgements between right and wrong and asserting the public good will be prominent.

In contrast, the universal application of equal treatment and equal rights emphasises the individual rather that the community. Indeed it seems to detach the individual from many community, moral and religious influences and pressures by giving universal equal rights to them.[19] The implicit view of the person here is one of an independent individual, choosing freely how to live, subject only to the similar equal rights of others. The individual is isolated and the state provides a neutral framework of equal rights, but it is increasingly unable to make traditional moral judgements about right and wrong, and thereby to discriminate to achieve such a public good.[20] This way of thinking is part of a broad tradition of thought that rejects traditional moral reasoning, that there are moral codes with universal application, and replaces it with an, apparently, neutral code.[21] This ethos of state neutrality about traditional morality allows one commentator to remark on the 'demoralisation of discourse'[22] and another on the 'demoralisation of society',[23] and another that people have 'lost the confidence with which they once spoke publicly about morality'.[24]

This movement towards individualism and moral neutrality can be seen in the way public policy in Britain deals with sexual issues that were once considered traditional moral ones, such as: marriage, divorce, abortion, homosexuality, sex education for children, welfare availability and the like. Behaviour in these areas is seen as a matter of individual personal choice, derived from individual's equal rights and need for equal treatment, rather than from traditional morality.[25] Stonewall's case, similarly, is that homosexuality and heterosexuality should be viewed as comparable activities, equally valid and equally meritorious,[26] and that therefore any discrimination against homosexuals is wrongful and based on prejudiced stereotyping. Stonewall wishes the current British military ban to be replaced with a neutral policy that restricts both heterosexual and homosexual unacceptable behaviour, akin to the one adopted in Australia.[27] Acceptance of this moves the argument from the earlier, pre-1967 view, that homosexuality should be discriminated against because it is wrongful and harms the community, to one where prejudice and discrimination against homosexuals is wrong.

This sketch of an aspect of contemporary public policy in Britain is relevant to the issue of homosexuality and the Army. The claim to equal treatment in the Army workplace based on merit alone would prohibit the Army from making judgements about the employee except in the, often quite narrow, sense of individual merit measured by objective criteria. Here, individuals receive equal treatment however they behave, unless their behaviour can be shown to be directly relevant to their job, and they choose how they want to live themselves. But service, not work, in the British Army has traditionally been seen as a much more holistic and fully rounded concept than this, a vocation, involving duty, honour, tradition, military virtue, self-sacrifice, courage and unlimited liability to give of one's life for the greater good of the community if that is necessary; the motto of the Royal Military Academy Sandhurst, 'Serve to Lead', expresses this thought succinctly.[28] This community of service theme resonates with Burke's argument that society involves a partnership, in virtue, over many generations, between the living, the dead and the yet to be born.[29] The words on the British Second World War memorial to those who fell in battle at Kohima seem perfectly to capture this sentiment:

> When you go home
> Tell them of us and say,
> For their tomorrow
> We gave our today.[30]

These are communitarian ideals and they are, subtly, challenged by the individualism inherent in equal treatment and equal rights arguments. Framing discussion in these individualistic terms makes it very difficult for the Army to sustain its traditional principles and thereby homosexuality becomes a matter of personal individual choice, detached from the reach of the wider, Army, community.

Community is a slippery and highly politicised concept capable of many meanings, but it might be possible to get broad agreement for the assertion that the closer and more united a community the greater the price expected and required of its members. Scruton has remarked on, 'the real price of community: which is sanctity, intolerance, exclusion and vigilance against the enemy'.[31] The British Army's policy towards many issues and with regard to homosexuality echoes this type of thinking. The Army's argument is that it is a tightly bounded group and it must create a strong community with a clear vision of its public good; 'fighting power': and it can't afford to be neutral about homosexuality since it regards it as something that will affect its community's cohesion deeply. The, probably, unsolvable dilemma here is that whilst the British Army is a close community, equipped, trained and paid to defend the nation-state and its interests, the nation-state is increasingly composed of an individualistic, equal-rights, morally neutral civilian society.

The other central argument apparent in Stonewall's case is the right to sexual privacy. The removal of the Army's ban is not seen by Stonewall as encouraging licence, but rather as respecting the privacy of individual's sexual lives.

> Our case, and it is the crux of the court case which will go to the European Court of Human Justice, is that we are arguing for a right of privacy, we are not arguing for licence, we are arguing for respect for people's private sexual lives.[32]

> For many lesbians and gay men, particularly those in the armed forces, their sexual relationships are a private matter. The effect of the changes we advocate will not mean that they will all rush to make their sexuality public knowledge ... In practice the effect of the policies we propose will not transform the armed forces. Life for everybody will be very much as it was.[33]

The Army's policy gives it an interest in preventing those whose homosexuality is public from becoming what it believes would be a disruptive influence and this may lead to it investigating people's sexual lives and subsequently to their dismissal from their employment. Stonewall disagrees and argues that the privacy of homosexual's sex lives should be respected and it is able to appeal for support to the European Convention on Human Rights that gives a right of privacy.[34] This claim for sexual privacy is discussed in the context of the Army's argument, considered below; however, the appeal to privacy raises an important issue that is best examined here.

One impression gained from examining the debate in the 1996 Select Committee Report is that the possible expression of homosexuality under consideration is not fully clarified. Broadly, there are two prominent ideals of the homosexual life in contemporary debate. One can be seen as the liberal one that argues that people have the right to be homosexuals as long as they don't harm others and this will occur if they are consenting adults and they practise in private. This view was famously expressed in the 1957 Wolfenden Report into homosexuality and prostitution where an area of private morality was identified that was not the business of public policy: 'there must remain a realm of private morality and immorality which is, in brief and crude terms, not the laws [sic] business'.[35] There always was an area of private morality, free from the law, but this argument sought to extend the boundaries of moral privacy and public morality. In doing so it was part of an ethos, that adults can do what they like with their own bodies as long as demonstrable harm is not caused to others, that has deeply shaped British social policy since the 1950s. It is this liberal view of privacy, that there is an area of private morality, in this case soldiers' homosexual behaviour, that is not the business of military law, which Stonewall represents in its evidence to the 1996 Committee.

However, the other prominent model of the homosexual lifestyle, a group-based one, is worth examining in some detail, since group understandings are of growing importance in British politics. Also, whilst this argument is not prominent in Stonewall's account, it is, perhaps somewhat surprisingly, implicit in the Army's argument. The goal of homosexual activists in the 1950s and 1960s was a liberal one of achieving civil rights, removing discrimination barriers and gaining public acceptance of the idea that what homosexuals did in private was their own business. However, for many, there was a move on from there, to support ideals of group rights, or 'Gay Pride'. An American philosopher has put this case for 'Gay Pride' succinctly:

> Today most gay and lesbian liberation advocates seek not merely civil rights, but the affirmation of gay men and lesbians as social groups with specific experiences and perspectives. Refusing to accept the dominant culture's definition of healthy sexuality and respectable family life and social practices, gay and lesbian liberation movements have proudly created and displayed a distinctive self-definition and culture ... Gay pride asserts that sexual identity is a matter of culture and politics, and not merely 'behaviour' to be tolerated or forbidden.[36]

On this view homosexuality is not simply a private matter, but rather it is a symbol of group identity that should be carried into the public arena and be affirmed.[37] It envisages a group-based pluralistic society bargaining in a manner that shows equal respect and affirmation for each group and its standards and its desires. It rejects the idea of common standards, or the dominant group's culture, that will, inevitably, impose itself onto other autonomous groups. Peter Tatchell, a well-known supporter of gay rights in Britain, appears to illustrate this view when he argues in his book about homosexuals and the military that;

> The modern queer agenda is post-equality. It's geared to a wholesale re-negotiation of sexual values and laws. We want ... more than mere equal treatment ... the *whole* [italics in the original] system has to change. That demands social transformation. It *means*, in the words of the Gay Liberation Front, moving 'beyond civil libertarian goals' to achieve a 'revolutionary change' which 'abolishes the gender system' and creates a 'new social order' which is not based on 'straight male privilege' ... The military is the incarnation of the gender system and the ultimate defender of that system. Its whole ethos is based on the straight male machismo which oppresses women and queers.[38]

These two models, liberal and radical, of the homosexual life seem to affect the argument about the British Army's prohibition on homosexuality a good deal. The liberal argument makes the issue of homosexuality a matter of individual private behaviour outside the purview of the wider, in this case, Army community's, opinions and laws. This argument is assimilationist; it denies any great differences between heterosexuals and homosexuals and encourages meritorious competition along individualistic equality of opportunity lines within the established heterosexual order. The radical Gay Pride argument rejects the existing heterosexual social order and brings homosexuality to the forefront of politics and allocates to it the role of a badge or symbol of group identity within a society that it wants to change. Stonewall's evidence to the Select Committee is expressed along liberal lines of seeking tolerance for what it argues to be private behaviour and personal choices. However, the politics of group rights are gradually becoming more important in Britain not least in the common claim that Britain is a pluralistic, multicultural, multi-religious, multi-racial society. It is not known, and no one can know, what model, the liberal or the radical, would eventually predominate if the ban on homosexuals in the British Army were lifted. Will homosexuals in the Army simply argue that their sexuality is a private matter and it is none of the Army's business as long as it is kept private? Or will they, in the Gay Pride tradition, argue that the Army must recognise their sexuality formally as a group within the Army and that the Army must therefore change its structure?

Traditionally, there are groups in the Army, indeed the regimental system makes a particular strength of group identity.[39] If Gay Pride became the ruling practice amongst homosexuals in the Army then probably regiments would eventually have groups within them based on sexual identity which would have an agenda that had to be taken into account by other groups within the regiment and the Army. This Gay Pride argument raises deep issues about Army community and social unity, and indeed fighting power, since it allocates important loyalties to the sexually identified group rather than to the wider community of the Army, and in doing so it raises concerns about the nature of common goals in such a community.[40]

The Army's case, although it is not presented as such, can also be seen to rest partly on a group rights basis. It is arguing that it is a group that has the duty and a preference to discriminate in its employment procedures with regard to homosexuality and that not being able to do this will cause great offence to its existing members and impaired efficiency in its performance of its group task. If this is true, then few things are likely to be more offensive or to cause more outrage than Gay Pride sentiments within the Army. Stonewall argues that nothing much will change if the ban is relaxed. However, in a group-rights-based community there is much room for members of groups to take offence at the activities of other groups. Stonewall's argument that not much will change rests, under-standably in its case, on the idea that homosexuality should no longer be considered a significant issue, but so much here depends on the strength of opinion of those heterosexuals already serving in the Army.

THE ARMY'S CASE

The Army's case, and it is the same as that of the other two services and the Ministry of Defence, was also presented to the Select Committee on the Armed

Forces Bill in 1996. As with Stonewall's submission, much of the Army's case consisted of rebuttal of its opponents' detailed arguments. The crux of the Army's justification for its ban on homosexuals was, however simply and succinctly expressed; it was on the grounds that military life is very different from civilian life:

> ... the special nature of Service life precludes the acceptance of homo-sexuality in the Armed Forces. The conditions of military life, both on operations and within the Service environment, are very different from those experienced in civilian life. To meet the exceptional demands of military operations members of the Armed Forces must work together as a close-knit and effective team. Their morale and ethos are crucial for their effectiveness. Service personnel can be required to live in close proximity with each other in shared, single-sex accommodation with very limited personal privacy. They may also be required to work together in physically close quarters sometimes under great stress ... these conditions, and the need for absolute trust and confidence between personnel of all ranks, must dictate ... policy towards homosexuality ... the primary concern ... is thus the maintenance of an operationally effective and efficient force. Coupled with this is the maintenance of discipline ... the policy derives from a practical assessment of the implications of homosexual orientation for Fighting Power.[41]

In support of this argument the Ministry of Defence submitted to the Committee its 1996 Report on Homosexuality that contained an internal survey that found that currently serving military personnel overwhelmingly did not wish to work alongside known homosexuals.[42] Of male Army respondents, 85 per cent agreed or strongly agreed that they would find the presence of known homosexuals offensive in a service environment, 3 per cent did not, and the overall figure agreeing or strongly agreeing for all three services was 84 per cent.[43] Females were more accepting of homosexuals, with 59 per cent of Army respondents finding homosexuals offensive.[44] Army males were also strongly offended by the thought of sexual acts between men with 83 per cent agreeing or strongly agreeing that they found this revolting, and 81 per cent of the tri-service sample were of the same view.[45] This Report made much of the thinking, feelings and sentiments of existing personnel towards homosexuals, and the Army's pro-fessional military judgement that known homosexuality would be harmful in its community. The Army's case is that future change in civilian society's attitudes towards homosexuals will possibly reduce the implications for fighting power, although it also suggests that there may be something immutable about the military environment that means that known homosexuals can never be accepted without adversely affecting fighting power.[46] More broadly, the Army's case is that its values should be the same as those of civilian society except when it is necessary to have different ones because of its function that necessitates a special military ethos.[47]

The Army is arguing here that its personnel are heterosexual, that they would be disturbed and offended by having to work in enforced close circumstances with known homosexuals, and that this would then consequently diminish fighting power. Stonewall, naturally, disputes the accuracy of the Army's internal survey[48] and views this argument as a weak justification for the ban on homosexuals in the military and one that rests on prejudice, stereotype and lack of factual evidence.[49] The Army justifies its policy by making two central, but overlapping, arguments for discriminating against homosexuals; one is for sexual privacy, the other is for fighting power.

In this debate both the Army and its critics are making claims for sexual privacy, but in different ways. Stonewall's desire is for a private homosexual sex life, free from the intervention of the Army. Gay Pride adherents, currently silent in this official debate, regard their sexuality as a very public issue and consequently can be seen to have a different concept of privacy. Their claim to privacy is in effect the privacy not to be stopped from making their sexuality public and having it recognised in the public arena. The Army's case is for a community that has little sexual privacy in it at all. The Army argues that its fighting effectiveness is based on being a close-knit community whose members have no choice but to work together in enforced closeness and who deserve privacy from unhelpful sexuality, be it homosexual or heterosexual. Indeed the Army's 1994 *Discipline and Standards Paper* does not necessarily recognise a private area of morality in some heterosexual relationships; for example it forbids heterosexual adultery and describes such behaviour in the following terms, 'The most serious cases of social misconduct involve adultery within the military community.'[50] Officers, married or single, who have adulterous relationships outside the military community hazard their jobs if this becomes publicly known.[51] So the Army discriminates against heterosexual behaviour when it believes that this serves its community purpose. Soldiers are expected to live open lives and for the Army to have access, if and when it desires, to all their lives. Yet the Army does support sexual privacy in that, as does civilian society, it separates men and women in accommodation and bathroom facilities, for all sorts of commonly accepted reasons, ranging from sexual privacy to the desire not to stimulate sexual activity between workplace colleagues.

Such considerations allow the Army, in turn, to make a claim for the rights of its heterosexual soldiers to sexual privacy.[52] Whilst Stonewall's case is that homosexuality is a private matter, the Army's case is the reverse: that, within the Army, homosexuality is a public matter. Its known, public existence, it argues, engenders hostile responses in the heterosexual soldier and diminishes fighting power and fighting spirit. Part of a judgment of the Master of the Rolls in the Court of Appeal was used by Stonewall to support its analysis;

> To dismiss a person from his or her employment on the grounds of a private sexual preference, and to interrogate him or her about private sexual behaviour, would not appear to me to show respect for that person's private and family life.[53]

This argument rests on the premise that homosexuality is a private sexual preference; something that the Army's argument rejects. From the perspective of the Army, the Master of the Rolls' argument can be easily reversed and then it can be argued that allowing known homosexuals to serve in the enforced closeness of military life does not show respect for majority heterosexual private and family life in the Army.

The Army's argument is not necessarily about overt actual homosexual behaviour, but it is about an attitude of mind; it is the thought of serving in enforced closeness with known homosexuals that is particularly offensive to soldiers. For example, for heterosexual soldiers the thought of showering with a known homosexual makes them feel threatened and, they argue, diminishes cohesion, unity and morale.[54] Stonewall strongly rejects this sense of military apprehension towards homosexuals and suggests that it is totally unwarranted and unnecessary.[55] In the circumstances of enforced communal living in the Army there would seem to be no way of resolving this dispute over privacy that will satisfy all the parties and ensure the right of privacy for each. This illustrates one of the dilemmas with anti-discrimination proposals; they almost inevitably curtail freedom of choice for someone or some group. Positively protecting one group very easily discriminates against another group that belongs to a different category. In this case there can be seen to be a clash of two public goods: the right of heterosexuals to sexual privacy and the right of homosexuals to sexual privacy. Even an appeal to equal human rights and equal treatment will not help here, since if they are allocated equally there will still be deadlock.

The other central claim of the Army is that fighting power or effectiveness depends on team work, leadership, discipline, mutual trust, morale and a military ethos, and that the presence of known homosexuals undermines these essential characteristics. This argument has a long history: it was supported in 1957 by the Wolfenden Committee which, whilst it argued for the decriminalisation of homosexuality in civilian society, argued that the military should be excluded from this.

> We recognise that within services and establishments whose members are subject to a disciplinary regime it may be necessary, for the sake of good management and the preservation of discipline and for the protection of those of subordinate rank or position, to regard homosexual behaviour, even by consenting adults in private, as an offence.[56]

James Adair's minority dissenting view in the Wolfenden Report included his belief that the removal of the ban on homosexuals in the military would create a situation where:

> ... an increase in the trend towards homosexual practices would be marked and intense while the effect on the morale of members of the services would be adverse and corrupting.[57]

This line of argument was characteristic of that of military speakers in parliamentary debates during the legislative initiatives that eventually became the Sexual Offences Act 1967. For example, Field Marshal Lord Montgomery said:

> What is the greatest single factor making for success in battle or for efficient and well trained armed forces in peacetime? It is morale. And what is the very foundation of morale? It is discipline. If these unnatural practices are made legal a blow is struck at the discipline of the British armed forces.[58]

In more recent times the same argument has been deployed, as, for example, in the Army's 1994 *Discipline and Standards Paper* which when referring to male or female homosexuality argued that it is:

> ... incompatible with military service because of the close physical conditions in which soldiers often have to live and work. Homosexual behaviour can cause offence, polarise relationships, induce violence and as a consequence morale and unit effectiveness suffer.[59]

It is this argument, that the presence of known homosexuals will harm the military community, that Stonewall is seeking to overthrow.

The Army's case is strikingly similar to one side of an important earlier debate about homosexuality in Britain. Following the Wolfenden Committee Report in 1957, Lord Justice Devlin and Professor Hart debated the issue of homosexuality and the law.[60] Professor Hart argued in the liberal tradition that there are areas in life, such as homosexuality amongst adults, which are simply not the law's business since they both are private and do not cause harm to others: and it is this viewpoint that has shaped contemporary civilian law. However, Devlin argued, in a conservative tradition, that society is held together by a common or public morality that acts as a unifying agent and which, or at least important parts of which, should be enforced or society will disintegrate.[61] Hence,

> What makes a society of any sort is community of ideas, not only political ideas but also ideas about the way its members should behave and govern their lives; these latter ideas are its morals ... If men and women try to create a society in which there is no fundamental agreement about good and evil they will fail ... without shared ideas on politics, morals and ethics no society can exist ... Societies disintegrate from within more frequently than they are broken by external pressures. There is disintegration when no common morality is observed ...[62]

Devlin sees a moral basis to social order and he argues that the law should preserve this order. He does not accept that a private area of morality exists in any real sense. Even some things, he suggests, done completely privately may ultimately be harmful to society, for they may harm the social order, social stability or individuals: things done privately, are he argues, a matter of concern to the wider community. Consequently he proposes that homosexuality done even in a concealed manner, if it becomes sufficiently widespread, will corrupt and harm the family and this could ultimately destroy or harm society. Hence in

Devlin's view the law should be used to protect public morality from acts which are believed to threaten it.

Devlin argued from a traditional, Christian inspired, moral position, but the Army's case in 1996, although it appears very similar to Devlin's, explicitly avows any moral stance or indeed any suggestion that homosexuals are less effective than heterosexuals as soldiers.[63] However, notably, Stonewall's argument is that the ban on homosexuals in the Army *is* a moral issue and that very little will actually change, except for the better, if homosexuals are allowed to serve openly in the Army.[64] Despite the Army's claim, it does seem to be arguing for common, or majority heterosexual standards, or indeed morals, implicit in existing Army morale, discipline and military ethos. Its views are those of the Army 'man on the Clapham omnibus', the reasonable man through whom Devlin would have society make moral judgements.[65] Known homosexuality, clearly, is viewed by the Army as introducing conflict, tension and disunity. Stonewall's case is based on the premise of equality between the two sexualities that therefore necessitates equal treatment. The Army's case is somewhat terse here and it does not directly challenge this argument of equality.[66] Rather, it can be seen to be reporting that open homosexuality in the enforced close context of Army life hooks into heterosexuals' emotions, their sexuality, psychology and sense of the person and leads to opposition to homosexuals. A remark by Peter Tatchell, in his book about homosexuals and the military in Britain, can be used to give support to this argument when he suggests that, 'At a deep unconscious level, there is a fundamental difference between the psyches of heterosexual males and queer men.'[67]

An important problem for the Army's argument here is that Britain, and indeed the Army, is increasingly pluralistic in outlook and practice. Homogeneous solutions are currently unpopular in contemporary Britain and there is diversity rather than homogeneity in people's behaviour as the British official statistics report, *Social Trends*, reveals.[68] The considerable homogeneity of the past has been replaced with a pluralism that involves diversity, not uniformity, of morality, practices and standards. A dilemma for the Army must be that it is maintaining here, out of what it argues is military necessity, a homogeneity of traditional moral standards. However, the civilian society that it protects and serves, and draws its recruits from, increasingly celebrates diversity and heterogeneity, as of course is likely if individuals are encouraged within a neutral moral framework to decide their own goals. One of the problems for any pluralistic society is what limits to set on diversity; where to set the boundaries of acceptable behaviour, since there is unlikely to be agreement about this in many cases. This problem seems to be particularly acute in the case of a British Army serving a pluralistic society. An effective army like the British one accepts some diversity, but within a tightly bounded community that insists on much conformity. In such an organisation, individualism, self-interest, tension and conflict, especially if they are given precedence, are viewed as disloyal, whereas uniformity, cohesion, trust and team work are seen as vital to success. The emphasis is on bonding together around shared virtues and goals, with unity of spirit, and of individuals deferring themselves to the whole. But these principles are significantly at odds with those of pluralistic society.

Another difficulty here is that the issue of fighting power is so hard to grapple with as, indeed, the Army concedes.[69] It is noticeable also that Stonewall, in its submission to the 1996 Select Committee, places its emphasis on discussion of communal living within the military, rather than on analysing issues of fighting power. Fighting power is defined by the Army as having three characteristics, concepts of war, the physical means to fight and the moral component.[70] It is this last that is troublesome here. The Army argues that morale is one of its ten Principles of War, both in war and peace, and that it fosters the 'will to win'.[71] The Army views morale as a mental state whose primary element is trust.[72] Cohesion is part of morale and cohesion is seen as stemming from high standards in training, the will to win, and from 'an ethically based code of personal conduct, in peace, which does not threaten or undermine cohesion on operations'.[73] Clausewitz argued somewhat similarly; he saw the moral components in war, which he identified, principally, as the skill of the commanders, the experience and courage of the troops and their patriotic spirit, as an essential part of the spirit of war, but one that was a mystery:

> ... the moral elements are among the most important in war. They constitute the spirit that permeates war as a whole and at an early stage they establish a close affinity with the will that moves and leads the whole mass of force, practically merging with it, since the will is itself a moral quantity. Unfortunately they will not yield to academic wisdom. They cannot be classified or counted. They have to be seen or felt ... it is paltry philosophy if ... one lays down rules and principles in total disregard of moral values.[74]

The Army views known homosexuality as adversely harming morale and cohesion and hence fighting power and it uses its survey of the views of existing military personnel as support for this contention.[75] This must be a matter of military judgement, since, if Clausewitz is correct, the spirit of war can only be 'seen and felt'. It is unlikely that the harm that the Army sees in allowing known homosexuality could be measured, or proven, as indeed Stonewall has emphasised when it attacks what it regards as prejudice, stereotype and lack of empirical evidence in the Army's account.[76] It is possible to argue that the major European powers which retained laws forbidding homosexuality until the 1960s, that is Britain, Germany and the Soviet Union, were the only ones able to fight the long Second World War with a mass army whose morale did not break.[77] However, morale, cohesion and fighting power are obviously subject to so many differing variables that making a causal link between them and allowing known homosexuality in soldiers is almost certainly impossible.[78]

This emphasis on trust resonates with the recent upsurge in interest in the place of trust in civil society and the discovery of social capital. Fukuyama argues for the importance of trust in civil society for creating the conditions necessary for prosperity. Societies with low trust, he argues, spend much effort protecting themselves from internal problems.[79] Social capital consists of those informal principles and rules that facilitate co-operation for the common good.[80] This argument is not new in military circles; a classic comparative study of the German and American armies in the Second World War found the German one to have had much more fighting power.[81] The main reason for this was that the German Army placed the creation of mutual trust between soldiers at the centre of its organisation in a way that the American Army did not.

This idea of the spirit of the effective military, a spiritual bond, is quite common. One authority speaks of new soldiers joining a 'mystical fraternity'.[82] Clausewitz suggested that soldiers see themselves as members of '... a special guild, in whose regulations, laws and customs the spirit of war is given pride of place'.[83] Winston Churchill once said of the British Army, 'The Army was not an inanimate substance, it was a living thing ... That was true of any Army, and it was still more true with regard to a voluntary Army.'[84] In Burma during the Second World War, General, later Field Marshal, Slim developed three principles; spiritual, intellectual, material, and in that order, to raise the fighting spirit of the 'Forgotten' British Army, which then went on to victory over the Japanese.[85] His spiritual principle, he argued was not necessarily religious, although he did view Christianity as very valuable in soldiers. Even the arch-realist Machiavelli wanted soldiers to be religious and to make oaths of allegiance to God and to the state to ensure their loyalty and obedience.[86]

The argument that morale, trust and cohesion constitute the spirit of war that must be seen and felt rather than measured is a Burkean-style argument about the wisdom of the ages and practical experience being more important than abstract rules. It resonates with the contemporary debate about homosexuality and the British Army, with one side making appeals to rules of human rights and the other to professional military judgement about the spirit of war. This under-standing of the mystical bonds that bind together soldiers in the Army does not of course tell us much in itself about what effect known homosexuals might have on this unity. However, these intuitive, enigmatic, bonds that unite soldiers together pose a great difficulty for the arguments of homosexual rights, sexual privacy and equal treatment. For these arguments lean towards individualism, factual analysis and measurement: I have rights or I do not: I have sexual privacy or I do not. These are concepts that see individuals as rational actors independ-ently achieving their own, measurable, goals as long as they don't hurt others. However the appeal to soldiers' mysterious metaphysical instinctive bonds that hold them together not by individualistic self-interest, but by membership, duty and moral obligation to the community are quite different.

CONCLUSION

The arguments used by the Army and by supporters of the homosexual argument in this debate raise a great many issues about the relationship between the British Army and civilian society. This is a controversy that reveals two differing views of the effective military and indeed of politics. For the Army, the ban on known homosexuals is about fighting power and sexual privacy which it believes involves morale, cohesion, trust, and heterosexual relationships. The Army's argument is a Devlin-like one that seeks the views of the Army reasonable man on the Clapham omnibus and honours unity and common standards and a social glue that holds its community together. Indeed this is an ideal of the good community which is a time-honoured one in British political thought.[87] The Army uses its experience of, and need to prepare for, effective fighting in battle to justify this ideal and its view that known homosexual practice weakens this community. Supporters of the homosexual case use a different perspective, one that emphasises individualism, human rights, equal treatment, sexual privacy, non-discrimination and legitimating homosexual activity. They can see no evidence that admittance of known homosexuals will adversely affect or harm morale and cohesion in the Army.

The two sides in this debate use different political languages and do not convince each other. One view is individualistic, the other is communitarian. However, there is little reason to suppose that the arguments deployed by Wolfenden in 1957 and accepted by Parliament in the debates that led to the Sexual Offences Act 1967 have lost their power when they are applied to the military. Military life is different from civilian life and this difference sometimes justifies different policies. It is not clear that an emphasis on individualism, sexual privacy and human rights will lead to a better or more fully effective military performance by the British Army. Given the evidence that serving Army personnel would find the presence of known homosexuals strongly offensive their presence in the Army would lead to diminished trust and social cohesion. The Army reflects society in many ways, but its prime task is to defend the nation-state efficiently.

NOTES

The opinions expressed in this paper are the personal views of the author and should not be understood necessarily to be those of the Ministry of Defence.

1. I am grateful for helpful suggestions from Brigadier Currie, Director of Personal Services (Army) in 1998 and from my colleagues Alan Ward and Nigel de Lee. As ever, responsibility for the argument is the author's alone. In places this paper draws on an earlier publication, see Stephen Deakin, 'The British Military: Community, Society and Homosexuality', *British Army Review*, 110 (August 1995), pp. 27–33.
2. Since policy amongst the three Services and the Ministry of Defence is the same on this issue, I conflate Army and Ministry of Defence sources in this paper, unless a reference is specifically an Army one.
3. Wolfenden Committee, *Report of the Committee on Homosexual Offences and Prostitution* (London: HMSO, 1957). Cmmd 247.
4. *Select Committee on the Armed Forces Bill* (London: HMSO, 1991), para. 38.
5. *Select Committee (1991)*, para. 40.
6. *Select Committee (1991)*, para. 40.

7. *Select Committee (1991)*, para. 41.
8. *House of Commons*, 17 June 1992, cols 989–96.
9. Ministry of Defence (1994). For details of these guide-lines see the *Guardian*, 11 May 1994.
10. *The Discipline and Standards Paper*, Ministry of Defence internal document (1993).
11. The issue does not seem to have been discussed in the 1961 Report. See *Special Report from the Select Committee on the Army and Air Force Bill* (London: HMSO, 1961). For subsequent discussions see *Special Report from the Select Committee on the Armed Forces Bill* (London: HMSO, 1966). *Special Report from the Select Committee on the Armed Forces Bill* (Lords) (London: HMSO, 1971). *Special Report from the Select Committee on the Armed Forces Bill* (London: HMSO, 1976). *Special Report from the Select Committee on the Armed Forces Bill* (London: HMSO, 1981). *Special Report from the Select Committee on the Armed Forces Bill* (London: HMSO, 1986). *Select Committee on the Armed Forces Bill* (London: HMSO, 1991).
12. *Select Committee on the Armed Forces Bill* (London: HMSO, 1996).
13. *Select Committee (1996)*, p. 99.
14. *Select Committee (1996)*, p. 178.
15. *Select Committee (1996)*, pp. 182–3.
16. *Select Committee (1996)*, p. 99.
17. Edmund Burke, *Reflections on the Revolution in France*. See, G.H. Sabine, *A History of Political Thought* (London: Harrap, 1963), pp. 607–19.
18. Burke, *Reflections*.
19. See Jonathan Sachs, *The Politics of Hope* (London: Jonathan Cape, 1997), p. 102.
20. See, Michael J. Sandel, *Democracy's Discontent* (Cambridge, MA: Harvard University Press, 1996), p. 7.
21. James Q. Wilson, *The Moral Sense* (New York: Free Press, 1993), p. 225. This morally neutral state may get into difficulties if it is asked to apply rights thinking to traditional moral disputes, such as the rights of the unborn child versus the right of the mother to choose abortion.
22. Jonathan Sachs, *The Persistence of Faith* (London: Weidenfeld & Nicholson, 1991), p. 42.
23. Gertrude Himmelfarb, *The Demoralization of Society* (London: IEA, 1995).
24. Sandel, *Democracy's*, p. 8.
25. Sachs, *Politics*, p. 42.
26. *Select Committee (1996)*, p. 186, para. 57. 'The prevailing and most respected scientific view is that homosexuality is a normal dimension of human sexuality and that homosexual conduct and behaviour is analogous to heterosexual behaviour.'
27. *Select Committee (1996)* p. 180. The relevant part of the Australian code reads, 'Sexual relations are a part of adult life and are predominantly a private matter for each individual.' See *Unacceptable Sexual Behaviour by Members of the Australian Defence Force* DI(G) PERS 35–3, November 1994, AL 1.
28. Moskos's I/O model is useful here and the British Army is usually viewed as an example of a very traditional army. See Charles Moskos and Frank Wood (eds), *The Military: More than Just a Job?* (London: Pergamon, 1988). Cathy Downes examines the British case in this work, see pp. 153–76. For the idea of 'unlimited liability' applied to the military see General Sir John Hackett, *The Profession of Arms* (London: Times Publishing, 1962), p. 63. For a recent article arguing the case for a traditional army see, 'How Soon Could Our Army Lose a War?', Sir Michael Rose, *Daily Telegraph*, 16 December 1997.
29. Sabine, *History*, pp. 607–19.
30. Arthur Swinsom, *Kohima* (London: Cassell, 1966), p. 254.
31. Roger Scruton, 'In Defence of the Nation', in Roger Scruton, *The Philosopher on Dover Beach* (Manchester: Carcanet, 1990), p. 310.
32. *Select Committee (1996)*, p. 99.

33. *Select Committee (1996)*, p. 185.
34. *Select Committee (1996)*, p. 182.
35. *Wolfenden Committee*, para. 61.
36. Iris Marion Young, *Justice and the Politics of Difference* (Princeton, NJ: Princeton University Press, 1990), p. 161. I owe this source to David Miller, *Nationality* (Oxford: Clarendon, 1997), p. 131. Miller's discussion of multiculturalism is very stimulating.
37. Miller, *Nationality*, p. 132.
38. Peter Tatchell, *We Don't Want to March Straight* (London: Cassell, 1995), pp. 32–3.
39. See, John Keegan, 'Regimental Ideology', in Geoffrey Best and Andrew Wheatcroft (eds), *War, Economy and the Military Mind* (London: Croom Helm, 1976), pp. 3–18.
40. For discussion of the difficulty of pluralistic societies having common goals see Raymond Plant, 'Community: Conception and Ideology', *Politics and Society* 8 (1), 1978, pp. 79–107.
41. *Select Committee (1996)*, p. 217.
42. *Report of the Homosexuality Policy Assessment Team* (London: Ministry of Defence, 1996).
43. *Report of the Homosexuality Policy Assessment Team*, p. 116. The statement was, 'In a Service Environment, heterosexuals would find the presence of known homosexuals offensive'.
44. *Report of the Homosexuality Policy Assessment Team*, p. 116.
45. *Report of the Homosexuality Policy Assessment Team*, p. 116. The statement was, 'The thought of sexual acts between two men revolts me'.
46. *Report of the Homosexuality Policy Assessment Team*, p. 227.
47. *British Military Doctrine* (London: HMSO, 1997), pp. 5, 10–11.
48. *Select Committee (1996)*, p. 99.
49. *Select Committee (1996)*, p.186, para. 55.
50. *Discipline and Standards Paper*.
51. *Discipline and Standards Paper*.
52. *Select Committee (1996)*, p. 91, para. 700.
53. *Select Committee (1996)*, p. 183, para. 23.
54. *The Report of the Homosexuality Policy Assessment Team* took considerable narrative evidence from serving military personnel along these lines.
55. *Select Committee (1996)*, p. 102, para. 776.
56. *Wolfenden*, para. 144. The replacement of military leadership by military management in this argument is revealing and possibly indicates a misunderstanding of military life.
57. James Adair in *Wolfenden*, p. 122, para. 11.
58. *House of Lords*, vol. 266, col. 247, 1965.
59. *Discipline and Standards Paper*.
60. Patrick Devlin, *The Enforcement of Morals* (Oxford: Oxford University Press, 1965), (12th impression, 1990); H.L.A. Hart, *Law, Liberty and Morality* (Oxford: Oxford University Press, 1963).
61. Devlin, *Enforcement*, p. 13.
62. Devlin, *Enforcement*, pp. 9–14.
63. 'It is not a question of moral judgement, nor is there any suggestion that homosexuals are any less courageous than heterosexual personnel.' *Select Committee (1996)*, p. 217.
64. *Select Committee (1996)*, p. 181.
65. Devlin, *Enforcement*, p. 15
66. The section in the Ministry of Defence's own report that deals with health issues and homosexual servicemen foresees relatively few health problems if homosexuals are admitted to the services. See *Report of the Homosexuality Policy Assessment Team*, pp. 181–6. However, conservative and pro–family supporters have little difficulty in making a case based on published medical journal papers to show the inequality of outcomes of the heterosexual and homosexual lifestyles. See, for example, Ronald Ray, *Gays in or Out?*

(London: Brassey's, 1993); T. Schmidt, *Straight and Narrow?* (Leicester: Inter Varsity Press, 1995); Stephen Green, *The Sexual Dead End* (London: Broad View, 1992). For an alternative interpretation of health issues in this area, see Gwyn Harries-Jenkins and Christopher Dandeker, 'Sexual Orientation and Military Service: The British Case', in W.J Scott and S.C. Stanley (eds), *Gays and Lesbians in the Military* (New York: Aldine de Gruyter, 1994). pp. 191–204.

67. Tatchell, *We Don't Want*, p. 21.
68. *Social Trends* (London: HMSO, 1996).
69. *Report of the Homosexuality Policy Assessment Team*, pp. 18–19.
70. *Report of the Homosexuality Policy Assessment Team*, pp. 18–19.
71. *British Military Doctrine*, p. A3.
72. *British Military Doctrine*, p. A3.
73. *British Military Doctrine*.
74. Carl von Clausewitz, *On War*, ed. and trans. Michael Howard and Peter Paret (Princeton, NJ: Princeton University Press, 1976), p. 184.
75. *Report of the Homosexuality Policy Assessment Team*
76. *Select Committee (1996)*, p. 178.
77. Christie Davies, *Permissive Britain* (London: Pitman, 1975), p. 138.
78. A useful and accessible overview of these issues is Gerald Garvey and John Dilulio, 'Only Connect', *The New Republic*, 26 April 1993, pp. 18–21. A critique of the argument that homosexuals affect military cohesion and morale can be found in Lois Shawver, *And the Flag was still There* (Binghampton, NY: Harrington Park Press, 1994), Chapter 7.
79. Francis Fukuyama, *Trust: The Social Virtues and the Creation of Prosperity* (London: Hamish Hamilton, 1995).
80. Francis Fukuyama, *The End of Order* (London: Social Market Foundation, 1997), p. 4.
81. Martin Van Creveld, *Fighting Power* (London: Arms and Armour Press, 1983).
82. Richard Holmes, *Firing Line* (London: Penguin, 1984).
83. Clausewitz, *On War*, p. 187.
84. Winston Churchill, House of Commons, *Official Report*, 8 August 1904; vol. 139, col. 1415.
85. Field Marshal Slim, *Defeat into Victory* (London: Cassell, 1956), pp. 182–3.
86. See Sebastian de Grazia, *Machiavelli in Hell* (London: Macmillan, 1996), p. 97.
87. One illustration of this in the legal debate about law and homosexuality is Hart's criticism of Devlin's views that they are typical, historically, of the English judiciary. Hart, *Law, Liberty*, p. 63; and Devlin, *Enforcement*, p. 125.

10

Race Relations in the Army

Stuart Crawford

This chapter is based almost entirely on the research I undertook during my Defence Fellowship at Glasgow University in 1995–96. I would stress, therefore, that I am describing in the main what I found then. Secondly, although I do not intend to talk about the recommendations of my Defence Fellowship Report, it is only fair to say at the outset that many of them have been taken up and implemented in the intervening period, although I suspect these developments were more the result of parallel work elsewhere than they were to do with my suggestions. That said, I believe that the evidence I produced to support my thesis is still relevant, if for no other reason than it has yet to be challenged either by re-interpretation by others or by the production of evidence to the contrary. I should also mention that this is the first officially approved airing of my Defence Fellowship work in public, although it has had unofficially sanctioned exposure in the House of Lords, the *Daily Telegraph*, and the BBC2 television programme *Black Britain*.

The armed services' inability to recruit and retain sailors, soldiers, and airmen from Britain's ethnic minorities has been brought increasingly to notice over the past decade. In 1986, HRH The Prince of Wales first publicly voiced his concern at the lack of ethnic representation in the Brigade of Guards and Household Cavalry, and his interest undoubtedly focused attention on the issues both in the general public and within the Ministry of Defence. Indeed, some expert observers believe he was the catalyst for the modern debate.[1] It is also clear that his interest did not diminish with time; as recently as September 1994 a meeting was convened at Highgrove at his request to discuss the lack of ethnic minority recruiting to the Household Division, during which it was agreed that 'decisive action was required if the situation were to improve'.[2]

The statistics speak for themselves; visible ethnic minorities[3] probably constitute some 6–7 per cent of the population of the United Kingdom today, and perhaps as much as 16 per cent[4] of the population in the vital 16–24 age bracket, the traditional recruiting ground for the services. In contrast, these same visible ethnic minorities made up just 1.4 per cent of the regular armed forces as at 1 October 1994, with the proportion of officers significantly lower at approximately 0.9 per cent.[5] Anecdotal evidence, including observations from serving commanding officers, suggests that this proportion has fallen in the last ten years or so.[6] This has been noted in Hansard, which recorded in 1991: 'Although no figures are available, some officers are certain that the number of black soldiers has declined in the last decade. One Green Jackets officer estimated that nearly 10 per cent of their soldiers were black in the 1970s.'[7] Proving this, however, is virtually impossible, for the services did not practise any formal system of ethnic monitoring in the period 1969–87, and, arguably, only in 1997 began to have a proper understanding of their ethnic composition.

ETHNIC MONITORING

Parliament has, in recent years, devoted a considerable amount of time and effort addressing equal opportunities in the armed services. Debates in both Houses have emphasised two major issues. The first has been the question of ethnic monitoring of service personnel, based on the premise that an accurate measure of ethnic minority servicemen is an essential prerequisite for dealing with racial problems. Ethnic monitoring was vigorously resisted by the Ministry of Defence for some considerable time. Monitoring at the recruitment stage, it was claimed, would undermine the services' declared policy of 'colour blindness' which allegedly ensured that all potential servicemen were treated equally regardless of race or ethnic background. Monitoring of serving personnel was resisted on the basis that it might prove 'divisive', in that promotion and employment could be positively or negatively affected if ethnic background was openly recorded.

Political pressure was a major factor in gradually overcoming the Ministry's objections. Ethnic monitoring was introduced from 1986 onwards, and by mid-1996 a comprehensive system of ethnic monitoring in the Regular Army had been introduced. From then on, every recruit entering the Army was obliged to declare his ethnic origin on a form provided for the purpose, whilst serving soldiers were surveyed yet again. A year into the initiative the Army felt it had a firm handle on its ethnic composition, and the Defence Analytical Statistics Agency now has sufficient material to carry out statistical analysis in some depth. However, while the Regular Army now has the necessary procedures in place to maintain its records appropriately, the scheme is only now being implemented in the Territorial Army and the Reserves.

RACIAL HARASSMENT AND DISCRIMINATION

The second major topic of parliamentary debate is that of racial discrimination and harassment within the armed forces. Questions on racial discrimination in the services have featured frequently in House of Commons debates over the past ten years. The government has persistently denied that there are major problems of this nature in the armed forces. Racial incidents, it has said, are few and far between and individually, as opposed to institutionally, inspired, although evidence to substantiate this statement has not to my knowledge been produced. Perhaps unsurprisingly the topic refused to go away and public pressure, expressed in the main through Parliament and the media, has led to a certain amount of action being taken.

In 1989, for example, concerned at under-representation from the ethnic minorities in the armed forces, the Ministry of Defence commissioned the management consultants, Peat Marwick McLintock, to assess the services' recruitment criteria and practices. Although their report[8] specifically concerned recruitment, and therefore considered matters outside the remit of this chapter, it produced one important finding. This was that the main disincentive to ethnic minorities joining the armed forces was fear of racial discrimination. From a sample of 511 Afro-Caribbeans and 512 Asians in the 15–24 age bracket, 60 per cent of the Afro-Caribbeans and 49 per cent of the Asians said they would expect to experience racial discrimination if they were in the armed forces. This attitude would appear to have been based largely on media reporting. The services were seen by them as racist, and no place for members of the ethnic minority population to attempt a career. This begged the question of how much racial discrimination there actually is in the armed forces. Answering this is far from straightforward and calls for the examination of a number of information sources.

OFFICIAL SOURCES

Given the high political profile of the topic, I was surprised to discover that no comprehensive records had been kept of racially motivated incidents in any of the services. As late as February 1989, Parliament was informed that central records were kept only of cases submitted to the Service Boards, which are discussed below. There *was* gradual progress over the years, however, and in January 1994 the government was able to inform Parliament that there had been a total of 29 complaints of racial discrimination made by Army and RAF personnel in the period 1988–93, and reiterated the Royal Navy's plan to introduce a recording system early that year.[9] These figures almost certainly recorded only a fraction of service racial discrimination incidents, as will be seen later.

Records of Service Boards of Inquiry *are*, however, one source of information on racial discrimination in the armed forces. These boards are convened in cases of alleged racial discrimination when servicemen have either been dissatisfied with the results of initial action taken or have applied formally for redress of grievance. Instigating such a formal and potentially damaging (both to the unit and, sadly, to the complainant) procedure is a daunting prospect, particularly to younger and more junior servicemen. It comes as no surprise to find, therefore, that relatively few Boards of Inquiry have been convened to investigate allegations of racial discrimination, and consequently as a source of statistical information, their records are of limited use. But they do provide a useful official record of the issues involved, and indicate the form and nature of racial discrimination inside the services. Records of proceedings from Army Boards of Inquiry in the period 1991–93, for example, illustrate the wide variety of problems that ethnic minority servicemen have encountered. These range across verbal racial abuse, victimisation, the unfair allocation of duties on account of race, physical abuse, and the changing of posting orders on account of a serviceman's colour. Not all allegations are substantiated in every case, but the most common experience was that of verbal abuse. Ethnic minority servicemen have been variously and routinely addressed as 'coon', 'coco', 'rubber lips', 'nigger', 'black bastard', 'black boy', and 'spade' amongst others, and it is obviously most distressing to the recipients when such unacceptable language is used by superior or employing officers. It is clear that such racial name calling was widespread, and one board remarked that it was 'disturbed by the view, expressed at all levels, that some degree of racial remarks and name-calling, referred to as "racial banter", was acceptable'. More than one board recorded in its findings that there was no extant Ministry of Defence policy on the use of racial language and that a permanent policy was required, providing clear instructions on racial language, for the benefit of both the Ministry of Defence and its soldiers.[10]

The few more recent official investigations into racial matters in the services have also attempted to define the extent of the problem. In late 1995 the Ministry of Defence commissioned the Office for Public Management to carry out a review of its equal opportunities policies, procedures, and practices, looking at the three services and the civilian part of the Ministry of Defence. Its Final Report[11] is essentially generalist in approach, but contains some fairly robust criticisms of the workings of the Ministry of Defence. In Chapter 3, for example, it pulls no punches in saying '[g]iven the level of scrutiny experienced by the Army (and by implication at least, the other two Services) we find it disappointing that there is still relatively little acknowledgement of the pervasive, long running and deeply entrenched problem of racism within the Armed Services ...'. It is also highly critical of the services' claims that they are proudly and intentionally 'colour blind' and that such racial problems as do exist are confined to the occasional and unintentional mistreatment of an individual. Such perspectives, states the Report, 'fall short of those which might be expected from a major employer who is actively and purposefully seeking to ensure equality of opportunity'.[12]

The Report also discusses a number of other aspects in its attempts to define the problem, including failures in leadership and the need for British society to be broadly reflected in a diverse armed service. In the latter case, it found 'a profound ambiguity and difference about whether this is a desirable goal among officers at both senior and middle levels'.[13] It also devotes considerable attention to the subject of racial name-calling observed, noting that it was widespread, particularly in training units. It concludes that such behaviour is unacceptable, but with a lack of clarity on attitudes to the phenomenon among senior officers which would not be reflected among senior managers in outside, i.e. non-service, organisations.

In summary, the Report is a fairly damning exposition of the state of race relations in the services as a whole. Indeed, it states that 'the negativity of public perceptions of race issues in the armed services is such that the civilian arm [of the Ministry of Defence] believes itself to be 'contaminated' by them'.[14] But, while clearly acknowledging that there are serious problems with race relations in the services, it does not produce any empirical evidence in the Report itself to support its opinion. The Report's recommendations are similarly broad, and thus we need to look elsewhere for further evidence of racial discrimination.

OTHER SOURCES

Other sources of information on the state of race relations within the armed forces are thin on the ground and largely anecdotal. There is very little in the way of recent British writing which concentrates exclusively on the issues of race and ethnicity in all or any of the three services. This in itself may be evidence of the reluctance to examine the problem. Such commentaries as do exist fall into three broad categories; those contained in books, military and other journals, and the press.

References to military racial and ethnic matters in British published books are limited. They tend to comprise anything from a couple of paragraphs to a few pages in military works of a more general nature, usually written by ex-serving officers. For example, in his book *Inside The British Army*, Antony Beevor, an ex-regular officer in the 11th Hussars, briefly discusses racial harassment and racism in the Army. He attempts to explain its existence by suggesting that '[m]ilitary life is likely to appeal to teenagers with skinhead prejudices, and one or two vitriolic characters are enough to stir up trouble against a black recruit' and that 'self appointed guardians of the barrack block flame think that to chase out blacks is to defend the honour of the regiment'.[15] He states, though, that racism is not endemic and that in 'elite' organisations like the Royal Marines and Parachute Regiment it is relatively rare. As the entrance procedure for both these units is relatively strenuous and highly selective, those who pass are much more likely to be judged on their merits than their race or ethnic background. He also suggests that overt racism is much less likely to occur in units where there are a number of ethnic minority soldiers already serving, as newcomers will not find themselves isolated.

Hugh McManners, another ex-regular officer and now Defence Editor of the *Sunday Times*, comments in *The Scars of War* that '[t]he Guards, Household Cavalry, and some other regiments, despite their regular denials, also practise an informal but effective colour bar'.[16] He goes on to suggest that in these regiments tradition has taken on a Masonic quality that has little to do with military efficiency, and the regiment itself decides who will be admitted. The suggestion is, of course, that these decisions are taken in a culture where ethnic minorities are not welcome. Neither of these authors are as forthright, however, as Yardley and Sewell, who in *A New Model Army* (published in 1989) were highly critical of the Army's response to allegations of widespread racism in the ranks. They argued that a large part of the problem was that the Army generally refuses to acknowledge that it has any racial difficulties. On the occasions when it does, it tends to blame attitudes from civilian society seeping into the Army. This, declared Yardley and Sewell, is nonsense, stating bluntly that '[a]nyone who has ever met any soldiers would know ... that they are amongst the worst racial bigots in society'.[17] They conclude that the Army does little to tackle its very real racial problems.

Unlike in the USA, in Britain there have been few articles in magazines and journals on the topic. In the Army's own in-house journal, *British Army Review,* the subject has been touched upon occasionally over the past ten years, most recently by my own essay in the December 1995 issue.[18] Elsewhere articles have occasionally appeared in such publications as *Equal Opportunities Review* and *Searchlight,* the 'International Anti-Fascist Monthly'.[19] It is clear, however, that the military debate on sociological issues in the UK is not nearly as well developed as it is in the USA, where journals such as *Military Review* and *Armed Forces and Society* carry articles on the sociological aspects of the military, in-cluding race and ethnicity, on a fairly regular basis. In short, little information on racial discrimination in the British armed services is currently available in journals in this country.

In contrast, racism, racial discrimination, and the interaction of ethnic minorities and the armed services have featured extensively in the press over the last decade. Indeed, the press has probably been, together with political pressure, one of the main factors behind the changes forced upon the Ministry of Defence and services in the period. And, although television and radio have participated, it has been the newspapers which have been most persistent and effective in their championing of the cause. Both 'quality' and 'tabloid' sections have been active throughout, and their collective reporting has been remarkably comprehensive; the course of the modern debate on race relations in the Army can be traced reasonably accurately from newspaper articles alone.

Newspaper coverage can be broken down into two broad categories; that which deals in general terms with the subject matter and that which focuses on specific incidents and individuals. Such a classification is fairly arbitrary, and there is considerable overlap between the two. Indeed, it is often a specific event which forms the basis of the general articles. The broadsheets have tended to carry more of the general articles while the popular press is much more likely to highlight the personal experiences of ethnic minority servicemen. Interestingly, newspaper reporting concentrates almost exclusively on the Army, and there is little mention of the other two services.

In 1986, around the same time as the first reports of the concerns of HRH The

Prince of Wales, the *Observer* carried what with hindsight might be described as the seminal newspaper article of the modern debate. In 'The Thin White Line', the result of two months' investigation, the then topical subject of lack of ethnic minority Guardsmen at Trooping the Colour was discussed, followed by a wide-ranging examination of the state of race relations in the Army in the same article. The *Observer* claimed that black and Asian soldiers were frequently subject to personal abuse and discrimination, were much less likely to be promoted because of their colour, and stood 'virtually no chance' of becoming officers. Additionally, the article claimed that a large number of black and Asian soldiers were to be found in service regiments such as the Royal Pioneer Corps, the Catering Corps, and the Royal Corps of Transport,[20] and that very few made it into the 'elite regiments like the cavalry'. A great deal of the *Observer*'s evidence came from interviews with soldiers and ex-soldiers from the ethnic minority community, and the researchers worked in close collaboration with the Commission on Racial Equality. Finally, the paper bemoaned the lack of relevant Ministry of Defence statistics and could only hazard a guess that between 3,000 and 6,000 of the Army's strength at that time of 163,000 was 'coloured'.[21]

The *Observer*'s lead was followed by other British newspapers in the following months, and the perceived need for the Army to introduce a system of ethnic monitoring was the favourite topic for discussion. The press campaign was partially vindicated in November 1986 when, as previously mentioned, ethnic monitoring of all new recruits from 1 April 1987 was announced. However, as *The Times* was again to point out in early 1987, recruit monitoring would not show whether blacks and Asians had equal access to elite units and whether they enjoyed equal promotion prospects.[22]

Around this time the Ministry of Defence commissioned the Peat Marwick McLintock Report to which reference has already been made. The major finding of that Report, that young people from the ethnic minorities were shunning careers in the forces mainly because of fear of racial discrimination, was seized upon eagerly by the press. Their interest was no doubt greatly increased by senior Ministry of Defence officials, despite the Report's findings, continuing to state that there was in fact scarcely any racial discrimination in the services at all![23]

More recently the press has given wide coverage to the Commission on Racial Equality Report on the Household Cavalry and its wider implications for the services as a whole.[24] This Report, discussed later on, prompted the media to revisit the whole topic of race and the services once more, with ethnic monitoring, racism and racial harassment, and the better known cases of racial discrimination, again featuring in the news. So too have official denials that 'there is widespread discrimination in the Army as a whole or in the other two Services'.[25] Overall, therefore, press coverage of the general aspects of race and the services has been steady and has kept the subject in the public domain. Coverage of the more prominent cases of racial discrimination which have arisen has also played its part.

All the cases which have achieved national press publicity involve more or less the same scenarios of abuse, victimisation, and general racial intolerance, but three are particularly worthy of mention. These are the cases of Guardsman Stokes, Private Anderson, and Corporal Malcolm.[26] Each of these have aspects which differentiate them from other recorded cases. Guardsman Stokes was the first modern day black Guardsman and therefore a press celebrity in his own right, Private Anderson's case led the Ministry of Defence to revise its procedures for dealing with such matters at Army Board level, and Corporal Malcolm's complaint led directly to the Commission on Racial Equality Report on the Household Cavalry.

Guardsman Richard Stokes took up guard duties at Buckingham Palace on 15 May 1988, in a blaze of publicity, watched by a crowd of some 2,000 people. He was the first black Guardsman to do so and his presence in the sentry box outside the Palace was seen as a major breakthrough in military race relations and vindication of the efforts of, amongst many others, The Prince of Wales. Sadly, Guardsman Stokes declined to serve more than his initial three year engagement. Although he left the service without making any formal complaints, some allegations of racial intolerance have since emerged. What had been trumpeted as proof of the Army's egalitarian regime had the opposite effect in the end, and Guardsman Stokes' experience only reinforced public perceptions of the Army, and the services, as racist.

Private Stephen Anderson joined the Devon and Dorset Regiment in 1983 and was the only black soldier in his platoon. Between then and his medical discharge from the Army in 1988 he claimed he had been both verbally and physically abused on several occasions on account of his colour. Anderson, after complaining unsuccessfully to his Commanding Officer, pursued the matter up the chain of command as far as the Army Board. The Commission on Racial Equality then backed Anderson in his quest for a judicial review of the Army Board's decision not to grant him redress or compensation. Anderson was successful, and in November 1990 the High Court quashed the Army decision. It was found that the Army's handling of the matter was 'flawed in a number of respects'. Subsequently, and after another military hearing, Anderson was awarded £600 compensation. The importance of this particular case is that it established the principles under which future cases were to be heard, but more generally the attention it drew was again unhelpful for the Army's record on race relations.

The last case is that of Corporal Jake Malcolm of the Royal Electrical and Mechanical Engineers (REME). Corporal Malcolm, a clerk, was posted to the light aid detachment (LAD) of the Life Guards on his return from the Gulf War. However, after being told by the senior Warrant Officer of the Life Guard's LAD that they 'were a difficult regiment to serve with at the best of times' without the problem of being black, he found himself reposted to the 4th Royal Tank Regiment.[27] Backed by the Commission on Racial Equality, Malcolm applied for redress of grievance and at a Board of Inquiry which sat in November 1992 it was found that he had in fact suffered discrimination. He was subsequently awarded

£6,500 in compensation. What made Malcolm's case particularly important, though, was that evidence given during his Inquiry persuaded the Commission on Racial Equality that racial discrimination of the kind Malcolm suffered might be widespread, and led directly to the two-year Commission on Racial Equality investigation into the Household Cavalry. This Report will be discussed below.

It was clear to me, therefore, that existing sources of information indicated that racial harassment, discrimination, and general racial intolerance did exist in the Army. The information from both official and other records also suggested, perhaps, that such problems might be widespread, despite constant official denials that this was the case. What was missing, however, were credible statistics to prove the extent and prevalence of these incidents. All that could be said up until this point, therefore, was that there was a suspicion of widespread racial discrimination with no means of proving it.

THE RACE RELATIONS QUESTIONNAIRE

Given this lack of statistical information, it became clear that for my study some attempt would have to be made to gauge the extent of racial problems in the services. I decided early on that the best way of collecting such information was by a self-completed postal questionnaire. Quantitative data secured by questionnaire should be reinforced by qualitative information, and so a number of interviews were conducted with serving ethnic minority personnel. Finally, the Commission on Racial Equality Report on the Household Cavalry was published on 27 March 1996, providing me at the time with an in-depth and up-to-date assessment of the state of race relations in one particular regiment.

Some problems immediately confronted the proposed questionnaire. The subject matter was undoubtedly controversial within military circles, and initial responses from the Ministry of Defence were not encouraging. The Army's Employment Policy branch was keen and ready to support the project but was not optimistic that it would be allowed. The Defence Analytical Services Agency (DASA) was most helpful and offered assistance at every stage, but naturally required me to have official permission to carry out the survey. Thankfully, eventually the Ministry of Defence sanctioned it and it went ahead.

The purpose of the survey was to collect information on the prevalence and extent of racial discrimination within the armed forces. However, there were a number of additional questions required to obtain a broader understanding of the major race relations issues. For example, I thought it important to discover the forms that racial discrimination took in the military, and what action was taken by the victims. Did they formally apply for redress, and if not, why not? What action was taken by the authorities on receipt of complaints, and were the complainants satisfied with the outcomes? Finally, all respondents were asked whether they thought there was racial discrimination in the services, regardless as to whether or not they had experienced it.

The questionnaire was sent out in early 1996 to a random, stratified sample of 1,600 Army personnel. In an attempt to secure a high response rate, question-naires were delivered in bulk to participating units with the request that they be returned in bulk on completion. Respondents were spread across all units and ranks, and the racial balance was established at 1,200 white respondents and 400 from the ethnic minorities. As expected, the survey caused a certain amount of controversy when questionnaires were received by units, but overall few complaints were made.

By late March 1996, some 803 individuals had responded, a 51.5 per cent return. I found this mildly disappointing, but DASA thought the response was good considering the anonymous and voluntary nature of the survey. What was more interesting was the difference in response rates between the ranks and different ethnic groups. The response rate for white officers and other ranks was 64.7 per cent and 55 per cent respectively. The corresponding percentages for black officers and other ranks was 35 per cent and 35.5 per cent, and for Asians 57.1 per cent and 18.9 per cent. In all, a total of 655 white and 146 ethnic minority servicemen responded, with two who declined to be classified. Why the response rate for the ethnic minority servicemen should be low compared to their white colleagues remains, sadly, a matter for speculation. There is some evidence that the administration of the survey was tampered with at unit level; this is unlikely, though, to have discouraged more than a handful.

Selected questions

Question 5   'Whilst serving in the Army, have you ever been, or have you ever felt that you have been, the victim of racial discrimination as defined by the Race Relations Act 1976?'

From the total of 803 respondents, 103 or 12.8 per cent answered 'yes' to this question. Those who answered 'no' constituted 86.6 per cent, while 0.6 per cent did not answer. At first glance this might appear to vindicate the official denial of widespread racial discrimination in the Army. However, when the statistics are broken down further, they show that while only 3.5 per cent of white respon-dents answered positively, 54.1 per cent of ethnic minority respondents stated that they had been the victims of racial discrimination. Accepting that most racial discrimination is perpetrated by whites on non-whites, this would seem to indicate that there was a significant problem.

Question 8   'Did you take any action to seek official redress for being a victim of racial discrimination?'

Of 103 respondents who had been victims of racial discrimination, only 14 individuals, 13.6 per cent, sought redress through official channels. This showed quite simply that the Army's grievance procedure at that time did not work for victims of racial offences.

Question 9   'Having been a victim of racial discrimination, why did you not seek official redress?'

The answers to this question show why the Army's grievance procedure was not working. Respondents could identify more than one reason if appropriate, and therefore absolute numbers do not match the 89 individuals who said they had taken no action. Forty individuals, approximately 45 per cent, said they did not complain because they believed such a step might adversely affect their careers. Twenty-seven (30 per cent) thought they would not be taken seriously; 23 (26 per cent) feared increased discrimination; while 20 (23 per cent) did not complain because the person to whom they would have had to make representations was the same person who was discriminating against them. Only 12 (14 per cent) said they did not know what to do about the discrimination they suffered. It is clear, therefore, that the majority of ethnic minority servicemen who suffered racial discrimination knew that something could be done about it, but most chose to take no action because they feared the consequences. Keeping quiet was seen as the best way of coping.

Question 15   'Even if you have not personally suffered racial discrimination, do you think there is racial discrimination in the Army?'
    Two-thirds (66 per cent) of all respondents to this question thought there was either a lot, some or a little racial discrimination in the Army. When analysed by ethnic group, 60.6 per cent of white respondents fell into these categories compared to 89.8 of those from the ethnic minorities. Perhaps the latter statistic is unsurprising, but the former suggests there is a general acknowledgement from white servicemen that racial problems exist.

Question 16   'If you have ticked "a lot of discrimination", "some discrimination" or "little discrimination" to Question 15, please describe why you think there is racial discrimination in the Army.'
    The answers to this question produced a vast amount of data and the bulk of it still awaits exploration. Responses varied from one or two lines to two or three pages, and examples of racial discrimination given by a large number of respondents gives a fascinating, and in some cases most disturbing, picture of the state of race relations in the Army. Respondents had witnessed or suffered all sorts of racial discrimination. As one might have expected, verbal abuse was most frequently recorded, and there was much discussion about whether any level of 'racial' language was acceptable. Denial of job opportunities or promotion was another frequent complaint, as was the unfair allocation of less pleasant tasks. Assessment of all replies to this question identified four major themes.
    First, a very large proportion of respondents held the opinion that the racial discrimination they acknowledged occurred in the Army was not the Army's fault. Society in general was to blame, and it was no surprise that racial intolerance in the civilian population was reflected in the services. Although all replies were anonymous, it was easy to discern that this rationalisation was particularly popular amongst officers. Some might say this provides a convenient excuse for not tackling the problem. Such statements inevitably led on to the argument that racial discrimination was therefore unavoidable and little could be done about it

until society changed. Regrettably, there seemed to be a common attitude of resigned acceptance that the organisation had a certain level of endemic racial intolerance.

Second, there was a widely held belief that certain units and regiments were well known for their racial intolerance. The Guards, Household Cavalry, and Scottish Division were frequently described as being bastions of racial discrimination. One officer reported being told at Sandhurst by an instructor that he could not apply for the Guards because he was black. Another respondent, who identified himself as a white Guardsman, stated quite bluntly '[i]f I were black, the last Regiment I would join would be the Guards'. Such widespread condemnation of these particular regiments is supported by evidence already presented, and it seems unlikely that such opinions are entirely unfounded. Indeed, evidence from the Commission on Racial Equality's recent investigation into one particular regiment, which I will touch on later, further endorses them. Inside the services, as well as outside, these organisations have an unenviable reputation as racist.

Third, there were many more descriptions of racism occurring within training organisations than there were of it taking place in regular units. Sadly, the training establishments have been the subject of allegations of misconduct before, particularly in cases of bullying of recruits, and accusations of racial abuse there sound all too familiar. Why racial discrimination in training units should be so prevalent is not entirely clear, but there are obvious links with bullying in the abuse of power by instructors, the singling out of distinctive individuals for attention, and the feelings of helplessness on the part of the victims. One would have thought that such establishments, which provide the bedrock of the Army, would be manned by instructors of the highest calibre who would be beyond such behaviour. From the evidence gathered here this would not appear to have been the case.

Finally, there was a certain amount of resentment that ethnic minority servicemen were seen to take advantage of racial sensitivity. Usually referred to as 'playing the race card', it was alleged that trumped-up claims of racial discrimination enabled soldiers of an ethnic minority background to avoid unpleasant tasks, pass training courses with marginal marks, and occasionally to gain undeserved promotion. In other words, many white respondents complained of positive discrimination in favour of blacks. In addition, some thought that ethnic minority servicemen brought many of their troubles upon themselves by isolating themselves from whites by forming groups and cliques and adopting overt racial or ethnic styles of dress and speech. This, it was claimed, created widespread resentment.

Taken overall, the answers to this particular question provide a most interesting source of internal attitudes to race and ethnicity in the Army. Perhaps the most appropriate and emotive summary was provided by one officer, who wrote thus: '[i]nstitutionalised racism is endemic in the British Army and is actively supported by senior officers as a means of preserving our "cultural heritage"; it is witnessed in the barrack block, on the sports pitch and, most noticeably, on the parade grounds of the Household Division. Whilst the WASP working practices are supported and enshrined in Queen's Regulations it will be ever thus.'

Overall, the survey seemed to indicate three main things. First, despite official denials over the years, racial discrimination was widespread[28] in the Army. Further examination of the data may show its extent geographically, regimentally, and by sex and rank. Next, only a small fraction of those who experienced it complained or made representations via the Army's internal grievance procedure; most did not because they believed that to do so would adversely affect their careers. Finally, just over half of those who did complain were not satisfied with the outcome. This last statistic, however, has to be treated with a certain amount of caution on account of the small sample size. Nevertheless, the results suggest that there was a significant problem of racial discrimination and that the grievance procedure in place was not adequate.

Interviews

The purpose of the interviews was to provide an initial qualitative cross-check on the quantitative results of the Race Relations Questionnaire. My academic supervisor, Mr John Money, undertook the interviews on my behalf and produced a short report.[29] The interviews were structured around a number of individual interviews, plus an extended focus group session. Personnel who took part in individual interviews were not involved in the focus group and vice versa, and both were carried out on different days. All sessions were completely confidential; individual soldiers were free to keep their identities private, which most preferred to do. After initial reticence, understandable in the circumstances, the dialogue of the interviews was characterised by a full and easy discussion of the soldiers' experience of, and views on, the problem of race relations in the Army.

A number of themes arose from the interviews. Without exception, all interviewees were of the view that racial discrimination did exist in the Army, and that it could at times be a serious problem. They claimed that it had detrimental effects on either their career prospects or the quality of their service lives, and in some cases both. They felt it had a detrimental effect on the recruiting and retention of black soldiers. Again, all but one were strongly of the view that until the Army accepted that racial discrimination was widespread there was no real chance that it would ever be tackled effectively.

The report on the interviews makes three general observations. The first is that a relatively low-level, background racism seems to be the norm in the Army today. It does not often seem to interfere seriously with either discipline or operational efficiency generally, possibly because it seems to be a point of pride amongst many blacks that they should not succumb to it, much less be driven out by it. However, the report suggests that racism in the Army may be a more widespread problem than the frictions normally found in an institutional environment, that it does nothing to encourage recruiting or retention amongst black soldiers, and that it may be a standing encouragement to the spread of more racist behaviour amongst those so inclined. Second, the evidence from the interviews suggests that there are, as in the rest of society, deeply bigoted individuals in the Army who tend to operate by covert administrative manipulation. Such individuals tend to use neglect, omission, falsification, and negative half-truths in their attempts to disadvantage ethnic minority servicemen. These are far deadlier weapons than outright abuse or intimidation, easier to camouflage, and harder to trace.

Finally, while none of the examples of racial discrimination identified in the interviews can be substantiated lest anonymity be betrayed, the interviewer felt that the frequency, sincerity, similarity, and the plausibility of the accounts given, considered alongside evidence garnered from other sources, suggested that they are representative of a much wider and deeper problem than has so far been acknowledged. Clearly, these interviews reinforced the evidence from elsewhere.

The last evidence I want to look at is in the Commission on Racial Equality Report on the Household Cavalry.[30] For some considerable time the Commission had been concerned about allegations of racial discrimination in the armed forces. As has been discussed, much of the evidence has tended to be anecdotal and unsubstantiated. However, allegations involving the Brigade of Guards and Household Cavalry had regularly arisen. At the same time, the Commission has been until recently unimpressed by the Ministry of Defence's efforts to implement equal opportunities policies. Against this background, the Commission was informed of the Army Board of Inquiry decision in 1993 in the case of Corporal Malcolm, whose posting to the Life Guards had been cancelled because of his colour. The circumstances of the Malcolm case, and the evidence it considered, confirmed the Commission's suspicions that there might be racial discrimination in recruitment, selection, and postings to the Household Cavalry. In January 1994, the Commission notified the Ministry of Defence of its intention of carrying out a formal investigation into these matters.

Approximately two years later, after review of all the evidence gathered during the investigation, and after representations from the Ministry of Defence on the Report's provisional conclusions had been considered, the Commission published its conclusions under five main headings. First, it concluded that there was indirect discrimination in officer recruitment and selection in the Household Cavalry which manifested itself in preference being given to candidates who had a connection with the regiment or who came from a particular background. Next, 'on a balance of probabilities' it decided that there had been unlawful discrimination in the arrangements made for determining who should be offered soldier employment in the Household Cavalry. Similarly, since even the Ministry of Defence accepted that Corporal Malcolm had been discriminated against when his posting was altered, the Commission found that there was direct discrimination in postings of other corps and regiments. Fourth, the Report concluded that there was abuse and harassment of ethnic minority soldiers in the Household Cavalry and that 'only serious and sustained efforts by all concerned would really eradicate racial abuse'.[31] Finally, the Commission found that instructions or inducements to discriminate had been made by a senior officer in the Household Cavalry in the form of an unlawful instruction to a subordinate officer. In short, the Report is a damning indictment of the state of race relations in that regiment at that time.

SUMMARY

In summary, there seems little doubt that there were indeed significant problems of racism and racial discrimination in the Army at the time of my work. The lack of official statistics on racially motivated or inspired disciplinary incidents, however, made it difficult to gauge its prevalence or extent, and little statistical evidence can be garnered from Records of Service Boards of Inquiry as these are few in number. For my Defence Fellowship, therefore, new research was carried out in an attempt to achieve a better understanding of the extent and prevalence of racial discrimination in the services, and the results support the suspicion that racial discrimination was widespread and endemic. Finally, the Report on the Household Cavalry by the Commission on Racial Equality with its in-depth investigation of the issues in one particular organisation, and subsequent related developments reinforce the evidence from elsewhere. Taken altogether, I believe the evidence to be persuasive.

Space does not permit me to describe or discuss the services' response to such criticisms properly. I think it is fair to say that the response has not always been enthusiastic, but undoubtedly progress has been made. In very general terms, however, the standard reply has tended to be that it is a minority of individuals, not the institutions themselves, who are at fault. I believe that my research lays this myth firmly to rest. The Army, which has received the bulk of the criticism, has gone furthest of all the services in an attempt to solve its problems. It has set up a specialist department to provide a focal point for the issues, has produced an Equal Opportunities Policy Directive, has sensible procedures for ethnic monitoring, has amended to some extent the cumbersome grievance procedure, and has more or less sorted out the training of its personnel. In addition, it has reached agreement with the Commission on Racial Equality on an action plan to sort out the more blatant aspects of racial discrimination identified during the investigation into the Household Cavalry, and the threat of a formal non-discrimination notice has recently been withdrawn. Admittedly, many of the changes now in train were forced upon a reluctant Army and Ministry, but the more enlightened within these organisations see them as essential. Whether the changes proposed go far enough, and indeed how and when they will all actually be implemented fully, remains to be seen.

The importance of their implementation for the future corporate health and well-being of the Army should not, however, be underestimated. I would suggest that only when the Army (and the other two services) loses its unfortunate racist reputation will the ethnic minorities be tempted to join in any numbers. The resultant increased participation from the ethnic minorities may help overcome many of the problems currently being experienced in the recruiting and retention field. More important, perhaps, is the cultural diversity which that increased representation would bring, enriching the collective skills, talents, and experience of the armed services. Ultimately, the services should become truly representative of all that is best in multicultural Britain and be a highly visible sign that Britain's ethnic minorities are indeed an integral part of the nation and its future. Such goals are, I believe, well worth pursuing.

NOTES

1. Interview with Jerome Mack, Equalities Associates, 3 July 1995.
2. Record of decisions taken at a meeting on Ethnic Monitoring Recruiting held at Highgrove on Monday, 12 September 1994.
3. As opposed to 'invisible' ethnic minorities such as Welsh, Irish, Scots, etc.
4. Unofficial figures quoted by Jerome Mack of Equalities Associates during interview on 3 July 1995. The 1991 Census gives the proportion of ethnic minorities in the UK as approximately 5.5 per cent.
5. Defence Analytical Services Agency, *Ethnic Composition of the Regular Armed Forces: Tri Service Personnel Statistics* (London: DASA), 1 October 1994.
6. Lt-Col. J.T. Jackson (1995), personal communication.
7. *Official Report*, 14 March 1991, col. 1267.
8. Peat Marwick McLintock, *Ethnic Monitoring Recruitment to the Armed Services*, Volumes 1–3 (London: KPMG, 1989).
9. *Offcial Report*, 13 January 1994, col. 268.
10. Records of Proceedings of Boards of Inquiry were provided by the Adjutant-General's department of the Ministry of Defence on the understanding that details of individual cases would remain confidential.
11. Office for Public Management, *Review of Ethnic Minority Initiatives: Final Report* (London: OPM, 1996).
12. Ibid., p 7.
13. Ibid., p. 11.
14. Ibid., p. 22.
15. A. Beevor, *Inside the British Army* (London: Corgi, 1991), p. 32.
16. H. McManners, *The Scars of War* (London: HarperCollins, 1993), p. 29.
17. M. Yardley and D. Sewell, *A New Model Army* (London: W.H. Allen & Co, 1989), p. 68.
18. Lt-Col. S.W. Crawford, 'Racial Integration of the Army: An Historical Perspective, *British Army Review*, 111 (1995), pp. 24–8.
19. See, for example, 'Armed Forces to Encourage Ethnic Minority Recruits', *Equal Opportunities Review*, 30 (March/April 1990), and 'Life Guards Abuse Black Recruit', *Searchlight*, 248 (February 1996).
20. All now subsumed into the Royal Logistics Corps (RLC).
21. 'The Thin White Line', *Observer*, 8 June 1986.
22. 'Racism in Forces is Denied', *The Times*, 29 January 1987.

23. See, for example, 'Blacks Shun Armed Services "Because of Discrimination"', *Independent*, 24 January 1990.
24. See, for example, 'Army Pledges to Stamp Out Racism in Ranks', *Independent*, 28 March; and 'Household Cavalry Ordered to Learn Gentle Art of Non-Discrimination', *The Times*, 29 March 1996.
25. See 'Five Year Plan to Combat Racism in the Armed Forces', *Daily Telegraph*, 29 March 1996, p 7.
26. Other cases examined by the author include those of Trooper McKay, Rifleman Ennals, Private Evans, Guardsman Lindsay, Fusilier Yeomans, Guardsman Janjua, Private Singh, Corporal Muir and Trooper Campbell. All contain allegations of racial discrimination and harassment.
27. Informally known as 'Scotland's Own Royal Tank Regiment' and easily the best of the four Royal Tank Regiments at the time in terms of attitude, style and sheer professional competence.
28. Defined as 'widely distributed or disseminated' in *The Concise Oxford Dictionary*.
29. W.J. Money, 'Race Relations in the Army Today' (1996). Report on interviews with black soldiers on behalf of Lt-Col. S.W. Crawford, RTR, Department of Social and Economic Research, University of Glasgow, unpublished.
30. Commission for Racial Equality, *Ministry of Defence (Household Cavalry): Report of a Formal Investigation* (London: CRE, 1996).
31. Ibid., p. 48.

11

Desegregation and Affirmative Action in the United States Armed Forces: A Comparative Model for British Reform?

Benjamin Foss

The United States military has an extensive record of addressing racism within the ranks over the past 50 years. While the military still stumbles when dealing with the issues of gay service personnel and the role of women in a modern force, through human resource management it maintains a level of racial harmony and even-handedness found in few other sectors of American life. The path to the present model has been uneven, at times reinforcing the ever-present racial prejudice in the United States. In a significant number of cases, however, the armed forces have pioneered anti-discrimination policies that proved practical, and were even replicated in civilian society with some success.

In a time when the British military has begun to recognise, and in some cases combat, bias within its recruitment and promotion procedures, it seems appropriate to examine the history of the changes in the US. The mistakes and successes that have shaped current policies in the US may offer some guidance as to how the UK can reduce prejudice in its ranks, improve its own recruitment and retention figures and generally build a more effective fighting force for the post-Cold War missions it must face. It should be made clear that it would be inappropriate to draw direct parallels between the US experience and the task that faces the British military. The US changes took place over a period of half a century in a different and changing political context. The American military and the British military are different in size and mission, and necessarily relate to both government and the public in divergent manners owing to their historical roles in the respective societies. Even the types of discrimination in question are different. While the US changes have had success in terms of race matters, the British military, in addition to being concerned over racial and ethnic prejudice, also needs to address issues of social exclusion, as well as the issues of the status of women and gays in the ranks. On these matters the US offers a poor model, and here no analysis will be made of the history on these fronts.

Despite all these divergent elements, in the midst of the pitched debate on how to improve the British military, adding a historical perspective to the discussion and injecting an analysis of another force wrestling with problems of bias helps identify the key elements of effective changes in a military organisation. There are a number of factors that make the US experience relevant to observers in the United Kingdom. There is a strong cultural similarity between the two nations. Both share a similar emphasis on individual liberty, rights and responsibilities. In political terms, both the United States and Britain are stable democracies in which civilian authorities have power over the country's military forces and in which the military must recruit rather than draft its members. It is also important to note that changes in the American military, as in the case of those that face the British military, were made because of practical necessity rather than on purely ideological grounds. In the US case, from the Second World War racial minorities were an increasingly important part of the military, and tension over race matters threatened to cripple the forces. In the UK current experience, significant shortfalls in the number of personnel requires that changes in recruitment and retention be made across the spectrum. Recognising the differences and drawing on the similarities, we can identify the main factors that motivated significant changes in US discrimination policy, the means used to identify changes and the reforms appropriate to the problems, as well as the effectiveness of these means.

The history of the recent change in the US armed forces on matters of race can be divided into two periods. The first period ranges from 1948 to 1974. This era began with President Harry S. Truman's announcement that the forces would be desegregated and ended when all the forces, including the most intransigent branch, the Navy, made equality and affirmative action cornerstones of policy. In this formative period, the notion that the military had to take an active role in the social construction of the forces, especially in terms of race matters, evolved and was cemented in place. From the mid-1970s this principle was put into action, expanding affirmative action programmes and fine-tuning the mechanism to reduce prejudice within the ranks. As the British military has only just begun to address its own problem of bias, beginning to keep statistics on the proportion of minorities in the late 1980s and just recently agreeing to work with the Committee on Racial Equality to fight racism in the ranks, the earlier period seems most relevant to the current discussion.

Finally, it should be made clear that this chapter focuses on issue of racial discrimination in the US force as a case study for changing the discrimination policy of a military organisation in general. It seeks to identify successful methods for change and therefore does not focus on the failures in discrimination policy that constitute the US military's efforts to deal with bias against women and openly gay personnel. There are many failures in the US policy concerning racial discrimination and these will be examined; but limiting this study to this coherent history, one that also has a number of successes, is a more effective way to understand and draw lessons from the US experience.

When President Truman issued Executive Order 9981 on 26 July 1948, he ended the segregation in the forces that had been maintained throughout most of the history of the US military.[1] Truman had shown resolve, pushing a controversial plank of his civil rights platform through just months before a re-election campaign that was clearly going to be a tightly contested battle against the Republican candidate, Governor Thomas E. Dewey of New York. It should be understood, however, that the President made this change in the armed forces in large part because he was under pressure. Indeed, the work of civil rights leaders and specifically A. Philip Randolph, the legendary head of the influential Sleeping Car Porters Union, pushed the issue into the public eye with such tenacity that Truman could not dismiss the concern.

Randolph, after losing battles with President Franklin D. Roosevelt over the desegregation of the US military during the Second World War, formed the Committee Against Jim Crow in Military Service and Training. In a private meeting with President Truman on 22 March 1948 he explained that he had 'found Negroes not wanting to shoulder a gun to fight for democracy abroad unless they get democracy at home'.[2] Owing to racial quotas established during the Second World War, black soldiers constituted over 10 per cent of the nation's manpower in the defence industry and more than that within the Army.[3] If black soldiers did not participate in the nation's military actions, the force's efficacy could be seriously threatened. Even if Randolph's threat lacked potency, the US was now in the Cold War and a rebuke by leaders in the black community would have been embarrassing, feeding the Soviet propaganda machine. The White House understood that it was now part of a slow-moving battle for the support of the leaders of various developing nations whose attention could become easily focused on racism within the US, especially if it was present in the heart of the fighting force that was ostensibly to defend freedom.[4]

Truman himself had a mixed record on race matters, at times supporting segregation and stating that he was 'not appealing for social equality of the Negro'.[5] In other instances, he showed an interest in justice for black people: 'My very stomach turned over when I learned that Negro soldiers, just back from overseas, were being dumped out of army trucks in Mississippi and beaten.'[6] His mind was open to persuasion on the topic, and faced with the challenge from Randolph and other civil right leaders, he determined to make a significant change in the armed forces, an area in which Truman, as Commander-in-Chief, could order immediate change without interference from Congress.

The same interest in change could not be found in the military leaders at the time. Indeed, the heads of the US military had already rejected an opportunity to begin the desegregation of the entire force. In December 1944, the US military, stretched thin by the war, had been forced to integrate a small number of black soldiers into combat units at the Battle of the Bulge. Expressly noting that he did not want the precedent of integrated units to encourage civil rights groups to ask for more changes, General Dwight D. Eisenhower asked Lieutenant-General John C.H. Lee to proceed but with a number of qualifications. Only 2,500 black soldiers were trained as riflemen, any press story about the integration was muted, and immediately after the campaign the black soldiers were unceremoniously returned to their segregated units.[7] A report by the Research Branch of the Information and Education Division of Eisenhower's European headquarters deemed the experiment successful. This information, however, was quashed by the Army Chief of Staff, General George C. Marshall. The lack of interest present in the senior ranks of the military in pressing the matter was again made clear by General Eisenhower in 1948 testimony before the Senate Committee on Armed Services. He suggested 'that if we attempt merely by passing a lot of laws to force someone to like someone else, we are just going to get into trouble'.[8] While Truman was able to listen to the arguments made by civil rights leaders, military leaders were against desegregation, as initiating such a controversial move ran counter to their ethos. They did not believe that the military was an appropriate place to push the bounds of social change. They saw their role as apolitical, maintaining a position in which the *status quo* was to be respected. The leadership was worried that changes could disrupt the forces' ability to defend the nation's interests, and therefore invoked the national defence as a justification for continuing their policies. The forces were only able to transform when reform was introduced from outside the organisation, and this outside impetus had to be prompted by vocal complaints from civilian society.

Once the original project of desegregation was deemed complete in 1954, however, there was little examination made of the role of racism in the forces. President Eisenhower, who reversed the segregationist position he had held in 1948 and came to support integration, did not, however, make the project a high priority and instituted no method of monitoring progress. As a result, the programme floundered, requiring the investigation and proposal of additional changes.

In the 1960s, a similar pattern of the military leadership resisting changes to eliminate discrimination emerged. Again external pressure from civilian authorities spurred by social activists pushed necessary changes to fruition. During the early 1960s, it became clear that problems of prejudice still faced black and other minority personnel in the forces. One of the more pressing issues was that of off-base housing for minority personnel stationed at bases in the still segregated American south. The President's Committee on Equality of Opportunity in the Armed Forces, formed in 1963, identified housing and the lack of adequate and integrated off-base schools for minority personnel and their children as the most important issue for the government to address. To meet this concern, the independent committee, composed of civilian experts, suggested that the military force off-base facilities to accept all military personnel, regardless of colour, by using the economic threat of denying such establishments all military patronage. Secretary of Defense Robert S. McNamara ruled this suggestion too aggressive and opted for a voluntary programme of off-base desegregation instead. The Department of Defense (DoD) later issued a report responding to critics of the independent commission's findings, stating that:

> *FACT:* No town, nor any part of a town, nor any single establishment in the United States has been placed off-limits because of racial discrimination ... [Commanders] are prohibited from using the off-limits power except as a last resort and then only with the approval of their Service Secretary.[9]

This emphatic refusal to challenge off-base discrimination remained policy until 1967. At this time, the military was coming under increasing pressure from the media and protest groups to improve the treatment of black service personnel. It had come to light that during 1965 and 1966, the casualty rate of black soldiers had soared to 25 per cent of all deaths and injuries, at which point the Pentagon ordered cutbacks in front-line participation by these soldiers.[10] The press reported on these figures and flawed policies regularly, with trenchant articles appearing in 1966 and early 1967.[11] Criticism also came from other fronts. Martin Luther King, Jr (1929–68), having received the Nobel Peace Prize in 1964, spoke out, condemning the war as a drain on resources that could be used to help the poor at home. Before being assassinated on 4 April 1968, he moved to unite the anti-war and civil rights movements, planning once again to march on Washington.[12]

One specific group targeted the DoD for its lack of action on the housing issue, Action Coordinating Committee to End Segregation in the Suburbs (ACCESS), a Washington area group that protested against housing discrimination.[13] In January 1967, members of the group learned:

> that there had been a standing order that would have allowed [the DoD] to make segregated housing off-limits and that they were not enforcing it ... and if individual commanders did not seem to be doing it, then our position was that it should be done on a national basis.[14]

In an interview, a former member of ACCESS, Lynn Chertkov, reported that the group had a clear motive when they paid McNamara a visit 'without an appointment', on 1 February 1967.[15] The group had learned about Directive 5120.36, which allowed segregationist establishments to be placed off-limits to all military personnel with the approval of the Service Secretary; the group now sought methods of 'forcing the issue into a matter of top priority'.[16]

After occupying McNamara's office briefly, they were granted a series of meetings with Cyrus R. Vance, the Deputy Secretary of Defense and McNamara's trusted friend.[17] Reflecting on the matter 28 years later, Vance declared that ACCESS had not been the impetus behind the changes undertaken by the DoD: 'They were just part of our overall effort to keep the thing moving.'[18] The former Deputy Secretary of Defense, who subsequently became a Secretary of State, suggested throughout an interview with the author that 'Bob [McNamara] and I' were interested in making the changes well before ACCESS became involved in 1967.

The *Washington Post*, however, contradicted Vance. A front-page article on McNamara's off-base housing plan on 22 June 1967, closed by adding that, 'William Hobbs, co-chairman of [ACCESS], said that he was pleased with the order. ACCESS has been campaigning since the beginning of the year to have McNamara issue a nationwide off-limits order.'[19] Following their meeting with Vance, the group members were invited back for a session in which they discussed the matter directly with McNamara. This direct protest, in the context of pressure from the press and other prominent activists, pushed the military into a radical rethinking of its anti-discrimination housing project.[20] As in the case of desegregation in the 1950s, the military proved unable to make the changes necessary to root out discrimination without first coming under direct pressure from civilian concerns. The military in both cases had the ability to make the changes under its own command structure, but the structure could not produce the radical measures needed to address the discrimination facing its minority members.

Placing the military under pressure to reform was not enough to ensure effective changes would happen. Undertaking such a complex process as combating racism in the ranks demanded research and deliberation by independent committees vested with the power to call witnesses and investigate the military's manpower information. To map his transformation, President Truman had formed the President's Committee on Equality and Opportunity in the Armed Services to review, plan and implement the integration. He named Charles Fahy, a Georgia-born Catholic who favoured integration, to head the Committee. The President gave the Committee broad powers to call witnesses, view documents and negotiate a solution with the Secretary of Defense.

The Fahy Committee, as it came to be known, spent 17 months conducting interviews, hearings and research into the issue of integration. In its final report, *Freedom to Serve: Equality of Treatment and Opportunity in the Armed Forces* (1950), the Committee offered a plan for the process of integration.[21] The Committee made detailed analysis of the current policies concerning race in each of the branches, and outlined changes that should be made immediately. Once the final agreement had been made between the Fahy Committee, the Secretary of Defense and the Service Secretaries in May 1950, the integration took place with speed and tranquillity. By 30 October 1954, the Secretary of Defense was able to announce that the last segregated units in the armed services, i.e. units with at least 49 per cent black soldiers, had been eliminated.[22] The Air Force integrated its units quickly. Between 1949 and 1956, the percentage of black airmen doubled from 5.1 per cent to 10.4 per cent of the total force.[23] The Navy moved more slowly. Indeed, by 1960, black sailors made up only 4.9 per cent of the service, a figure less than half of any other service and half that of the proportion of blacks in the US population generally.[24]

The Army and Marine Corps remained segregated until 1951. The US military would become committed in Korea starting in the summer of 1950. Combat facilitated the integration of the infantry and other ground combat units.[25] The commanders in the Army and the Marines found that keeping units segregated restricted their ability to move troops and adapt quickly. In 1951, General Matthew B. Ridgway, the Far East Commander, suggested that black riflemen be integrated into white fighting forces, as they had been during the Battle of the Bulge in 1944 and 1945.[26] The Army asked an independent team of social scientists to examine the implication of integrating the forces. The group, working under the auspices of the Operations Research Office, used the code name *Project Clear*.[27] They released their report advocating the transition to a desegregated force on 29 July 1951. These changes spread through the ranks rapidly and soon changed the Army's entire structure, including that outside the east Asian theatre. This is not to say that there were not large parts of the military hierarchy in which black participation remained extremely limited, but the principle of separation had been rejected. While many military leaders and conservative politicians had suggested that integration would hinder morale and efficiency, as the *Project Clear* team of social scientists report and subsequent success of the changes show, this proved not to be the case.

Following the success of using independent committees to review and suggest military policy in 1948 and 1951, Adam Yarmolinsky, Assistant to the Secretary of Defense, suggested adopting the model to address concerns in 1961. McNamara reported that:

> [Yarmolinsky] said the way to do it would be to bring in some outsiders who would not be biased by relations with the individual who might be implicated in the racial tensions, ... I said 'They probably will not come up with anything.' But I was willing to do it.[28]

McNamara, a champion of bureaucratic efficiency, embraced the notion of a committee, one drawing directly on the Fahy precedent. Having 'read about the Fahy Committee', Yarmolinsky 'thought "Ah-ha! Maybe that's what we should do: set up an outside committee"'.[29] President Kennedy, following McNamara's and Yarmolinsky's advice, announced the creation of the President's Committee on Equality of Opportunity in the Armed Forces on 24 June 1962. Though the President lent his name to the Committee, it was a creature of the DoD. Indeed, calling it the President's Committee was largely 'window dressing' according to McNamara.[30] While the Gesell Committee, named for its chair, Gerhard Gesell, whom Yarmolinksy suggested to head the group, was able to ferret out the information it needed by inspecting bases, requesting documents and calling witnesses drawing on the authority of the President, it was responsible to McNamara, not the President himself. This would later make it difficult for the Committee to see its recommendations through to fruition. When McNamara objected to proposals regarding fighting off-base discrimination, the focus of over half the Committee's report, the careful plan floundered as there was no one outside the DoD to press the matter. It was not the quality of the work but the lack of will to implement the recommendations, ones that would be adopted half a decade later by the same Secretary, that stifled the proposals. Once they were enacted, sanctions against segregationist establishments would prove effective, but for now the lack of political support at the highest level killed the ideas.

The Gesell Committee had one key element of a successful oversight group: its members were not of the organisation it was attempting to review. But it lacked another key element: the authority to see its recommendations through. The Fahy Committee had had both of these elements, independence and authority, and its recommendation had precipitated the desegregation of the entire US military in under four years. This achievement is much more remarkable when one notes that this was in an era when the public schools remained segregated and civil rights bills died in Congressional filibusters. Indeed, the influence of this programme was so pronounced that while considering the 1954 *Brown* vs. *Board of Education* case, the prosecution presented the Justices of the US Supreme Court with a detailed account of the success of integration in the military in the form of Lee Nichols's manuscript for his 1954 book *Breakthrough on the Color Front*.[31] The Gesell Committee lacked the independence and the authority to make changes, and therefore proved impotent until external pressure during the Vietnam War forced the leadership to reverse its position.

Independence and authority for the committees in question were not the sole factors in determining the success of their proposals. Indeed, much of the outcome of their work rested on the implementation. Accountability, monitoring and responsiveness to the concerns of military personnel were vital to the effectiveness of the successive proposals. In the earlier case of the Fahy Committee's recommendations, the DoD kept detailed statistics on the proportion of white and minority soldiers in each unit, as well as of the number of minority personnel at each rank across the forces. The forces also took time to interview individual soldiers and collect impressions through operations such as *Project Clear*, the investigation by social scientists into the impact of integration on the effectiveness of the forces. Each of the Service Secretaries was required to report on the status of his efforts to desegregate the forces on a regular basis, entering his statistics with the Secretary of Defense, who was able to report the rapid desegregation of the forces less than four years after the project began.[32] As President, Eisenhower had put no such system in place to monitor further progress. Lacking any system of accountability, the effort to reduce racism in the forces faltered.

In the series of changes following the 1963 report, the changes for which base commanders were made responsible happened quickly and with great impact. While directives to deal with off-base housing were given little attention by the DoD and therefore by base commanders, a firm system of accountability was put into place regarding school desegregation. With the 1954 *Brown* vs. *Board of Education* case backing them, and facing the reality that a majority of bases relied heavily on local schools, the military required that local officers in charge report regularly on the status of the school near to their bases and that they intervene if the situation was unsatisfactory.

By 1963, the office of the Secretary of Defense issued a memorandum to the

Secretaries of all the services affirming 'the constitutional right of every child to be assigned to and to attend public schools without regard to race, color, religion or national origin'.[33] Citing the *Brown* decision on the matter, the department required virtually every base commander in the South to initiate a detailed pro-gramme to encourage desegregation in the off-base schools. Each commander was told to pressure the local school and community leaders, and to advise parents of the law, explaining how they could 'secure constitutional rights protecting against assignment on a racial basis through the courts'.[34]

The DoD and the Service Secretaries followed the schools issue closely enough to become involved in individual cases that demanded intervention. On 25 October 1963 Electronics Technician First Class James B. Williams wrote to Paul B. Fay, at the time Acting Secretary of the Navy, requesting assistance. In a memorandum sent via his Commanding Officers, he reported that according to the Dallas Independent School system integration plan:

> both of my children are eligible to attend the Sudie L. Williams (white) School ... [but that] my application was denied on the grounds that my children would have to cross a main thorough-fare. This crossing is a patrolled school crossing which is used by white children.[35]

Suspecting that his children, who were black, were denied a transfer to the Williams school on the basis of race, Technician Williams requested that the school administration relinquish the application form he had submitted. He was denied access, as was his Commanding Officer who also entered a formal request. When the pair were informed that the office of the Superintendent of Schools would 'not relinquish a copy unless a court order made this necessary', they entered a request through the Secretary of the Navy that the Justice Department intervene.[36] A Department of Justice letter, dated 12 December 1963 responded to an inquiry regarding the Williams case by Fay, the Acting Secretary of the Navy. Burke Marshall, Assistant Attorney General for the Civil Rights Division, reported that the department was already seeking 'legal relief on behalf of servicemen who are in the situation of Technician Williams'. As soon as the ruling happened, the Justice Department hoped that these precedents could be used to support Williams in his claim.[37]

A base commander, previously instructed to pursue cases of school segre-gation aggressively by McNamara, had assisted one of his men by first seeking to intervene locally, and then forwarding a request directly to the Secretary of the Navy. The Secretary pursued this request directly with the Justice Department Civil Right Division and received a prompt assurance that they would take all possible action to help integrate the Dallas school. The system of accountability and a directive to use the chain of command to assist in the integration of the local school was effective in this case.

The effectiveness of the measures in this instance appear to have been repre-sentative of the national experience. In a 25 May 1964 DoD assessment of progress concerning off-base discrimination, the agency reported that bases 'in

Maryland, Tennessee, Virginia, North Carolina, South Carolina, Georgia, Florida and Alabama all reported successful school desegregation efforts by commanders'.[38] The report qualified this statement, conceding a 'varying degree' of success, and that changes were 'not brought about solely because of command intervention'. But the memorandum underscored that 'the importance and impact of command support in achieving constitutional school assignment procedures has been repeatedly demonstrated'.

The same could not be said of efforts to desegregate housing and commercial establishments near bases. The same report recounted that

> a number of commanders have had no success whatever in persuading local white leaders to consider the off-base problems facing Negro servicemen, much less sit down and discuss those problems with Negro spokesmen.[39]

The language of the orders regarding housing desegregation had made it clear that Commanding Officers were not to intervene in the community without prior consent from their superiors. Indeed, orders regarding off-base discrimination, other than that concerning schools, were so vague and lacking in measures of accountability that in the four years following the initiation of the 1963 programme, only two requests to use sanctions were filed; both of these were denied.[40] On the controversial community issue of school desegregation, the base commanders were given direct responsibility and required to report on their efforts, and therefore great progress was made. In the case of desegregation of housing and commercial establishments, a tense community concern in which Commanding Officers were not given the responsibility to initiate change or monitor progress, few gains were made. In both cases, the commanders had the law supporting them, but they succeeded only when military policy forced them to monitor success.

Monitoring became an important concern in 1967 when Secretary McNamara decided to focus the military's efforts on housing desegregation. The department had conducted a 'nationwide census of equal opportunity in off-base rental housing' beginning on 11 April 1967.[41] Following McNamara's characteristic wishes to have detailed data on the matter, the Department asked each base commander for a large initial report including a precise list of facts on local housing, and then for meticulous reports each month thereafter. In a press conference on 22 June 1967, McNamara conceded that DoD Directive 5120.36, the original 1963 order, had had little impact on the 'humiliating discrimination' against black service personnel, and that a new programme was necessary.[42] McNamara would now enact and even exceed the provisions recommended by the Gesell Committee in 1963. Moving quickly, he forbade all military personnel stationed at Andrews Air Force Base in Prince Georges County, Maryland from living in segregated apartments or trailer parks within a three-and-one-half mile radius of the installation. The Secretary stated that the programme, which encompassed the Washington area, would be a test case for a national model, suggesting that 'we anticipate moving elsewhere in the country'.[43] The base command would now be absolutely required to sanction any local landlord who would not give a written promise to rent to any and all military personnel.

In his June announcement, the Secretary also indicated that high level Pentagon officials would meet with Washington area apartment operators and insist that housing be desegregated if military personnel were to live in their facilities. In the preceding four years, the responsibility for the programme had been delegated to a Deputy Assistant Secretary of Defense under the Assistant Secretary for Manpower. The primary responsibility was now given to Vance, McNamara's close associate and the second in command of the DoD. This involvement of senior officials, in combination with a rigid and detailed programme for change indicated that the DoD intended to place the full force of the agency behind the new rules. Over the following six months the policy grew in a series of successive stages, until on 7 September, the department 'expanded [the new programme] to cover the entire nation'.[44]

As part of the new system of accountability, the DoD established two categories for equal opportunity housing: 'open' and 'listed'. Open housing included establishments declared open to all by the owner upon personal inquiry by the base commander or his senior assistant. Listed facilities were placed in base housing directories and required a signed certificate by the manager or the base commander affirming that the housing was accessible to all. Within four months of the 22 June institution of the programme, the initial programme in the Washington and Maryland area resulted in a 275 per cent increase in the number of 'open' buildings (175), and a 195 per cent increase in the number of individual units (13,603).[45] By 31 December 1967, the DoD, having begun a nation-wide programme, announced that the number of 'listed' housing units had risen from 646,700 to 802,200, an increase of 155,500 units. Of the 1,096,200 housing units near military bases, this represented an increase in the percentage of open housing from 59 to 73 percent nation-wide.[46] This trend continued: by 20 June 1968, the percentage of open housing had increased to 83 per cent of the total.[47] Shortly thereafter, the 1968 Civil Rights Act specifically addressing fair housing passed into law. Building on these laws and a number of recent US Supreme Court precedents, the DoD became even more aggressive in its demands for open housing. By 31 August 1969, the department had signed pledges that 91 per cent of housing near military bases was open nation-wide, a monumental turn around from the 35 per cent rate of desegregation two years previously.[48] Fast and effective changes in segregation across the South were generated by these three elements: placing responsibility for the new changes directly in the bailiwick of base commanders, moving monitoring of the programme to a higher office, and initiating a system to verify progress.

Not all major changes in the US military's policy concerning racial discrimination emanated from outside the command structure. The period 1948 to 1974 can been seen as an era in which the culture of the military changed. By the close of this period, the senior members of each of the services came to understand the value of integration and anti-prejudice programmes. Shortly thereafter, the force would institute programmes of affirmative action in which members of minority groups were offered additional training and support in their effort to advance through the ranks. These programmes are outside the focus of this study, but it is interesting to note that the plans for many of the programmes came from within the ranks.

One of the best example of the change in culture that began to permeate the forces can be found in the story of Admiral Elmo R. Zumwalt, Jr. When he became Chief of Naval Operations (CNO) on 1 July 1970, the Navy was under tremendous internal strain due to racial tensions.[49] On the date of Zumwalt's promotion to the Navy's top service position, ships and bases were riddled by gangs and other forms of factionalism and racial tension. Morale was low, with only 10 per cent of the force choosing to re-enlist; by the end of Zumwalt's four years this rate more than doubled to 26 per cent.[50] At the age of 49, Zumwalt was the youngest US Naval Commander in history, and was closely attuned to the needs of the enlisted sailor. The Admiral recognised that radical changes in the way the Navy treated its men, regardless of race, needed to be implemented immediately. His solution was to begin sending out personal orders to the entire Navy in the form of 'Z-grams'. Over his four-year term, he would send out a total of 121.

Through these orders, Zumwalt was 'striving to make Naval service a more satisfying and enjoyable way of life'.[51] These changes were significant to enlisted sailors and their dependants, who were known to line the dock and cheer the C.N.O whenever he arrived at a new port.[52] Moreover, they revised a long tradition of polished and rigid discipline within the Navy, instead emphasising a 'two-way dialogue at all levels of command', and 'respect and ... a commensurate degree of responsibility'.[53]

Zumwalt also created a new lattice of programmes to deal with race relations within the Navy. The Admiral established a 'Human Resource Program' which trained a corps of personnel in mediation, communication skills and 'the management of human resources'.[54] This programme would evolve over the next few years, creating an elaborate set of workshops and forums that dealt with issues of conflict resolution and race and class relations. Former Captain Steve Shelby remembered that the 'Navy finally understood that they were dealing with human beings when they started the human resource management program'. He continued, remembering that:

> I had an E-9 who would rather throw you across the room than talk to you ... it was just outright bad; he was from the South, he was hard ... He went through the human resources course and when he left he said, 'You know what? This is a new Navy; I have got to change'. I know it had a positive effect.[55]

Captain Thomas Callaham concurred with this positive assessment of the Human Resource Program, reporting that 'I always thought that I was not a racist ... but in this process I found out I had hang-ups just like everyone'. Sounding more like a counsellor than a Navy captain, Callaham recounted 'that there was an effort to bring us all down to one level and show us that each one of us was good in our own way, not but that we had to force everyone into our own view'.[56] This careful attention to human relations and race issues greatly relaxed tensions within the forces and helped change the Navy's attitude on race.

Zumwalt also established a programme of minority affairs, which included an officer on each ship who became a clearing-house for concerns. Understanding that the chain of command could stifle valid complaints by sailors who felt that they had been mistreated, Zumwalt also set up an 'Action Line' phone messaging system which allowed enlisted men to report concerns over their commander's actions.[57] He also established 'many local councils and committees' to deal with 'minority affairs' and named a number of 'special assistants for minority affairs' in his Washington office.[58] The comprehensive programme dealing with minority affairs also focused on recruiting new sailors from minority groups, and retaining those who were already in the force.

The results of these changes were dramatic. In 1968, two years before Zumwalt arrived, the percentage of black sailors in the Navy was a paltry 4.8 per cent; the level had floated within one-half of 1 per cent of this for the past 15 years.[59] When he left the position and the Navy in 1974, the figure had jumped to 7.8 per cent and the number of minority officers had more than doubled. This trend would continue over the next decade, with black Naval personnel reaching a partici-pation rate of 10.4 per cent by 1980.[60] While the numbers still did not match the other forces', the figures had shot up after decades of stagnation. These increases were not solely because of Zumwalt's changes; when the draft ceased in 1973, blacks became an even larger proportion of all the forces. Yet the disparity between the Navy and the other services declined, suggesting that the branch had been able to improve its policy, and reputation, substantially. This was as a result of Zumwalt's attention to the details of integration and affirmative action, an attentiveness that emerged from within the force once the precedent addressing racial matters had been established by the DoD as a whole.

Zumwalt's work was made possible by earlier work in the forces. In reflecting on the 26 years that constitute this initial period of addressing racism in the US military, we should recognise a number of trends. In a number of cases, it made political sense to initiate change in the government civil rights programmes in the context of the forces.

Implementing changes in this traditionally conservative organisation allowed President Truman a degree of political cover that would not have been afforded if he had attempted to make similar changes in society at large. In the US context, the President, as Commander-in-Chief, has absolute power over the forces. This allowed Truman to push the integration through without approval from Congress. Many generals, admirals and political leaders had argued that pioneering desegregation and affirmative action in the armed forces was risky, insisting that the military could only ape the practices of the society that surrounded it. Instead, because of the political cover afforded and the logistical ease of implementing sweeping changes, the forces became the proving ground for anti-discrimination policy. Throughout the period, the forces had a highly symbolic relevance, influencing the action of the Supreme Court in the *Brown* decision and serving as a focus for civil rights leaders.

Consistent themes emerged as to the manner in which the forces were able to change. For the changes to begin, strong pressure had to be brought to bear from outside the military establishment. For the new rules to be effective, an independent body of observers had to review the actions of the military, establishing clear goals and offering a system of verification and accountability for the proposed changes. Finally, political leadership at the highest level had to push these changes through the services. In cases where the three elements – external pressure on the military, independent review with clear standards and political leadership – were present, change was quick and dramatic. The initial integration under Truman took less than four years; the integration of off-base schools in the early 1960s took less than two years and the effort to desegregate housing beginning in 1967 took just over 18 months.

If any of the elements were missing, problems persisted. Lacking external pressure or oversight, military leaders had resegregated the forces in 1945 after the limited desegregation at the Battle of the Bulge. Between 1954 and 1960, racial discrimination and problems in community relations concerning race matters persisted in the absence of the three key elements for change. Despite an independent review, the lack of political leadership and accountability in verification of changes allowed the housing desegregation problem to continue through the middle 1960s.

Learning from the US experience is a delicate process. No nation can adopt another nation's methods of change entirely. But many of the experiences of the US military on matters of race do seem to speak to the dilemma facing the British military at present. As the current government implements its Strategic Defence Review, it seems logical to inspect the experience of the US and ask what lessons can be found.

NOTES

1. 'Executive Order 9981', in *Blacks in the Military: Essential Documents*, Bernard C. Nalty and Morris J. MacGregor, Jr (eds) (Wilmington, DE: Scholarly Resources, 1981), p. 239. Hereafter cited as *Essential Documents*.
2. Richard M. Dalfiume, *Desegregation of the US Armed Forced: Fighting on Two Fronts 1939–1953* (Columbia, MO: University of Missouri Press, 1969, 1975), p. 163.
3. Martin Binkin *et al., Blacks in the Military* (Washington, DC: Brookings Institution, 1982), p. 43.
4. Morris J. MacGregor, Jr, *Integration of the Armed Forces, 1940–1965* (Washington, DC: Centre for Military History, United States Army, 1981), p. 291.
5. MacGregor, *Integration*, p. 293
6. David McCullough, *Truman* (New York: Simon & Schuster, 1992), p. 588.

7. Ulysses Lee, *The Employment of Negro Troops* (Washington, DC: United States Army, 1966), p. 690.
8. United States Senate, Committee on Armed Services, *Hearings … on Universal Military Training* (Washington, DC: United States Government Printing Office, 1948), National Archives, Military History Branch, Washington, DC.
9. 'Office of Assistant Secretary of Defense (Manpower), *Straightening Out the Record*, 19 August 1963, with attachments 4' as reproduced in *Essential Documents*, v. XIII, beginning p. 225.
10. *New York Times*, 29 April 1968, p. I:16. It is interesting to note that while the US draft board system skewed the selection of soldiers towards blacks – in 1967, 98.5 per cent of the 17,123 persons serving on local draft boards were white, and no board in the states of Alabama, Arkansas, Louisiana or Mississippi had an African-American member – this was not the only factor in tilting the composition of the fighting force away from white participation. (Bernard C. Nalty, *Strength for the Fight: A History of Black Americans in the Military* (New York: The Free Press, 1986), p. 299.) It is true that the draft system allowed those with the money for education or the connections to join the reserves to avoid combat service. In this period, few blacks had these luxuries. Once black soldiers enlisted, however, economic factors continued to contribute to the problem. Many black soldiers volunteered for the paratroopers and other combat positions to earn more pay. One soldier reported that, 'I found out I could earn $55 a month extra for being a paratrooper, so I went for jump school' (*New York Times Magazine*, 24 July 1968, p. I:48). This pay raise constituted a 50 per cent increase for a first-time enlisted man, serving as a strong incentive for poorer, and often black, soldiers to take on dangerous missions. By 1965, black re-enlistment rates stood at 49.3 per cent while whites volunteered for another tour only 13.7 per cent of the time (*New York Times*, 29 April 1968, I:48). This trend peaked in 1967 when blacks began leaving the military, but by this time as much as 60 per cent of some airborne rifle platoons were black.
11. Binkin *et al.*, *Blacks in the Military*, p. 32.
12. W. Augustus Low and Vigil A. Clift (eds), 'King, Martin Luther, Jr', in *Encyclopedia of Black America* (New York: McGraw-Hill, 1981), p. 488.
13. Lynn Chertkov, former ACCESS member, personal phone interview between Bethesda, Maryland and Middletown, Connecticut, 28 February 1995.
14. Chertkov, personal phone interview,
15. *Washington Post*, 2 February 1967, p. I:3.
16. Ibid.
17. *Life*, 10 May 1968, p. 90.
18. Cyrus R. Vance, New York, personal interview, New York City, 6 March 1995. Hereafter cited as Interview with Vance, 6 March 1995.
19. *Washington Post*, 22 June 1967, p. I:4.
20. It is interesting to note that the two major histories on the integration of the US military written by Bernard Nalty and Morris J. MacGregor, Jr, respectively, neglect the role of outside protest. Instead they emphasise the agency of the President and McNamara in pushing through changes. As both of these authors were official historians of the military, there may have been bias in their presentation of the material, owing to the military's interest in colouring the past to show its past leaders as opposing discrimination of their own will and effort.
21. *Freedom to Serve: Equality of Treatment and Opportunity in the Armed Forces; A Report by the President's Committee* (Washington, DC: Government Printing Office, 1950), National Archives, Military History Branch, Washington, DC.
22. *New York Times*, 31 October 1954, p. I:1.
23. MacGregor, Integration, p. 412.
24. Binkin *et al.*, *Blacks in the Military*, p. 43.

25. *Essential Documents*, p. 295.
26. This is not to suggest that a war is necessary to facilitate major changes in military organisation. It is, however, interesting to note that much of the integration of forces, in this case race, as well as the opportunities that have been afforded women in the Russian and Israeli militaries, have happened when the force's strength is stretched to capacity. While many people dismiss non-traditional soldiers, the luxury of prejudice disappears in times of great military need.
27. *Project Clear, Social Research and the Desegregation of the United States Army*, Leo Bogart (ed) (New Brunswick, NJ: Transaction Publishers, 1992), p. 1.
28. Robert S. McNamara, personal interview by phone between Middletown, Connecticut and Washington, DC, 21 February 1995.
29. Adam Yarmolinsky, personal interview, Washington, DC, 9 January 1995.
30. MacGregor, *Integration*, p. 536.
31. Adam Yarmolinsky, *The Military Establishment* (New York: Harper & Row, 1971), p. 350.
32. *New York Times*, 31 October 1954, p. I:1.
33. Memorandum from Norman S. Paul, Assistant Secretary of Defense to Service Secretaries, Subject: Assignment of Dependants of Military Personnel to Public School, 15 July 1963, National Archives, Military History Branch, Washington, DC.
34. Ibid.
35. Memorandum to the Secretary of the Navy, from James B. Williams, ET1, via Commanding Officer, US Naval and Marine Corps Reserve Training Center, Dallas, Texas, 25 October 1963, National Archives, Military History Branch, Washington, DC.
36. Ibid.
37. Letter to Paul B. Fay, Acting Secretary of the Navy, from Burke Marshall, Assistant Attorney General, Civil Rights Division, 12 December 1963, National Archives, Military History Branch, Washington, DC.
38. Memorandum to the Secretaries of the Army, Navy and Air Force, from Alfred B. Fitt, Deputy Assistant Secretary of Defense (Civil Rights), Off-base Equal Opportunity Inventories, 25 May 1964, National Archives, Military History Branch, Washington, D.C.
39. Fitt, 25 May 1964.
40. David Sutton, 'The Military Mission Against Off-Base Discrimination', in *Public Opinion and the Military Establishment*, vol. I, Charles Moskos, Jr (ed.) (Beverly Hills, CA: Sage Publications, 1971), p. 172.
41. Memorandum from Deputy Secretary of Defense Cyrus R. Vance for Secretaries of Military Departments, 11 April 1967 1, National Archive, Military History Branch, Washington, DC.
42. *Washington Post*, 23 June 1967, p. I:1.
43. *New York Times*, 23 June 1967, p. I:1.
44. *New York Times*, 8 September 1967, p. I:1.
45. Yarmolinsky, *Military Establishment*, p. 352.
46. Press Release, 'Defense Department Reports Progress in Eliminating Housing Discrimination', Office of the Assistant Secretary of Defense (Public Affairs), 31 December 1967, National Archives, Military History Division, Washington, DC.
47. News Conference by Clark M. Clifford, Secretary of Defense, Pentagon, 20 June 1968, National Archives, Military History Division, Washington, DC.
48. Yarmolinsky, *Military Establishment*, p. 352.
49. Elmo R. Zumwalt, Jr, *On Watch: A Memoir* (New York: Quadrangle, 1976), p. 272.
50. *Wall Street Journal*, 13 May 1974.
51. Z-93, Z-gram file, Operational Archives, Naval Historical Center, Washington, DC. All Z-grams cited are from this source.
52. Zumwalt, photo following, p. 272.

53. Z-93.
54. Z-55.
55. Steve Shelby, Navy Captain (ret.), personal telephone interview between Honolulu, Hawaii, author in Middletown, Connecticut, 10 February 1995.
56. Thomas Callaham, Navy Captain (ret.), personal interview by phone between Deltaville, VA, author in Hanover, NH, 3 January 1995.
57. Z-60.
58. Z-93.
59. Binkin *et al.*, *Blacks in the Military*, p. 42.
60. Ibid.

12

On 'The Need to be Different': Recent Trends in Military Culture

Christopher Dandeker

ALL CHANGE FOR THE ARMED FORCES

For the armed forces the pace of change since 1989 has been extraordinary with simultaneous changes in both international security and domestic society. Despite calls for a period of stability, after a series of reviews from Options for Change to the recent Strategic Defence Review (SDR), one of the few things they can be certain of is further change. One of the effects of the period of domestic and international turbulence since 1989 is that the 'people dimension' of the British armed services has become a central problem in defence debates. As is evident from the outcome of the SDR, a range of personnel issues – equal opportunities in employment and 'over-stretch' for example – have moved up the political agenda.[1]

A key issue for those concerned with the people dimension of the armed services – and thus with making a success of the SDR – is the extent to which the military way of life needs to be different from that of civilian society.[2] This problem has always been at the heart of the academic study of civil–military relations. The starting point in the literature is that armed forces are 'Janus-faced' organisations. On the one hand, they and their political masters have to respond to the strategic context by building militarily effective organisations. On the other hand, especially in democracies, they have to ensure that the armed services are responsive to the changing society which they defend, that pays for them, and without whose support they can do little. The issue is how responsive?

MILITARY CULTURE AND THE NEED TO BE DIFFERENT

Conservatives tend to be suspicious of tempering military culture in order to accommodate changes in wider society, even to the extent of arguing that military effectiveness requires a supportive framework of robust conservative values in civilian society. In contrast, liberals tend to expect the armed services to conform to civilian values, and in so doing underestimate the unique character and demands of military life.[3] Closer examination of the issues shows that the most sensible approach is a pragmatic one that lies somewhere between the conservative and liberal positions; it is misleading to assume that military accommodation to civilian social values must necessarily undermine military effectiveness.[4] The challenge for the personnel strategist is to ensure that a balance is struck between these, sometimes competing, demands. Furthermore, in adjusting to changes in society and international security, the personnel strategist has to take into account the history and traditions of the individual services, which are normally critical factors in sustaining their identity, sense of shared purpose and morale.

The problems associated with the military's 'need to be different' – how such differences are to be drawn in practice and how to generate support and legitimacy for them in civilian society – have moved centre-stage in recent years.[5] This is because of a series of interconnected challenges to military culture. The new strategic context has raised questions about the continuing relevance of warrior values in military operations where high-technology, 'push-button' warfare seems to have a higher profile, and where warfare itself may come to be displaced by a variety of peace-support operations. In society, social, cultural and legal changes provide a less robust supporting framework for the core values of military culture. Indeed, a new generation of prospective recruits is less accepting of some of the traditional demands of a military way of life. Meanwhile, there are cost-pressures at work that have led to a civilianising influence on the ethos of the services through the introduction of what are considered to be best business practices such as the wider employment of civilians and contractors. Before considering these challenges in more depth it is as well to focus first on the distinctive features of military culture.

In general terms, culture comprises a set of ideas, beliefs and symbols that provide a definition of the world for a group or organisation and guides for action.[6] The functional imperatives of war and military operations ensure that the services stand apart from civilian society. Of course, there are important ways in which the armed services are similar to civilian enterprises. For example, one can point to the importance of teamworking, leadership, the idea of loyalty to the organisation and its mission and – of ever-increasing importance – the need to work with advanced technologies particularly in the information field. Furthermore, the services share with other organisations such as those in the fields of education, health and religion an 'institutional' quality. In institutional organisations, the main drivers are values rather than the market. People carry out their tasks of educating, caring for the sick, of managing armed force primarily not to make a profit but in order to implement the values that provide the overall purpose of the organisation. In contrast, for market-based organisations, the main driver is the need to monitor and adjust to the demands of the market in order make a profit on the capital invested.[7]

As institutional organisations the armed services also have their own unique culture and resulting contract with their personnel. Ensuring that service personnel are prepared to fight involves leadership, management and motivation. For the military the core values of military culture are subordination of the self to the group and the idea of sacrifice: the individual must be willing to subordinate him or herself to the common good – the team and common task. Furthermore, there must be a willingness to sacrifice one's life for the team in peace and war – without this an armed force will risk defeat. Ideally, by dint of leadership and training, these values will be upheld voluntarily as a result of conscience. However, if necessary, coercion may be required. This is what makes military discipline – an effective structure of command for the giving and receiving of orders – quite different from other organisations in terms of the demands it places upon personnel. These demands include the obligation to train to kill and to sacrifice self; to participate in a military community where one works, lives and socialises with other service personnel; and, when necessary, a 24-hour commitment with the risk of separation from family at short notice.

Of course, individual services also have their own specific cultures: for example, the combat units of different services. With the Army there is a requirement to close with and kill the enemy in comparison with the greater 'action at a distance' characteristic of the other services. Especially in the teeth arms of the Army, people are asked to do a variety of tasks in changing and hostile territory. In the Royal Navy, by contrast, the ship and the demands of the sea, whether in peace or war, tie the individual into the web of obligations comprising a cohesive unit. This seems to be connected with the fact that as far as off-duty personal life, away from the ship, is concerned, the Royal Navy is, generally speaking, less apprehensive than the Army. In the case of the British Army this concern is particularly evident due to the peculiarly tribal nature of the regimental system.[8]

CHALLENGES TO MILITARY CULTURE – THE STRATEGIC CONTEXT

As I indicated earlier, challenges to military culture stem from changes in both international security and society at large. In this discussion, I focus on the impact of the strategic context on the civil–military relationship before reversing the focus and turning to the effects of a changing society on that relationship. In responding to these challenges, the armed services need to sustain bonds of 'civil–military understanding'. I use this term to refer to a mutually supportive relationship between the armed services and the civilian community; this is a relationship of communication and perception, trust and legitimacy.

After a decade of reductions in military establishments and a seeming widening of the spectrum of missions that they are expected to perform, the services face an inevitable question by the public: what is the relevance and purpose of the armed services? Two particular difficulties arise here. The first concerns the connection between strategy and public perceptions. There has been a *perceived* decline in major, direct, military threats to the UK, and an increase in the apparent priority given to non-war fighting roles such as peacekeeping and military assistance to humanitarian operations. Accordingly, the question may be asked: why should scarce resources continue to be expended on maintaining a high-intensity war machine – the core of a distinctive cultural identity of the military? There is some concern among military personnel that the core war-fighting role is being obscured in public perceptions.[9] The public needs to be made more aware of the following view: that it makes good sense to train the armed forces for war-fighting and then to 'train down' in order to cater for the needs of missions in which a more restrained use of force is appropriate.

The task of building a national consensus on what armed forces the UK needs for its security and defence policy is not made any easier by a second difficulty: the decline in the 'knowledgeability' of military affairs in the civilian community – both opinion formers and the general public. It appears that respect for and support of the armed forces is quite robust in the UK, US, France, and the Netherlands.[10] However, support for the current level of funding for defence is less so, particularly in the face of demands from other areas of public expenditure such as health, education, the environment and public transport. In countries which no longer have conscription, especially the UK and USA, direct experience and appreciation of military affairs have declined markedly over the past 20 years, both in the political elite as well as in broader sections of the population. Most people's experience of the military is gained second-hand from the media and the information produced in this way often reflects past rather than current realities of life in the armed forces.

In the UK, there has been a reduction in the number of people with direct experience of military affairs.[11] As a consequence of the long-term decline in the size of the military establishment since the end of conscription, there has been a corresponding diminution in the number of military and ex-military personnel in society. In addition, with base closures and rationalisation, the 'footprint' made by the military on society has diminished. This process has been reinforced by the security problems in Northern Ireland since 1968, which have led to the military becoming 'invisible', until very recently, owing to the lack of public display of uniforms.[12] The number of those – especially opinion formers – who can speak knowledgeably about the services has declined in recent decades. Linkages between the services and MPs are being improved but this has to be part of a broader investment effort in public relations, and in making more of the role of reserve forces as a means of sustaining civil–military understanding. Whatever operational advantages are to be gained from a more closely integrated regular/reserve mix, there remains a concern that the reduction in the size of the Territorial Army and unit amalgamations will leave significant areas of the country having little or no military presence. All this will not provide favourable conditions for sustaining the public profile of the armed forces and the legitimacy of its core war-fighting mission, let alone the legitimacy of regenerating a stronger military capability should the need arise in future. The warning times of threats may be shorter than those required to garner public support for action designed to address them.

Whatever mix of missions is established for the armed services, their organisational structure and culture designed to meet them have changed significantly in recent years and will continue to do so. In the more established all-volunteer forces the key developments in this connection are: cadreisation, force packaging, the integration of the individual services into a more purple mode of operation and culture, and the idea of 'delayering' organisational hierarchies. While, as will become apparent later, there are societal factors that help to account for these changes, I focus here on the strategic and operational drivers.

Cadreisation refers to the gap between the wartime and peacetime establishments of a military formation. Together with 'force packaging' of military structures it allows for the regeneration of military capacity of a customised or 'mix and match' kind, suited to the specifics of particular contingencies. Force packages can be assembled at short notice to form a mix of force appropriate for the specific demands of an unforeseen crisis demanding the use of armed forces. Such modular structures can be geared to war-fighting as well as other, and more controversial, roles, such as aid to the civil authority on matters of internal security, and assisting the police and customs in anti-terrorism and drugs law-enforcement activities.[13]

Force packaging involves the participation of elements from all three services. It is in this context that one can refer to the increasing importance of 'jointery'. The increased focus on inter-service integration – what can be called the purple trend – has implications for the expertise and education required for personnel at different points in the military hierarchy. In addition, inter-service integration involves units drawn from the armed forces of different countries, posing additional issues of 'cultural interoperability':[14] how to ensure effective co-operation among different national traditions.

Increasingly, in modern armed forces senior commands will not be available for officers above lieutenant-colonel rank unless they have served on a 'purple staff'. Preparing military professionals for these complex roles, which Charles Moskos has termed soldier statesman and soldier scholar roles, requires innovation in education and organisation. This can be seen, for example, in arrangements for the efficient management of complex joint operations involving components not only from all three services but from other countries as well.[15] To take a specific example, the Joint Rapid Deployment Force structure and Permanent Joint Headquarters, set up in 1996, and the establishment of the Joint Services Command and Staff College are designed to develop the joint ethos required of future operations. This process extends much further the 'purple' developments of the Cold War era, when in the NATO structure far greater allowance was made for national and service 'stovepipes' in the organisational hierarchies. One could foresee the development of a more robust central defence staff manned by officers with the ethos to put defence above individual service interests. There may even be a career structure for this defence staff, although with officers moving back to their own service regularly, for example, for command appointments, so that they would keep in touch with the military basis of their role. It is worth noting that these educational developments will increase the transferability of skills of officers who have experience of such staffs once they return to civilian society.[16]

In addition to the organisational developments I have just discussed, the military will also make greater use of the less hierarchical and lengthy chains of command characteristic of contemporary leading businesses. The drivers of the process are both strategic and societal: the pace of military operations and the pressure to borrow, where relevant, from business organisations in the search for efficiency gains. However, critics point out that this development will be limited by the need for a coercive, disciplined structure in a war-fighting organisation. Despite the critics, the Bett team remain committed to the idea of delayering, arguing that:

> the civilian world has pointed the way to the delayering and simplification of organizations. Much of this is driven by cost pressures, which the services are themselves feeling, but also by changing technology and the need to react speedily to information in fast-moving situations, which is also very much a requirement of Service operations. It seemed to us that eighteen layers from five-star officer to basic grade serviceman in an overall organization of 250,000 people (and within each of the much smaller individual Services) would look less and less credible to taxpayers and potential recruits. We saw the need for a rank structure, of course, particularly on operations; our argument was that the Services should adapt it, sooner rather than later, to a changing world – and to changing operational needs. All the most senior officers we spoke to wanted some reduction in ranks.[17]

Some officers have argued that the delayered format together with the 'matrix' principle[18] is probably likely to work best in very specific circumstances. These are where a formation is operating some distance away from the front line, where the nature of the task at hand should determine the composition of the staff employed, rather than principle of rank.[19] It is worth noting that, in the Permanent Joint Headquarters of the Joint Rapid Deployment Force discussed earlier, project teams comprise a significant feature of the working pattern. This is necessary because of the rapidly evolving complex emergencies with which these organisations are concerned.

Although the British armed services have to plan to operate alone, the most likely scenarios will see them working in a variety of complex coalitions with the military of other countries; this will include the possibility of not working closely with the United States. Consequently, the problems of service jointery will need to be addressed in a wider context of combined and multinational operations. Here the armed services confront a range of 'cultural inter-operability' issues arising from the meshing of a variety of military and doctrinal cultures. In addition, there will be social issues arising from co-operation between formations working under quite different national personnel policies. We thus turn from the challenges to military culture stemming from the international security context to those within the wider society.

CHALLENGES TO MILITARY CULTURE – THE WIDER SOCIETY

Here we find that changes in society are themselves connected with the international context. Thus, social change in the UK is connected with transformations in other societies, processes which are reinforced by participation in the European Union and its legal regulations. It is, therefore, difficult to consider social change in one country in isolation from other countries with which it is connected in relations of mutual influence.

Compared with 20 years ago, today's society is more positively disposed to the free market compared with the central state as a basis for economic life (although whether this will be reversed with the evolution of the European Union over the next decade is debatable). The armed services have to establish how far commercial practices such as privatisation, contracting out, and the formation of agencies in the logistic and support sectors can be used in an institutional organisation without compromising operational effectiveness.

When considering recent developments in military organisation, it is interesting to note the striking parallels between the drivers of change facing the armed forces and those encountered by private sector organisations. Six dimensions are worthy of note. First, the end of an immediate direct threat to national territorial sovereignty is paralleled by the lack of a stable market for business. Second, military establishments such as those in the UK are at their lowest level since the Second World War. The trend of company downsizing since the 1980s parallels this process. Third, the military has to address a range of missions involving operations other than major war, namely, intervention abroad in multinational contributions to international peace and stability. This focus on the projection of force to dispersed points on the globe from a home base parallels the ways in which companies are having to respond to increasingly global markets. Fourth, the military are having to think through the possibilities offered by the application of business models to the military, such as contracting-out of functions, restructuring of hierarchies and so on – processes that echo civilian developments in the empowerment and restructuring of companies. Fifth, both military and civilian organisations have to respond to the social and cultural challenges of a changing society. This society is more individualistic (in which, for example, people wish to be actively involved in how their working lives are structured and expect employers to respect their private and family commitments), egalitarian, and litigious. Sixth, both sets of organisations are seeking to make best use of the new information technologies in enabling them to achieve a competitive edge over their rivals. This is evident in all aspects of organisations from the personnel functions (such as the administration of pay, personnel records and so on) to operational areas – not least in the offensive and defensive aspects of 'information warfare'. As I indicated in the discussion of delayering, the drivers of organisation structure are both strategic and societal.

As in the private sector, armed forces are increasingly reviewing their core activities, identifying which might be contracted out in order to cut costs but not at the sacrifice of quality – indeed, costs may be reduced while quality improves as appears to have occurred in the field of catering services. Outsourcing can involve one or more of the following activities: privatising a function; awarding a fixed-term contract to provide a contracted out service – an exercise often conjoined with market testing; the submitting of an activity to a competition in which the existing in-house provider has to compete with a private sector bid to provide the service for a subsequent period; creating a quasi-independent agency, say, to provide personnel services (as in the RAF's Personnel and Training Command). As the Strategic Defence Review reports, currently:

> most of defence support is now delivered through 44 Defence Agencies. A number of Agencies have achieved savings on their operating costs of over 20 per cent in their first two or three years and several of the programmes involve rationalisation of activities from, anything up to 220 sites to a single location … Many of the Defence Agencies will be affected by SDR outcomes … which include the formation of new Agencies in such areas as aviation repair, strategic movements, storage and distribution and, probably, Army equipment support.[20]

In addition to outsourcing, civilianising is a significant trend in the armed services. Civilianisation involves the substitution of civilian for military personnel with 2,000 such posts being civilianised at present. Civilians are, for the most part, at least in the UK, cheaper to employ than expensively trained military personnel. Also civilians often stay in their posts longer than military personnel do, providing valuable continuity of experience and expertise. Since the mid-1990s, the objective has been to 'civilianise posts and so release valuable military resources to the front line wherever it makes operational and economic sense to do so'.[21]

The challenge placed before the military is to identify what is the core uniformed regular military personnel requirement, beyond which functions could be performed by civilians, employed either by the Ministry of Defence or by private companies under contract. For example, with the RAF's officers constituting about 18 per cent of the service total compared with 5 per cent for some other countries such as the Israeli Defence Forces, further civilianising of non-core functions can be anticipated, not least because of the savings in costs that can be achieved.[22] In establishing such core figures the assumptions are that, if a post is required in time of peace and war, then a regular is needed. If a task is required in wartime only, then a reservist could perform it. In the case of tasks required in peacetime only, then it could be contracted out or civilianised. The trend is thus towards smaller forces with fewer regulars, and more reservists, civilians and contractors.

In addition to applying best business practices to the armed services, the military has to adjust to a socio-cultural context, which is less convergent with the core assumptions of traditional military culture. A higher value is placed upon individualism and social equality with citizens attuned to the 'blame and compensation' culture more disposed to enforce their rights in the courts. Previously the Crown, together with the Ministry of Defence and services, was exempt from legislation. This is no longer the case and the policy has been for some years to behave as if the law did apply. In future, exemptions are only likely to be supported if and when it can be demonstrated that the imposition of law would be incompatible with essential training and operations of the military. A case in point would be minimum wage legislation, and another the possibility of preventing the employment of soldiers below the age 18. In a climate that is less deferential, it is now up to the military to prove that conforming to the changing norms and values of wider society would be likely to damage operational efficiency rather than the burden of proof being on the proponents of change. More often than not these issues will have to be addressed in a legal context. A series of rulings and directives will continue to flow not so much from the UK legislature but from such bodies as the European Union Commission and European Court, especially in the fields of employment law, health and safety at work, and freedom of information.

Deference to authority figures – especially in institutional organisations – has waned: authority has to be earned and not taken for granted. This trend poses questions for the armed forces with their highly structured authority relations, as for example in recent discussions on whether service personnel ought to have the right to be able to air and represent their grievances in forums that are outside the formal chain of command. It is in this context that Major Eric Joyce has argued that the Army need no longer prepare for war in time of peace. This is because peace-keeping is the only thing that is likely to occur. Presumably, long warning times will allow such a shift in the *modus operandi* of an army at peace. This development will allow a loosening of the chain of command to incorporate a more rights-based system of command and consultation, more akin to non-military organisations. Yet such arguments seem more persuasive if they are wedded to an assessment of the nature of modern war or of operations other than war, including muscular peace-keeping, as I mentioned earlier in connection with the Bett team's views on the modern chain of command.

In a more individualistic society a lower priority is given to the values of the community and the subordination of the self to that of the team. Also in a 'postmodern' subjective culture it is more difficult to sustain objective definitions of right and wrong. Furthermore, significant sections of the youth population are less physically fit than before. In order to maintain standards the costs of the training machine are likely to rise in order to bring poorer quality recruits up to the standard required. It will also be a challenge to maintain the traditional expectation that military personnel should conform to a code of moral conduct that is more demanding than that expected in civilian life with respect to issues of honesty, integrity, and adultery. Focusing on the needs of the individual will be of critical importance in both recruitment and retention. This is why the Strategic Defence Review is right to stress the importance of looking after the individual and the individual's family. Laudable initiatives include, for example, those such as ensuring that with new accommodation, 'in most instances, individuals of all ranks will be provided with a single room'.[23] The same can be said for the recognition that the services need to take 'individual aspirations for family stability into account as far as practicable' when managing postings, although operational requirements must be paramount.[24]

In recent years, the basis of the separate military community has been eroded significantly, although the effects on operational effectiveness remain unclear.[25] It is likely that with the home basing of the RAF and Army, they will converge with civilian arrangements, which have been long shared by the Royal Navy. While much of the military community will be dispersed into civilian society, service accommodation will tend to be focused on the younger service families. Jessup shows how the welfare of military families will increasingly be shared between the armed services and the civilian community (echoing the American experience).[26]

Within the family itself, increasingly both parents work, with employers facing rising demands for career breaks and more flexible working practices, demands that are also having to take into account the growing number of single-parent families. For the armed services much work will need to be done to provide more flexible working conditions and to recognise that women are no longer prepared to place their own career second to that of their military partners. Women are of course pursuing careers in the military and it is likely that the remaining rules excluding them from the front-line positions will be removed, although issues connected with the training and working relations of gender-integrated units will remain.

A further challenge to military culture concerns the issue of social representation and diversity. In recent years, the armed forces have experienced a transformation in the wider employment of women, a process that may, depending upon an ongoing review, erode the combat arms as a male preserve. In addition, they are likely to have to replace the current formal prohibition on homosexuals being employed in the services with a code of conduct that forbids inappropriate behaviour at work.[27] Recently, the political focus on equal opportunities and the armed services has shifted to the dimension of race and ethnicity. Society is also more ethnically heterogeneous than 20 years ago, raising issues of equal opportunities for all employing organisations and the need to ensure that the services are broadly representative of the society they are supposed to defend. There has been a good deal of discussion about the need for the armed services to be broadly 'representative' of the society of which it is a part. The 'Policy for People' chapter of the Strategic Defence Review includes the statement that:

> We are determined that the Armed Forces should better reflect the ethnic composition of the British population. Currently some 6 per cent of the general population are from ethnic minority backgrounds, but they make up just 1 per cent of the services. This must not continue. We have set a goal of attracting 2 per cent of new recruits this year from ethnic minority communities for each Service. We want that goal to increase by 1 per cent each year so that, eventually, the composition of our Armed Forces reflects that of the population as whole.[28]

The key question arising here is whether the goal of 'closing the gap' is defensible and achievable. The idea of representativeness can be given at least two rather different interpretations. First, one can refer to a socio-demographic match between military and society. In this context this would involve the military matching the 6 per cent statistical profile in the wider population – a goal achieved through planned targets if not quotas. As Sir Michael Howard has pointed out, this is very much an American value.[29] Second, one might argue that the armed services should subscribe to core societal values such as equality of opportunity, decency, fairness, careers open to all, and advancement in the organisation on merit. Accordingly, the services could feel relatively comfortable about the task of explaining the mismatch between their profile and that of society, but with one proviso. The gap would need to be explained not by a failure to have an effective equality of opportunity programme, but in terms of the propensity of particular groups to select certain kinds of occupations, military or civilian.[30] Given this differential propensity rate among groups in society, it is most unlikely that the services will be able to achieve the goals of representation in the first sense of that concept. Reaching such a goal would require programmes of affirmative action that are illegal in the UK and, perhaps, on the wane in the USA.[31]

Significant progress is achievable as far as the second meaning of representation is concerned. Thus over the past three years, the armed services, having been held up as a problem case by such agencies as the Equal Opportunities Commission and the Commission for Racial Equality, are now regarded in a rather different light. For example, the Commission for Racial Equality has been impressed with the changes introduced concerning ethnic monitoring, equal opportunities training, and the right of resort to tribunals outside the chain of command.[32] In addition, there have been changes such as the disciplinary code on racial harassment as well as attempts to build effective bridges between the services and ethnic minority communities. Meanwhile, having championed the cases of pregnant servicewomen in a number of costly (to the Ministry of Defence) disputes, the Equal Opportunities Commission now uses the services as a case study in how to introduce an equal opportunities policy.

It might be asked why the services should be (as they are) devoting so much attention to the issue of equal opportunities, whether in the context of ethnic minorities or gender. This question raises far broader issues concerning the evolution of military culture. In recent discussions, it has become clear that, in this area at least, some people perceive a 'zero-sum' conflict between functional and societal imperatives. That is to say meeting (so-called 'politically correct') equal opportunities objectives detracts from operational effectiveness. Such action diverts investment from more worthy objectives such as platforms or other equipment. Also, equal opportunities could, perhaps, undermine the traditional cohesion of the military community; here is another area where the military, rather than being used to defend the country, is being used as a 'social experiment' or part of a project to build a new, more inclusive society.[33]

However, other commentators have identified a number of reasons why this objective is a desirable one from the point of view of the *operational effectiveness* of the armed services.[34] First of all, it can improve access to a wider recruitment pool, as the armed services compete with civilian companies for scarce labour, both in terms of quantity and quality. In this context, one can point to the fact that ethnic minorities, although about 6 per cent of the national population, constitute over 19 per cent of the 16–24 military recruitment pool. In addition, there is a predisposition among some ethnic minority populations to pursue education as a means of improving their labour market positions, thus providing the services with a useful additional pool of skilled labour. Second, the armed services would benefit from a diversity of skills and backgrounds that a broader-based entry would produce. With the need for more intelligent and flexible service personnel likely to increase rather than decrease, such diversity will probably prove an advantage in future years. Third, a military freed from racial discrimination and focused instead on diversity, tolerance and decency would be more operationally effective than one in which racial harassment was permitted.[35] Fourth, the services could benefit from being seen to live up to the ideal of an equal opportunities employer. While this may enhance their standing in ethnic minority communities, it is just as important to sustain the legitimacy of the armed services and thus the fount of goodwill among the general public. In any case, the legal pressure to conform to this ideal is real enough. While the services have much to gain from recruiting a greater proportion of the ethnic minority communities than they currently do, those communities themselves would also derive some benefit. Lt-Col. Stuart Crawford has argued (drawing on the work of Cynthia Enloe[36]) that, if American experience is anything to go by, military service can provide ethnic minority communities with a sense that they are valuable elements of the social and political system. That is to say, people from these backgrounds are and feel included, not excluded: they develop skills that enhance their socio-economic mobility as well as acquiring a range of leadership skills that can be transferred back to local communities. This would suggest that all three could be seen as facets of a process of citizenship building.

CONCLUSION

As I suggested earlier, a pragmatic perspective leads one to the conclusion that it is misconceived to view meeting functional and societal imperatives as a zero-sum game. The armed services confront a series of challenges to their unique culture. They need to develop a personnel strategy that does not damage operational effectiveness – or make the services feel that they are permanently under attack from outsiders who do not fully appreciate the strategic imperatives impinging on them. However, at the same time, the supportive links between armed forces and society must be cultivated. Doing so need not weaken, but can actually strengthen, the services. In a healthy democracy it is vital that the armed forces do not remain too far apart from the society they are charged to defend. After all, it is society that funds them and bestows on them their legitimacy; and it is society from which they recruit their personnel and to which they return them to continue their working lives as civilians.

NOTES

1. 'Past defence reviews have concentrated on strategy and equipment, sometimes with insufficient consideration of people. This Review has given people their proper place at the centre of our plans', *The Strategic Defence Review*, Cm 3999 (July 1998), 36, para. 138.
2. The idea of the 'right to be different' (and whether the formulation is better put as a need to be different) came to prominence during the tenure of General Sir Michael Rose as Adjutant-General. A number of in-house studies explored this theme. Some of the issues were discussed in October 1997 at a seminar sponsored by the British Military Studies Group. See *The Future of British Military Cultures: Social and Legal Change in Britain and Europe: The Personnel Implications for the Armed Forces of the 21st Century* (BMSG, February 1998).
3. For a review of these traditions see Bernard Boene, 'How Unique Should the Military Be? A Review of Representative Literature and Outline of a Synthetic Formulation', *European Journal of Sociology*, (1990), pp. 3–59.
4. The most influential of the conservative thinkers on these issues is S.P. Huntington, *The Soldier and the State: The Theory and Practice of Civil–Military Relations* (Cambridge, MA: Harvard University Press, 1957). For those seeking to steer a pragmatic, midway path between conservatism and liberalism the most persuasive is the work of Morris Janowitz, *The Professional Soldier* (Glencoe, IL: Free Press, 1960).
5. I refer to need, not right, to be different because, in democracies, the rights of the armed services are pre-given but devolved to them by the civilian political leadership. Normally, a professional military is given the right to be heard not least on such matters as what it feels it needs to do its job properly. It thus may have a need to be different, but a right to be so presupposes a civilian decision to grant it.
6. See Karen O. Dunivin, 'Military Culture: Change and Continuity', *Armed Forces and Society*, 20 (1994), pp. 531–47; Dunivin, 'Military Culture: A Paradigm Shift', *Air War College Maxwell Paper*, No. 10, Maxwell Air Force Base, AL, USA, February 1997.
7. On the distinctive features of institutional organisations and the implications for the armed services see the useful discussion in H. Sorensen 'New Perspectives on the Military Profession: The I/O Model and Esprit de Corps Re-evaluated', *Armed Forces and Society*,

20 (1994), pp. 599-617, 610. See also C. Moskos and F.R. Wood, *The Military: More Than Just a Job?* (London: Brassey's, 1988).

8. This point emerged in discussions with a number of officers from both services. For a recent discussion of the regimental system in the British Army (with a particular focus on the political aspects) see Hew Strachan, *The Politics of the British Army* (Oxford: Clarendon Press, 1997), pp. 195–233.

9. Of course, there is a case for not retaining this capability, or that by overly focusing on it one diverts attention from the key tasks of the armed forces for the foreseeable future: peace support and humanitarian relief. In a recent paper for the Fabian Society (one which has triggered much social and political debate within and outside the services) Major Eric Joyce has argued that the Army no longer needs to prepare for war in time of peace. This is because peace-keeping is the only thing that is likely to occur. Presumably long warning times will allow such a shift in the *modus operandi* of an army at peace. Eric Joyce, *Armed Forces and the Man – Renewing the Armed Services*, (Fabian Society, 1997).

10. See B. Boene, W. von Bredow and C. Dandeker, 'The Military in Common Risk Societies: Elements of Comparison Among Nine Countries of West Central and East Europe', in J. Kuhlmann (ed.), *The Military in Common Risk Societies* (forthcoming).

11. '[T]here is ... roughly 10 per cent of the residual military experience in contemporary society compared to even 20/30 years ago.' See keynote address: 'The Future of British Military Cultures: Social and Legal Change into the 21st century–Britain in Comparative Perspective'.

12. In November 1998, the ban on wearing uniform while on duty, in public at least in mainland UK, was lifted in order to raise the public profile of the armed services.

13. C. Guthrie, 'The British Army at the Turn of the Century', *RUSI Journal,* June (1996), p. 5.

14. Professor Bernard Boene, of the Military Academy, St Cyr and the University of Toulouse, France, has coined the phrase 'cultural interoperability'.

15. C. Moskos and J. Burk, 'The Postmodern Military', in J. Burk (ed.), *The Military in New Times: Adjusting Armed Forces to a Turbulent World* (Boulder, CO: Westview Press, 1994), pp. 154–5.

16. B. Robertson, 'Joint Needs in 2010', in G.A.S.C. Wilson (ed.), *British Security 2010, Proceedings of a Conference held at Church House, Westminster* 1995, pp. 284–5.

17. C. Dandeker, Martin Edmonds, James Higgs and Fiona Paton,'The Independent Review of Armed Forces, Manpower, Career, and Remuneration Structures (The "Bett Report"), Context, Commentary and Response', with a foreword by Martin Edmonds, *Bailrigg Paper*, University of Lancaster, 1997, p. 21.

18. In many companies one can observe a shift from a multi-layered hierarchy to team or matrix structures. Specialisation of functions is still retained but less so than before and focused on projects working across functions. The matrix format provides the basis for more flexible organisation structures. One effect of a delayered, matrix organisation is the need to ensure that the workforce has the skills to be empowered effectively and to produce quality output. One conclusion from all of this is that throughout such flexible forces the need for intelligent soldiers is likely to increase rather than diminish. David Segal has taken up the wider application of matrix and related ideas to military organisations. See D.R. Segal, 'Organizational Designs for the Future Army', United States Army Research Institute for the Behavioral and Social Sciences, *Special Report*, No. 29 (1993), pp. 39–40.

19. Some officers have suggested to me that, with the absence of Army corps and groups, the scope for delayering is actually rather limited. For example, there is, in fact, little that could be delayered within the battalion, although there is scope for giving more responsibility to officers of junior ranks, as in making more use of captains as company commanders.

20. *Strategic Defence Review*, Supporting Essay Eleven, 11-8, para. 48.

21. Statement on Defence Estimates: 1994, p. 77

22. Discussions with RAF officers.
23. *Strategic Defence Review*, 9-5, para. 29.
24. *Strategic Defence Review*, Supporting Essay Nine, Policy for People, 9-3, p. 17. Leave and facilities for improved communication with families are also welcome improvements to service family life.
25. See the excellent work by C. Jessup, *Breaking Ranks: Social Change in Military Communities* (London: Brassey's, 1996).
26. Jessup, *Breaking Ranks*, p. 180.
27. On this, see C. Dandeker and F. Paton, 'The Military and Social Change', *London Defence Studies*, 39 (1997).
28. *Strategic Defence Review*, Supporting Essay Nine, 9-8, 41.
29. Sir Michael Howard, 'The Armed Forces and the Community', *RUSI Journal*, August (1996), p. 10.
30. This point raises difficult and complex issues, especially the extent to which an inclination not to pursue a military career is the result of perceived or real racism in the prospective employing organisation. This point is part of a related study by the author with Professor David Mason of the University of Plymouth.
31. Crawford points out that the Race Relations Act 1976 permits the provision of help to members of under-represented groups in their efforts to enter certain occupational sectors (personal communication). This can be in the form of education and training or encouragement through advertising and promotional initiatives. However, the selection process must be clearly on grounds of merit.
32. On 1 October 1997, service personnel were given the right of appeal to an industrial tribunal (although complaints had first to be referred to the chain of command).
33. Some personnel in the services have taken this view, one that is hardly absent in wider society. It was strongly criticised by the Chief of the Defence Staff, General Sir Charles Guthrie, at a conference sponsored by the Ministry of Defence on 'Equal Opportunities: Learning from Experience', held at the Royal Society of Arts, London, 10 November 1998.
34. The work of Lt-Col. Stuart Crawford is particularly noteworthy in this connection. The arguments developed here draw on Crawford's work and on a number of conversations with him over the past two years. See Crawford's 'Racial Integration in the Army – An Historical Perspective', *British Army Review*, 111 (December 1995), pp. 24–8. His Defence Fellowship thesis on this subject is, as yet, unpublished and not available to the public.
35. Speech by General Colin Powell and subsequent discussion at the Equal Opportunities Conference, Royal Society of Arts, 10 November 1998.
36. See C. Enloe, *Ethnic Soldiers: State Security in Divided Societies* (Athens, GA: University of Georgia Press, 1980). Also see Charles Moskos and John S. Butler *All That We Can Be: Black Leadership and Racial Integration the Army Way*, Twentieth Century Fund Book (New York: Basic Books, 1996).

PART III:
SOCIAL CHANGE AND FIGHTING EFFECTIVENESS

13

Fit to Fight: The Conceptual Component – An Approach to Military Doctrine for the Twenty-first Century

Sebastian Roberts

As Colonel Land Warfare 2, responsible for 'high-level doctrine' in the British Army, I have often been asked 'What is doctrine?' The facile answer, 'What is taught', disguises an important distinction. There are two distinct parts to doctrine. The greatest part, 'what is taught', is current best thought and practice, collated and published in digestible form, to inform education, training and operations. These are essentially the TTPs – tactics, techniques and procedures – which even at the highest levels of defence provide *aides-mémoire* for practitioners. But there is also the corpus of core thinking, which is the conceptual basis for all that we do in delivering fighting power. This is the stuff of enduring principles and characteristics, the relatively unchanging foundations upon which we approach the future. I say 'relatively' because change is continuous, and in the case of defence, unless our core thinking is designed to embrace change and retain the intellectual initiative, we are doomed to fail in our duty to succeed in conflict. This short paper is designed to examine these conceptual foundations, and propose those which offer a good basis for what we teach – for our doctrine for the twenty-first century.

Major-General Tony Pigott, Director General of Development and Doctrine, has outlined the key elements of the British Army's approach to the future as follows:

- combination of ends, ways and means;
- vision – shared, enduring, inspirational;
- embrace totality of future operational environment – combined, joint, multinational, inter-agency;
- concepts, doctrine, force development – an essential trinity;

- core tasks are combat operations – an enabler for wider tasks;
- train as you intend to operate;
- sharpen future-oriented processes and lines of development;
- attend to the people (moral) component;
- keep a healthy margin for uncertainty.

These precepts are universally applicable; I will pick up most of these themes, concentrating on our national doctrinal perspective, with the observation that before any other consideration, doctrine must be right for the nation or organisation concerned. Effective joint, multinational or inter-agency doctrine must be the harnessing of thoroughbreds, not a chimera. In our case, the United Kingdom's geography, history and politics (membership of the United Nations Security Council, a leading role in NATO, the European and Commonwealth dimensions and global and regional interests generally) lead to a distinctive British view of the nature of conflict, which is a foundation stone for the future development of our doctrine. The term 'spectrum of conflict' is widely used to describe conflict: a linear model which runs from low to high intensity, or from other operations to war. The British Army increasingly uses the model shown in Figure 1, which portrays a continuum of conflict prevention, through conflict, to post conflict and conflict resolution. The external arrows portray the ever-present imperative to reduce the conflict segment of the continuum:

Figure 1 The spectrum of conflict

It is important to note that this two-dimensional model describes a complex spiral through time of inter-related conflicts. The key deductions that we can make about future conflict are:

- the importance of a full spectrum approach, recognising especially the new challenges and opportunities in conflict prevention and post-conflict operations;

- the political imperatives to expand the conflict prevention 'zone', and to minimise time (and money and casualties) in conflict;
- that full spectrum capability requires a combined, joint, multinational and inter-agency mix of players;
- that the mix, role and relative importance of those players will differ in each crisis, and their balance will change as each crisis develops;
- that fighting in war continues to be the central focus for armies;
- that armies must be designed to conduct operations simultaneously in different 'zones' of the spectrum;
- that simultaneous operations in different 'zones' are likely to have complex inter-relationships: allies in one crisis may not be friends in another.

In its approach to these challenges of future conflict, the United Kingdom has the advantage that because of its geography, history and politics, all its military operations in the past 300 years have been expeditionary. This long history of expeditionary operations has included many of the greatest wars that have afflicted mankind, but it has also meant a continuum of other operations – creating and policing an empire, colonial and post-colonial counter-insurgency and constabulary operations, and the full range of peace support operations. This means that there is nothing new or strange for the British Army in conducting operations other than war. Geography, history and politics have also meant that we have not needed a large standing army designed for national defence, except in the two world wars; and even then our operations were all expeditionary. In the same way, we have never had to resort to full conscription: even in the First World War, conscription was not universal; it never occurred, for instance, in Ireland. The British Army has remained essentially volunteer and professional as well as expeditionary ever since medieval times.

From the expeditionary nature of our approach to operations it follows that for the British Army, 'Joint is a given'. The British Army cannot deploy abroad without going overseas; and this simplistic truth is reflected in the degree of integration of our armed forces, manifest in such organisations as the Joint Services Command and Staff College, the Permanent Joint Headquarters, and Joint Rapid Reaction Forces, and their missions. This jointness is also a function of economy and scale, both of which negate the realistic possibility of the United Kingdom establishing a 'third force' for operations other than war.

This leads to another core tenet of British military doctrine: that focusing on war is absolutely essential to approaching all military operations. All military activities, including training, involve risk, but warfare is the most demanding, in terms of national will, resources and the demands it makes on the individual – whether the most senior commander, the most junior soldier, or a member of their families. For this reason, it is a fundamental tenet of British military doctrine that the Army should be organised, trained and equipped first and foremost for war. By preparing for war, other operations are made easier. If this focus were ever to be lost it would be massively difficult in time, resources, attitudes and ethos to regain it. This is not to underestimate the complexity and demands of other operations, such as peace support operations, but to recognise the simple truth that it is *relatively* easier to change gear from training and preparing for warfare to peace-support operations, than the other way round.

It is for this reason that British military doctrine is founded on the principles of *war*, and defines military effectiveness in terms of *fighting* power, of which it distinguishes three components: conceptual, physical and moral. The conceptual component is the thought process behind the ability to fight. The physical component is the means to fight, and it comprehends the main elements of combat power – the resources for combat. The moral component is that to which Napoleon was referring when he declared that in war 'the moral is to the physical as three is to one'. The term 'moral component' means more than either morale (*le Moral*), morals (*la Morale*) or morality (*la Moralité*). It is defined as:

> The ability to get people to fight. Simplified as the possession of high morale, the ability to get people to fight has three fundamental elements: the motivation to achieve the task in hand; effective leadership from those placed in authority; and sound management of all personnel and resources.[1]

Related to the British Army's focus on war and fighting power is its essentially operational nature. Operational effectiveness is the core criterion upon which the British Army is judged and justified. Ever since the Cold War ended, approaching 30 per cent of the British Army has been committed to operations – that is to say actually deployed, preparing for deployment, or recovering from deployment – at any one time. This compares to the 11 per cent regarded as the maximum acceptable over prolonged periods in the US Army. It means that the British Army is exceptionally operationally experienced throughout its arms, services and ranks, compared to almost any other army in the world. There are very few British soldiers without at least one campaign medal; and because of the limited size of an all-Regular Army, all are trained, and many have operational experience, in multiple roles and skills. For instance, units and individuals of all arms have served in the infantry role in Northern Ireland. This enhances the fighting focus of the whole Army, including the many members of the Reserves and the Territorial Army, all volunteers, who serve alongside their regular counterparts on operations.

High operational use also feeds the 'can-do' attitude of the Army. This is a double-edged sword, because the enthusiasm to 'do the business' which is so characteristic of volunteer professionals can, over time, detract from the readiness for war of the whole Army: operations can be the enemy of training. But the fact remains that the Army exists to conduct operations, and the positive side of the can-do attitude is that it breeds a culture of coping with the unexpected, of accepting responsibility, in all ranks.

This attitude, born of constant experience of expeditionary operations, leads instinctively to embracing the next two core conceptual tenets of the British Army: the manoeuvrist approach and mission command. The manoeuvrist approach to warfare 'seeks to destroy an enemy's cohesion and his will to win through a series of rapid, violent and unexpected actions that create a turbulent and rapidly deteriorating situation with which he cannot cope' (*British Defence Doctrine*). This requires an attitude of mind which grasps the initiative and seeks originality and surprise. It demands improvisation, initiative, freedom and speed of action, decentralised command and delegation of authority, and resources to the level at which chaos can be exploited and its effects transformed to advantage. This is the essence of mission command. Its tenets are mutual trust, timely decision-making, the importance of understanding a superior commander's intention, and, by applying this to one's own actions, a clear responsibility to fulfil that intention.

Delegation is a key aspect of mission command, and another core tenet of the British approach to defence. The friction and complexity of land operations demand that all commanders are trained to delegate authority, responsibility and resources to the level at which they can best be used to achieve the tempo which defeats the enemy by beating his decision/action cycle – and that subordinates at all levels are trained to accept the appropriate responsibilities. This ideal would easily descend into utopian anarchy, if not for the next vital characteristic of the British armed forces: professionalism.

The British Army is essentially professional. This means that all British soldiers, including those in the Territorial Army and Regular Reserves, must recognise their legal right and duty to fight and if necessary kill, according to their orders, and their unlimited liability to give their lives in doing so. Both duty and liability are shared with all members of the armed forces, but the particular circumstances of the land environment, in which every soldier is a weapon bearer, means that all must be prepared personally to make the decision to engage the enemy and place themselves in harm's way. This is the unique nature of soldiering. This professionalism originates in the volunteer nature of the British armed forces; it is honed by constant, progressive, realistic and demanding training, in which the ethos, as well as the doctrine of the Army is inculcated.

Another distinctive core facet of the British Army is to be found in its common basic training. All officers in the British Army are trained at one military academy, the Royal Military Academy Sandhurst, and receive all their subsequent command and staff training at the Joint Services Command and Staff College, along with all their peers in the Royal Navy and the Royal Air Force. As a result, the British Army is led by an officer corps with an exceptionally unified professional education. Irrespective of arm of service or type of commission, the common background of Sandhurst means that all British officers arrive in their regiments or corps with the same professional foundations; the basics of an ethos which is honed throughout their careers by superiors, peers and subordinates with the same military education. By the same token, the other ranks also receive an increasingly uniform basic training, which begins, like that of the officers, with basic infantry skills. After their basic training – in the case of the officers, a year at Sandhurst – all ranks receive their special-to-arm training, and, within a total of less than 18 months (less than a year for many other ranks), join the regiments to which in most cases they will return throughout their careers.

This is a highly significant difference from most other NATO armies: at a stage when the officers of most other armies are not half way through their initial training, British subalterns are leading their first commands – and, given the high deployment rate, they are probably on operations within 18 months. This is not to commend less training: far from it. The real lesson is that if economy, scale and the recruiting market allow, there is much to be said for a single basic military education for all officers, focused exclusively on the fundamentals of the profession, bringing together both short service (usually three years in the first instance) and regular (career) officers. Apart from preventing the discrimination that can arise in armies with exclusive military academies, it also means that the majority, who have not chosen to spend a full career in the Army, infuse the whole officer corps with an open-mindedness born of expecting a life after soldiering, probably after only three years or so. It helps to ensure that the common ethos is not narrowly military, but provides an external reference founded on deeper and broader principles. Furthermore, the relative brevity of basic training means that British soldiers get the operational experience they join for very early.

Of course the commonality and relatively short duration of basic training are not purely the result of good planning – as in everything else, economy and scale play their part. They are also part of the reason for the modular structure which is another fundamental facet of the British Army. Since we cannot afford the luxury of formations with single, distinct missions, it is a tenet of the British approach to operations that we tailor our forces for specific operations by grouping capabilities and units for the task in hand, in the process of task-organising. This modular approach is a feature of the British Army as old as its expeditionary, operational focus. Our history suggests that there is a lower limit for 'modularity' in the combat arms in warfare – the unit. The twentieth century history of a British infantry regiment is instructive. To use the one I know best, the Irish Guards, its first operations were as mounted infantry in South Africa in 1900; the Great War saw the regiment raising several battalions, which fought mainly as main defence infantry in the trenches, but also saw it contributing to a new regiment, the 6th (Machine Gun) Guards. Imperial policing between the wars was followed by infantry fighting in all theatres save south-east Asia in the Second World War, and by mechanised infantry and tank battalions in the Guards Armoured Division in north-west Europe. Since the war, the single battalion has served in the airportable, mechanised and armoured infantry roles in every theatre, in operations ranging from counter-insurgency to peace support operations. Many other battalions could add all-arms warfare in the Falklands or the Gulf to their similar list.

One of the most important facets of the British Army, which is a key factor in its ability to task-organise, is its volunteer ethos. The British Army is made up entirely of volunteers, and a volunteer army differs fundamentally from a conscript one. A conscript army is the citizens in arms. Service is a function of citizenship. Service in such armies is compulsory by law. Soldiers serve because they are citizens, so a conscript army's ethos is based on belief in the state and service to it. This applies to the regular cadres as well as the conscripts. Conscript armies reflect national society directly because they are drawn from every part of it. The British Army, on the other hand, is composed of volunteers who are servants of the Crown. British soldiers are professionals who choose to serve because they want to be soldiers. Their service must be based on mutual trust rather than law or contract. Many British soldiers – those from Eire or Nepal for example – are not even British citizens. So the British Army is not a citizen army either, and therefore does not reflect national society like others. Rather it reflects the volunteers of which it is composed. Volunteers come at a price, not only in financial cost, but in terms of ethos; unless they want to do so, volunteers neither join nor stay. As in any organisation, output is dependent on input. Hence a volunteer army cannot be engineered by law or fiat without risk. Any change to the ethos demands a change in the volunteers. Equally, a change in the volunteers will affect the ethos. Changing either will affect the output – ultimately shaping the military effectiveness which the nation wants. This is why the Army must always be in touch with the aspirations and attitudes of its soldiers; it must train and educate them as necessary; and it must be sensitive to the demands of society. Conversely, social engineering of the British Army will affect its fighting power.

The volunteer nature and international composition of the British Army make it more usable throughout the spectrum of conflict than citizen or conscript armies. Citizen and conscript armies focus essentially on national defence; as conflict becomes more complex, volunteer professionals focused on their profession become increasingly useful. One has only to look at the relative utility of the French or Spanish Foreign Legions, or the Netherlands Marines, compared to the conscript elements of their armed forces.

Another related facet of the British Army is its multinational outlook and experience. A function again of geography, policy and economy, the British Army has very seldom fought or operated without allies. Even imperial policing and counter-insurgency have always included co-operation with indigenous troops; the Falklands War stands out as a unique example of a British national joint campaign.

In a similar vein, the British Army is used to the inter-agency dimension, not least, in its recent history, from its experience of serving under the lead of the Royal Ulster Constabulary in Northern Ireland. The increasing significance of a widening variety of other agencies throughout the spectrum of conflict raises an absolutely vital issue. Given the new categories of players, what now constitutes a soldier? The presence on operations of contractors like Brown and Root, of organisations with hitherto military capability like HALO, the British anti-mining trust, of civilian policemen, and of new categories of reserve soldiers, such as the British sponsored reserves (civilian contractors' employees whose contracts commit them to being called up in certain circumstances) or even the new mercenary 'private military companies', such as Sandline International, mean that the distinctions between soldiers and civilians are becoming blurred. If traditional citizen armies have less utility in the new spectrum of conflict, volunteer professional soldiers will be far from the only ones involved in conflict.

While armies remain nations' first choice tools for managing conflict, it is vital that they continue to attract high quality people. To achieve this, the Army must be in touch with what the best young people want, value or aspire to. Dying for king and country would probably attract less votes now at the Oxford Union than it did, famously, in the 1930s. There are signs that idealism, like so much of life, is focused much more on global than on national issues, and that people are increasingly prepared to offer their service for more than patriotism. More young people than ever before may be able to answer Baron Percy's strikingly modern call: *'Allez où la Patrie et l'humanité vous appellent ... soyez-y toujours prets a servir l'une et l'autre!'*[2] At the same time, fewer and fewer young people, especially the ablest, expect traditional single careers. Armies want the same people who in Switzerland join the International Committee of the Red Cross, or in France, Médecins sans Frontières, not necessarily as a career for life, but as a vital part of their lives. This implies the need for ever-greater flexibility in Army career management, making perhaps a virtue of the trend which sees many top quality young soldiers leave after relatively short service to join other agencies, by re-employing experts as required.

One of the most important aspects of the growing part played in conflict by other agencies is the recognition that defence is not just a matter for soldiers, civil servants and politicians. It is increasingly necessary to engage a wider community in defence and security issues, in understanding conflict. This is why seminars such as that for which this paper was prepared are so important; they contribute tremendously to vital cross-fertilisation, and improve the synapses of defence. This is crucial in approaching what is perhaps *the* fundamental challenge of current and future conflict, the imperative need to determine the legal, moral and ethical framework for future operations.

The spectrum of conflict in Figure 1 shows that as the old simplicities of war and peace, of victory and defeat between sovereign nations or alliances recede into the past, the key question both for soldiers and societies is 'What is worth fighting – or killing or dying – for?' The soldier's ultimate responsibility to fight – and if need be kill and die – remains, and as ever it requires a moral and ethical basis which is shared and understood by all; but the societies from which we recruit have increasingly diverse ethical and moral codes, while conflict is becoming ever more complex. The crucial dichotomy is between increasing ethical and moral diversity in society, and the absolute necessity of a rock solid, common ethical and moral basis for all our soldiers on all operations. The aim of the British Army's forthcoming Doctrine for the Moral Component (with the working title 'Soldiering') is in effect to provide the algebra with which to do the complex equation to resolve this dichotomy between current pressures on societies and individuals, and the challenges of future operations.

The sole purpose (and measure) of our armed forces remains military effectiveness; that is to say success in war and other operations. But military effectiveness cannot be based on functional output alone, and unless it is focused on higher, external ethics, an army risks the moral bankruptcy of the Waffen SS. Soldiers must know that what they do is right, and that they have the support of their nation, their society and their government:

> If serving military officers are now required to study wider public relations and political issues, can we not encourage facilities for MPs to increase their knowledge of military matters and begin to understand in particular the practical utility of military ethos? There may be those who sneer at such concepts, who just do not understand this element of fighting power and its practical implication. British troops will advance through minefields under fire because they trust they are not being sacrificed for a political bungle, know that the British public is behind them, implicitly trust their comrades and enjoy an ethos which sees all ranks as a 'band of brothers'. And they have a robust self-confidence and pride in their superiority over everyone else. To destroy these qualities is effectively to threaten the fighting power of the British Armed Forces. Doctrine can be taught and resources can be bought, but it doesn't matter how clever your doctrine is or how well equipped you are if your soldiers will not close with and kill the enemy. Martial spirit is a precious and fragile commodity.[3]

There are no quick fixes. Since there are ever greater demands on the individual soldier to address complex ethical and moral issues in every type of operation, under the omnipresent eye of the media, and in the absence of ethical and moral values held commonly throughout society or the nation, the Army must assert and inculcate its own ethos. In the words of Iain Torrance, 'the fragmentation of moral authority and the cult of individualism in society'[4] pose fundamental problems for any organisation which requires the willing subordination, or at least realignment, of the needs, desires and aspirations of the individual to those of the group, which for every soldier may amount to the ultimate extent of giving one's life for a higher purpose. To answer this challenge, the Army must accept its responsibility to be a 'moral community'.[5]

The British Army has another core facet, which has much to offer here: the regimental system. In many ways a historical survival from the times when officers were commissioned to raise, train and command regiments, the system has certain aspects which offer tremendous utility in modern conflict. First, the unit of about 500 to 600 soldiers seems to be the right size to balance the needs, aspirations and desires of the individual, with the functional utility – the fighting power – of the organisation. It seems to be the optimum size for each to know everyone, and their own place. Second, in the case of the United Kingdom, most of these regiments are sustained in recruiting terms from geographical areas with strong existing loyalties and characteristics. Third, each regiment has the history and trappings – colours, uniforms, music and mottoes – to inspire the deepest pride and loyalty. All of these mean, most importantly, that the regiment is regarded as a family – a community which embraces the individual from cradle to grave. It has been observed that they are akin to tribes; certainly the 'family regiment' is a very real and potent organisation: it is the one in which most British soldiers, certainly in the combat arms, do all their operational service. When a British soldier is not on the staff or at a training establishment, he or she will return throughout their career to the same regiment.

The continuity of service in the same operational unit is what makes the high rate of operations and flexibility of units and individuals possible, and goes to the heart of the volunteer, professional Army. Loyalty is to the professional family, and so the answer to the key question 'What is worth dying for?' is simple, and the same for any operation: your mates are *always* worth dying for.

Such professional families *are* moral communities; it is vital to ensure that their ethos is right. There are plenty of instances of armies and units with magnificent morale and superb effectiveness which were based on a depraved ethos: the Waffen SS is an obvious example. One of the risks inherent in military organisations is that they can be effective in any cause if their internal components, conceptual, physical and moral, are strong. The thing that sets a good army or a good soldier apart from an effective one is an external moral reference, and in achieving this, as in all else, leadership is the key.

I am conscious that this seems a pretty rosy view of the British Army; it is certainly that of one who loves it. But no one is blind to the challenges of both conflict and society. Understanding conflict is a matter not just for soldiers, civil servants and politicians. The growing part played by other agencies in its conduct and management underlines this point. True ethical military effectiveness is achieved only by constant vigilance, analysis and diligence throughout the wider community.

The core conceptual facets of the British Army – its expeditionary, volunteer, professional nature; its doctrine of manoeuvre and mission command; its modular, joint, multinational and inter-agency approach to operations; its focus on warfare, the principles of war and fighting power; its strong historical basis, with such manifestations as the regimental system; its emphasis on leadership and training; and perhaps above all, its constant operational experience – have honed the existing organisation into an effective instrument for national policy in the very complex and uncertain world of future conflict. With continuing good leadership, from the highest political level to the most junior commander, and constant vigilance and analysis, engaging all the wider community, the British Army will continue to be fit to fight – conceptually, physically and morally.

NOTES

1. Army Doctrine Publication, vol. 1, *Operations*, June 1994, pp. 1–7.
2. Baron Percy, *Chirurgien Militaire de l'Empire* (1754–1825).
3. Dr John Reid MP, 'The Armed Forces and Society', *RUSI Journal*, April (1997) (as Opposition Spokesman on Defence).
4. Dr Iain Torrance, *Ethics and the Military Community* (Strategic and Combat Studies Institute, Occasional No. 24, 1998)
5. Ibid.

14

The Moral Component

Iain Torrance

According to the 1989 booklet, *Design for Military Operations – The British Military Doctrine*,[1] ingredients in fighting power (the ability to fight) are: (1) the physical component (the means to fight); (2) the conceptual component (the thought process); and (3) the moral component (the ability to get people to fight). The booklet allows that the moral factor is difficult to define, and is often, following Napoleon, summed up in the term 'morale'. Yet it acknowledges that the ability to get people to fight is not just a question of morale, but also involves motivation, leadership and management.

Perhaps because we tend to think spatially, aided by diagrams and flow charts, it is evident that, once the moral component is set alongside the physical and conceptual, as if it were something external to both of them, it is tempting to equate it with matters of morale, and see it as the raisins in the fruit cake along with the flour and the butter, rather than as the heat in the oven, which binds all the other ingredients together. So a first issue is to suggest that the diagram is misleading. I am taking as a point of entry the instinct of the drafters of British military doctrine that the moral component is *more* than morale, although morale follows from it. I want first to consider: When is war *moral* or *immoral*? And the ethics of soldiering follow reasonably clearly from that. I then want to ask: What are the virtues of the soldier (that is, the specific moral skills a good soldier must acquire)? This should clarify the approach to questions like leadership, integrity and self-discipline, by locating them in a more intelligible context. None of these questions is straightforward, and they feed into each other. I am not promising formulae or cut and dried answers, but offer it as a sympathetic contribution to a very important continuing debate.

Let us begin with the 'just-war' arguments. They are particularly relevant and interesting at the end of the 1990s, as at least three assumptions are under review. These are: (1) broadly Protestant understandings of justice and rationality which call in question the easy applicability of the just war arguments; (2) broadly Roman Catholic understandings of the immorality of violence which signal a change in the just war perspective; and (3) the changes in the nature of war itself. We can take these in turn.

The earliest Christian perspective on war was to follow the teaching of Jesus that when struck one should turn the other cheek. However, it gradually began to be taken that the prohibition on self-defence did not imply that one may not defend one's neighbour. This was first formulated by Ambrose of Milan (c. 339–97) and his pupil, Augustine of Hippo (354–430). There was a logic behind this. It implied that the impetus behind the Christian sanctioning of just war was the duty of love, which led to protecting the innocent. The foundation was *not* a Christian presumption that it was sinful to inflict harm. Two other consequences then follow: (1) considerations of restraint in the use of violence are *temporally* subsequent to the decision to apply force; and (2) considerations of restraint are *logically* derived from the same duty of love, which is now directed towards the aggressor. So restraint is also rooted in the duty of love, rather than in a presumption that it is intrinsically sinful to inflict harm.[2] Classic just-war argument evolved from this and was rooted in those instincts.

Thus, Thomas Aquinas (c. 1225–74) argued that three conditions were necessary for a war to be just.[3] These were: war should be declared by a legal authority; it required a just cause; and a just intention. For both *just cause* and *just intention* St Thomas quoted Augustine. On cause, 'Those wars are generally defined as just which avenge some wrong, when a nation or a state is to be punished for having failed to make amends for the wrong done, or to restore what has been taken unjustly.'[4] On right intention: 'For the true followers of God even wars are peaceful, not being made for greed or out of cruelty, but from desire for peace, to restrain the evil and assist the good.'[5] This classic formulation was developed in the early modern period under Francisco de Vitoria (1492–1546) and Hugo Grotius (1583–1645) in response to new questions raised by the propriety of colonial wars against non-Christians, and by the Protestant Reformation, where both sides claimed just cause. The issue of colonial war led to just-war doctrine being removed from the realm of theology and located instead within the sphere of secular natural law, and the issue of war between Christians with the possibility of justice on both sides led to greater emphasis being given to restraint, which in turn led to the formulation of rules limiting the conduct of war.[6] As everybody knows, thinking on these matters was accelerated at the end of the nineteenth century, agreed at The Hague and Geneva Conventions, and incorporated in resolutions of the United Nations.

The details of that need not concern us here, as what we are concerned with first is the kind of misgivings advanced about the applicability of the just war arguments in general. And evidently, if it is not accepted that war may be just, *that affects the moral component of fighting power.*

Since the 1960s, there has been a steady loss of confidence in our ability to resolve moral dilemmas in a satisfactory and definitive way. There were various reasons for this. Traditionally, in Christian ethics, moral dilemmas were resolved through appeal to scripture, reason and tradition. However, post-war biblical criticism has undermined the authority of the Bible, and an increasing realisation of the *social location of reason* – an understanding that what is held to be reasonable varies from culture to culture and through the course of time – has undermined confidence in the authority of reason and tradition. Secular ethics have not fared much better. There, traditionally, dilemmas were resolved either consequentially (looking at consequences, and selecting that course which produced most benefit) or deontologically (anchoring one's decision on a fundamental principle). Problems here included the insoluble question of where do consequences end and what is to count as a consequence; and on the other side, what is the origin of our moral principles, how are such principles recognised, and how are conflicts between principles to be resolved.

Into this vacuum or flux, in 1981 Alasdair MacIntyre launched his remarkable book *After Virtue*.[7] Here, among other things, MacIntyre argued that reason *by itself* was unable to resolve moral argument. As an example he showed the interminable (irresolvable) nature of the disagreement over justice between John Rawls and Robert Nozick. Did justice simply require equal distribution of goods, or did it take account of the past (how people came to be in need)? The insufficiency of reason was grounded in: (1) the acknowledgement that what is *reasonable* is socially constructed – different things appear reasonable to different cultures and historical periods; and (2) reason, by itself, is not sufficiently concrete to persuade, and so to motivate, action. MacIntyre's resolution was to suggest that we should desert universal (foundational) post-Enlightenment moral principles based on reason, and instead construct local moralities based on communities. This has fostered a shift towards more local and communitarian thinking. It has been characterised as non-foundational or post-modern ethics, and, in certain senses, it lends itself to the current debate about the Army's self-understanding. According to this, the Army is a culture, a moral community with its own distinctive ethos, and the 'right to be different' claim is put into a philosophical context. *That impacts sharply on the moral component in fighting power*, and we shall return to it, but the non-foundational perspective has other consequences which are less congenial for the armed forces.

As soon as we become more sharply aware of what the tradition-dependent account of morality implies, we come to see just how 'local' arguments based on 'justice' may become. If justice, at least in certain dimensions, is shaped by *whose justice* it is, *and which rationality* it is located within, then we may have far less confidence in appealing to the principles of just war as being universally applicable and recognisable. MacIntyre's argument warns us that where moral argument is couched in general terms and justified by appeal to reason, then there is a risk of 'slippage' and manipulation of the standard. An extension of the argument is that it is then important to distinguish between just war, realism and crusade. This needs to be explained. *Just war*, in the proper sense, would be extremely rare, and could only be waged if there were a genuinely shared culture and ecology of values between opponents. Both sides would need to have a comparable understanding of just cause, proportion and restraint. *Realism* would be technically unjust war, war fought with few strictly moral pretensions, but businesslike, and where coercion was seen as the most efficient means of gaining an objective. Realism might be the professional soldier's war, and here war would end immediately the limited military objective has been gained. *Crusade* would be war conducted in the name of some higher value under the rhetoric of 'victory at any cost'. It would again be unjust in terms of the classic arguments, but its injustice would be cloaked by political and media rhetoric, and it would be a politicians' war. The warning which follows from MacIntyre's analysis of contemporary ethics is, I suggest, that we must take account of the danger of *slippage*: the slide *from realism* in the conduct of war *into crusade* through manipulation of the just-war criteria. The traditional just-war language permits this because it is so generalised and abstract that it has little purchase on reality and provides no friction. Historically, armies, as do all disciplined communities, have understood the importance of restraint. But once war is driven either politically or by the press in terms of crusade, it becomes actually impossible to make sense of proportion and appropriateness. Two issues follow from this. First, if MacIntyre is right and values are found within a moral community, then the military community, disciplined and characterised by firmly held values of its own, will tend to be resistant to slippage and may even find itself morally in conflict with a more bloodthirsty public. This is a reverse of the picture usually portrayed of callous and licentious soldiers. Second, it may be argued that the fundamental issue is, as the American ethicist Stanley Hauerwas puts it, to determine: 'how democracies are to develop virtues in their citizens to fight wars with limited purposes, not crusades'.[8] If the armed services are authorised by democracies, and if democracies are at risk of losing their grasp on justice, then our understanding of the moral component of fighting power is complicated by having the tension between Army and civilian society built into it. The armed services may well be the more moral community. My first suggestion was that the usual diagram may be misleading. The moral component of fighting power may be more like the heat from the oven rather than the raisins in the cake. A complication now is that the cake may have been pre-heated or half baked in a civilian oven which may be at a different temperature.

This brings us, second, to changes in the Roman Catholic attitude to the just war arguments. Though these are arguments from outside the military community they have considerable effect on the moral component to fighting power, as they threaten its moral legitimacy.

James Turner Johnson traces the beginning of this shift in perspective to 1870 when a *Postulatum* was presented to the First Vatican Council. The purpose of this was to challenge 'the justice of the form of war practised by modern states'.[9] The objection was rooted in reaction to the Franco-Prussian War, and possibly the American Civil War. It pointed to the nationalistic ambitions of various states, the militarism of national armies, and 'hideous massacres' which the Church could not accept as just. The *Postulatum* dismissed the idea that a first use of force could be just, though it allowed the justice of a second use of force in defence.[10] That was a first step. Following the carnage of the First World War, the Conventus of Fribourg in 1931 distinguished between defence, which was lawful, and the argument for war from national 'necessity', which was judged illicit. These documents changed the agenda, setting in motion a 'presumption against war'.

This trend was carried forward implicitly in a Christmas message of 1956 by Pope Pius XII, and explicitly in the 1963 encyclical *Pacem in Terris* of Pope John XXIII. Here the Pope said: '[I]n this age which boasts of its atomic power, it no longer makes sense to maintain that war is a fit instrument with which to repair the violation of justice.' Quite what the Pope intended is still disputed, but one interpretation is that this was an outright rejection of all just-war theory,[11] not simply a condemnation of first strike. The same trend was continued by Pope Paul VI in his 1965 address to the United Nations General Assembly: 'Never again war, war never again!', and in the 1983 pastoral letter of the American Catholic bishops, *The Challenge of Peace*. This document crystallised presuppositions which had been implicit in papal statements for three decades. It maintained that: 'Catholic teaching begins in every case with a presumption against war and for peaceful settlement of disputes. In exceptional cases, determined by the moral principles of the just war tradition, some uses of force are permitted.'[12]

It was suggested earlier that the fundamental root of the just war perspective was the duty of love, which authorised defence and the restoration of justice. The *presumption against war* which has developed over the past 30 years is a change of direction; an innovation, which could undermine the moral authority of fighting power. How justifiable is this change?

I want to bring two criticisms against this change in perspective, and then make a comment. First, the change requires a different logical sequence, which has not been justified. That is, it makes *ius in bello* (the restraints on conduct in the prosecution of war) prior to *ius ad bellum* (the justification for initiating war). As has been suggested before, restraint follows from the fundamental duty to love, rather than from a fundamental presumption that it is sinful to cause harm. Second, the change in perspective may be empirically misguided, in that it fails to address the contemporary nature of war. Its expression during recent decades has been rooted in the context of deterrence and the nuclear threat. But it may be objected that modern war is not concerned with mass destruction, that it relies on conventional, not nuclear weapons, and indeed, if one follows the spectrum model of war in the 1998 paper on 'soldiering', then the nature and boundary of war will continue to change considerably, and may become highly focused. Modern soldiering may well be for humanitarian non-nationalistic purposes, and thus the moral fear of nationalistic militarism may now be out of place. All of this suggests that the innovation in just-war thinking is unjustified, and that there is still work for the traditional arguments to do.

But whether justified or not, I suggest that there is a way in which this shift in perspective risks *compromising* the moral element in fighting power. I referred earlier to the slippage which may occur when the generalised just war arguments have lost their grittiness in a post-modern secular culture, and can fail to prevent a drift from realism to crusade. That, in a sense, is a drift from the right, urging the military community into a fight it does not believe in. What I am suggesting now is that there may equally dangerously be a drift from the left, questioning the morality of forcibly restoring justice, and obliging the military community to sit down for dinner with murderers.[13] I suggest that this is as serious a question for the integrity of the moral component.

So far we have looked at the moral appraisal of war, asking how shifting perspectives affect *and compromise* the moral component in fighting power. Let us now change direction and consider what are the virtues of the soldier, that is the specific moral skills a good soldier should acquire.

Current discussion of this issue has been shaped, understandably, by the 1996 'right to be different'[14] paper. I suggest that the line taken there has been driven in part defensively, to respond to secular (non-military) comments on matters like the previous ban on homosexuals, and on codes of practice which forbid similar private acts like adultery. To some extent, the Army has been wrong-footed by this line of questioning. In a liberal climate, when even the Church of England is revisiting its attitude to homosexual practice, it is very difficult for the Army to refer to the Bible *simpliciter*. Thus, we have seen the 'right to be different' move. As this move has flaws as well as real advantages, it provides a useful point of entry for discussion of military virtues.

In its concern to be non-moralistic, this perspective tends to portray virtues and vices purely functionally. Thus, the Army is held to derive its culture primarily from its central *raison d'être*, which is land-based war-fighting. The nature of the Army's ethos follows directly: it is taken to be based on the *unique* requirement that all Army personnel must be capable of armed conflict, and ultimately, be prepared to close with the enemy at short range, face to face and kill them. It is suggested that all British soldiers have an unlimited liability to fight, kill and if necessary die. Consequently, it is combat effectiveness, rather than the pursuit of a moral high ground, which is the sole criterion for the Army's standard of behaviour. Functionality requires friction-free work teams, and thus it has been maintained that homosexual behaviour is incompatible with military service, as it can cause offence and create conflict between soldiers, damaging teamwork and so putting operational effectiveness at risk. Similarly, and here adultery is given as an example, any personal behaviour which puts at risk the trust and respect that must exist between individuals who may, at some stage, depend on each other under operational conditions must be avoided.

One may make several comments on this. First, if one is going to embrace a functional approach, how realistically may it still be maintained that the central *raison d'être* is land-based war-fighting? There has been much discussion recently of the role of the Army in operations other than war.[15] An especially interesting contribution of the 1998 paper on 'soldiering' is its account of the future security environment, the spectrum of conflict, and the nature of the future battlespace. This acknowledges that straightforward distinctions between war and peace are gone, and military operations will be but one strand in future conflict. I believe that this must be taken extremely seriously. But when the nature of conflict is being so radically rethought, how viably may one still try to specify a soldier's virtues from a *single* function?

Second, one has to ask how adequately one may derive a satisfactory account of a profession with its attendant virtues from functionality alone, especially when that function is set by a secular post-modern society. The various professions, through training, discipline and history, form identifiable moral communities. How separate that moral community will be from wider society will vary. However, if the smaller, more intensive moral community of professionals allows its function to be set entirely from outside, it risks becoming morally bankrupt. This is the risk of slippage or drift referred to earlier in discussion of the just-war arguments. The professional community may well be more moral than the outside world, and that qualifies the meaning of the claim that it *exists to serve*. It may also have a professional duty to question. A sobering illustration of this is provided by the current debate in the United States about death and the beating heart organ donor.[16] Traditionally, organs for transplant have been taken from cadaver donors who have been declared *brain* dead, but whose heart beat has been maintained mechanically to ensure the vitality of the donor organ. Because the supply of donor organs does not match demand, there has been a search for a new source. The University of Pittsburgh Medical Centre has recently turned to non-heart-beating cadaver donors. These are donors who have been declared dead on *cardiopulmonary* criteria, after their relatives have decided to forgo further treatment. So here, the still living patient is taken to theatre, treatment is withdrawn and the organs are removed. The sociologist Renée Fox has described that is an 'ignoble form of cannibalism'.[17] But that is not the worst recent example of slippage. Because of the extreme shortage of donor organs for newborn and very young children, up to half of whom die before surgery, in 1994 the Council on Ethical and Judicial Affairs of the American Medical Association gave an opinion that it was 'ethically permissible' to use anencephalic neonates as organ donors, even though, under current law, anencephalic babies are not dead.[18] The Council suggested: 'Permitting such organ donation would allow some good to come from a truly tragic situation …'.[19] This recommendation was reversed in December 1995, but it is still a warning of what may happen when a profession allows itself to be functionally driven by demands from outside. In this case, the profession retained sufficient grittiness to remain morally critical. We will return to this. The old argument is that peaceful, wider society should fear the militaristic ambitions of armies. I am suggesting that the reverse should at least be considered. The professional community may well have more going for it morally than wider society, and relating the Army's entire ethical perspective to functionality is to pay homage to a regime which is long gone. Commenting on recent happenings in the United States, the ethicist William F. May recalled the story by the brothers Grimm of the child who had to be sent away to learn how to shudder because he had so little horror that he even tried to play with a corpse. Retaining the capacity to shudder is an important part of moral grittiness.

Third, speech of a 'right to be different' and 'unlimited liability', though expressing something important, in certain senses sounds odd. Though we may admire the saint or the hero, and though he may say, 'I was only doing my duty', it is by no means clear that we may say that people have a *moral obligation* to perform such acts. Duty, in J.S. Mill's phrase, is something which can be 'extracted from a person like a debt', but heroism is not thus. It is something which is more generous and has to be inspired by a particular vision.[20] Acts of heroism or sainthood are excesses of virtue rather than excesses of duty, for to go beyond justice is not to be more just.[21] This kind of consideration will affect the way we give an account of the virtues and excesses of a profession, and is a point to which we will return.

Fourth, to take this further, let us for a moment return to the prohibition of adultery in the 'conduct and standards' paper. It is prohibited on the grounds that it undermines combat effectiveness! I believe this argument should not be dismissed out of hand, as it points towards something wider. Let us consider the specifically Christian prohibition of adultery. This does not simply require blind obedience to a command. For Christians, fidelity in marriage is crucially linked to belief in the faithfulness of God. Marital infidelity erodes our ability to proclaim that faithfulness, and so to derive comfort from it, which is one of the primary internal goods of Christianity.[22] I suspect that something very similar could be elaborated from the military prohibition of adultery. Thus, what is grammatically a rule, 'do not commit adultery', is spelled out as a practice, and the practice is located in the wider narrative of what it is to be a Christian. Communities are groupings of people formed by shared narratives, and distinctive communities are made different by distinctive narratives.

Let us now take this argument further, for it leads, I suggest, to a development in recent thinking about the Army. Latterly there has been a fair amount done on military ethos, with much contributed by Patrick Mileham,[23] who, as a soldier and military historian, is well placed to do this. A renewed interest in the role of ethos is part of the move to what is called 'communitarian ethics', which was referred to earlier. According to this perspective, moral thinking relies less upon abstract moral principles (like 'do not commit adultery'), and instead relates decision-making to character, which is in turn shaped by community and ethos. When we discover who we are, much of the dilemma over what we should do has been solved. Rule, or doctrine, is spelled out as practice.

As a perspective, this has been persuasive and successful in helping a variety of groups to recover identity. An example is the restoration of US Marine discipline and self-confidence since Vietnam by an uncompromising process of recruit training. However, even good ideas may be taken too far and absolutised. The thesis that values are located in separate moral communities involves buying into post-modernism,[24] which has been described as 'the laziest of orthodoxies'. It tends towards arrogance.[25] Hermetically sealed communities are uncomfortably like cults. A telling criticism is that 'communitarianism runs the risk of giving individual members of a particular tribe or community no critical distance

[from] their own situatedness'.[26] Thus, if one were a slave and one's entire identity, role and duties were defined by one's community, then one would have no moral vocabulary left with which to object to one's status. Similarly, if a soldier's identity and virtues were defined purely in terms of the military community (military communitarianism), and he was ordered to commit an atrocity, he would be left without a vocabulary of moral disobedience. A fear of getting into this position underlies my hesitation about the 'right to be different' perspective.

How then can one retain the benefit of seeing the impact of ethos and community in fostering specific military virtues, which allows rules or codes to be embedded in practices, but avoid falling into the trap of producing morally uncritical members of an inward looking cult? I will try to answer this by looking more carefully at the work of Alasdair MacIntyre. The argument is important because the 1998 paper on 'soldiering' warns that future operations will make unprecedented demands on the individual intellectually and morally; issues of proportionality will become increasingly complex; *each* soldier will be *more* battlespace aware, *more* mobile, *more* lethal, and so bear *greater* responsibility.

MacIntyre's book explores the interrelations between practices, traditions, narratives and virtues. All of these terms are used in a technical way, but we need only be concerned with the outline structure. A *practice* is a co-operative human activity which produces an *internal good*. An internal good is a value which is appreciated *only* by practitioners of the practice.[27] I would suggest that MacIntyre is pointing here to something which underlies what is right in 'right to be different'. Internal goods have their own standards of excellence. Again, this points to something underlying in 'right to be different'. A set of practices constitute *a tradition*. MacIntyre understands a tradition as a 'long-standing argument'. A tradition only remains alive so long as it is discussed and passed on. This discussion is both internal and external, as the tradition is defined and redefined. *Narrative* is what provides the context in terms of which an action makes sense. Therefore, the question, 'What should I do?' presupposes the prior question, 'Of which narratives am I a part?' For example, the question, 'Should I commit adultery?' presupposes the question, 'Is this action part of the on-going story of the Army?'(!), 'Does this action equip me for the roles the tradition will expect me to discharge?' Now, unlike the ancient world, or even the world of three generations ago, we do not have a totally fixed account of which narratives we belong to, but the concept of 'narrative embeddedness' still gives *some* explanation of (partial) moral boundaries and moral momentum. Putting this more concretely, *by and large* we expect people to act in character (to remain within moral boundaries); *by and large* we have some expectation that they will be able *to improvise* on certain themes. And I suggest that this *qualifies* the 'right to be different' perspective, as it allows for more fluidity.

In conclusion, MacIntyre's perspective is an important resource in rethinking the 'right to be different'. First, in relation to saints and heroes, by taking us out of the language of obligation, it allows us to understand such acts of moral generosity not as duties but as inspired *improvisations*. They may be understood as the excellences of internal goods. Such virtues may not be demanded, but they may be inspired, and they are supported and cultivated within a tradition. That may say something to military training, which should require history and literature so as to develop the imagination. Second, and this is what is crucially important, MacIntyre's account of living tradition as being *a sustained argument* both gives an account of moral embeddedness (what has been called 'right to be different') and provides for moral critical distance. The military community, if it is to retain vitality, needs to respond to changes in the nature of war (as set out in 'soldiering'), and I suggest it can only do this through engaging in sustained dialogue with a series of partners, the Church, politics and the academic world.

NOTES

1. Army Code No. 71451, pp. 33–5.
2. For this discussion, see James Turner Johnson, 'Just War: A Broken Tradition', *The National Interest*, 45 (Fall 1996), pp. 27–36. Turner argues, very importantly, that some current versions of the just war arguments form a 'broken tradition' as they have shifted in recent Catholic thought *from* their foundation in the duty of love protecting the innocent *to* a Christian presumption against doing harm.
3. The reference is *Summa Theologica, Secunda Secundae, Quaestio XL, De bello*, in *Aquinas: Selected Political Writings*, ed. A. P. D'Entrèves (Oxford: Basil Blackwell, 1948), pp. 158–60.
4. *Summa Theologica*, Iusta bella solent diffiniri, quae ulciscuntur iniurias, si gens vel civitas plectenda est, quae vel vindicare neglexerit, quod a suis improbe factum est, vel reddere quod per iniuriam ablatum est.
5. *Summa Theologica*, Apud veros Dei cultores etiam illa bella pacata sunt, quae non cupiditate aut crudelitate, sed pacis studio geruntur, ut mali coerceantur, et boni subleventur.
6. On these points, see Johnson, 'Just War', pp. 29–30.
7. *After Virtue* (London: Duckworth, 1981). See also *Whose Justice? Which Rationality?* (London: Duckworth, 1988).
8. *Dispatches from the Front* (Notre Dame, IN: University of Notre Dame Press, 1994), p. 147.
9. Johnson, 'Just War', p. 30.
10. Johnson sees this, the undercutting of the first use of force, along with the acceptance of the second use (defined as defence) as being a factor not only in Catholic thought, but also in twentieth-century international law (p. 31).
11. Evidently, another, weaker interpretation would be that he saw war as being now so inherently destructive that it could no longer serve justice.
12. National Conference of Catholic Bishops, *The Challenge of Peace* (Washington, DC: United States Catholic Conference, 1983), p. iii (quoted in Johnson, 'Just War', p. 33).
13. See, for example, the thought-provoking article by Noel Malcolm, 'Bosnia and the West: A Study in Failure', *The National Interest*, spring (1995), pp. 3–14. Malcolm's thesis is that the Western world's reaction to the destruction of Bosnia has been 'a triumph of diplomacy'. He distinguishes between *diplomacy* and *foreign policy*. Diplomacy seeks 'to assuage, to conciliate, to reassure: the end state at which it aims is a psychological one'; foreign policy has concrete aims, 'to make things happen' to 'stop things happening'. On Bosnia, Western governments have been unsure about what their policy interests are, and they have taken refuge in diplomacy. My suggestion is that this risks deserting genuinely moral issues.

14. British Army Board policy papers: 'The Extent to Which the Army Has the Right To Be Different' (1996). See also Patrick Mileham's 'Military Virtues I: The Right to be Different', *Defense Analysis*, 14, 2, (1998). I am grateful to Patrick Mileham for allowing me to read the typescript prior to publication.

15. In the more serious press, see the report, 'Where Have All the Soldiers Gone?', *The Times* magazine, 7 March 1998 (pp. 26–30), with its account of the views of Major Eric Joyce, and the *Sunday Times* News Review of 1 February 1998, p. 7, which gave a very similar report.

16. See discussion by Gilbert Meilander, *Bioethics* (Grand Rapids: Eerdmans, 1996), pp. 90–103.

17. Renée Fox, '"An Ignoble Form of Cannibalism": Reflections on the Pittsburgh Protocol for Procuring Organs from Non-Heart-Beating Cadavers', *Kennedy Institute of Ethics Journal*, 3 (June 1993), p. 236. Referred to in Meilander, *Bioethics*, p. 101.

18. For discussion of this, see Meilander, *Bioethics*, pp. 98–9.

19. Meilander, *Bioethics*, p. 99.

20. See J.O. Urmson, 'Saints and Heroes', in J. Feinberg (ed.), *Moral Concepts* (Oxford: Oxford University Press, 1969), pp. 69–73.

21. See Onora O'Neill, *Towards Justice and Virtue: A Constructive Account of Practical Reasoning* (Cambridge: Cambridge University Press, 1996), p. 208.

22. See Nancey Murphy, 'Using MacIntyre's Method in Christian Ethics', in N. Murphy, B. Kallenberg and M. Nation (eds), *Virtues and Practices in the Christian Tradition* (Harrisburg, PA: Trinity Press International, 1997), p. 39.

23. See Patrick Mileham, *Ethos: British Army Officership 1962–1992* (Strategic & Combat Studies Institute, Occasional No. 19, 1996). See also 'Military Virtues 1: The Right To Be Different?' and 'Military Virtues 2: Ethos of the British Army', *Defense Analysis*, 14 (1998). See also Iain Torrance, *Ethics and the Military Community* (Strategic & Combat Studies Institute, Occasional No. 24, 1998).

24. It goes hand in hand with a rejection of 'foundationalism', the thesis that there are underlying universal values which straddle different cultures and communities.

25. It is not an accident that some of the self-consciously post-modern British theologians have formed a group called 'Radical Orthodoxy'.

26. Frank G. Kirkpatrick, 'Public and Private: The Search for a Political Philosophy that Does Justice to Both Without Excluding Love'. This was a paper given to the conference on John Macmurray at the University of Aberdeen in April 1998, which will be published subsequently. A similar criticism of communitarianism is made by Martha Nussbaum in 'Virtue Revived', *Times Literary Supplement*, 3 July 1992, pp. 9–11. John Webster similarly criticises communitarian Christianity, on the ground that the Christian faith is *both* local *and* catholic. See J. Webster, 'Locality and Catholicity: Reflections on Theology and the Church', *Scottish Journal of Theology*, 45 (1992), pp. 1–17.

27. Practices may produce external goods. Many people may appreciate the performance of an outstanding pianist. But only a pianist can appreciate the particular satisfaction of playing well.

15

People not Personnel:
The Human Dimension
of Fighting Power

Alan Hawley

Terminology while seeking to illuminate frequently creates smokescreens and obfuscation. Mindful of that danger, let us state at the outset that the use of the term 'physical' in this paper refers to the physicality of the individual not the more generally understood doctrinal interpretation. The subject of this study is the individual soldier and his relationship with the Army's organisation. As such it encapsulates elements of physiology, psychology, anthropology, social science and history. This is inevitable given the complexity and ramifications of the subject. There can be no meaningful simplistic approach to such complicated and important topics as motivation, capacity and fighting power. The whole consists of multi-tiered, inter-branching elements which may be synergistic or antagonistic to each other. The results of this complex weaving are the effectiveness and utility of the military instrument. As such it is a matter of no small importance.

There are a number of separate strands to this consideration. The first component is that of the individual soldier. Since no man is merely a biological entity operating solely on pre-programmed responses, but is rather a sensate individual within a set of personal characteristics, the individual is a fascinating underpinning of military effectiveness. He simultaneously holds the key for military success and for its failure. Each individual's mixture of personal physical strengths and weaknesses, psychological characteristics and philosophical beliefs collectively form the building blocks of military success or failure. This mixture is the essence of the human condition which is the challenge of leadership.

The exercise of leadership is another fascinating component of the mixture. In order to organise, enthuse and energise individuals the application of effective leadership is paramount. It is axiomatic in a military population that fighting power requires appropriate leadership. Indeed, armies throughout history have greatly prized leaders and leadership. They have recognised the battle winning contribution which such qualities endow. However, armies are social organisations and leaders work within the parameters accepted by these uniformed societies. As such they are both constrained and liberated within the accepted limits. Military leadership is based upon conditional obedience and the wise leader understands and accepts the limits of this concept of duty. It is the prevailing climate of ethics, mores and customs which set this milieu. Such a constellation of factors comprise the organisational health of the military community. As with all aspects of the human condition, these are constantly changing; it is a dynamic mixture.

The contention of this paper is that there are three components to be considered in fighting power; the individual, the organisation and the relationship between them all. Each of these is a major study in itself but the key is their interaction. The whole is greater than the sum.

THE INDIVIDUAL SOLDIER

Most societies throughout history have felt the need to complain about the shortcomings and inadequacies of their young. The tension between a hierarchy and its successors is one which has been evident in all Western civilisation, with frequent derogatory references to the young being the hallmark. Modern society is no different with unfavourable comparisons being drawn between the generations particularly in terms of physical standards. It is almost a truism to hear that modern youth are not the physical equals of their forefathers; that they are not as hardened. The evidence on this matter is at best mixed.

The trend in child health over the last century is one of steady and frequently dramatic improvement. This reduction in infant mortality rates, serious childhood illness leading to disability and the significant decrease in infectious diseases have all been the result of social, economic and medical improvements. Reflecting this change are the physical aspects of improved personal well-being; the young are taller, and heavier. This improvement has been gradual with each generation being an improvement on the preceding one. Balancing these welcome developments is the growing evidence of cardiovascular problems. Thus, many authorities have identified that the young, in some cases as young as 5 years old, have the beginnings of atheroma in their arteries, particularly the coronary arteries. These atheromatous plaques may cause heart attacks or strokes at some stage and are the result of a complicated set of risk factors. High amongst them are diet and lifestyle. Quite clearly, the increasing proportion of individuals who are overweight and even obese is an extreme illustration of this phenomenon. It is a trend which feeds the perception that many of the young spend too much time in front of television or video screens and too little on the sports field.

An interesting comparison can be made with the situation of 100 years ago. An analysis of acceptance rates into the British Army between the years 1893 and 1902 shows very little difference with the modern equivalent rates. The figures do disguise differences in the reasons for rejection; a century ago the main causes were tuberculosis, skeletal abnormality and chronic disability as opposed to back pain, anterior knee pain and asthma today. However, the similarity in the overall rates is a striking feature notwithstanding the great changes in morbidity that have occurred in the intervening period.

Equally interesting are the comments which were being made 100 years ago. The same debate about the quality of the young was taking place then with the same sentiments and doubts being expressed. The following comments were made in explanation of the data of a century ago:

> Had it not been for the persistent teaching of sanitation during the last generation, the state of our larger towns might possibly have been worse. But may not the beneficial working of hygienic enactments in reducing directly the bills of mortality have contributed indirectly to the bringing about of the facts which we now deplore, namely, the existence of a race of physical degenerates? Under conditions prevailing in what may be termed the pre-sanitary period, the living would represent largely the survival of the fittest. Under the fostering influence of Hygeia many survive who, under ruder conditions, would have died. These survivals are sexually mature; weak men marry girls as weak as themselves, and beget sickly children who grow up more weak than their parents. Add to this the effects of ignorance on the part of mothers, scarcity and impurity of milk, overcrowding and the ever-present strain of the struggle for existence, and we get a sequence of facts which must tend towards physical deterioration.[1]

The debate had been triggered by Sir F. Maurice's paper 'National Health: A Soldier's Study' which had examined critically the state of the nation's health and the requirement for military manpower. Significantly, despite the frequently expressed concerns about the situation the answering paper to Maurice concluded, 'We are disposed to think that there is no need for pessimism as to national physique; what we need is a broader conception on the part of the nation of each man's duty to the state.' Leaving aside the tones of social Darwinism, which jar against the modern ear, there is still a kernel of relevance to the contemporary context. In particular, the final conclusion about undue pessimism about youth's physical condition would seem to have echoes which reverberate down the century.

In today's Army there can be heard voices carrying on the same debate. At the practical level there is, however, an acceptance that some individuals joining the Army need additional physical preparation in order to meet the demands of soldiering. It is likely that there has always been this tendency and that in any population of humans there is a distribution of capabilities that will always see a gradation. However, a sensible policy of manpower planning will seek to maximise all available resources. The present approach is the pragmatic embodiment of this. At this point then we can establish that the physical aspect of an individual's capacity for a military life is unlikely to have changed substantially over the years. Despite the fears surrounding physical degeneration in the young there is little evidence that this is profound or even irremediable. Indeed, in direct contradiction to this, the process of additional physical fitness training has been introduced. Fundamentally, defects and shortcomings in physical fitness can be remedied by progressive and appropriate training provided that health is good enough.

But what is it for which we are to prepare an individual soldier? There may be some core competencies which are required of all soldiers, but what are they and what are the additional specific needs? An indication can be gained from a quick survey of some of the great captains of history. Napoleon famously declared the requirements as, 'The first qualification of a soldier is fortitude under fatigue and privation. Courage is only the second; hardship, poverty and want are the best school for a soldier.' These are challenging views with obvious implications for both recruiting and training policies. Another perspective can be found in an address by Field Marshal Wavell speaking at the Royal United Services Institute in 1933: .

> What are the qualities of the good soldier, by the development of which we make the man war-worthy – fit for any war? – The following four – in whatever order you place them – pretty well cover the field; discipline, physical fitness, technical skills in the use of his weapons, battle-craft.

So, here are two experienced commanders differing in their interpretation of the requirements for a soldier. Perplexing though this might seem at first sight, on reflection it should not be surprising. Combat and the experience of it have moved on from the massed action, colour and direct fire of the Napoleonic era to the complexities and complications of modern operations. The confusing array of weapon systems, speed of manoeuvre and technological potential of war in the information age, is counterbalanced by the more direct human contact of peace support operations. Such a wide spectrum of possible deployment and utility does not necessarily serve to simplify the requirement and its definition. An attempt to create order out of this potentially overwhelming task has been made by General Sir Rupert Smith. He has suggested that a defence capability can be seen in terms of the ability to ameliorate, contain, compel, deter and destroy. The context in which these options are chosen will be defined by the political imperative informing the military mission. Conceivably, in some situations two or more of the options may be used simultaneously; more usually they will be employed sequentially.

So, what is the relevance to the individual soldier and what are the implications? It is clear that there is a continuing requirement for the traditional role of closing with the enemy and destroying him in the most personal and demanding manner. The clearance of Argentinean positions in the dark on Mount Tumbledown would have been immediately recognisable to the soldiers of Wellington's and Haig's armies. The pressures and tensions of this intense and violent type of engagement are well researched and recorded in the body of literature and knowledge covering combat stress reactions and post-traumatic shock disorder. The toll on men involved in these operations is understood in terms of the physiological and psychological reactions. This is the norm for the fighting soldier and is used as the model for his training. However, the more recent operations involving peace-support and humanitarian activities are not without their human costs. The demands range from the non-involvement when faced by gross acts of barbarity, as was faced by many British soldiers in the early days of the United Nations operation in Bosnia and Croatia, through the helplessness faced by many in the face of overwhelming human despair, disease and desperation in the refugee camps of Rwanda, to the patient patrolling in the face of intimidation, hostility and terrorism as evident at times in Northern Ireland. Hence, we can begin to sketch in the qualities which are required of the modern soldier. In addition to the traditional virtues of fortitude, courage, physical fitness and battle skills which Napoleon and Wavell described, there are the additional requirements demanded by the range of contemporary deployments: patience, intelligence, self-control, understanding, sympathy, readiness to accept responsibility and an ability to work in teams. Such a list is a most demanding amalgam of the old and the new with considerable selection and training implications.

So what of the individual? Has he changed as well as the requirement? We have already established that on the physical side there has been no great change so perhaps that is the answer. Unfortunately, that is not the whole answer. Comforting though it may be to think that individuals are as least as able as their forefathers, it ignores the fact that man is a social animal. Each of us develops as a result of a balance between nature and nurture. Our totality is the result of these two influences. Man has evolved as part of a co-operative venture in competition with other groupings. These twin themes of co-operation and conflict run throughout history. It is therefore fundamental to examine the whole social context as well as the physical aspect to be able to give an adequate response to the question 'Has the individual changed?'

Having started a comparison with the situation of a century ago, it is appropriate to continue it. Such an analysis has to include the context in which the individual lives, since the whole is composed of many parts of which social conditions, prevailing customs and genetic inheritance all have a part to play. An army is a social organisation with its own distinctive codes and ethos which may reflect or differ from its parent society. It sets the context in which soldiers live and operate and its idiosyncrasies and eccentricities are derived from its history and traditions. They are the means by which the stresses and strains of the battlefield are resisted so that combat capability can be delivered most effectively. Quite clearly, they are culturally derived.

One hundred years ago the expectations and beliefs of the individual soldier were rather different from today. The British empire was at its zenith, the practice of organised religion was virtually universal, the class structure was clear, hierarchical and accepted, the definition of the enemy was unequivocal and the requirement to destroy him was similarly uncluttered. When going into action, all engagements were group activities which maintained the social cohesion of the unit and all units were of a size that gave each man only one job to do. In his everyday life, the presence of death was familiar with mortality rates from both disease and accidents being high. All of this produced an individual with a set of certainties about life, society and the Army and his part within them.

Today these certainties no longer exist. The individual is less likely to see himself in terms of a co-operative venture. The growth of a culture of private enterprise and individual search for reward may have advantages in the generation of wealth, but it is less likely to produce men and women willing to put mission before self. This divergence in the philosophical basis of the state and its army may be uncomfortable for all concerned creating tensions and disagreements, if not frank incomprehension, on both sides. In addition, the loss of certainties underpinning rightness of cause, religious conviction and the decreased frequency and significance of massed group action also erode the psychological robustness of the individual. On the battlefield itself the experience of combat has also changed. Instead of being a shared experience under fire with a real appreciation of a shoulder-to-shoulder bonding, the modern battlefield is just as likely to be a lonely place. The manoeuvrist approach tends to the concentration of fire on a temporary and overwhelming basis. If you are on the receiving end of just such a lightning application of joint firepower, given the adoption of tactical dispersion as a norm, it is possible that the experience of it might seem to be entirely personal; all the enemy's spite is being vented on you alone. There are limited numbers of comrades with which to share it. The sudden and immediate realisation of one's own mortality may be overwhelming. As to the experience of death, this has largely been relegated to hospitals and hospices in everyday life. The high mortality rates of infants and adults have been replaced by the institutionalisation of death. The practice of laying out the dead in the parlour and involving the whole family in the ritual and proximity of death has gone. In its place is an increased expectation about individual rights to health care. The advent of the Patient's Charter is merely the latest evidence of this development.

What then has been established about the individual soldier? Whilst the evidence about physical capability is at best mixed, it is clear that any shortcomings can be rectified with an appropriate training regime. The situation regarding the other aspects that together comprise a healthy and effective soldier is rather more problematical. The changes in society have been a mixed blessing. The great social advances which have taken place over the past century have empowered the individual and introduced a vastly improved standard of living, but the other side of the coin has tended to diminish exactly those elements which are most useful to a military life. Selflessness, commitment to the common good and the submersion of private gain in the pursuit of a higher intangible, all run counter to the prevailing ethos in civilian life. This philosophical divergence risks gradually eroding traditional military virtues and weakening the cohesion of the warrior community. The effects are felt both by the individual soldier and the

Army as a whole; the individual is more prone to the stresses of the battlefield and the whole system suffers from the increased fragility of its component parts.

To redress the balance, is a comparison with our forefathers appropriate? After all, we are not required to compete against our predecessors on a contemporary battlefield. A more relevant exposure is with our likely antagonists. In this respect, the picture is possibly more comforting. A healthy respect for an enemy is a sensible precaution and some are especially deserving of such regard. Again this is little different from our grandfather's day as evidenced by Kipling's respectful poetry on colonial opponents. In his case he especially selected the Mahdi's followers, the 'Fuzzies' in his idiom, for particular mention. Despite a similar regard for many of the opponents of recent years, the comparison on the battlefield has underlined the quality of the British soldier. He may not have all the resilience of his grandfather but the evidence suggests that currently he has sufficient quality for the demands of contemporary conflict.

THE ARMY AND ORGANISATIONAL HEALTH

We have already stated that the Army can be regarded as a distinctive community within the larger society. It has developed its own ethos and mores which enable it to cope with the stresses and strains of operations and to bring combat power to bear in the most effective manner. While ideally not being isolated from society, it is nevertheless distinctive from it by virtue of its function. After all, it is authorised by the consent and support of the wider community to threaten and ultimately to deliver lethal force. This is a most serious and heavy responsibility which demands appropriate training, equipment and control measures to be introduced. Similarly, the application of this lethal force is not without risk so that soldiers are at hazard of their own lives in the pursuit of the mission. This is the essence of what General Sir John Hackett described as the 'unlimited liability'; the preparedness to risk life and limb in the furtherance of the mission. The nature of this liability is such that it is all demanding and is shared with very few other groups in society. In this sense, a soldier is set apart from others.

The voluntary acceptance of this unlimited liability is the first step in the individual becoming a soldier. The organisation then prepares and trains him for the full acceptance of the challenge. To do this the recruit is put through a series of training phases at the completion of which the fundamentals of battlefield survival and skills are learnt. Inevitably, the defence mechanisms used by the military community to maintain group cohesion in the face of the rigours, both physical and psychological, may seem eccentric to outsiders. This has been described by Alan Hanbury-Sparrow in the following graphic terms: 'The real enemy was Terror, and all this heel-clicking, saluting, bright brass and polish were our charms and incantations for keeping him at bay.'[2]

For those unfamiliar with the exertions of operations and the demands of the battlefield, the customs and traditions of the military can seem eccentric or even slightly ludicrous. Indeed, there is a danger, given the complexities of human psychology both collective and individual, that some customs are retained and propagated merely for their own sake. There will always be this tension within a hierarchical organisation let alone between it and the rest of society. These pressures can only grow during periods of rapid social change. This is exactly the situation with which the Army has had to cope since the Second World War. It is therefore not surprising that the inherent social conservatism of the military has been challenged by both the scale and pace of change in the wider society. The difficulties which various social issues have raised for the military have been well recognised and reported. Chief amongst these are the problems associated with women in the military, racism and homosexuality. These have all been questions which reach to the heart of the Army's self-image.

It is interesting to note that the difficulty experienced by the Army in relation to some social issues is at marked variance with its ability to accommodate the rapid change in technology. Indeed, the military has been particularly adept at adopting and using the new technologies. It has even managed to incorporate them into its existing structure with only minimal disruption. These new technologies become accepted and integrated once their combat worth is established. In this sense there is a collective pragmatism about the Army; it allows the incorporation of new technologies and techniques whilst preserving the still useful and valuable aspects of the traditional. This tendency to evolution rather than revolution, a practical and pragmatic approach to battlefield problems, an ingrained scepticism regarding intellectual and academic debate and a separation from mainstream civilian life (partly due to the terrorist threat, partly as a matter of tradition) means that the military is not well placed to handle the difficult social issues of the day. Indeed, in the British Army it has meant that the scepticism surrounding intellectual debate as opposed to 'proper soldiering' has meant that the development of doctrine and its importance has taken some time to become accepted. Characteristically, upon acceptance there has been a substantial commitment to it and some excellent doctrinal thinking has been produced. However, this is not in the historical tradition of the British Army; it is a new development.

The core of the question of organisational health as it affects the Army revolves around the issues of insiders and outsiders. Additionally, this is interwoven with the complicated problems of self-image. In essence, the identification of insiders as the definition of outsiders is central to the way in which the Army interacts with non-uniformed agencies and also within itself. At a time of rapid social change in society, the hierarchical community of the Army is challenged by the new philosophies and emerging thinking of the younger generation. This has probably always been a cause of tension. For instance, the experience of conscription and National Service after the Second World War was a period of self-examination for the Regular Army. Quite clearly, the accommodation of civilians, some of them unwilling, into the Army was achieved with some success. The various campaigns successfully fought throughout the 1950s and the retreat from empire bear witness to this. However, the universality of conscription, the example of wartime conscription service and the immediacy of the campaigns in the post-war period make any comparisons with the contemporary situation somewhat tenuous.

The current social and political context is particularly complex for the traditional structures and ethos of the Army. In comparison with the period of National Service, there is a reduced overt political presence of the military. This is partly the result of the loss of single service ministers and their ministries as the Ministry of Defence has become a truly joint endeavour. It is also due to the reducing collective experience of military service amongst the population at large and decision-makers in particular. It will become increasingly unlikely that Secretaries of State for Defence and their cabinet colleagues will have personal experience of military service. Whilst this is not of itself necessarily a weakness in matters of strategy and higher-level resource management, it does run the risk of producing a rift between uniformed and civilian elements of the defence estate particularly when questions of ethos and custom are concerned.

At the same time, due to a combination of factors the military has become more separated from mainstream civilian experience. The terrorist threat has forced both a withdrawal of military uniforms from the streets of the United Kingdom for anything other than security operations or set piece parades. Exacerbating this trend has been the enclosure of barracks with security fences and armed guards. Necessary as these measures have been, their combined effect is to remove the Army from civilian life. At the same time increased financial stringency has led to some cuts in ceremonial and presentational events. None of these decisions has been lightly taken, but the cumulative effect has been to increase the degree and sense of isolation of the Army within British society.

The very success of the Army in the many operations in which it has been involved since the passing of National Service has paradoxically strengthened this tendency. How can the experience of operations in Bosnia, the Gulf and Rwanda be easily accommodated into the normal frame of everyday experience in the United Kingdom? The exertions of armoured warfare in the Middle East and the deprivations of cholera and refugee camps in central Africa are entirely foreign to the routine of life at home. Their very distinctiveness and difference sets them apart. The successful completion of these various operations is a cause of national satisfaction, but their achievement is the business of the unfamiliar grouping/tribe of the Army. This sense of extraordinariness is shared by the military. It is well aware that much of its work is of a completely different nature from the normal. This very difference is the reason that many choose to join. It is also clear that these experiences are seen to matter; they are widely reported in the media and are the subject of widespread debate and comment. These aspects serve to reinforce the feeling of distinctiveness; the essentials of defining the insiders' and outsiders' group have been confirmed.

Further adding to these identification pressures have been the introduction of management techniques from the wider society. While there have been clear advantages in incorporating civilian management techniques for the crucial areas of resource planning and allocation, some of the approaches are not without difficulties. Hence, the introduction of agencies for many support areas have led to disputes between different users of the resources. Nor should this be a surprise. The philosophy underlying a successful agency is one of maximum efficiency in competition with others; it is essentially a competitive process. The application of combat power is also a competitive process but its successful exploitation depends upon the highest degree of co-operation. Furthermore, this co-operation runs through all the elements of the force, from combat through to combat service support. Yet these relationships, which are crucial on operations, are not fostered by the peacetime agency approach that promotes competition between and involving exactly those elements that are so vital to each other in the all-arms approach. Such philosophical schizophrenia exemplifies the importing of commercial practice into an environment which is anti-commercial in its entire ethos and existence. The tensions which are generated by this process are not conducive to the cohesion of the organisation.

Another recent experience which has had a major effect on the collective psyche of the Army has been the turmoil of the reductions and redundancies consequent upon the break-up of the Warsaw Pact. This whole process including both voluntary and compulsory redundancies brought the experience of down-sizing right to the heart of the Army. Not only were individuals affected but hard decisions about units were made. These deliberations cut to the heart of the military, challenging many assumptions about the nature of the relationship between the military and its paymasters. The corollary of Hackett's unlimited liability is that the individual who accepts the burden of the liability should have maximum support afforded, and this appeared to be challenged by the entire experience. Furthermore, the widespread concern amongst those who might be affected by the redundancy programme was then aggravated by worries about retaining regiments. In a very real sense, this importing of civilian management processes was perceived to be targeting the fabric of the Army. It served to increase the unease amongst many about the social pressures coming to bear on the Army.

Nowhere has this been felt more keenly than the traditional fighting elements of the Army. Not only were the infantry and armoured corps the most vociferous in their defence of the regiment during the Options for Change debates, they have also found themselves to be most affected by the other social tensions. This is particularly true of the infantry. It is the British infantry that encapsulates for many the very essence of the Army. The Thin Red Line of Balaclava and the massed ranks of the Household troops at Trooping the Colour are popular manifestations of this regard. However, there are specific tensions which may be acting upon the viability of the infantry in its traditional sense. Most of these are the products of divergent trends in civilian life and the traditional requirement of the infantry.

It is the task of the infantry to close with the enemy and to destroy him. This may require the extreme application of personal violence at the most basic and visceral level. Clearing trenches of an enemy or forcing him out of buildings is a bloody and exacting experience testing the resolve of the soldier to the ultimate. Whilst this is the worst case requirement, it is used as the litmus test of the infantry's capability. Hence, all infantrymen are physically and technically trained to close with the enemy as necessary. This is a style of fighting whose very essence can be traced in a direct lineage over the centuries to the soldier and warrior castes of early history. The shared experience of this personal battlefield helps define the infantryman. However, this heritage is completely foreign to the normal experience and aspirations of the young in society. To many it is anathema to consider, let alone to undertake, such bloody personal conflict. The whole requirement runs counter to the ethos of personal advancement which is the prevalent theme of successful commercial enterprise. Instead, to volunteer for privation, hardship, danger and the risking of personal harm in the pursuit of a common good whilst the financial recompense is essentially moderate, is not a choice which sits comfortably with conventional civilian ethos. Hence, it is unsurprising that many infantry regiments have experienced continuing recruiting difficulties. The clash of competing basic philosophies acts to the disadvantage of the infantry.

On the other hand, recruiting to the more technical corps of the Army is consistently buoyant. In particular, the Royal Engineers and the Royal Electrical and Mechanical Engineers combine obvious military utility with a clearly recognisable training with potential for usefulness in the civilian employment market. This potent combination helps to ensure that these corps are well recruited. Individuals who join them will receive a training which will ensure an option to pursue a full career in the Army or to leave and find appropriate employment in civilian life. These factors make the technical corps a more attractive career choice. Civilian equivalence is a positive attraction. These manning pressures worsen the existing pressures within the Army's internal structure. The politics of the British Army have been comprehensively examined elsewhere.[3] It is sufficient to note that competition for manpower is not a basis on which the internal cohesion of the organisation is likely to be improved. As far as manning is concerned the continued shortfall in the infantry compares badly with the strength of recruiting to the Royal Engineers and Royal Electrical and Mechanical Engineers. It is a comparison which merely serves to damage further the self-image and confidence of the traditional fighting arms.

So far the picture painted is a relatively gloomy vista. Perhaps this is inevitable in a critique. However, notwithstanding these fault lines and difficulties it is evident that the Army remains an operationally potent force. Its performance in the whole range of operations throughout the spectrum of conflict since the Berlin Wall came down has been impressive and effective. It has managed to deal with the problems of a philosophical schizophrenia and an adverse manning climate, as well as the challenges of social and legal change, whilst maintaining a high tempo of operational involvement. It is a testament to a number of factors that this has been achieved; the basic high quality of the personnel within the Army, the pragmatism of the organisation and the continued high level of political commitment. These are of clear importance. However, they are likely to be temporary bulwarks against the social tide unless a cohesive and appropriate approach to issues is adopted. Failing this, the organisational health will be degraded and the individual soldier will also inevitably suffer.

APPROACHES FOR THE FUTURE

The future Army will continue to be faced with the challenges of social change. These are the most problematical of all issues for the hierarchical social organisation of the military to face. It has always been the same for the British Army with its social conservatism and pragmatic approach to problems. These are not weapons which are maximally effective against an expansionist rights culture or ideological precepts. Indeed, they directly challenge the benign paternalism which has underpinned so much of the leadership ethos of the Army. Paternalism is a concept of the past; the approach now is based much more on personal autonomy and choice. These are difficult concepts for the social structure of the military.

The future military must somehow maintain the balance between the legitimate demands of the wider society for change and conformity to the civilian norm with the need to safeguard its distinctive ethos. Such an approach may well demand the judgement of Solomon on occasions, but the task must be undertaken so that the pertinence and utility of the Army is appreciated by all. The military must be brought within the purview of mainstream society and its developments so that the right degree of cross-fertilisation can be ensured. The re-appearance of uniformed soldiers amongst the civilian community is a welcome step in this direction. Equally, the close links between civilian academics and the military system are helpful. This is also an entirely understandable development given the increasing proportion of Army officers who are graduates (the majority of Sandhurst-trained officers are graduates). The old suspicion of academics, if not frank anti-intellectualism, is rapidly being replaced by a more valuable two-way intercourse between the military and academia. Indeed, civilian academic advisers are now formally part of the whole system of defence policy formulation. This is a welcome and mutually productive relationship.

However, it remains crucial for the Army to define its philosophical approach to its business. Whilst this is being done in a most impressive fashion in the fields of doctrine and war-fighting policy, it is once again the rock of social change which is being repeatedly re-visited. For example, the fundamental relationship between the officer and the soldier has been subtly altered without any coherent policy or thinking. Instead, a gradual incremental change has been wrought as a consequence of a generation of junior officers bringing a slightly modified version of their own civilian beliefs and practices into their commands. As a result we have edged away from benign paternalism in effect, but without a clear commitment to this change or a stated alternative.

This does then beg the question of the avenue of approach which is most appropriate. Given that the Army's social structure is dynamic what should be its purpose? Ultimately, the measure of the utility of a change or a structure is the effectiveness of the delivered combat capability. Should this be degraded, then the causal change is not welcome. The wider context has to be set by the acceptable legal and ethical constraints emanating from society. Within these parameters, the position of the Army has to be considered using the measure of operational effectiveness.

In order to be effective, the value of the individual officer and soldier has to be appreciated. Man is a social animal and a soldier is a social animal par excellence. He needs the support of the organisation so that he can play his part in the delivery of combat capability. The requirement is to select, train and then to nurture the individual so that he is able to take up Hackett's unlimited liability. Failing this then the execution of the individual's commitment is likely to be flawed.

Training is obviously a central component of this whole process. It is a method by which the technical skills can be imparted to the soldier as well as the ethos of the organisation. Yet it is an area which is perpetually hostage to budgetary pressures. Such pressures, whilst understandable, are not helpful. In an earlier time of financial review, when the fledgling Army Medical College which had been established after the incompetence and criticism of the Crimean War, was threatened with closure, the then commandant retorted with the rejoinder, 'If you think education is expensive, try ignorance!' This is still pertinent advice. The training given to the individual should be more than the narrowly defined battle craft requirements. Instead, by a progressive process, the ethos and philosophy of the organisation can be imparted, converting the willing civilian in uniform into a soldier. This takes time and resources. It will also involve a mixture of novel and traditional methods. However, it is essential if there is to be a possibility of not only keeping but developing the appropriate philosophical and psychological balance. Such a balance is essential to give both organisation and individual the necessary shoring against the rigours and exertions of operations. It remains as true that conflict is an act of applied psychology. The tools available are violence and the threat of violence, whilst the targets are the perceptions of military commanders, individual soldiers and the populations from which they are drawn. Once this fact is understood, then the direction and priorities in military training and education can be defined.

The bottom line in combat effectiveness is still the soldier. It is he who mans the equipment, who maintains, who fights it and who keeps on fighting until the victory is won. The role of the Army is to prepare the soldier for this duty and to sustain him in it. As a concluding comment it is appropriate to turn to another experienced commander for his thoughts. General Creighton Abrams, speaking in 1985, gave a complete and telling summary of the human dimension in armies when he said:

> By people I do not mean personnel ... I mean living, breathing, serving, human beings. They have needs and interests and drives. They have spirit and will, and strengths and abilities. They have weaknesses and faults; and they have means. They are the heart of our preparedness ... and this preparedness – as a nation and as an Army – depends upon the spirit of our soldiers. It is the spirit that gives the Army life. Without it we cannot succeed.

NOTES

1. W. Taylor, 'The Physique of Recruits', *Journal of the Royal Army Medical Corps*, 1 (July–December 1903), pp. 221–30.
2. R. Holmes, 'The Real Enemy', in *The Firing Line* (Harmondsworth: Penguin Press, 1987), pp. 204–69.
3. H. Strachan, 'The Politics of the Regiment', in *The Politics of the British Army* (Oxford: Oxford University Press, 1997), pp. 195–233.

16

A Model for the Analysis of Fighting Spirit in the British Army

Charles Kirke

An army has many necessary ingredients – such things as equipment, command and staff structures, fighting doctrine and procedures – but probably the most basic of all are the fighting soldier and the human group in which he fights. Military human groups can be considered special in many ways because of the unique requirement that they should operate effectively under extreme stress, and indeed continue to do so even after suffering sudden and traumatic reduction through casualties. It is this unique and special nature of military human groups, and the bonds that define and sustain them, that led to the choice of research area out of which this paper arises. The particular area which this paper addresses is the description and analysis of fighting spirit in the British Army, viewed from the perspective of the academic discipline of social anthropology.

SOCIAL ANTHROPOLOGY AND SOCIAL STRUCTURE

Examination and analysis of military groups is not new. Military sociology and military psychology are well-established academic disciplines.[1] However, one potentially fruitful area has largely been neglected: this is the approach of the social anthropologist. Social anthropology is an evolving discipline which had its origins in the late nineteenth century, and can no longer be thought of as a single body of theory and practice. This paper uses as its basis the concept of 'social structure', which arose initially from the writings of Emile Durkheim[2] but was subsequently developed by the 'British school' of structural-functionalism in the inter-war years. This British school almost exclusively studied exotic small-scale societies (groups with a population of a few hundred, usually of what were then called 'primitive' peoples) and placed its emphasis on three main elements: first, fieldwork – prolonged participant observation of the peoples being studied; second, the study, as far as possible, of the totality of the social institutions and customs of the people, rather than the single themes which had been the preoccupation of sociologists; and, third, attempting to provide the means for comparison between cultures.

It seems self-evident that human groups have by their very nature some sort of structure, or framework for daily life. Indeed, 'social structure' is much talked about in the social anthropological and sociological literature, and has been a fundamental concept for over 100 years. However, there is no agreed or 'standard' definition of the term among sociologists or social anthropologists. The definition used here has been generated with reference to two basic works of British social anthropology and is as follows:

> 'Social structure' is a body of ideas, rules and conventions of behaviour which governs how groups of people or individuals organise themselves *vis-à-vis* each other. Social structures therefore provide the indispensable background to, and framework for, daily life.[3]

I have used this definition as the basis for the construction of a model for describing, analysing and predicting British soldiers' behaviour.[4]

A SOCIAL ANTHROPOLOGICAL STUDY OF THE BRITISH ARMY

It need hardly be stated that the interaction of human beings is a highly complex matter, and that the life of soldiers is no different from life in any other human group in this respect. The detection and identification of all the complexities of social structures are no easy matters, and can only be achieved by prolonged and close observation of the people involved. Indeed, even after prolonged investigation the social anthropologist can only expect to provide ever better theoretical models of the social processes and constructs that he observes. Such models should be viewed as heuristic devices that are necessarily simplifications of a more complex picture, but nevertheless have value in enabling the observer better to describe, analyse and predict the human behaviour he or she is examining.[5] What is presented here is therefore no more than a model: no study of this kind can claim the authority of 'truth'.[6]

The study started from the base case of a unit[7] which is virtually all male, and in barracks. Life in the field and on operations was considered where appropriate. The methodology of the study was based on three main thrusts, which exploited the researcher's unique position as a social anthropologically trained participant observer with insider status. First, data were gathered in contemporary British Army units. This data capture was achieved by participant observation in 13 units over the year of formal research (supplemented by the personal observations of the researcher over the previous 21 years, rank ranged from second lieutenant to lieutenant-colonel), by one-to-one interviews lasting between 30 minutes and over two hours conducted with 117 serving individuals rank-ranged from private soldier to lieutenant-colonel, and a smaller number of group discussions. Second, an historical perspective was attained by extensive library-based study of soldiers' first-hand accounts over the past 300 years. Third, the data were subjected to analysis from the social anthropological perspective, from which emerged the model which this paper seeks to present.

It should be borne in mind that the study was aimed at identifying general rules and trends across combat units, rather than detailed analysis of particular units. This paper therefore concentrates on the common ground rather than differences in detail.

Social structures

Because of the novelty of the approach, some of the terms used in this paper have been coined specifically to cover and delineate novel concepts. Whenever these words are used, they are printed in *italics* and defined on first use. Thereafter they are used rigorously and may be treated as exclusive technical terms.

The study identified four separate social structures (as defined above) existing in all the forward combat units of the British Army, which can be summarised as follows:

1. The *formal command structure*, which is the structure through which a soldier at the bottom receives orders from the person at the top. It is embedded in and expressed by the hierarchy of rank and the formal arrangement of the unit into layer upon layer of organisational elements. It contains the mechanisms for the enforcement of discipline, for the downward issue of orders and instructions and for the upward issue of reports, and it provides the framework for official responsibility.

2. The *informal structure*, which consists of the web of relationships of friendship and association within the unit. Individuals come into personal contact with other people within the unit, of any rank, and establish interpersonal relationships with them. Although it might appear at first sight that the quality and intensity of such relationships are determined by free choice on the part of the individual (because they are informal), the network of a soldier's informal relationships is for the most part constrained by his rank and position in the unit.

3. The *loyalty/identity structure*, which consists of a nesting series of different sized groups which are defined by opposition and contrast to other groups of equal status in the *formal command structure*. Thus an infantry soldier would feel loyalty to his platoon in competition with other platoons of the same company, to his company in competition with other companies and so on. It is important to note that at every stage the soldier is equally a member of all his potential groups in the *loyalty/identity structure*. It is also important to note that this structure ultimately defines his identity as a member of a particular regiment or corps, as expressed in his cap badge, and that this identity is exportable to, and unaltered by, all military contexts.

4. The *functional structure*, which is expressed in the formation of groups to carry out specific purposes. These task-oriented functional groups might exactly reflect the *formal command structure* or they might be independent of it. For example, an infantry platoon (a basic element in the infantry command structure) tends to go on exercise and operations as a formed body, whereas a 'rear party' which remains in barracks while the rest of the unit is away (for example on leave or on an operational tour of duty) is usually made up of an *ad hoc* grouping of soldiers from all over the unit, with a similarly *ad hoc* chain of command.

These four social structures are all at work simultaneously and as a result are interwoven into a complex and intricate whole during the business of daily life. They are summarised in Figure 1:

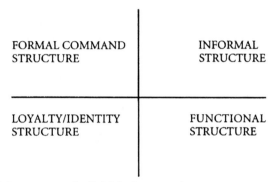

Figure 1 Social structures in British Army units

This model may initially appear less than helpful in that it provides a potentially bewildering collection of variables. However, there are precedents in the social anthropology literature for such a form of social organisation (see, for example, Geertz's description of village structures in Bali,[8] where there are seven interwoven 'planes of social organisation'), and experience has shown that, in spite of its complexity, it can be used to good effect to understand the lives of soldiers.

The operating group

Because all the four structures are at work simultaneously, an individual soldier feels that he belongs simultaneously to a large array of potential groups (defined by the structures in Figure 1).

For example, a Royal Artillery soldier on sentry at the edge of a gun position[9] could feel a potential member of many groups, including:

• *Formal command and loyalty/identity structures*: the Royal Regiment of Artillery; his unit; the troop and battery in which he is serving.

- *Functional structure:* his gun detachment; the group of sentries guarding the position; the group of soldiers on the gun position.

- *Informal structure:* his group of friends in general (including those away from the gun position); those people on the gun position with whom he is friendly.

However, it would be unrealistic to assume that the soldier was equally committed to all of these groups simultaneously. Indeed, under normal circumstances an individual will feel at any one time that one group in particular demands his attention and energy above all others. As an aid to analysis the concept of the *operating group* is used to denote this particular group. It is important to note that this *operating group* varies with changing circumstances: thus in the case of the Royal Artillery soldier above, his *operating group* would probably be the functional group of sentries with whom he is working at the time. However, this would change as soon as he goes off sentry duty, perhaps to the other functional group consisting of his gun detachment or perhaps an informal group of soldiers with whom he is friendly, if he is allowed to rest. A parallel term, *operating structure,* can be used to denote the structure to which the *operating group* belongs.

The most complex case – the informal structure

By its very nature, the *informal structure* was found to be considerably more complex than the other three, because the rules and conventions of which it is composed are generated and reproduced entirely by the mutual consent and co-operation of those operating within it, and it has no basis in deliberate design. Accordingly, a separate sub-model was developed to describe the various social bonds that operate within it. These can be summarised as follows:

1. *Close friendship.* As defined in the study, '*close friendship*' consists in a durable relationship that transcends the military environment, where there is a large measure of trust and respect between the parties and few barriers to discussion of highly personal matters. In interviews with soldiers of all ranks it was established that, for virtually every one, a useful test to identify *close friendship* would be to determine whether the relationship would survive unchanged if one of the parties was prepared to shed tears in the presence of the other. It is a rare and special relationship. In the words of a warrant officer in an infantry battalion during an interview for this study, 'I've maybe made only two or three close friends in my career, though I've had plenty of military friends.'

2. *Friendship.* The term '*friendship*' was used specifically in the study to refer to a less intense relationship which is frequently found to exist between soldiers within the *informal structure*. It can have all the appearance of *close friendship*, in that individuals constantly seek each other's company, will

help each other if they are in trouble, and will be prepared to share almost anything if the need arises, but it falls short of the depth and intensity of the other relationship. Thus, during an interview one soldier said of his particular circle of mates that he would be more than prepared to help any one of them: 'If a bloke was feeling unhappy then his friends would naturally take him out drinking to cheer him up. However, if a mate said, "I'm worried because I think I might be gay" or something, then I wouldn't want to know!' Bonds of *friendship* are usually formed within narrow bands of rank. For example, private soldiers may form *friendships* with lance corporals, but a *friendship* with a full corporal may attract disapproval. Similarly, warrant officers may form *friendships* with sergeants that they have known for some time, but there will always be a certain distance in the relationship (particularly if they are in the same sub-unit). Senior lieutenants may form *friendships* with captains, but junior second lieutenants are unlikely to do so. Although there are no formally stated regulations which proscribe *friendships* growing up between people of widely diverse rank, such relationships are frowned upon because they are held to be potentially compromising for discipline.

3. *Association.* It is often found that two soldiers separated by rank distance wide enough to exclude *friendship* between them will come into regular contact and will form an informal bond of mutual trust and respect that falls short of *friendship* as defined above, but is nevertheless an important mechanism in the *informal structure*. Such a relationship will probably arise, for example, between an infantry platoon sergeant and his platoon commander, between an artillery battery sergeant major and his battery commander, or between a tank commander and his crew. This relationship was given the name '*association*' in the study.

4. *Informal access.* It is recognised, though not officially laid down, that each individual has a right to speak informally and without a formal appointment with certain other people who are at a certain degree of structural distance (superiors in his chain of command for instance), even though a link of *association* does not exist between them. Thus a junior officer can expect to be able to have '*informal access*' to his sub-unit commander, as the sub-unit commander can to his Commanding Officer. Similarly, any member of a Sergeants' Mess can expect to have opportunities informally to approach the Regimental Sergeant Major (RSM).

5. *Nodding acquaintance.* The term '*nodding acquaintance*' encompasses all the informal relationships which are not encompassed by the other terms. In essence, it is a relationship where the parties know each other by sight, but not necessarily by name, and they acknowledge each other's existence and common participation in the same segment of the *formal command structure*. The relationship may remain as it is, or it may grow into any one of the others listed above.

Apart from *close friendship*, which is by definition a strong mutual bond, and *nodding acquaintance*, which is essentially weak, a significant variable in any particular case is the intensity of the relationship. Thus, for instance, a soldier will like some of his *friends* more than others, and will find *informal access* easier with some people than others.

These relationships are illustrated in Figure 2.

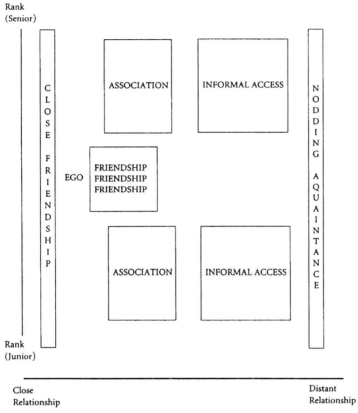

'EGO' is a soldier of no particular rank (but neither the most junior nor the most senior)

Figure 2 Diagram of relationships in the *informal structure*

The structures in operation

Although the four social structures in the model have been described separately, they should be seen as intertwining with and balancing each other in a way that prescribes soldiers' behaviour (individually and in groups) in an array of different contexts. As the context changes, so do the prescribed behaviour and *operating group* identification and membership. This feature gives the overall system a flexibility and suppleness that under normal circumstances prevent insurmountable personal or structural barriers growing up within the unit. It also ensures that communications exist within and between all parts of the unit and it provides an array of checks and balances against dysfunctional behaviour.[10] When group cohesion and military effectiveness are high, the structures are in an appropriate balance and operating in harmony: where there are serious tensions and low effectiveness in a unit then they are out of balance in some way.

The wider context

Although this model is powerful in its ability to explain much of what goes on in British combat units and to describe the social environment in which British soldiers live, it can not of course cover every aspect of the experience of each individual. In particular, it is not designed to cover the wider context in which the soldier's specifically military milieu is embedded. The two major components of this wider context are the personality of the individual, which determines how he reacts to pressures exerted upon him, and social forces outside the military environment, which he experiences through human contact and from the media.

It is questionable whether the model could ever be expanded to encompass these external factors, given the very large array of variables which they would introduce. The four-structure model should therefore be regarded as providing a zoomed-in picture of the essentially military area rather than a panoramic view of the complete social and personal context in which soldiers live.

Validation

Some considerable thought has been given to testing the model's validity, and accordingly an historical study and a cross-cultural study were carried out. The historical study was based mainly on first-hand accounts written by British soldiers from the early eighteenth century to the Second World War. It revealed that the model fitted the material throughout the period studied. All four social structures regularly appeared, and the informal relationships deducible from the material could be clearly categorised according to the fivefold range described above. Furthermore, no identified features of social organisation within military units fell outside them.[11]

The cross-cultural study examined a United States Air Force (USAF) unit and a Gurkha unit. The USAF material did not test the model beyond its limits. Instead, the case material suggested that even in an organisation which had different national origins and different structural and functional emphases, the model could provide a framework for analysis and thus understanding of the lives of those involved. However, the Gurkha material provided a stark contrast: the model was insufficient to portray accurately the social structures in the

Gurkha battalion which was studied. Although all four social structures were present, some extra dimension was required. This extra dimension had to encompass the special Nepalese/Gurkha features which seemed to penetrate all four of the military structures.

The exercise in analytical control therefore demonstrated that the model provided a useful unifying framework for analysis under many circumstances, but that it would not cover all types of military unit in all cultures. It therefore can and should be used with confidence, though the analyst must be aware of its limitations and be awake to the possibilities of the existence of important factors which it does not reveal (as in the Gurkha case).

ANALYSIS OF FIGHTING SPIRIT

Having described the model, it is now necessary to apply it to the consideration of fighting spirit in the British Army.[12]

Let us take the case of a company of British infantry moving forward in the attack and thereby preparing to close with an enemy who is expected to resist fiercely. Although this is an abstract case with no concrete context it will serve its purpose here as an unambiguous example of violent combat and one in which the infantry soldiers' fighting spirit will be tested. For each individual, going forward to inflict and risk death or maiming is neither a logical nor an instinctively natural action, but against all apparent logic the individuals do go forward, as has happened countless times in history. One might well ask why they are doing so rather than leaving the field either physically or mentally. The model outlined above provides the following explanation, in that the social structures of the unit each provide a context where there is no option but to go on:

Formal command structure – The soldiers have their orders to attack, and there is a chain of command in place to ensure that they do so.

Informal structure – They are part of a group of individuals who are bonded together in informal relationships of *friendship* and *association*.

Functional structure – They are performing a common task which they are trained and equipped to do, which is a defining task in the business of being a soldier.

Loyalty/identity structure – The reputation of all the loyalty/identity segments of which they are members is at stake.

So, whatever the *operating group* or the *operating structure*, each soldier is in a context where continuing the attack is the only option. According to the model, therefore, their fighting spirit is a function of their participation in the social structures, and of the provision in each structure of a context where attacking is the appropriate thing to do. While things remain as they are here described, therefore, an individual can only cease to go forward by denying the *operating structure* and removing himself from the *operating group*.

The question then arises as to how the social structures that promote this militarily desirable situation can be nurtured and strengthened, so that no individual wishes to deny the *operating structure* or absent himself from the *operating group*.

There are many different ways of using the model to examine this question. First, for example, we can take the individual soldier's case, checking through the headings in the model:

Formal command structure. If a soldier is to fight, he must know what he is supposed to do, what his chain of command is, to whom he is supposed to give orders, from whom to take orders, and to whom to send reports. In essence, he must know where he stands in the formal command structure.

Informal structure. He must be comfortable with the relationships he has in the informal structure. They ought to be appropriate, and as strong as possible. It is obvious that chaos and uncertainty are large factors in war, and it is more than likely that at various times in combat the *informal structure* will be the *operating structure* by default (in the absence of relevant formal orders). It is vital therefore that it is properly ordered and maintained because that is the point at which the fighting group could informally melt away.

Loyalty/identity structure. He must be a fully participant member of the loyalty/identity structure of the people on whose side he is fighting.

Functional structure. A soldier needs to be master of his military skills and to be as familiar as possible with the conditions that he is encountering – he needs to be properly trained. He also needs to know what he has to do – what is the job that is highest priority – and he needs to feel that he has the right resources to do it – the right equipment, the right ammunition, and to be in the right human group (that he is not in a platoon that has to carry out a company task, for example).

Second, we can take a view from the top of the unit by asking what the Commanding Officer can do to promote the strength of the social structures, and mutual support between them. The model indicates that he will need to ensure that all of his soldiers are members of groups in all four structures, and are comfortable with them. He must ensure that each structure is given its turn in his soldiers' lives. There must, for example, be times when orders are given and taken, when salutes are exchanged, where the machinery of discipline is seen to be exercised (*formal command structure*). Similarly, his officers and men must be able to relax in each other's company and they must all be in the appropriate set of relationships for their positions and status in the unit (*informal structure*). Again, they must be properly trained and organised for the tasks in hand (*functional structure*). They must exercise membership of the various segments in the *loyalty/identity structure* at every possible level. Finally, the Commanding Officer must ensure that there is an appropriate balance between the stress that he places on each of the structures so that none becomes over-important in the eyes of his men.

Third, we can look at the roles and performance of leaders within the unit at any level. It is widely accepted that they make a vital contribution to the fighting spirit of their men by their conduct and example, and reference to the model can enlighten us as how they can do so. Using the model, we can see that each leader must be able to function as such whatever the *operating group* or the *operating structure*. For example, if a leader has a positive personal rapport with his men (*informal structure*) and fully participates in and supports the *loyalty/identity structure*, but does not have the iron in the soul that enables him to receive or to give with equanimity orders that are unwelcome (*formal command structure*), then he will fail when he attempts to give such orders to unwilling subordinates.

The past

Before we look at the implications of the model for the future fighting spirit of the British Army it would be as well to revisit the historical element of the study to try to obtain a perspective on this issue over time. Regrettably there is no space here to give the details, but in summary the model was found to work well in the analysis and understanding of first-hand accounts of British soldiers' behaviour over a very long period. First-hand material back to 1640 was examined and the model was found to give insights at least as far back as 1700, and probably further – though it must be understood that there is not really enough material in the period before the mid-eighteenth century to be certain. The research conclusion was that the patterns of behaviour described by the model have a remarkably long history and a tenacious persistence through considerable social and technological change.

The future

So, what about the future? What insights can the model give? What follows is of course a personal view, but one based on the model described above and so, it is hoped, free from emotional bias in a highly charged area.

In considering the future, I am making the assumption that the formal internal organisation of our combat units will not undergo radical change. This appears to be a safe assumption because it has a history of operational success and it is well suited to British soldiers' social behaviour. It provides an appropriate and effective milieu in which soldiers can work and fight.

On the other hand, changes in wider British society may well have an effect on the military unit, for two reasons. First, all recruits to the services have spent their lives so far embedded in that wider society and are bound to bring its effects with them in the form of personal dispositions.[13] Second, mature serving soldiers are not isolated from that society but receive its influence through human contact and through the media.

Three particular changes in British society seem to have a potential impact on the social structures in a military unit:

- The first is an aspect which I shall call 'civilianisation of attitudes'. By this I mean the idea that being a soldier is less and less a way of life and more and more 'just a job' to be done between certain hours of the day, leaving the rest of the time for non-military pursuits. It is perhaps best expressed in the Bett Report[14] which implied that the military was out of date in its application of management techniques to everyday lives and that changes were needed to bring it into line with civilian best practice.

- The second is post-modernism. In essence, post-modernism is a collection of ideas which amount to a statement that there is no such thing as established reality – nothing is absolute and all perception is conditioned by the standpoint of the observer. It is a widespread influence on the culture of current Western societies. In particular, it questions the validity of rules, frameworks and conventions.[15] It has been expressed over the past century or so in the arts by the rise of such things as abstract painting and the abandonment of musical keys and conventions of harmony. In more recent times it has entered popular culture on a wide scale; for example:

  - The idea that personal experiences are more important than things which are taught by those in authority or passed on from other people. This has found expression in such ideas as self-realisation by 'doing your own thing' and in the drugs culture, where individuals consider the unreal experiences induced by drugs to be as valid as the experiences of everyday mundane life.

  - The rise of New Age religion, where each individual is invited to acquire the set of religious beliefs and practices that 'work for them'.

- The third is what is called here 'moral liberalism'. The basis of moral liberalism is the morally upright idea that nobody should be seriously disadvantaged by circumstances beyond their control. It has been applied in turn over the past 25 years to the social emancipation of women, black people, homosexuals and those with physical disabilities. It has led to labelling as in some way shameful many attitudes towards such 'minorities' which are still widely held in British society. Its most obvious expression is in the phenomenon of 'political correctness'.[16] Resistance to moral liberalism usually provokes a hostile public reaction, which in many cases has been enshrined in the law. In the current British Army this attitude has already led to the acceptance of the idea of employing women in a far wider array of military roles than could possibly have been envisaged 15 years ago. In the future it may well lead to the acceptance of self-declared homosexuals as full and appropriate members of the Army.

In the light of these three changes, I can offer two scenarios depicting the future fighting spirit of the British Army:

- In the first, we can take a lesson from the past: the social structures, on which I believe my model shows the ingredients of fighting spirit rest to a substantial degree, will remain fundamentally unchanged. In the same way as they have endured great changes, for example changes in weapons technology and in the class structure of British society, they will endure the social changes that are upon us now. This is depicted in the classic diagram of stable equilibrium (Figure 3). It represents a ball in a cup – no matter how far up the cup you push the ball it will return eventually to its stable position in the bottom. We can call this 'View One'.

Figure 3 *Stable equilibrium*

The second scenario is somewhat different:

- First, the idea that being a soldier is simply another form of employment, rather than a way of life, will undermine the cohesion of military units simply by reducing the time that the individuals spend in the context of the social structures. One might describe this as a dilution of the military culture. Second, the influence of post-modernism in the popular culture will make it less and less acceptable to live by rules, discipline, self-discipline and self-control. This will put a larger and larger burden on the *formal command structure* at just the time when individuals spend less and less time under it as the operating structure. The *formal command structure* will therefore have to be used increasingly in a diminishing envelope of time, thus reducing the time available for the other structures to be exercised. The system of social structures will therefore become unbalanced. Third, the liberal humanist changes will make it – indeed are already making it – possible to have sexual relationships (heterosexual now, homosexual later perhaps) with fellow-members of the unit, sub-unit or primary group. This change introduces a new set of relationships into the informal structure – so different that they cut across the bonding influence of mutual trust. Jealousy, envy and rivalry will become part of everyday life in the arena where *friendship* and *association* have hitherto been the majority of relationships. This is a significant qualitative change that will alter the informal structure fundamentally.

These changes will alter the body chemistry of military units. They will push the social structures beyond their elastic limit and lead to an unwelcome change in the social structures that have been operating for at least 200 years and have been an important element of our fighting spirit.

I offer another model of equilibrium, this time of stable equilibrium with an elastic limit – a point beyond which everything changes.

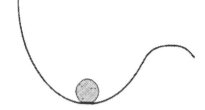

Figure 4 *Stable equilibrium with elastic limit*

In Figure 4 things are stable so long as the ball remains in the lower half of the cup, but if it is pushed too far up the sides of the cup then it will escape to a completely new state.

Moreover, even if the military establishment is able at all to counter the difficulties posed under this scenario, and thus partly restore the stability of the equilibrium, it might in doing so lose the support of a public which embraces as natural, reasonable and just the views and values which it is trying to resist. And an armed service needs public support.

We can call this 'View Two': and in this view the fighting spirit of the British Army will be changed for the worse. We may lose the next war.

Nobody can say at this point which of these two views is the more realistic. However, military caution dictates that the dangers represented in View Two are examined in great detail, as they represent a significant threat if they are found to be realistic.

NOTES

Although the author of this paper is a serving officer in the Army, the views expressed are the author's own, and do not reflect official opinion or thought.

1. Examples are too numerous to set out comprehensively, but would include works of military sociology such as Morris Janowitz, *The Professional Soldier: a Social and Political Portrait* (Glencoe, IL: The Free Press, 1960), and *Sociology and the Military Establishment* (New York: Russell Sage Foundation, 1965); John Baynes, *Morale: A Study of Men and Courage* (London: Cassell, 1967), and *The Soldier in Modern Society* (London: Eyre Methuen, 1972); John Hockey, *Squaddies: Portrait of a Subculture* (University of Exeter, 1986); Ruth Jolly, *Military Man Family Man: Crown Property* (London: Brassey's Defence Publishers, 1987); Mary Wechsler Segal, 'The Military and the Family as Greedy Institutions', in Charles Moskos and F. Wood (eds), *The Military: More then Just a Job?* (London: Pergamon-Brassey's, 1988), pp. 79-97, and works of military psychology such as Reuven Gal, and David Mengelsdorff, *Handbook of Military Psychology* (Chichester: Wiley, 1991), and Eli Ginzberg, *Breakdown and Recovery*, Vol. 2 of *The Ineffective Soldier: Lessons for Management and the Nation* (New York: Columbia University Press, 1959).
2. See, for example, Emile Durkheim, *Rules of the Sociological Method*, ed. George Catlin (Chicago, IL: University of Chicago Press, 1938) and Emile Durkheim, George Simpson (ed.), *Suicide: A Study in Sociology* (London: Routledge & Kegan Paul, 1952).

3. I have composed this definition using John Beattie, *Other Cultures: Aims, Methods and Achievements in Social Anthropology* (London: Routledge & Kegan Paul, 1966), and Lucy Mair, *An Introduction to Social Anthropology* (Oxford: Clarendon Press, 1965).

4. The model was refined during a one-year postgraduate study based at the University of Cambridge, Department of Social Anthropology.

5. See, for example, Brian Chapman, *The Science of Society: An Introduction to Sociology* (London: George Allen & Unwin, 1967) p. 32, and N. Paul Loomba, *Management – A Quantitative Perspective* (London: CollierMacmillan, 1978), pp. 39, 85.

6. However, in the case of the present study, although it has involved only one year of full-time research (1993/94) the author's time of deliberate observation has been considerably longer (25 years) and the participation of the author, as a serving officer, has been close. It is therefore suggested that the resulting model can be taken as well founded and authoritative.

7. A unit is a formed body of soldiers organised into an HQ and sub-units and commanded by a lieutenant-colonel. It is usually between 350 and 600 strong.

8. Clifford Geertz, 'Form and Variation in Balinese Village Structure', *American Anthropologist*, 61 (1959), pp. 991–1012.

9. A 'gun position' is an area of ground occupied by a number of deployed artillery pieces, their local command system and the soldiers to man them. It is distinct from the administrative area ('wagon lines') and the forward areas, where observer parties and the battery commander are normally deployed.

10. Examples of these processes taking place are given in Charles Kirke, 'Social Structures in the Combat Arms Units of the British Army' (paper offered to *Armed Forces and Society*).

11. A paper summarising the results of the historical study is in preparation.

12. This paper is written with special reference to the British Army because that army was the central area for the study out of which it arises. It may well be that other armies have similar social structures and that the model could be extended to considering fighting spirit in those armies as well.

13. See, for example, Pierre Bourdieu, *The Logic of Practice* (Cambridge: Polity Press, 1990), pp. 52–65.

14. Michael Bett *et al.*, *Managing People in Tomorrow's Armed Forces* (London: HMSO, 1995).

15. An informative introduction to post-modernism is given in David Harvey, *The Condition of Postmodernity: An Enquiry into the Origins of Social Change* (Oxford: Basil Blackwell, 1989).

16. See Sarah Dunant (ed.) *The War of the Words: the Political Correctness Debate* (London: Virago Press, 1994) for a useful set of essays on the topic of moral liberalism.

17

Fighting Spirit: Has it a Future?

Patrick Mileham

'War always interested me ... the reality of war, the actual killing ... to know in what way and under the influence of what feeling one soldier kills another ...'

Tolstoy

'Fighting, Sergeant, is an activity, but it's also a state of mind.'
'Sir, get real, try telling that to the lads!'

ETHOS AND MILITARY VIRTUE

'Fighting spirit', roughly the equivalent of the US term 'warrior spirit', has recently gained prominence in the context of military policy and 'defence capability' – that formal collection of mainly physical pre-requirements and enabling factors needed for projecting British military power. The mental activity needed to articulate the modern-day meaning and implications of fighting spirit, particularly for the Army, remains incomplete, although begun in the early 1990s at the time of the two major Ministry of Defence reviews.[1] A feeling quickly grew at the time that a number of intangible aspects of the Army and other services were under threat. What constituted these intangibles – broadly the corporate concepts, traditions, procedures, habits and emotions – was uncertain. They could be described up to a point of course, but explanations, ready to be defined convincingly in policy publications or robust Whitehall *viva voce* argument, were much more difficult to find. Even at the cultural level, when such intangibles are supposedly values in themselves, meeting value for money scrutiny revealed an embarrassing weakness in the politico-military intellectual armour of policy-makers and uniformed debaters. The cost to soldiers of their efforts and cost to the taxpayer are often not of the same value category.

A word widely invoked in the debate was 'ethos', seemingly appropriate to express the gravity and complexity of what was to be defended. It soon became part of the military terminology of the period. Then in 1995 the term was formally addressed in three Army Board papers, the instructive one in respect of this chapter was entitled *The Extent to Which the Army Has The Right to be Different.*[2] Known informally as the 'Army Ethos Paper', it was a most difficult paper both to research and draft. Its chief purpose was to draw the line between what was deemed essential to the Army's purpose as a militarily effective force, and any major incursion of employment law and civilian personnel practices into the preserve of military terms of service and discipline, seen in the context of trends in social behaviour. The paper's chief value was the articulation of the Army's 'characteristic spirit or ethos', which was deemed to be:

> That spirit which enables soldiers to fight. It relies principally on motiv-ation, which in turn calls for high degrees of commitment, self-sacrifice and mutual trust.

This 'ethos statement' [*sic*] briefly proclaims the Army's 'distinguishing function'. Implicitly the context is of the soldiers' collective emotional and spiritual life:[3] the second sentence reinforces the self-evident claim with the psycho-philosophical pre-requirement of 'mutual trust'. While 'fighting spirit' is not the same thing as 'enabling spirit', for practical purposes the former term, used by the Adjutant-General of the day, acknowledges the Army's self-professed core purpose. If this statement has any meaning at all, however, it must be raised far above the level of sentimentality and identify military endeavour with the highest hopes and aspirations of humanity.

With this statement as a starting point, the aim of this chapter is to analyse the assumptions which lie behind fighting spirit as both concept and practice, while considering the British Army's future as an effective fighting force.

One of the premises of this chapter is that all contact and activity between two or more persons immediately places them in a moral relationship, which may range from that of substantial and obvious moral significance, to one of an only slight or almost imperceptible degree. It follows that soldiers joining together to fight an enemy, conducting any sort of task and even living together in formed units, should recognise that almost everything they do has moral significance, including the relationship with the enemy, in that case one of mutual antipathy. In operations and war they are governed by the full panoply of just war theory and law (*jus ad bellum*) and the laws of war (*jus in bello*): military disciplinary codes and working practices also guide soldiers' peacetime behaviour.

Another premise is that ethos can be described as a collective aspiration towards virtuous conduct amongst an identifiable group of persons. While virtue is a first-order predicate and can only really be ascribed to individuals, values are the carriers (in the ethnographical sense) of mutual understanding of a number of persons, while culture is the behaviour and actions – a third-order predicate[4] in the hierarchy of ethics in an institution. As a consequence of a soldier being ordered to fight, it becomes his virtuous duty to break one set of laws and simultaneously devote all his energies, and maybe his life, to abide by another. But refraining from disobedience to legal orders and avoiding war crimes is not enough for a virtuous corporate spirit or desirable and prevailing ethos; there is a sense in which ethos implies additional understanding and conduct within the spirit of the law. That is the meaning of conduct beyond the call of duty, and the substance described in thousands of citations honouring bravery and exceptional combat performance in the history of the British armed forces. As civil laws take precedence over military law in democratic nations, civilised conduct demands levels of self-control and self-discipline at the personal, group and corporate level, and in the context of the British Army, distinguishes the civilised soldier[5] as a representative public servant of a democratic nation from a militarised brute.

A list of military virtues can easily be drawn up by anyone with military experience or an intelligent commentator, and frequently are. A modern soldier in the author's opinion[6] should possess:

- *Personal integrity* – accepting hazard, courageous, honourable, humane, a whole person (i.e. not duplicitous).
- *Trustworthiness* – showing intelligent obedience, self-confidence, self-discipline, loyalty and honour.
- *Competence* – proving functional expertise, in adverse conditions, acting with judgement, possessing leadership qualities (if a leader) and with high personal standards.

One can read much into such statements. As an expression of military virtues these are the stuff of military hyperbole and ideology, but giving them a different orientation one is left with blatant militarism. The true significance of these virtuous traits, however, is that they are not absolutes but variables. They are variable within a unique individual, his (or her) predisposition at the moment of enlistment or officer selection, and at times of subsequent training, operational experience, and stage of career over many years. They are also variables within a military unit, and an army. They are variable according to the mood of the day, the presence or absence of danger, stress, physical deprivation, cognitive clarity or confusion, the state of morale and the course of operational or non-operational events. Human variables are factors in the promotion of synergy (force-multiplication) on the battlefield, and are dependent on linear and non-linear interconnections with vast numbers of other battlefield variables of a physical and conceptual nature. Negative synergy is the symptom of collapse. As with courage, which Lord Moran pointed out was not inexhaustible, soldiers draw on military virtues on account. The approach to these variables, whether positive or negative, in reality characterises the spirit of the institution, that is – more or less – its ethos.

Virtues as abstract concepts, it must be admitted, are more often than not diminished between an individual's or group's intentions and their actions. Similarly it does not mean that it is possible or perhaps even desirable, to seek a superabundance of every virtue within every soldier, unit, formation or army. There can be a dangerous excess of supposed virtue – according to Aristotle's widely accepted theory of the 'mean' – as well as a deficiency. But extrapolating the word integrity or wholeness applied to a virtuous individual, an army above all needs fully integrated units, those which do not easily disintegrate physically and morally and are thus potentially successful in battle.

So fighting spirit, while itself a virtue both in anticipation and actual conduct in a fight, is accorded a high place in the list of military virtues, and in the British Army is *a fortiori* officially now claimed as an expression of drawing together all the virtues of the soldiers' profession. However, the corporate spirit of individuals within a military group attempting (or failing) to live up to these virtues is not easily subject to prescription by policy-makers or remote military commanders. Neither ethos nor fighting spirit can be ordered up in the ordinary sense of military orders, and they can only be manifestations of an effective spirit of leadership and the activity of leaders at all levels. Also, defining fighting is not as straightforward as it may seem.

FIGHTING: A TRADITIONAL DEFINITION

Historically before the advent of gunpowder, fighting was for most combatants primarily a matter of close quarter, or relatively close quarter, physical actions with hand-held weapons – knives, swords, clubs and thrusting spears of various shapes and sizes. Even with the introduction of projectile spears and arrows, together with the stand-off firepower of such weapons when massed together, the expression closing with the enemy still meant the direct person-to-person, face-to-face act of fighting. Otherwise defined as mortal combat, it actually resulted in the death of opponents, their running away in fear of their lives or their capture after submission. Treatment of prisoners depended on reciprocal attitudes of the combatants.

So fighting spirit drew on physical strength, hostile intention, fear of the enemy, wrath generated in response to hostile action; in short the most direct physical emotional commitment to the act of fighting. Such close quarter combat was an intensely personal matter, whether the individual was animated by personal circumstances, habit or acculturation in his group, even when modified by rudimentary or sophisticated inhibitions we would recognise as of moral or civilised behaviour, a code of soldierly honour. A soldier was fighting simultaneously for his life and the death of the enemy, and in some cultures his immortal soul – the full meaning of 'warrior' caste and culture. Moving forward to modern history, indigenous soldiers of the British Indian Army were warriors in this sense, displaying such zeal based on their religion. In Britain, military fervour of religious spirituality and intensity was only present in Cromwell's army and some Highland regiments in royal service into the early years of the nineteenth century. Christian beliefs and sensibilities certainly genuinely inspired many British individuals during the Indian Mutiny, as a counter to the mutineers' religious zeal. It could be said the 'regimental system' encouraged an intense, integrating and exclusive quasi-religious spirit in some British regiments in their heyday, the defining moment being August 1914.

Of course, fighting could be and usually was a desperate affair, with a high chance of pain and/or capture or death, whether instantaneous or lingering. The anticipation of these personal occurrences and the anger and fear generated – these emotions are always closely linked – could be and frequently were mitigated by a fatalistic attitude to life which had driven the soldier from the scum of society to enlist in the first place in, for instance, Marlborough's regiments or Wellington's Peninsular Army. Iron discipline, an unquestioning and determinist militarism, often itself generating greater physical and moral fear than the fear of combat, remained essential for unit integrity well into the twentieth century. Life was cheap, nasty and brutish, and men were fatalistic: the survivors' feelings could be anaesthetised by post-battle catharsis and alcohol.

Long before the eighteenth century, however, the value of avoiding close quarter fighting had been learnt. Firearms and early artillery gave a soldier a greater chance of survival, and the ability to destroy the enemy *en masse*. Fighting then included the spirited animation needed to fire small arms at observed enemies, but also reliable close artillery support. The general's art was to maintain that distance, prudently keeping casualty rates low, thus sustaining the physical integrity of the army. Rapidly closing distance at the right moment, particularly with the use of cavalry to destroy the enemy's physical and moral integrity by swift manoeuvre, became a means of achieving strategic and battlefield advantage. Exposure of troops to close quarter mortal combat was compressed into as short a time as possible, enabling the final *coup de grâce* to be administered, if the enemy had not by then run away. That became the full significance of the modern term 'closing with the enemy' and destroying the enemy's morale and willingness to continue to fight was part of the military art, long before von Clausewitz codified it.

Two descriptive extracts will suffice for literally countless acts of traditional fighting in numerous wars fought by the British Army around the world. The first is a description of the storming of Badajoz in 1812.

> A tremendous firing now opened upon us, but the troops were no ways daunted ... the whole division rushed to the assault with the most amazing resolution ... The soldiers flew down the ladders and the cheering from both sides was loud and full of confidence. Grapeshot and musketry tore open their ranks ... It was a volcano! Up we went; some killed, and others impaled on the bayonets of their own comrades.[7]

When looking back at the actual killing with modern understanding and imagination, one wonders at the quality of the variables of 'confidence', 'resolution' and undauntedness, as well as the presence of anger and fear. The traditional language used by the officer eyewitness does not allow for complexity and variableness of the emotions of the thousands of soldiers present. For every man of demonstrable bravado there is almost certainly one present of more normal and more fragile human feelings, and the commentary of an 18-year-old private soldier at Vimeiro in 1808 gives a different account of soldiers' feelings.

> In our first charge I felt my mind waver; a breathless sensation came over me. The silence was appalling. I looked along the line. It was enough to assure me. The steady determined scowl of my companions assured my heart and gave me determination.[8]

Stirring stuff, but emotions, although variables, do not alter much in the sum of human experience over the generations, and the chief one in battle or operations must be fear. Fear, as Richard Holmes points out in *Firing Line,*

> involves a struggle between the demands of the instinct and the dictates of conscience. This is especially true before a soldier's first battle ... the conflict between an instinctive prompting to seek safety and a desire not to deviate from the standards expected of him by his leaders and comrades. 'I am afraid of being afraid', as one officer admitted in a letter home in 1917.[9]

There are countless narratives by ordinary soldiers of fighting and killing in the two World Wars, but almost always written after a period of reflection of days or even years, their authentic feelings being modified. Holmes also cites a medical study of our century.

> Most soldiers on approaching the firing line, displayed uneasiness and apprehension by restlessness, irritability, artificial jubilancy or silence and withdrawal, or by unusual perspiration, diarrhoea and frequency of micturition.[10]

If a soldier can, with the help of his comrades,[11] overcome his fear sufficiently, then he may well be able to display the fighting spirit reciprocally imitated by his comrades. Equally so there almost certainly comes a point when many soldiers do not have the time to be aware of their fear when charging the enemy; their instincts prompting their physical actions to destroy the enemy before he can destroy them. But compulsion – the British subaltern and his pistol – was not uncommon in the Great War,[12] nor the retaliatory 'fragging' of US officers in Vietnam.

RISK

The final significant factor in the traditional definition of fighting is the element of risk. Danger and risk in the physical sense are used interchangeably in the English-speaking world, but looking at the linguistic roots of each helps to define fighting spirit more accurately.

Danger derives from Latin *dominium*[13] and in the context of physical harm implies soldiers are at the mercy of circumstances of a life-threatening nature. The soldier of any age can therefore be a passive recipient of physical harm, even if his energies are actively engaged. Bayoneting the enemy, he can be struck by shrapnel from a haphazard shell fired by either side: having no choice, he had been ordered into the artillery killing zone and was killed by a seemingly accidental occurrence. The nature of danger is circumstantial, random and anonymous, and is thus of a different order of moral engagement with the enemy than hand-to-hand fighting.

On the other hand, Peter Bernstein recommends a more precise definition of terms and argues in *Against the Gods: The Remarkable Story of Risk* that 'Risk derives from the early Italian *riscare*, which means to dare. In this sense, risk is a choice rather than a fate.'[14] Although Bernstein writes of risk in general, his meaning touches directly on our understanding of what is really happening in combat. With danger or peril, there is little or no choice for soldiers, whereas to risk or hazard one's life implies personal choice, personal commitment and the direct moral contingency and engagement of a soldier with his enemy, face to face in a physical and practical sense. This reinforces the premise that all such contact, hostile as well as benign, has a moral element. Risk gains even greater moral significance when placing others in danger through one's own choice as a leader or comrade, whether at the precise moment acting bravely or in cowardly fashion. Thus traditional fighting places the soldier in a position of both danger and risk: the closer he is in direct mortal combat with an enemy, the more likely he is to have to make hazardous choices, even if individual micro-tactical ones.

The implication for the soldier's traditional trade is that personal commitment, the manifestation of soldierly virtues even now in the 1990s, are linked in the traditional military paradigm with direct mortal combat. Before moving on to more up-to-date implications of fighting spirit, it should be stated that a list of physical fighting qualities based on bodily physique, energy and endurance, is of one categorical order, while intellectual and moral qualities are of a different order. The recognition and calculation of hazard and acceptance of danger span both sets of qualities.

MODERN SOLDIERING

Modern-day soldiers are not solely employed to fight, they are employed to *be* soldiers and take part in all the activities of soldiering.[15] During war, operations or peacetime, and any state in between, they include a wide range of sub-activities, many near to the traditional activity of fighting, some exclusively military and others parallel with or directly equivalent to civilian pursuits and occupations. Specialisation and the division of military labour is of course a feature of all modern armies.

The underlying concept of aggressively closing with the enemy in mortal combat has since 1909 been expressed succinctly as one of the British Principles of War, offensive action. Another principle is security. Ninety years on, after all the politicians' and commanders' deliberative processes of establishing war and operational aims, risk analysis, selection of battlefield objectives, matching troops to tasks and provision of resources of every imaginable kind, British soldiers are still likely to be ordered into battle to conduct 'offensive action', and fight aggressively in intense war, even to the extent of hand-to-hand fighting. What has changed is the nature of 'security' or defensive action.

The 'Revolution in Military Affairs' (RMA), defined as those conceptual and physical components of military power that 'fundamentally alter[s] the character and conduct of conflict',[16] has characterised fighting in the twentieth century by a combination of force multiplication, exponential growth in the extent of the geographical battlefield, speed of manoeuvre, capability for dispersion, distancing of weapons from human targets, artillery fire power, aerial delivery of weapons and the addition of weapons of mass targeting and destruction. This change from 1914 onwards, together with mass conscription from sections of society with different values and a wholly different mental approach to fighting compared with that of the traditional career British soldier, was bound to affect the moral component of fighting power, as well as the approach to danger and risk in battle. Writing of 1914, Samuel Hynes states:

> The minds of the fighting men changed. The new soldiers came to the war believing that individual wills would have a role there; what man did – his decisions, his actions – would affect whether he lived or died. The new weapons of war challenged that conviction; they made death accidental. It wasn't the violence or the power or the cruelty of those weapons that made the war different; it was the *vast* [author's italics] randomness and anonymity of their ways of killing.[17]

Categorically, fighting spirit, however defined, must itself have changed as the physical nature of fighting has changed. Whether he should act according to imposed determinist principles of action, or draw on his own voluntarist intuition, became the source of many a soldier's internal mental conflict in action.

While the individual soldier and units of previous generations could expect to take part in close-quarter combat, the RMA provides for an ever increasing range of methods of distancing him from the enemy, while enabling him more effectively to achieve military objectives and war aims efficiently, quickly, decisively and as safely as possible. The function is to defeat the enemy conclusively, closing with him in mortal combat only at the final 'moment of truth'[18] for both sides, ideally to enact a symbolic surrender with the enemy in a supreme moment of *moral* truth.

Designed to condense the danger time to the minimum, every advance in technology and conceptual practice in modern armies has had the purpose of promoting the physical integrity of units and thereby their moral integrity. Whether in weapons, ground vehicles, airlift and air offensive platforms, communications equipment and information technology, security has taken literally a quantum leap at every new scientific discovery. The moral as well as technical concepts behind technologies are part of the perpetuating battlefield revolution.

Thus, fighting spirit must be a vastly more complex and sophisticated experience and concept at the end of the twentieth century than at the beginning, particularly as the full extent of the possibilities for total war that the nuclear age enables lies solely in the imagination, and in a moral sense is totally unimaginable.

Indeed, the modern generation of the British Army has only twice gone to war and fought in intense battle. The 1982 Falklands conflict produced this narrative.

> The CO then shouted out 'Follow me', wrote Sergeant Barry Norman, and ran down the hill and headed towards the enemy position. I immediately followed and was followed by ... others of Tac 1 and A Company ... Someone to my rear shouted: 'Watch out, there's an enemy position on the left'. I immediately looked left and saw an enemy trench ... it opened fire on me. I hit the ground ... I returned fire to the enemy trench and the Colonel ... proceeded up the hill towards the enemy position. As he got within three feet of the position ... he was shot in the back from a trench in the rear. I remained there for some considerable time, possibly ten minutes – it felt for ever – pinned down. Eventually two 66s [66mm rockets] were used on the enemy trenches and they surrendered.[19]

This passage, which could have equally been an encounter in any theatre in the Second World War, realises the dilemma of really understanding how a professional soldier feels in rushing into intense combat. He distances himself from his feelings. 'It felt forever' is the telling phrase: the remainder is descriptive, as one expects from a trained, mature, self-disciplined, objective professional soldier of a self-authenticating elite combat unit.

In the virtually unopposed armoured thrust in the Gulf War of 1991, British troops experienced encounters with the enemy of a different nature. British infantrymen expressed their experiences more tellingly three days after the event as follows.[20]

> It's not like an exercise when you hear the contact [enemy firing] ... you're paying a *lot* of attention to it ... The guys in the back were pretty apprehensive. There's total isolation in the Warrior [armoured personnel carrier with 30 mm cannon], total silence ... there's an artificiality about it ... get out of the vehicle and all hell is let loose.
>
> We won the fire fight ... gave the trenches a jolly good blasting ... taking them out at 800m with HE. The difficulty was to make a decision to commit men to the ground [dismount] to clear trenches and take the surrender of the enemy. There was an indication that the enemy wanted to surrender. The company commander wanted to push forward ... my worry was we were going too fast ... going through trenches that hadn't been cleared.

When we went in, there was relatively nothing for us to do ... there wasn't the will to fight from the enemy.

It makes a huge difference if the enemy infantry's fighting spirit has been utterly destroyed before one's own soldiers have to go in on foot and hazard their lives. Declaring the moment of cease-fire trench by trench was reportedly easier in this war than the Falklands. So the Gulf War was an ideal military experience in the Clausewitzian sense for the Coalition troops, although their part in the fighting can probably best be described almost as a surreal experience.

These two encounters with modern-day enemies are exceptional for the vast majority of post-National Service volunteer professional soldiers in the last 40 years of the British Army's record of service. British soldiers have rarely fought in the traditional sense in the second half of the twentieth century, and the question emerges: What is the nature of the function of soldiering that takes up most of their time? While the primary function of those in the combat arms – infantry-men, tank crewmen and armed helicopter crew – is still to fight, the combat support arms and combat service support arms have primary tasks which are not in a direct sense fighting. While trained to fight for self-protection *in extremis*, they are not expected or trained to take offensive action in formed units of any size. Their soldierly activities are centred around high-technology weapons, weapon platforms and logistic support and for them a true professional spirit – to the extent of facing danger and risking their lives (i.e. involving personal choice) in the faithful conduct of their work – is the equivalent of fighting spirit. The quality of one is of course dependent on the quality of the other in a truly integrated force: the physical integrity of a unit, formation or force continues to require the individuals' moral integrity to sustain it.[21]

How the fighting spirit of the British Army has been promoted, preserved, undermined or destroyed at various times, is linked to the substance of its history during the course of the century. The concept of operations practised by today's British Army is based on the minimum length of time that can be achieved in exposing soldiers to close-range fighting and face-to-face encounter – that is armoured vehicles duelling at close range and infantrymen dismounting for the final assault. It is the rare, unprotected moment when traditional fighting spirit is needed and the individual, or his leader making decisions for him, knows intuitively what risk, hazard and daring really are. Facing reality is conceptually and intellectually one thing, but as G.K. Chesterton suggested 'practical facts as facts do not always create a spirit of reality, because reality is a spirit'. A person's sense-awareness equally makes the realisation of the moment of truth an intensely philosophical-emotional experience.

Tolstoy, when trying to answer the question 'under the influence of what feeling one soldier kills another',[22] sought to probe the presumably timeless moral awareness involved in 'the *actual* killing' process. This process is a psycho-philosophical as well as practical experience, which underlies the essence of fighting spirit. We have to admit that there is little objective research data on fighting spirit available within the modern intense warfare experience, so, like Tolstoy, we can only give a partial answer.

THE FUTURE OF THE FIGHTING SPIRIT

There can be few human organisations other than armies that require a stronger deterministic paradigm to ensure effective performance. The modern truly professional Army, however, is recognised to be a voluntary one, that is based on voluntarist principles. Voluntarism means choice, choice on joining, and a stream of conscious or unconscious choices during service, whether in peacetime, or on limited or intense operations. Voluntarism self-evidently needs to be sustained by high degrees of self-discipline.

Without insulting the motivation of those who have served and are currently serving, it should be recognised that it is very unlikely that many officer or soldier entrants to the British Army have in recent generations consciously conducted any sort of actuarial risk analysis, that is assessing the likelihood of their taking part in combat and the consequent risk of death, injury, capture or any other circumstantial or incidental possibilities which may affect their future lives. There is, however, much evidence that modern, educated entrants are much more conscious of what they want to gain for themselves from service in the Army and what they are not prepared to do. The preponderance of the Army which is employed to close with and kill the enemy has now dropped to 30 per cent.[23] Seventy per cent of entrants, one assumes, decided that 'professional spirit' described above, rather than 'fighting spirit', was their first consideration. In fact for some period now, much of the sort of spirit that willingly accepts risk or hazard seems to have become that of specialists, the preserve of the Parachute Regiment, Special Air Service Regiment and the Royal Marines, not a general Army-wide moving spirit. With peace-keeping and peace-enforcement operations now becoming the normal activity of soldiers, and fighting in the traditional sense becoming abnormal, a high degree of fighting spirit can hardly be encouraged in these politically charged circumstances, even when physical danger is prevalent. The careful control or concealment of virtually all aggressive intentions has now become a self-discipline necessarily instilled by training and the rules of engagement in all soldiers.

While such conceptual and personal motivational changes seem set to continue to move away from a traditional definition of fighting spirit, there are technology factors which are already planned for the dismounted infantrymen, as he closes with and kills the enemy in future intense conflict. The Future Infantry System Technology (FIST) – a mind-boggling range of portable military equipments – will be designed for him to be a walking (or running) technologically communicating, locating, navigating, reporting, intelligence-gathering, virtual reality observing, self-sustainable, cyber-space robot – but still a human being.[24] How the intellectual or moral components of his conduct will fit in with the technology is uncertain, including fighting spirit, unit cohesion and leadership. The problems ramify if the enemy is organised, equipped and, above all, motivated differently from one's own troops.

So what of the fighting soldiers of the future?

There is an assumption that young males will continue to apply for combat arm service. Inexperienced, gullible, malleable by maturer men, young males are demonstrably 'those in the population who are prone ... to risky behaviour .... They consistently overestimate their own ability to handle difficult situations ... while simultaneously underestimating the personal danger they face.'[25] They supposedly make ideal infantrymen for use in traditional fighting, where older more pragmatic men tend to seek a greater chance of survival through more personally secure means of defeating the enemy. Cynically, one can say that the Army has always relied on young turks, both soldiers and officers, to do the fighting and provide cannon fodder. Anyone with any sense would avoid volunteering for such foolhardiness. The contradiction of course is that courage, innate or induced, if it is to engender fighting spirit and simultaneously reduce foolhardiness, requires considerable maturity.

It must not be forgotten that all combatants for the British Army agree to volunteer by 'signing the most fearsome contract of employment devised', in the opinion of a serving officer considering the open-ended nature of Army service. 'How can one quantify that contract of employment ... and particularly what the life and death clause would be worth in monetary terms?'[26] There is no answer, but a 'psychological contract' for the armed services is currently being considered by personnel policy-makers. Drawn from current society, the same young people[27] face the modern world of existential angst, individualism, inflation of expectation, egalitarianism, widescale distrust, as well as scepticism about institutions and authority. In the civilised Army, potential recruits are not asked about 'the actual killing': they state that the reasons for joining, both male and female, are '85 per cent for a sense of adventure, 75 per cent always wanted to be a soldier; and 68 per cent for gaining a trade'.[28] A sense of adventure is not necessarily the same as *riscare*, to hazard one's life.

I believe increasingly that young persons, both male and particularly female, are conducting their own actuarial risk analysis about the likelihood of being killed, wounded, captured or inflicted with a lifelong health problem, if they sign the 'fearsome contract'. Life is not cheap. There is evidence of less voluntary suspension of disbelief about military self-esteem and glory. Death is not so easily swallowed up in victory. Battlefield catharsis is replaced by post-traumatic stress disorder. Similarly, as a consequence of the repeal of Section 10 of the Crown Proceedings Act 1947, hundreds or thousands or servicemen and women are seeking compensation through the courts from the Secretary of State, for injuries sustained in peacetime training or current peace-keeping operations. Recruiting for the combat arms, particularly infantry, has sharply declined during the late 1990s.

The possibilities and nature of intensive fighting in wars of the future are subject to much imaginative analysis, by such writers as Paul Kennedy, Christopher Bellamy and Alvin and Heidi Toffler.[29] British military policy-makers have also been busy speculating in broad geo-strategic terms in anticipation of future technologies and capabilities, not only on a single-service basis but also on a fully integrated joint-service and coalition partner basis. *Two Speculative Views of Future Warfare and their Implications* was a paper produced for the Ministry of Defence in 1996, for the Army's planning purposes. The contents include highly imaginative forecast requirements for concepts and technologies of command and control, information and intelligence firepower, protection, manoeuvre, control of the electro-magnetic spectrum, sustainability and deployability. The implanting of pre-programmed microchips in would-be warriors or genetic engineering of such a human sub-type is getting closer, 'bringing into question exactly what is human'.[30] While the conduct of fighting is described in terms of the conceptual and physical components of fighting power, some of the variables, such as non-state enemy forces, degrees of professionalism and training, as well as motivation, contain implicit moral variables which remain uncalculated and probably incalculable.

Coming at a time of military recession and low morale, after a golden age for the British Army,[31] the Strategic Defence Review of 1998, involving 'a re-examination of British defence requirements from *first principles* [author's italics],[32] recognises the extent of the human factor and particularly intellectual development to a degree as never before. The fighting spirit of the future British Army is not mentioned, but within the desire to continue to employ 'highly skilled and motivated people', there must lie concealed a continuing aspiration for effective fighting troops – as a first principle.

Whilst there has been confusion recently caused by having to search for a new role for an existing world-class army, the Army is working hard on personnel policies and understands much more about what motivates the modern man or woman than hitherto. Comprehension of the advanced leadership development requirements by commanders of all levels down to junior NCOs may be sufficient to deal with the intellectual difficulties of peace-keeping and peace-enforcement which preoccupy much of the Army's energies at the present time, i.e. that type of operation requiring at least some offensive action and fighting spirit when appropriate. The corresponding moral leadership and comradeship needed to deal with the human implications of intense technological future warfare, may also be sufficient, if it proves to be better than any potential enemy's cohesiveness, comradeship and moral leadership. The development of socio-moral aspirations in a military unit, which can endure over time and seem to be external to the individualistic life of feelings, ideally should become an institutional fact.[33] Mutual trust has been claimed as a defining feature of the British Army, and it needs to be perpetuated whatever future operations may entail. The best sort of training must include developing the moral component as well as the physical and conceptual.

There is one final factor about future wars which reflects back on one's half-formed assumptions about the general war that never happened during the past half century. That is the dominance of the human spirit despite the utter moral incomprehensibleness of total nuclear war. Fighting spirit now as always, depends on real, live, direct human contact with comrades – with collective frenzied and maddened physical reactions to the fear of the moment becoming battle-winning. Desperate conditions and awful experiences can bind together troops ever more closely in already strongly cohesive armies. The British Army's cohesiveness and comradeship over the years compare well with most other armies of the advanced nations.

CONCLUSIONS

From being a personal and very subjective experience, fighting has developed additionally into a vast range of highly objective physical and intellectual activities. The sophistication of the means of killing and destroying the enemy's will increased exponentially between each generation of soldiers. While fighting still implies direct mortal combat, fighting spirit must constitute an enduring and defining military virtue, which has no direct and legitimate parallel in any other occupation or profession.

With regard to future war, with endless possibilities for confusing virtual and real realities, it will be apparent from the foregoing sections that the quality of fighting spirit cannot really be extrapolated from past experience of war with any certainty. The nature of conflict has already changed so radically and knowledge about people's motivation in operations being subject to so many and different human, physical and conceptual variables, that specific assumptions about moral and spiritual matters cannot be guaranteed in advance.

That is not, however, an excuse to suspend belief or ignore analysis, debate and other activities to develop the deepest understanding about human nature in warfare. There is a higher possibility of achieving self-fulfilling prophecy for operational success, if high degrees of faith and confidence are projected by leaders and strongly held beliefs are engendered amongst intelligent volunteers of all ranks drawn from contemporary society. There is evidence, despite some forebodings of the difficulties ahead, that commanders are coping professionally with the expectations and stresses of modern operations short of war and the necessary training for them. There is also hope that the British Army is making progress towards being a more intelligent, more self-disciplined and more self-confident Army than it has ever been before.

NOTES

1. Ministry of Defence, *Options for Change* (London: HMSO, 1991, Cmnd 1595), *Front Line First: Defence Cost Studies* (London: HMSO, 1994).
2. The author was involved in its drafting. *BA2000: Towards an Army of the Twenty-first Century* (May 1995) and *The Development Agenda* (June 1995) were the other two.
3. Logically ethos must refer to persons in the plural. In the act of simplifying what are highly complex phenomena, the papers' authors unwittingly admit to a difficulty differentiating inductive and deductive reasoning. The recommendations of the paper included the eventual publication of a 'Code of Conduct' for the Army and 'a programme of education to explain these issues to the Army'.
4. This hierarchy is argued in Patrick Mileham, 'Military Virtues 1: The Right to be Different?', *Defense Analysis*, 14, 2 (1998), p. 173. Virtues are connected with the trait theory of personality, with applications for occupational and clinical psychology, as well as in the light of the armed forces' own professional ideas. See Gerald Matthews and Ian Deary's *Personality Traits* (Cambridge: Cambridge University Press, 1998).
5. Mileham, 'Military Virtues', pp. 183–7. See also discussion in *Proceedings of Workshop on Armies in Transition: New Realities, New Opportunities, Volume I* (Headquarters US Army Europe and Seventh Army, Deidesheim, Germany, 1997), p. C-3-1.
6. Mileham, 'Military Virtues', pp. 182–3, derived from work on the Army Board Paper *The Extent to which the Army Has the Right to be Different.*
7. An eye witness of the 4th Division, quoted in Michael Glover's *Wellington's Peninsular Victories* (London: Pan Books, 1963), pp. 49–50.
8. The extremely articulate (but un-named) soldier also witnessed the ignominious retreat to Corunna and victory at Waterloo. Christopher Hibbert (ed.), *A Soldier of the Seventy-First* (London: Purnell Books, 1975), p. 18.
9. Richard Holmes, *Firing Line* (London: Penguin Books, 1987), p. 141.
10. Holmes, *Firing Line*, p. 138.
11. This is the direct connection between a soldier's moral integrity and the integrating force of a well-motivated unit, sub-unit, section or crew.
12. John Keegan, *Face of Battle* (London: Penguin Books, 1983), p. 282.
13. *Oxford English Dictionary on a Historical Basis* (Oxford: Oxford University Press, 1997). Via Old French *dangier*, it is a noun, while the verb is 'to endanger'. The Latin noun is *periculum*, from which derives the word 'peril'.
14. Peter L. Bernstein, *Against the Gods: The Remarkable Story of Risk* (New York: Wiley, 1996), p. 8. Tolstoy asks the question 'Does it not depend on whether the choice is prompted by a noble feeling or a base one, whether it should be called courage or cowardice?' *The Raid and Other Stories* (Oxford: Oxford University Press, 1982), p. 2.
15. See *The Moral Component of Fighting Power: Soldiering*, the forthcoming MOD Army Doctrine Publication.
16. A. Krepinevich in Steven Metz and James Kievit in 'Strategy and Revolution in Military Affairs: From the Theory to Policy' (Strategic Studies Institute, US Army War College, 1995), p. 3. All British Military Doctrine is based on these three 'components' of military power, first published in *Design for Military Operations: The British Military Doctrine*, 1989, Army Code 71451.
17. Samuel Hynes, *The Soldier's Tale: Bearing Witness to Modern War* (London: Pimlico, 1998), p. 56.
18. Categorised in various occupational contexts by Richard Normann in *Service Management* (Chichester: Wiley, 1984) and Jan Carlzon, former Chief Executive of Scandinavian Airways Systems.
19. In Robert Fox, *Eyewitness Falklands* (London: Methuen, 1982), p. 175. The Colonel, 'H' Jones of 2nd Bn Parachute Regiment, was awarded the Victoria Cross posthumously for

this incident.

20. TV Interview of officers and soldiers of 1st Bn Royal Scots, shortly after the end of *Operation Desert Sabre* 1 (UK) Armoured Division video production.

21. While 'co-operation' is a Principle of War, all current MOD policy and doctrine leads to one to conclude that 'integration' should replace it for the reasons stated. See also note 11 above.

22. Tolstoy, *The Raid*, p. 1, this author's italics. Quoted in Hynes's *The Soldier's Tale*, p. xi. This book most nearly answers Tolstoy's question.

23. *Strategic Defence Review*; MOD commentary in a letter to the author dated 30 July 1998.

24. MOD Concept Paper, *Future Infantry System Technology*, draft of February 1997. David Mercer writes of future difficulties of human beings working in cyber-space 'where our identity is split between one's physical being and our electronic *alter ego*, who is to say who or what we are? It will take some time before this new *Homo Integrans* is accepted psychologically ... and legally.' David Mercer, *Future Revolutions: A Comprehensive Guide to Life and Work in the New Millennium* (London: Orion Books, 1998), p. 66.

25. Aston University research, reported in the *Times Higher Education Supplement*, 17 January 1992.

26. Colonel D.A. Protheroe in 'The Armed Forces in the 1990s: Personal Problems and the Future of the Military Contract', in *Record of Proceedings* of the inaugural meeting of the British Military Studies Group, 1989, p. 52.

27. Ninety per cent of the Army is under the age of 30, according to the MOD, quoted in *The Times*, 27 February 1997.

28. Unpublished Army attitude survey by David Tickner in 1994 conducted at an Army Training Regiment.

29. For instance, Paul Kennedy, *Preparing for the Twenty-First Century* (London: Harper-Collins, 1993), Christopher Bellamy's 'Spiral Through Time: Beyond "Conflict Intensity"', *Occasional* No. 35 (Camberley: Strategic and Combat Studies Institute, 1998) and the Tofflers' *War and Anti-War: Survival at the Dawn of the 21st Century* (London: Little, Brown, 1993).

30. David Mercer, *Future Revolutions: A Comprehensive Guide to Life and Work in the Next Millennium* (London: Orion, 1998), pp. 37 and 65, in which he states that 'almost two thirds of our individuals [questioned] suggest that microchips will be implanted in the brain (by 2035)'. See also Christopher Bellamy, *Knights in White Armour: The New Art of War and Peace* (London: Pimlico, 1997), pp. 203–6.

31. The Chief of the General Staff, General Sir Peter Inge, stated in *Soldier*, 50 (2), 24 January 1994, 'The Army is going through a dark tunnel at the moment.' Four years later the 'overstretch' of matching troops to tasks is deepening the crisis.

32. Ministry of Defence, *The Strategic Defence Review: Modern Forces for the Modern World*, p. 1.

33. See, for instance, John R. Searle writing on the sociology of 'institutional facts' in *The Construction of Social Reality* (London: Allen Lane, 1995), and General Sir John Hackett's wish for ethnological studies 'on group resistance to stress' as proof of the regimental system in his *Profession of Arms* (London: Sidgwick & Jackson, 1983), p. 224. Significantly the 'Index of Martial Potency' prepared by the Royal United Services Institute in *International Security Review 1999* (London: RUSI, 1998) which places Britain's armed forces as lying fourth in the world behind the US, Chinese and Russian forces, does not measure respective 'efficiencies and morale'.

Notes on Contributors

S.J. Ball is lecturer in modern history at the University of Glasgow. His books include *The Royal Air Force and Strategic Deterrence* and *The Cold War*.

Lt-Col. Sir John Baynes was a regular soldier and held a Defence Fellowship at the University of Edinburgh. He has authored *The Soldier and Modern Society*, *Morale*, *No Reward but Honour? The British Soldier in the 1990s*, among other books.

Antony Beevor served in the 11th Hussars, and is the author of *Inside the British Army*, as well as *The Spanish Civil War*, *Crete*, and *Stalingrad*.

Peter Bracken served in the Adjutant-General's Corps, where his postings included responsibility for equal opportunities.

Jeremy Crang is lecturer in history at the University of Edinburgh, where he is also Deputy Director of the Centre for Second World War Studies.

Stuart Crawford was commissioned into the Royal Tank Regiment and as lieutenant-colonel commanded the City of Edinburgh Universities Officers Training Corps. He has held a Defence Fellowship at the University of Glasgow, and is currently Deputy Defence spokesman for the Scottish National Party.

Christopher Dandeker is professor of military sociology and head of the Department of War Studies, King's College, London.

Stephen Deakin is a senior lecturer in the Department of Defence and International Affairs, Royal Military Academy Sandhurst.

Ben Foss has held a White House internship; his paper was written while he was Marshall Scholar at the University of Edinburgh.

Col. Alan Hawley enlisted in the Royal Artillery, but after commissioning studied medicine. He was the first of the Royal Army Medical Corps to complete the Higher Command and Staff Course, and is currently Chief of Staff, Army Medical Directorate.

Mohammed Ishaq is research associate in the Department of Management and Marketing, University of Paisley.

Christopher Jessup is senior lecturer in adult education, University of Bristol, where he directs the Services Welfare Training Programme. He is the author of *Breaking Ranks: Social Change in Military Communities.*

Lt-Col. Charles Kirke is a serving officer in the Royal Artillery. He has held a Defence Fellowship at the University of Cambridge, and is currently working on a PhD.

Patrick Mileham completed the MPhil in International Relations at Cambridge, while serving in the Royal Tank Regiment, and is now lecturer in management studies at the University of Paisley.

Brigadier Sebastian Roberts served in the Irish Guards, was Military Assistant to the Chief of Defence Staff, then Colonel Land Warfare (2), responsible for the Army's doctrine, and is now Director of Public Relations (Army).

Hew Strachan is professor of modern history and director of The Scottish Centre for War Studies, University of Glasgow. His most recent book is *The Politics of the British Army.*

Iain Torrance is professor of patristics and Christian ethics in the Department of Divinity with Religious Studies, University of Aberdeen, and a former Territorial Army padre.

Reggie von Zugbach de Sugg is professor in management, University of Paisley, and a former Regular Army officer. He is the author of *Power and Prestige in the British Army.*

Index

Printed in the United Kingdom
by Lightning Source UK Ltd.
128155UK00001B/17/A